CHILTON BOOK COMPANY

REPAIR & TUNE-UP GUIDE

CHEVY ASTRO
GMC SAFARI
1985-87

All U.S. and Canadian models of Chevrolet Astro and GMC Safari minivans

President LAWRENCE A. FORNASIERI
Vice President and General Manager JOHN P. KUSHNERICK
Executive Editor KERRY A. FREEMAN, S.A.E.
Senior Editor RICHARD J. RIVELE, S.A.E.
Editor RICHARD T. SMITH, S.A.E.

CHILTON BOOK COMPANY
Radnor, Pennsylvania
19089

SAFETY NOTICE

Proper service and repair procedures are vital to the safe, reliable operation of all motor vehicles, as well as the personal safety of those performing repairs. This book outlines procedures for servicing and repairing vehicles using safe, effective methods. The procedures contain many NOTES, CAUTIONS and WARNINGS which should be followed along with standard safety procedures to eliminate the possibility of personal injury or improper service which could damage the vehicle or compromise its safety.

It is important to note that repair procedures and techniques, tools and parts for servicing motor vehicles, as well as the skill and experience of the individual performing the work vary widely. It is not possible to anticipate all of the conceivable ways or conditions under which vehicles may be serviced, or to provide cautions as to all the possible hazards that may result. Standard and accepted safety precautions and equipment should be used during cutting, grinding, chiseling, prying, or any other process that can cause material removal or projectiles.

Some procedures require the use of tools specially designed for a specific purpose. Before substituting another tool or procedure, you must be completely satisfied that neither your personal safety, nor the performance of the vehicle will be endangered.

Although the information in this guide is based on industry sources and is as complete as possible at the time of publication, the possibility exists that the manufacturer made later changes which could not be included here. While striving for total accuracy. Chilton Book Company cannot assume responsibility for any errors, changes, or omissions that may occur in the compilation of this data.

PART NUMBERS

Part numbers listed in this reference are not recommendations by Chilton for any product by brand name. They are references that can be used with interchange manuals and aftermarket supplier catalogs to locate each brand supplier's discrete part number.

SPECIAL TOOLS

Special tools are recommended by the vehicle manufacturer to perform their specific job. Use has been kept to a minimum, but where absolutely necessary, they are referred to in the text by the part number of the tool manufacturer. These tools can be purchased, under the appropriate part number, from the Service Tool Division, Kent-Moore Corporation, 29784 Little Mack, Roseville, MI 48066-2298, or an equivalent tool can be purchased locally from a tool supplier or parts outlet. Before substituting any tool for the one recommended, read the SAFETY NOTICE at the top of this page.

ACKNOWLEDGMENTS

Chilton Book Company expresses appreciation to the Chevrolet Motor Division, General Motors Corporation, Detroit, Michigan 48202; and GMC Truck and Coach Division, General Motors Corporation, Pontiac, Michigan 48053 for their generous assistance.

Information has been selected from Chevrolet and GMC shop manuals, owner's manuals, data books, brochures, service bulletins, and technical manuals.

Manufactured in the United States of America
1234567890   6543210987

Chilton's Repair & Tune-Up Guide: Chevrolet Astro/GMC Safari 1985–87
ISBN 0-8019-7750-9 pbk.
Library of Congress Catalog Card No. 86-47772

CONTENTS

Quick Reference Specifications For Your Vehicle

Fill in this chart with the most commonly used specifications for your vehicle. Specifications can be found in Chapters 1 through 3 or on the tune-up decal under the hood of the vehicle.

 ## Tune-Up

Firing Order_____

Spark Plugs:

    Type_____

    Gap (in.)_____

Torque (ft. lbs.)_____

Idle Speed (rpm)_____

Ignition Timing (°)_____

    Vacuum or Electronic Advance (Connected/Disconnected)_____

Valve Clearance (in.)

    Intake_____   Exhaust_____

Capacities

Engine Oil Type (API Rating)_____

    With Filter Change (qts)_____

    Without Filter Change (qts)_____

Cooling System (qts)_____

Manual Transmission (pts)_____

    Type_____

Automatic Transmission (pts)_____

    Type_____

Front Differential (pts)_____

    Type_____

Rear Differential (pts)_____

    Type_____

Transfer Case (pts)_____

    Type_____

FREQUENTLY REPLACED PARTS

Use these spaces to record the part numbers of frequently replaced parts.

PCV VALVE	OIL FILTER	AIR FILTER	FUEL FILTER
Type_____	Type_____	Type_____	Type_____
Part No._____	Part No._____	Part No._____	Part No._____

General Information and Maintenance

HOW TO USE THIS BOOK

Chilton's Repair & Tune-Up Guide for the Astro Van is intended to help you learn more about the inner working of your vehicle and save you money in it's upkeep and operation.

The first two chapters will be the most used, since they contain maintenance and tune-up information and procedures. Studies have shown that a properly tuned and maintained van can get at least 10% better gas mileage than an out-of-tune van. The other chapters deal with the more complex systems of your van. Operating systems from engine through brakes are covered to the extent that the average do-it-yourselfer becomes mechanically involved. This book will not explain such things as rebuilding the differential for the simple reason that the expertise required and the investment in special tools make this task uneconomical. It will give you detailed instructions to help you change your own brake pads and shoes, replace points and plugs, do many more jobs that will save you money, give you personal satisfaction and help you avoid expensive problems.

A secondary purpose of this book is a reference for owners who want to understand their van and/or their mechanics better. In this case, no tools at all are required.

Before removing any bolts, read through the entire procedure. This will give you the overall view of what tools and supplies will be required. There is nothing more frustrating that having to walk to the bus stop on Monday morning because you were short one bolt on Sunday afternoon. So read ahead and plan ahead. Each operation should be approached logically and all procedures thoroughly understood before attempting any work.

All chapters contain adjustments, maintenance, removal/installation and repair or overhaul procedures. When repair is not considered practical, we tell you how to remove the part and then how to install the new or rebuilt replacement. In this way, you at least save the labor costs. Backyard repair of such components as the alternator is just not practical.

Two basic mechanic's rules should be mentioned: One, whenever the left side of the vehicle or engine is referred to, it is meant to specify the driver's side of the vehicle. Conversely, the right side of the vehicle means the passenger's side. Secondly, most screws and bolts are removed by turning them counterclockwise and/or tightened by turning them clockwise.

Safety is always the most important rule. Constantly be aware of the dangers involved in working on an automobile and take the proper precautions. (See the section in this chapter, Servicing Your Vehicle Safely and the SAFETY NOTICE on the acknowledgment page).

Pay attention to the instructions provided. There are 3 common mistakes in mechanical work:

1. Incorrect order of assembly, disassembly or adjustment. When taking something apart or putting it together, doing things in the wrong order usually costs extra time, however, it CAN break something. Read the entire procedure before beginning the disassembly. Do everything in the order in which the instructions say you should do it, even if you can't immediately see a reason for it. When you're taking something apart that is very intricate (for example, a carburetor), you might want to draw a picture of how it looks when assembled at one point, in order to make sure you get everything back in its proper position. (We will supply exploded views whenever possible). When making adjustments, especially tune-up adjustments, do them in order. Often, one adjustment affects another and you cannot expect satisfactory results unless each adjustment is made only when it cannot be changed by any other.

2. Overtorquing (or undertorquing). While it is more common for overtorquing to cause damage, undertorquing can cause a fastener to vibrate loose causing serious damage. Especially, when dealing with aluminum parts, pay attention to torque specifications and utilize a torque wrench in assembly. If a torque figure is not available, remember that if you are using the right tool to do the job, you will probably not have to strain yourself to get a fastener tight enough. The pitch of most threads is so slight that the tension you put on the wrench will be multiplied many, many times in actual force on what you are tightening. A good example of how critical torque is can be seen in the case of spark plug installation, especially where you are putting the plug into an aluminum cylinder head. Too little torque can fail to crush the gasket, causing leakage of combustion gases and consequent overheating of the plug and engine parts. Too much torque can damage the threads or distort the plug, which changes the spark gap.

NOTE: *There are many commercial products available for ensuring that fasteners won't come loose, even if they are not torqued just right (a very common brand is Loctite®). If you're worried about getting something together tight enough to hold but loose enough to avoid mechanical damage during assembly, one of these products might offer substantial insurance. Read the label on the package and make sure the product is compatible with the materials, fluids and etc. involved before choosing one.*

3. Crossthreading occurs when a part such as a bolt is screwed into a nut or casting at the wrong angle and forced. Crossthreading is more likely to occur if access is difficult. It helps to clean and lubricate the fasteners, then start threading with the part to be installed going straight in. Start the bolt, spark plug or etc. with your fingers. If you encounter resistance, unscrew the part and start over again at a different angle until it can be inserted and turned several turns without much effort. Keep in mind that many parts, especially spark plugs, use tapered threads so that gentle turning will automatically bring the part you're threading to the proper angle if you don't force it or resist a change in angle. Don't put a wrench on the part until it's been turned a couple of turns by hand. If you suddenly encounter resistance, and the part has not been seated fully, don't force it. Pull it back out and make sure it's clean and threading properly.

NOTE: *Always take your time and be patient, once you have some experience working on your vehicle, it will become an enjoyable hobby.*

TOOLS AND EQUIPMENT

Naturally, without the proper tools and equipment, it is impossible to properly service your vehicle. It would be impossible to catalog each tool that you would need to perform each or any operation in this book. It would also be unwise for the amateur to rush out and buy an expensive set of tools on the theory that he may need one or more of them at sometime.

The best approach is to proceed slowly, gathering a good quality set of tools that are used most frequently. Don't be misled by the low cost of bargain tools. It is far better to spend a little more for better quality. Forged wrenches, 6 or 12 point sockets and fine tooth ratchets are by far preferable to their less expensive counterparts. As any good mechanic can tell you, there are few worse experiences than trying to work on a vehicle with bad tools. Your monetary savings will be far outweighed by frustration and mangled knuckles.

Begin accumulating tools that are used most frequently; those associated with routine maintenance and tune-up.

In addition to the normal assortment of screwdrivers and pliers you should have the following tools for routine maintenance jobs:

1. SAE (or Metric) or SAE/Metric wrenches – sockets and combination open end/box end wrenches in sizes from $1/8$–$3/4$" (6–19mm) and a spark plug socket ($13/16$" or $5/8$" depending on plug type).

NOTE: *If possible, buy various length socket drive extensions. One break in this department is that the metric sockets available in the U.S. will all fit the ratchet handles and extensions you may already have ($1/4$", $3/8$" and $1/2$" drive).*

2. Jackstands, for support
3. Oil filter wrench
4. Oil filler spout, for pouring oil
5. Grease gun, for chassis lubrication
6. Hydrometer, for checking the battery
7. A container for draining oil
8. Many rags for wiping up the inevitable mess.

In addition to the above items there are several others that are not absolutely necessary but handy to have around. These include oil dry, a transmission funnel and an usual supply of lubricants, antifreeze and fluids, although these can be purchased as needed. This is a basic list for routine maintenance but only your personal needs and desires can accurately determine your list of tools. If you are serious about maintaining your own vehicle, then a floor jack is as necessary as a spark plug socket. The greatly increased utility, strength and safety of a hydraulic floor jack makes it pay for

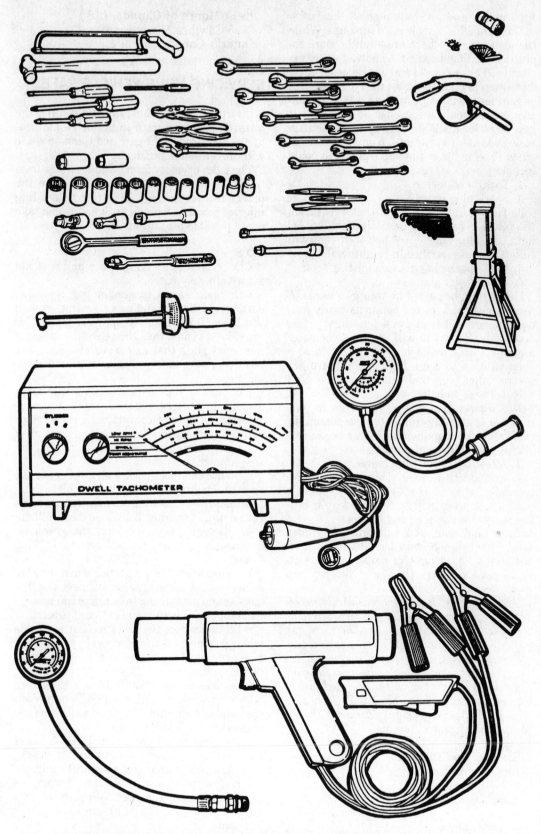

You need only a basic assortment of hand tools for most maintenance and repair jobs

itself many times over throughout the years.

The second list of tools is for tune-ups. While the tools involved here are slightly more sophisticated, they need not be outrageously expensive. There are several inexpensive tach/dwell meters on the market that are every bit as good for the average mechanic as an expensive professional model. Just be sure that it goes to at least 1,200–1,500 rpm on the tach scale and that it works on 4, 6 or 8 cylinder engines. A basic list of tune-up equipment could include:

1. Tach/dwell meter.
2. Spark plug wrench.
3. Timing light (a DC light that works from the vehicle's battery is best, although an AC light that plugs into 110V house current will suffice at some sacrifice in brightness).
4. Wire spark plug gauge/adjusting tools.
5. Set of feeler gauges.

Here again, be guided by your own needs. A feeler gauge will set the points as easily as a dwell meter will read dwell but slightly less accurately. Since you will need a tachometer anyway ... well, make your own decision.

In addition to these basic tools, there are several other tools and gauges you may find useful. These include:

1. A compression gauge. The screw-in type is slower to use but eliminates the possibility of a faulty reading due to escaping pressure.
2. A manifold vacuum gauge.
3. A test light, volt/ohm meter.
4. An induction meter. This is used for determining whether or not there is current in a wire. These are handy for use if a wire is broken somewhere in a wiring harness.

As a final note, you will probably find a torque wrench necessary for all but the most basic work. The beam type models are perfectly adequate, although the newer click type are more precise.

NOTE: *Special tools are occasionally necessary to perform a specific job or are recommended to make a job easier. Their use has been kept to a minimum. When a special tool is indicated, it will be referred to by manufacturer's part number, and, where possible, an illustration of the tool will be provided so that an equivalent tool may be used. A list of tool manufacturers and their addresses follows:*

In the United States, contact:

Service Tool Division
Kent-Moore Corporation
29784 Little Mack
Roseville, MI 48066-2298

In Canada, contact:

Kent-Moore of Canada, Ltd.
2395 Cawthra Mississauga
Ontario, Canada L5A 3P2.

SERVICING YOUR VEHICLE SAFELY

It is virtually impossible to anticipate all of the hazards involved with automotive maintenance and service but care and common sense will prevent most accidents.

The rules of safety for mechanics range from "don't smoke around gasoline," to "use the proper tool for the job." The trick to avoiding injuries is to develop safe work habits and take every possible precaution.

Do's

• Do keep a fire extinguisher and first aid kit within easy reach.

• Do wear safety glasses or goggles when cutting, drilling, grinding or prying, even if you have 20/20 vision. If you wear glasses for the sake of vision, then they should be made of hardened glass that can serve also as safety glasses or wear safety goggles over your regular glasses.

• Do shield your eyes whenever you work around the battery. Batteries contain sulphuric acid. In case of contact with the eyes or skin, flush the area with water or a mixture of water and baking soda, then get medical attention immediately.

• Do use safety stands for any under vehicle service. Jacks are for raising the vehicle. Safety stands are for making sure the vehicle stays raised until you want it to come down. Whenever the vehicle is raised, block the wheels remaining on the ground and set the parking brake.

• Do use adequate ventilation when working with any chemicals. Like carbon monoxide, the asbestos dust resulting from brake lining wear can be poisonous in sufficient quantities.

• Do disconnect the negative battery cable when working on the electrical system. The primary ignition system can contain up to 40,000 volts.

• Do follow the manufacturer's directions whenever working with potentially hazardous materials. Both brake fluid and antifreeze are poisonous if taken internally.

• Do properly maintain your tools. Loose hammer heads, mushroomed punches/chisels, frayed or poorly grounded electrical cords, excessively worn screwdrivers, spread wrenches (open end), cracked sockets, slipping ratchets and/or faulty droplight sockets cause accidents.

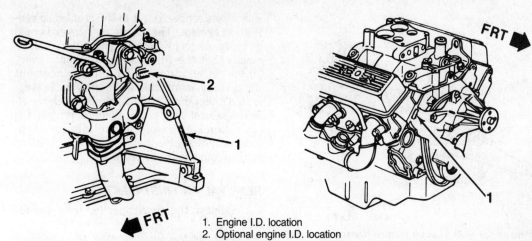

1. Engine I.D. location
2. Optional engine I.D. location

Location of the Engine Identification Number—2.5L and the 4.3L engines

Engine

The 2.5L engine identification numbers are stamped on the left side of the rear engine block flange; the 4.3L engine identification numbers are stamped on a pad of the engine block which is located at the lower front edge of the right side cylinder head. The eighth digit of the serial number identifies the engine used in the vehicle.

Transmission

4-SPEED AND 5-SPEED MANUAL

The transmission serial numbers are located on the front right side of the main housing.

TURBO HYDRA-MATIC 4-SPEED

The TH-M 700-R4, 4-spd automatic transmission serial numbers are located on the rear

Transmission Usage

Year	Engine L (cu. in.)	Manual 4-spd. ①	Manual 5-spd. ②	Automatic ③
1985	2.5L (151)	MR2	MH3	MD8
	4.3L (262)	MR2	MH3	MD8
1986–87	2.5L (151)	MR2	ML3	MD8
	4.3L (262)	MR2	MH3	MD8

① 76 mm
② 77 mm
③ THM 700-R4

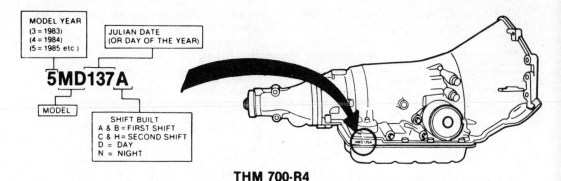

MODEL YEAR
(3 = 1983)
(4 = 1984)
(5 = 1985 etc)

JULIAN DATE
(OR DAY OF THE YEAR)

5MD137A

MODEL

SHIFT BUILT
A & B = FIRST SHIFT
C & H = SECOND SHIFT
D = DAY
N = NIGHT

THM 700-R4

Location and description of the THM 700-R4 automatic transmission serial number

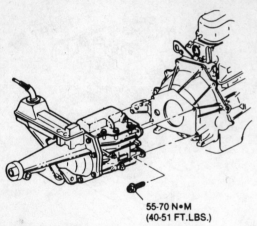

55-70 N•M
(40-51 FT.LBS.)

View of the MH3 5-speed manual transmission; the
MR2 4-speed is similar

right side of the transmission case, above the
oil pan.

Drive Axle

All Astro Vans have the drive axle serial number located on the forward side of the right axle
tube. The two or three letter prefix in the serial
number identifies the drive axle gear ratio.

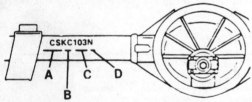

CSKC103N

A   C   D

B

A. Axle code
B. 7½" (1900 mm) Chevrolet St. Catherines
C. Day built
D. Shift (D = Day, N = Night)

Location and description of the drive axle serial
number

ROUTINE MAINTENANCE

Air Cleaner

The air cleaner consists of a metal housing
with a replaceable paper filter and the neces-

sary hoses connecting it to the crankcase ventilation system. The air cleaner cover is held
by two nuts on all models. The factory recommends that the filter be replaced once every
30,000 miles. Inspection and replacement
should come more often when the vehicle is operated under dusty conditions. To check the effectiveness of your paper element, remove the
air cleaner assembly, if the idle speed increases noticeably, the element is restricting
airflow and should be replaced.

REMOVAL AND INSTALLATION

1. Remove the air cleaner top nuts and lift
off the top.
2. Remove the filter from inside the filter
housing.
3. Clean the inside of the air cleaner housing before reinstalling the air filter.

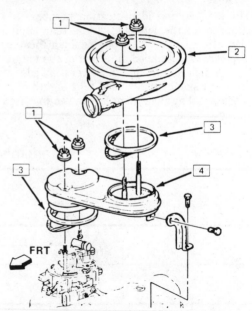

FRT

1. Nut-tighten to 50 N·m (37 ft. lbs.)
2. Air cleaner
3. Seal-remove paper if new seal
4. Adapter

View of the air cleaner assemblies used on the 1986–
87 2.5L and 4.3L engines

Rear Axle Specifications

Model	Ring Gear Diam.	Standard Axle Code	Limited Slip Axle Code	Axle Ratio	Axle Usage
M10905	7.5″	FSA	FSD	4.11	HO4
M10905	7.5″	FAA	FBA	2.56	GM8
M10906	7.5″	FCA	FCB	2.73	GU2
		FFA	FFB	3.08	GU4
		FMA	FMB	3.42	GU6
		FRA	FRB	3.73	GT4

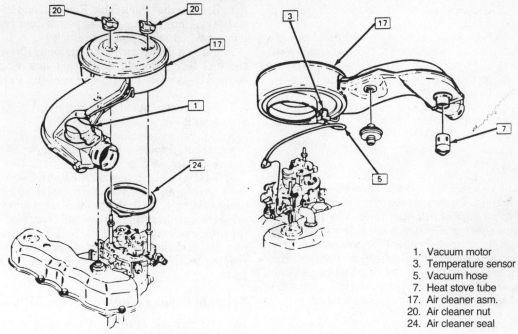

1. Vacuum motor
3. Temperature sensor
5. Vacuum hose
7. Heat stove tube
17. Air cleaner asm.
20. Air cleaner nut
24. Air cleaner seal

View of the air cleaner assembly used on the 1985 2.5L engine

4. To install, use a new filter and reverse the removal procedures. Torque the nuts to 37 ft.lb.

Fuel Filter

There are three types of fuel filters used: The internal (1985 4.3L carburetor models), the inline and the intank.

CAUTION: *Before removing any component of the fuel system (TBI models), be sure to reduce the fuel pressure in the system. The pressure regulator (TBI models) contains an orifice in the fuel system; when the engine is turned Off, the pressure in the system will bleed down within a few minutes.*

REMOVAL AND INSTALLATION

Internal — 1985 Carbureted models

1. At the carburetor, disconnect the fuel line connection at the fuel inlet filter nut.
2. Remove the fuel inlet filter nut from the carburetor.
3. Remove the filter and the spring, then discard the old filter.

NOTE: *A check valve MUST be installed in the filter to meet the Motor Vehicle Safety Standards for roll-over. When installing a new filter, pay attention to the direction the fuel must flow through it; it MUST be installed with the check valve end facing the fuel line. The new filter is equipped with ribs on the closed end to ensure that it will not be installed incorrectly unless it is forced.*

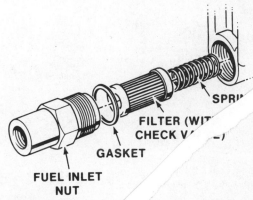

Exploded view of the internal fuel filter—1985 4.3L carburetor

4. Install the spring and the new filter/check valve assembly into the carburetor inlet, followed by the fuel inlet nut. Torque the nut to install the fuel line and tighten the ... Start the engine and check for

Inline

The inline fuel filter is located in the fuel feed line under the hood.

NOTE: *If the engine was just turned Off, allow it to rest a few minutes to give the fuel system time to bleed down.*

1. Using two wrenches (one for backup), remove the fuel lines from the filter.

2. Loosen the filter-to-bracket bolt, remove the filter and discard it.

NOTE: *When installing a new filter, pay attention to the direction the fuel must flow through it.*

3. Install the new filter into the bracket, then install new O-rings and the fuel lines. Using two wrenches, torque the fuel lines-to-filter to 22 ft.lb. Start the engine and check for leaks.

Intank

The intank filter is constructed of woven plastic and is located on the lower end of the fuel pickup tube in the fuel tank. The filter prevents dirt and water from entering the fuel system; water will enter the system if the filter becomes completely submerged in water. The filter is normally self cleaning and requires no maintenance; should this filter become clogged, the fuel tank must be flushed.

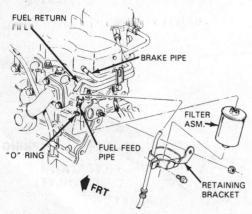

FUEL RETURN
PIPE
BRAKE PIPE
FILTER ASM.
FUEL FEED PIPE
"O" RING
FRT
RETAINING BRACKET

Exploded view of the inline fuel filter on the 2.5L engine—the 4.3L engine is similar

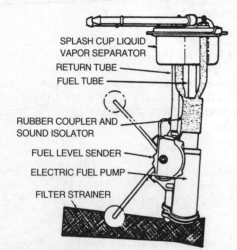

SPLASH CUP LIQUID VAPOR SEPARATOR
RETURN TUBE
FUEL TUBE
RUBBER COUPLER AND SOUND ISOLATOR
FUEL LEVEL SENDER
ELECTRIC FUEL PUMP
FILTER STRAINER

View of the intank fuel filter—TBI fuel systems

1. Refer to the "Fuel Tank, Removal and Installation" procedures in Chapter 4 and remove the fuel tank from the vehicle.

2. Using a drift punch and a hammer, drive the fuel lever sending unit's cam lock ring counterclockwise, the lift the sending unit from the tank.

3. Remove the fuel filter from the fuel pump and clean it.

NOTE: *When installing the intank fuel filter, be careful not to fold or twist it for this may restrict the flow.*

4. To install, use a new sending unit-to-fuel tank O-ring and reverse the removal procedures. Using a drift punch and a hammer, drive the cam lock ring, of the fuel lever sending unit, clockwise. Install the fuel tank, connect the fuel lines and electrical wire to the sending unit. Start the engine and check for leaks.

Positive Crankcase Ventilation (PCV)

The PCV valve is attached to the valve cover by a rubber grommet and connected to the intake manifold through a ventilation hose. Replace the PCV valve and the PCV filter (located in the air cleaner) every 30,000 miles.

REMOVAL AND INSTALLATION

1. Pull the PCV from the valve cover grommet and disconnect it from the ventilation hose(s).

2. Inspect the valve for operation: (1) Shake it to see if the valve is free; (2) Blow through it (air will pass in one direction only).

NOTE: *When replacing the PCV valve, it is recommended to use a new one.*

3. To install, reverse the removal procedures.

Evaporative Canister

To limit gasoline vapor discharge into the air, this system is designed to trap fuel vapors, which normally escape from the fuel tank and the intake manifold. Vapor arrest is accomplished through the use of the charcoal canister. This canister absorbs fuel vapors and stores them until they can be removed to be burned in the engine. Removal of the vapors from the canister to the engine is accomplished by a canister mounted purge valve (2.5L TBI and 4.3L carbureted engines), the throttle valve position (2.5L and 4.3L TBI engines), a thermostatic vacuum (TVS) switch (4.3L carbureted engines, non-Calif.) or a computer controlled canister purge solenoid (4.3L carbureted engines, Calif.).

In addition to the modifications and the can-

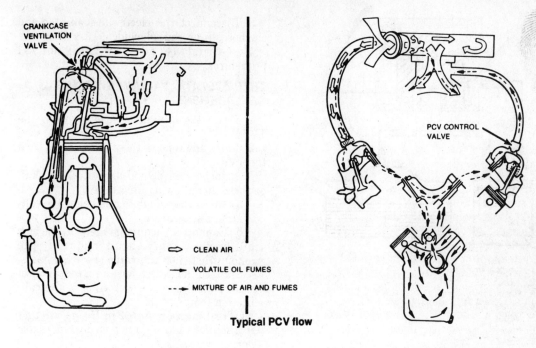

CRANKCASE
VENTILATION
VALVE

PCV CONTROL
VALVE

⇨ CLEAN AIR

→ VOLATILE OIL FUMES

-→ MIXTURE OF AIR AND FUMES

Typical PCV flow

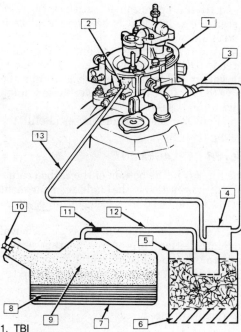

1. TBI
2. Canister purge port
3. Vacuum signal
4. Purge valve
5. Vapor storage canister
6. Purge air
7. Fuel tank
8. Fuel
9. Vapor
10. Pressure-vacuum relief gas cap
11. Vent restricter
12. Fuel tank vent
13. Purge line

Cross-sectional view of the evaporative emission control system—2.5L TBI engine

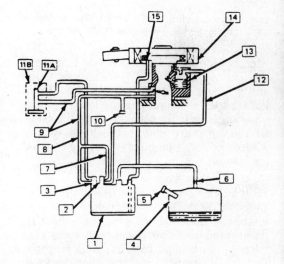

1. Canister
2. Vapor vent control valve
3. Canister purge control valve
4. Fuel tank
5. Fuel cap
6. Fuel tank vent line restriction
7. Vacuum signal for bowl vent valve
8. Vapor purge line (full manifold vacuum)
9. Ported manifold vacuum
10. PCV valve
11A. TVS-federal application
11B. Electric purge solenoid-California application
12. Carburetor bowl vent line
13. Carburetor
14. Air cleaner
15. Fuel vapor canister vent

Cross-sectional view of the evaporative emission control system—4.3L carbureted engine (1985)

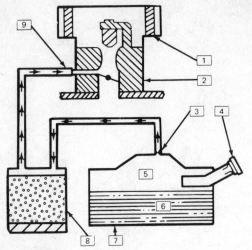

1. Air cleaner
2. T.B.I. unit
3. Restrictor
4. Press-vacuum relief gas cap
5. Vapor
6. Fuel
7. Fuel tank
8. Charcoal canister
9. Purge

Cross-sectional view of the evaporative emission control system—4.3L TBI engine (1986 and later)

ister, the fuel tank requires a non-vented gas cap. The domed fuel tank positions a vent high enough above the fuel to keep the vent pipe in the vapor at all times. The single vent pipe is routed directly to the canister. From the canister, the vapors are routed to the intake system, where they will be burned during normal combustion.

SERVICING

Every 30,000 miles or 24 months, check all fuel, vapor lines and hoses for proper hookup, routing and condition. If equipped, check that the bowl vent and purge valves work properly. Remove the canister and check for cracks or damage, then replace (if necessary).

REMOVAL AND INSTALLATION

1. Disconnect and mark the charcoal canister vent hoses.
2. Remove the canister-to-bracket bolt.
3. Lift the canister from the bracket.
4. To install, reverse the removal procedures.

CHARCOAL CANISTER SOLENOID REPLACEMENT

1. Disconnect the negative battery cable.
2. Remove the solenoid retaining bolt, the cover and the solenoid.

3. Disconnect the electrical connector and the hoses from the solenoid.
4. To install, reverse the removal procedures.

THERMOSTATIC VACUUM SWITCH (TVS) REPLACEMENT

1. Drain the coolant to a level below the TVS.
2. Mark and remove the vacuum hoses from the TVS.
3. Remove the TVS and check it. To check it, perform the following procedures:
   a. Allow the switch to cool below the calibration temperature.
   b. Connect a vacuum gauge(s) to the output port(s), apply vacuum equal to the amount listed on the valve or switch base.
   c. Place the switch base in a container of water, then heat the water above the calibration temperature.
NOTE: *Leakage of up to 2 in.Hg in 2 minutes is allowable and does not mean a defective part.*
   d. If the operation is satisfactory, reinstall the valve; if it is defective, replace it with a new one.
4. Apply soft setting sealant to the valve threads (DO NOT apply sealant to the end of the valve) and install the valve. Torque the valve to 10 ft.lb., then turn it clockwise to align it with the hoses.
5. Reinstall the vacuum hoses. Refill the cooling system.

FILTER REPLACEMENT

The filter is in the bottom of the carbon canister which is located in the engine compartment should be replaced every 30,000 miles or 24 months.
1. Refer to the "Charcoal Canister, Removal and Installation" procedures, in this section and remove the canister from it's bracket.
2. At the bottom of the canister, grasp the filter with your fingers and pull it out.
3. To install, use a new filter and reverse the removal procedures.

Battery

All Astro Vans have a Maintenance Free battery as standard equipment, eliminating the need for fluid level checks and the possibility of specific gravity tests. Never-the-less, the battery does require some attention.

Once a year, the battery terminals and the cable clamps should be cleaned. Remove the side terminal bolts and the cables, negative cable first. Clean the cable clamps and the battery terminals with a wire brush until all corrosion, grease, etc. is removed and the metal is

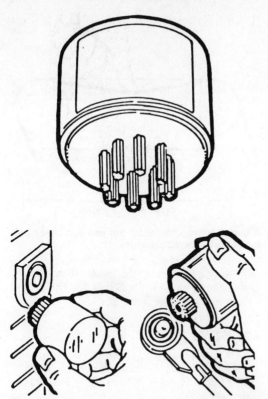

A special cleaning tool is available for cleaning the side terminals and clamps

shiny. It is especially important to clean the inside of the clamp thoroughly, since a small deposit of foreign material or oxidation there will prevent a sound electrical connection and inhibit either starting or charging. Special tools are available for cleaning the side terminal clamps and terminals.

Before installing the cables, loosen the battery holddown clamp, remove the battery and check the battery tray. Clear it of any debris and check it for soundness. Rust should be wire brushed away and the metal given a coat of anti-rust paint. Replace the battery and tighten the holddown clamp securely but becareful not to overtighten, which will crack the battery case.

NOTE: *Batteries can be cleaned using a solution of baking soda and water. Surface coatings on battery cases can actually conduct electricity which will cause a slight voltage drain, so make sure the battery case is clean.*

After the clamps and terminals are clean, reinstall the cables, negative cable last. Give the clamps and terminals a thin external coat of nonmetallic grease after installation, to retard corrosion.

Check the cables at the same time that the terminals are cleaned. If the cable insulation is cracked, broken or the ends are frayed, the cable should be replaced with a new one of the same length and gauge.

CAUTION: *Keep flames or sparks away from the battery. It gives off explosive hydrogen gas. The battery electrolyte contains sulphuric acid. If you should get any on your skin or in your eyes, flush the affected areas with plenty of clear water. If it lands in your eyes, seek medical help immediately.*

Testing the Maintenance Free Battery

Maintenance free batteries, do not require normal attention as far as fluid level checks are concerned. However, the terminals require periodic cleaning, which should be performed at least once a year.

The sealed top battery cannot be checked for charge in the normal manner, since there is no provision for access to the electrolyte. To check the condition of the battery:

1. If the indicator eye on top of the battery is dark, the battery has enough fluid. If the eye is lit, the electrolyte fluid is too low and the battery must be replaced.

2. If a green dot appears in the middle of the eye, the battery is sufficiently charged. Proceed to Step 4. If no green dot is visible, charge the battery as in Step 3.

3. Charge the battery at this rate:

Charging Rate Amps	Time
75	40 min
50	1 hr
25	2 hr
10	5 hr

NOTE: *DO NOT charge the battery for more than 50 amp-hours. If the green dot appears or if the electrolyte squirts out of the vent hole, stop the charge and proceed to Step 4.*

It may be necessary to tip the battery from side-to-side to get the green dot to appear after charging.

CAUTION: *When charging the battery, the*

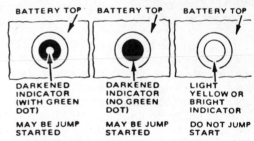

Maintenance-free batteries contain their own built in hydrometer

Battery	Test Load (Amps)
1981099	150
1981102	170
1981104	250
1981108	370

Battery load test values

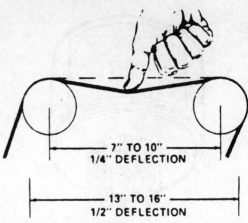

A gauge is recommended, but you can check belt tension with thumb pressure

electrical system and control unit can be quickly damaged by improper connections, high output battery chargers or incorrect service procedures.

4. Connect a battery load tester and a voltmeter across the battery terminals (the battery cables should be disconnected from the battery). Apply a 300 amp load to the battery for 15 seconds to remove the surface charge. Remove the load.

5. Wait 15 seconds to allow the battery to recover. Apply the appropriate test load, as specified in the following chart:

Apply the load for 15 seconds while reading the voltage. Disconnect the load.

6. Check the results against the following chart. If the battery voltage is at or above the specified voltage for the temperature listed, the battery is good. It the voltage falls below what's listed, the battery should be replaced.

ESTIMATED TEMPERATURE	MINIMUM VOLTAGE
70° F. (21° C.)	9.6
50° F. (10° C.)	9.4
30° F. (0° C.)	9.1
15° F. (−10° C.)	8.8
0° F. (−18° C.)	8.5
0° F. (BELOW: −18° C.)	8.0

Temperature versus voltage drop

Belts
INSPECTION

Check the drive belt(s) every 15,000 miles/12 months (heavy usage) or 30,000 miles/24 months (light usage) for evidence of wear such as cracking, fraying and incorrect tension. Determine the belt tension at a point halfway between the pulleys by pressing on the belt with moderate thumb pressure. The belt should deflect about ¼″ (6mm) over a 7–10″ (178–254mm) span, or ½″ (12.7mm) over a 13–16″

(330–406mm) span, at this point. If the deflection is found to be too much or too little, perform the tension adjustments.

ADJUSTING TENSION

NOTE: *The following procedures require the use of GM Belt Tension Gauge No. BT-33-95-ACBN (regular V-belts) or BT-33-97M (poly V-belts).*

1. If the belt is cold, operate the engine (at idle speed) for 15 minutes; the belt will seat itself in the pulleys allowing the belt fibers to relax or stretch. If the belt is hot, allow it to cool, until it is warm to the touch.

NOTE: *A used belt is one that has been rotated at least one complete revolution on the pulleys. This begins the belt seating process and it must never be tensioned to the new belt specifications.*

2. Loosen the component-to-mounting bracket bolts.

3. Using a GM Belt Tension Gauge No. BT-33-95-ACBN (standard V-belts) or BT-33-97M (poly V-belts), place the tension gauge at the center of the belt between the longest span.

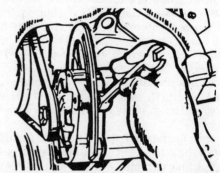

To adjust belt tension or to replace belts, first loosen the component's mounting and adjusting bolts slightly

Belt Tension Specifications

Engine	Tensioning	Alternator	Power Steering	Air Cond.	A.I.R. Pump
2.5L	Before Operating The Engine (New Belt)	②	146 Lb.	169 Lb.	—
	After Operating The Engine (Old Belt) ①		67 Lb.	90 Lb.	
4.3L	Before Operating The Engine (New Belt)	135 Lb.	146 Lb.	169 Lb.	146 Lb.
	After Operating The Engine (Old Belt) ①	67 Lb.	67 Lb.	90 Lb.	67 Lb.

① At no time should belt exceed "After Operating The Engine" tension. Tension to be checked within 15 minutes after operating the engine. For belts driving more than one adjustable accessory, use highest tension specified. Any tensioning of replacement belts or the retensioning of previously installed but unrun belts, must adhere to above specifications (maximums prior to engine operation and minimums after engine operation). Any re-tensioning of previously run belts must be set to the "After Operating The Engine" specification.

② Generator belt with C60 air conditioning (new belt) 169 Lb.; old belt 90 Lb.
Generator belt with C41 heater (new belt) 146 Lb.; old belt 67 Lb.

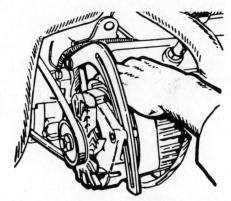

Pull outward on the component and tighten the mounting bolts

4. Applying belt tension pressure on the component, adjust the drive belt tension to the correct specifications.

5. While holding the correct tension on the component, tighten the component-to-mounting bracket bolt.

6. When the belt tension is correct, remove the tension gauge.

REMOVAL AND INSTALLATION

1. Loosen the component-to-mounting bracket bolts.

2. Rotate the component to relieve the tension on the drive belt.

3. Slip the drive belt from the component pulley and remove it from the engine.

NOTE: *If the engine uses more than one belt, it may be necessary to remove other belts that are in front of the one being removed.*

4. To install, reverse the removal procedures. Adjust the component drive belt tension to specifications.

Hoses

The upper/lower radiator hoses and all heater hoses should be checked for deterioration, leaks and loose hose clamps every 15,000 miles or 12 months.

REMOVAL AND INSTALLATION

1. Drain the cooling system.

2. Loosen the hose clamps at each end of the hose.

3. Working the hose back and forth, slide it off it's connection and then install a new hose, if necessary.

NOTE: *When replacing the heater hoses, maintain a 1½" (38mm) clearance between the hose clip-to-upper control arm and between the rear overhead heater core lines-to-exhaust pipe.*

4. To install, reverse the removal procedures.

NOTE: *Draw the hoses tight to prevent sagging or rubbing against other components; route the hoses through the clamps as installed originally. Always make sure that the hose clamps are beyond the component bead and placed in the center of the clamping surface before tightening them.*

Air Conditioning

NOTE: *This book contains simple testing procedures for your van's air conditioning system. More comprehensive testing, diagnosis and service procedures may be found in* CHILTON'S GUIDE TO AIR CONDITIONING SERVICE AND REPAIR, *book part number 7580, available at your local retailer.*

SAFETY WARNINGS

Because of the importance of the necessary safety precautions that must be exercised when working with air conditioning systems and R-12 refrigerant, a recap of the safety precautions are outlined.

• Avoid contact with a charged refrigeration system, even when working on another part of the air conditioning system or vehicle. If a

HOW TO SPOT WORN V-BELTS

V-Belts are vital to efficient engine operation—they drive the fan, water pump and other accessories. They require little maintenance (occasional tightening) but they will not last forever. Slipping or failure of the V-belt will lead to overheating. If your V-belt looks like any of these, it should be replaced.

Cracking or weathering

This belt has deep cracks, which cause it to flex. Too much flexing leads to heat build-up and premature failure. These cracks can be caused by using the belt on a pulley that is too small. Notched belts are available for small diameter pulleys.

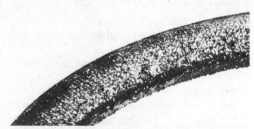

Softening (grease and oil)

Oil and grease on a belt can cause the belt's rubber compounds to soften and separate from the reinforcing cords that hold the belt together. The belt will first slip, then finally fail altogether.

Glazing

Glazing is caused by a belt that is slipping. A slipping belt can cause a run-down battery, erratic power steering, overheating or poor accessory performance. The more the belt slips, the more glazing will be built up on the surface of the belt. The more the belt is glazed, the more it will slip. If the glazing is light, tighten the belt.

Worn cover

The cover of this belt is worn off and is peeling away. The reinforcing cords will begin to wear and the belt will shortly break. When the belt cover wears in spots or has a rough jagged appearance, check the pulley grooves for roughness.

Separation

This belt is on the verge of breaking and leaving you stranded. The layers of the belt are separating and the reinforcing cords are exposed. It's just a matter of time before it breaks completely.

HOW TO SPOT BAD HOSES

Both the upper and lower radiator hoses are called upon to perform difficult jobs in an inhospitable environment. They are subject to nearly 18 psi at under hood temperatures often over 280°F., and must circulate nearly 7500 gallons of coolant an hour—3 good reasons to have good hoses.

A good test for any hose is to feel it for soft or spongy spots. Frequently these will appear as swollen areas of the hose. The most likely cause is oil soaking. This hose could burst at any time, when hot or under pressure.

Swollen hose

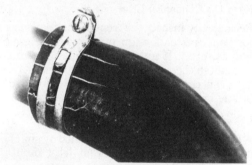

Cracked hoses can usually be seen but feel the hoses to be sure they have not hardened; a prime cause of cracking. This hose has cracked down to the reinforcing cords and could split at any of the cracks.

Cracked hose

Weakened clamps frequently are the cause of hose and cooling system failure. The connection between the pipe and hose has deteriorated enough to allow coolant to escape when the engine is hot.

Frayed hose end (due to weak clamp)

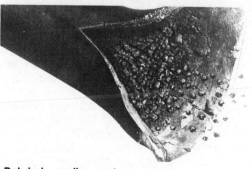

Debris, rust and scale in the cooling system can cause the inside of a hose to weaken. This can usually be felt on the outside of the hose as soft or thinner areas.

Debris in cooling system

heavy tool comes into contact with a section of copper tubing or a heat exchanger, it can easily cause the relatively soft material to rupture.

• When it is necessary to apply force to a fitting which contains refrigerant, as when checking that all system couplings are securely tightened, use a wrench on both parts of the fitting involved, if possible. This will avoid putting torque on the refrigerant tubing. It is advisable, when possible, to use tube or line wrenches when tightening these flare nut fittings.

• DO NOT attempt to discharge the system by merely loosening a fitting or removing the service valve caps and cracking these valves. Precise control is possible only when using the service gauges. Place a rag under the open end of the center charging hose while discharging the system to catch any drops of liquid that might escape. Wear protective gloves when connecting or disconnecting service gauge hoses.

• Discharge the system only in a well ventilated area, as high concentrations of the gas can exclude oxygen and act as an anaesthetic. When leak testing or soldering, this is particularly important, as toxic gas is formed when R-12 contacts any flame.

• Never start a system without first verifying that both service valves are back-seated (if equipped) and that all fittings throughout the system are snugly connected.

• Avoid applying heat to any refrigerant line or storage vessel. Charging may be aided by using water heated to less than 125° to warm the refrigerant container. Never allow a refrigerant storage container to sit out in the sun or near any other heat source, such as a radiator.

• Always wear goggles when working on a system to protect the eyes. If refrigerant contacts the eyes, it is advisable in all cases to see a physician as soon as possible.

• Frostbite from liquid refrigerant should be treated by first gradually warming the area with cool water and then gently applying petroleum jelly. A physician should be consulted.

• Always keep the refrigerant drum fittings capped when not in use. Avoid any sudden shock to the drum, which might occur from dropping it or from banging a heavy tool against it. Never carry a drum in the passenger compartment of a vehicle.

• Always completely discharge the system before painting the vehicle (if the paint is to be baked on), or before welding anywhere near the refrigerant lines.

NOTE: *Any repair work to an air conditioning system should be left to a professional. DO NOT, under any circumstances, attempt to loosen or tighten any fittings or perform any work other than that outlined here.*

SYSTEM INSPECTIONS

Checking For Oil Leaks

Refrigerant leaks show up as oily areas on the various components because the compressor oil is transported around the entire system along with the refrigerant. Look for oily spots on all the hoses and lines, especially on the hose and tubing connections. If there are oily deposits, the system may have a leak, have it checked by a qualified repairman.

NOTE: *A small area of oil on the front of the compressor is normal and no cause for alarm.*

Checking The Compressor Belt

Refer to the Drive Belts section in this chapter.

Keep The Condenser Clear

Periodically inspect the front of the condenser for bent fins or foreign material (dirt, buts, leaves, etc.). If any cooling fins are bent, straighten them carefully with needlenose pliers. You can remove any debris with a stiff bristle brush or hose.

Operate The A/C System Periodically

A lot of A/C problems can be avoided by simply running the air conditioner at least once a week regardless of the season. Simply let the system run for at least 5 minutes a week (even in the winter) and you'll keep the internal parts lubricated as well as preventing the hoses from hardening.

Refrigerant Level Check

The first order of business when checking the sight glass is to find the sight glass. It will either be in the head of the receiver/drier or in one of the metal lines leading from the top of the receiver/drier. Once you've found it, wipe it clean and proceed as follows:

1. With the engine and the air conditioning system running, look for the flow of refrigerant through the sight glass. If the air conditioner is working properly, you'll be able to see a continuous flow of clear refrigerant through the sight glass, with perhaps an occasional bubble at very high temperatures.

2. Cycle the air conditioner ON and OFF to make sure what you are seeing is clear refrigerant. Since the refrigerant is clear, it is possible to mistake a completely discharged system for one that is fully charged. Turn the system OFF and watch the sight glass. If there is refrigerant in the system, you'll see bubbles during the off cycle. If you observe no bubbles

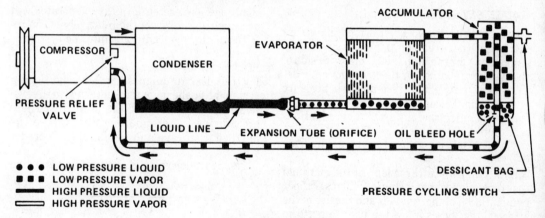

LOW PRESSURE LIQUID
LOW PRESSURE VAPOR
HIGH PRESSURE LIQUID
HIGH PRESSURE VAPOR

Air Conditioning System

when the system is running and the air flow from the unit in the vehicle is delivering cold air, everything is OK.

3. If you observe bubbles in the sight glass while the system is operating, the system is low on refrigerant. Have it checked by a professional.

4. Oil streaks, in the sight glass are an indication of trouble. Most of the time, if you see oil in the sight glass, it will appear as a series of streaks, although occasionally it may be a solid stream of oil. In either case, it means that part of the charge has been lost.

Leak Testing the System

There are several methods of detecting leaks in an air conditioning system; among them, the two most popular are (1) halide leak detection or the open flame method and (2) electronic leak detection.

The halide leak detection is a torch like de-

vice which produces a yellow-green color when refrigerant is introduced into the flame at the burner. A purple or violet color indicates the presence of large amounts of refrigerant at the burner.

An electronic leak detector is a small portable electronic device with an extended probe. With the unit activated the probe is passed along those components of the system which contain refrigerant. If a leak is detected, the unit will sound an alarm signal or activate a display signal depending on the manufacturer's design. It is advisable to follow the manufacturer's instructions as the design and function of the detection may vary significantly.

CAUTION: *Caution should be taken to operate either type of detector in well ventilated areas, so as to reduce the chance of personal injury, which may result from coming in contact with poisonous gases produced when R-12 is exposed to flame or electric spark.*

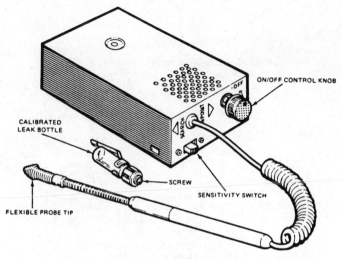

Electronic leak detector

GAUGE SETS (USE)

Most of the service work performed in air conditioning requires the use of a set of two gauges, one for the high (head) pressure side of the system, the other for the low (suction) side.

The low side gauge records both pressure and vacuum. Vacuum readings are calibrated from 0–30 in.Hg, and the pressure graduations read from 0–60 psi.

The high side gauge measures pressure from 0–600 psi.

Both gauges are threaded into a manifold that contains two hand shut-off valves. Proper manipulation of these valves and the use of the attached test hoses allow the user to perform the following services:

1. Test high and low side pressures.
2. Remove air, moisture and/or contaminated refrigerant.
3. Purge the system of refrigerant.
4. Charge the system with refrigerant.

The manifold valves are designed so they have no direct effect on the gauge readings but serve only to provide for or cut off the flow of refrigerant through the manifold. During all testing and hook-up operations, the valves are kept in a Closed position to avoid disturbing the refrigeration system. The valves are Opened ONLY to purge the system of refrigerant or to charge it.

When purging the system, the center hose is uncapped at the lower end and both valves are cracked (Opened) slightly. This allows the refrigerant pressure to force the entire contents of the system out through the center hose. During charging, the valve on the high side of the manifold is Closed and the valve on the low side is cracked (Opened). Under these conditions, the low pressure in the evaporator will draw refrigerant from the relatively warm refrigerant storage container into the system.

Service Valves

For the user to diagnose an air conditioning system he or she must gain entrance to the system in order to observe the pressures. There are two types of terminals for this purpose, the hand shut off type and the familiar Schrader valve.

The Schrader valve is similar to a tire valve

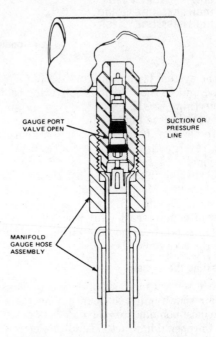

Manifold gauge hose connected to a Schraeder type service port

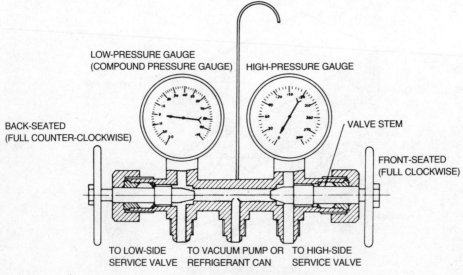

Typical manifold gauge set

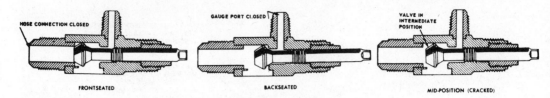

Manual service valve positions

stem and the process of connecting the test hoses is the same as threading a hand pump outlet hose to a bicycle tire. As the test hose is threaded to the service port the valve core is depressed, allowing the refrigerant to enter the test hose outlet. Removal of the test hose automatically closes the system.

Extreme caution must be observed when removing test hoses from the Schrader valves as some refrigerant will normally escape, usually under high pressure; observe safety precautions.

Some systems have hand shut-off valves (the stem can be rotated with a special ratcheting box wrench) that can be positioned in the following three ways:

1. FRONT SEATED – Rotated to full clockwise position.

a. Refrigerant will not flow to compressor but will reach the test gauge port. THE COMPRESSOR WILL BE DAMAGED IF THE SYSTEM IS TURNED ON IN THIS POSITION.

b. The compressor is now isolated and ready for service. However, care must be exercised when removing service valves from the compressor as a residue of refrigerant may still be present within the compressor. Therefore, remove the service valves slowly observing all safety precautions.

2. BACK SEATED – Rotated to full counter clockwise position. Normal position for system while in operation. Refrigerant flows to compressor but not to test gauge.

3. MID-POSITION (CRACKED) – Refrigerant flows to entire system. Gauge port (with hose connected) open for testing.

Using The Manifold Gauges

The following are step-by-step procedures to guide the user to the correct gauge usage.

CAUTION: *Wear goggles or face shield during all testing operations. Backseat hand shut-off type service valves.*

1. Remove the caps from the high and low side service ports. Make sure both gauge valves are closed.

2. Connect the low side test hose to the service valve that leads to the evaporator (located between the evaporator outlet and the compressor).

3. Attach the high side test hose to the service valve that leads to the condenser.

4. Mid-position the hand shutoff type service valves.

5. Start the engine and allow it to warm-up. All testing and charging of the system should be done after the engine and system has reached normal operating temperatures (except when using certain the charging stations).

6. Adjust the air conditioner controls to Max. cold.

7. Observe the gauge readings.

When the gauges are not being used it is a good idea to:

a. Keep both hand valves in the closed position.

b. Attach both ends of the high and low service hoses to the manifold, if extra outlets are present on the manifold or plug them (if not).

c. Keep the center charging hose attached to an empty refrigerant can. This extra precaution will reduce the possibility of moisture entering the gauges. If the air and moisture have gotten into the gauges, purge the hoses by supplying refrigerant under pressure to the center hose with both gauge valves open and all openings unplugged.

DISCHARGING THE SYSTEM

When it is necessary to remove (purge) the refrigerant pressurized in the system, follow this procedure:

CAUTION: *Be sure to perform operation in a well ventilated area.*

1. Operate the air conditioner for at least 10 minutes.

2. Attach the gauges, turn Off the engine and the air conditioner.

3. Place a container or rag at the outlet of the center charging hose on the gauge. The refrigerant will be discharged there and this precaution will avoid its uncontrolled exposure.

4. Open the low side hand valve on gauge slightly.

5. Open the high side hand valve slightly.

NOTE: *Too rapid a purging process will be identified by the appearance of an oily foam. If this occurs, close the hand valves a little more until this condition stops.*

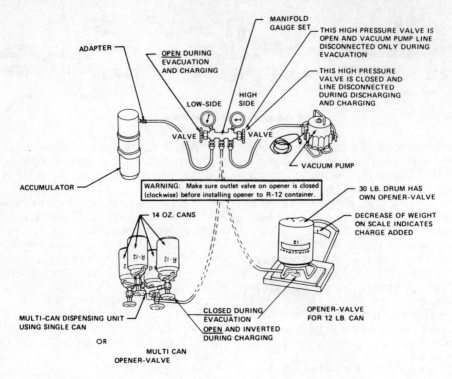

MANIFOLD GAUGE SET

THIS HIGH PRESSURE VALVE IS OPEN AND VACUUM PUMP LINE DISCONNECTED ONLY DURING EVACUATION

THIS HIGH PRESSURE VALVE IS CLOSED AND LINE DISCONNECTED DURING DISCHARGING AND CHARGING

ADAPTER

OPEN DURING EVACUATION AND CHARGING

LOW-SIDE   HIGH SIDE

VALVE   VALVE

VACUUM PUMP

ACCUMULATOR

WARNING: Make sure outlet valve on opener is closed (clockwise) before installing opener to R-12 container.

30 LB. DRUM HAS OWN OPENER-VALVE

DECREASE OF WEIGHT ON SCALE INDICATES CHARGE ADDED

14 OZ. CANS

MULTI-CAN DISPENSING UNIT USING SINGLE CAN

OR

MULTI CAN OPENER-VALVE

CLOSED DURING EVACUATION

OPEN AND INVERTED DURING CHARGING

OPENER-VALVE FOR 12 LB. CAN

Typical gauge connections for discharge, evacuation and charging the system

6. Close both hand valves on the gauge set when the pressures read 0 and all the refrigerant has left the system.

Evacuating the System

Before charging any system it is necessary to purge the refrigerant and draw out the trapped moisture with a suitable vacuum pump. Failure to do so will result in ineffective charging and possible damage to the system.

Use this hook-up for the proper evacuation procedure:

1. Connect both service gauge hoses to the high and low service outlets.

2. Open the high and low side hand valves on the gauge manifold.

3. Open both service valves a slight amount (from the back seated position), then allow the refrigerant to discharge from the system.

4. Install the center charging hose of the gauge set to the vacuum pump.

5. Operate the vacuum pump for at least one hour. If the system has been subjected to open conditions for a prolonged period of time, it may be necessary to "pump the system down" overnight. Refer to the System Sweep procedure.

NOTE: *If the low pressure gauge does not show at least 28 in.Hg within 5 minutes, check the system for a leak or loose gauge connectors.*

6. Close the hand valves on the gauge manifold.

7. Turn Off the pump.

8. Observe the low pressure gauge to determine if the vacuum is holding. A vacuum drop may indicate a leak.

System Sweep

An efficient vacuum pump can remove all the air contained in a contaminated air conditioning system very quickly, because of its vapor state. Moisture, however, is far more difficult to remove because the vacuum must force the liquid to evaporate before it will be able to be removed from the system. If the system has become severely contaminated, as it might become after all the charge was lost in conjunction with vehicle accident damage, moisture removal is extremely time consuming. A vacuum pump could remove all of the moisture only if it were operated for 12 hours or more.

Under these conditions, sweeping the system with refrigerant will speed the process of moisture removal considerably. To sweep, follow the following procedure:

1. Connect the vacuum pump to the gauges, operate it until the vacuum ceases to increase, then continue the operation for ten more minutes.

2. Charge the system with 50% of its rated refrigerant capacity.

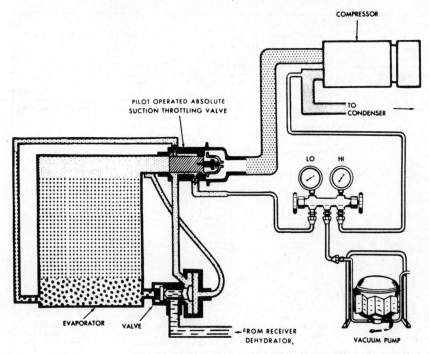

COMPRESSOR

PILOT OPERATED ABSOLUTE
SUCTION THROTTLING VALVE

TO
CONDENSER

LO   HI

EVAPORATOR   VALVE

FROM RECEIVER
DEHYDRATOR,

VACUUM PUMP

Schematic for evacuating the system

3. Operate the system at fast idle for ten minutes.

4. Discharge the system.

5. Repeat (twice) the process of charging to 50% capacity, running the system for ten minutes, then discharging it for a total of three sweeps.

6. Replace the drier.

7. Pump the system down as in Step 1.

8. Charge the system.

CHARGING

CAUTION: *Never attempt to charge the system by opening the high pressure gauge control while the compressor is operating. The compressor accumulating pressure can burst the refrigerant container, causing sever personal injuries.*

Systems With a Sight Glass

The air conditioning system uses a sight glass to check the refrigerant level, it should be carefully inspected to avoid under or over charging. The gauge set should be attached to the system to verify the pressures.

To check the system, clean the glass and start the engine. Operate the air conditioning controls on Max. for approximately five minutes to stabilize the system. The room temperature should be above 70°. Check the sight glass for one of the following conditions:

1. If the sight glass is clear, the compressor clutch is engaged, the compressor discharge line is warm and the compressor inlet line is cool; the system has a full charge of refrigerant.

2. If the sight glass is clear, the compressor clutch is engaged and there is no significant temperature difference between the compressor inlet and discharge lines; the system is empty or nearly empty. By having the gauge set attached to the system, a measurement can be taken. If the gauge reads less than 25 psi, the low pressure cutoff protection switch has failed.

3. If the sight glass is clear and the compressor clutch is disengaged, the clutch is defective, the clutch circuit is open or the system is out of refrigerant. By-pass the low pressure cut-off switch momentarily to determine the cause.

4. If the sight glass shows foam or bubbles, the system can be low on refrigerant. Occasional foam or bubbles is normal when the room temperature is above 110° or below 70°. To verify, increase the engine speed to approximately 1500 rpm and block the airflow through the condenser to increase the compressor discharge pressure to 225–250 psi. If the sight glass still shows bubbles or foam, the refrigerant level is low.

CAUTION: *DO NOT operate the vehicle engine any longer than necessary with the condenser airflow blocked. This blocking action also blocks the cooling system radiator and will cause the system to overheat rapidly.*

Amount of refrigerant / Check item	Almost no refrigerant	Insufficient	Suitable	Too much refrigerant
Temperature of high pressure and low pressure lines.	Almost no difference between high pressure and low pressure side temperature.	High pressure side is warm and low pressure side is fairly cold.	High pressure side is hot and low pressure side is cold.	High pressure side is abnormally hot.
State in sight glass.	Bubbles flow continuously. Bubbles will disappear and something like mist will flow when refrigerant is nearly gone.	The bubbles are seen at intervals of 1 - 2 seconds.	Almost transparent. Bubbles may appear when engine speed is raised and lowered. No clear difference exists betwen these two conditions.	No bubbles can be seen.
Pressure of system.	High pressure side is abnormally low.	Both pressure on high and low pressuré sides are slightly low.	Both pressures on high and low pressure sides are normal.	Both pressures on high and low pressure sides are abnormally high.
Repair.	Stop compressor immediately and conduct an overall check.	Check for gas leakage, repair as required, replenish and charge system.		Discharge refrigerant from service valve of low pressure side.

Using a sight glass to determine the relative refrigerant charge

When the system is low on refrigerant, a leak is present or the system was not properly charged. Use a leak detector to locate the problem area, then repair it. If no leakage is found, charge the system to capacity.

CAUTION: *If equipped with a suction throttling valve, is not advisable to add refrigerant to a system, because the amount of refrigerant required to remove the foam or bubbles will result in an overcharged and potentially damaged system components.*

Windshield Wipers

For maximum effectiveness and longest element life, the windshield and wiper blades should be kept clean. Dirt, tree sap, road tar and so on will cause streaking, smearing and blade deterioration if left on the glass. It is advisable to wash the windshield carefully with a commercial glass cleaner at least once a month. Wipe off the rubber blades with the wet rag, afterwards.

If the blades are found to be cracked, broken or torn, they should be replaced immediately. Replacement intervals will vary with usage, although ozone deterioration usually limits blade life to about one year. If the wiper pattern is smeared, streaked or if the blade chatters across the glass, the elements should be replaced. It is easiest and most sensible to replace the elements in pairs.

BLADE REPLACEMENT

1. Lift the wiper arm assembly from the windshield.
2. Depress the wiper arm-to-blade assembly pin to disconnect the blade assembly from the wiper arm.
3. To install, use new blade assemblies and reverse the removal procedures.

Tires

TIRE ROTATION

Tire wear can be equalized by switching the position of the tire about every 6000 miles. Including a conventional spare in the rotation pattern can give up to 20% more tire life.

CAUTION: *DO NOT include the new Space Saver® or temporary spare tires in the rotation pattern.*

There are certain exceptions to tire rotation, however. Studded snow tires should not be rotated and radials should be kept on the same side of the vehicle (maintain the same direction of rotation). The belts on radial tires get set in a pattern. If the direction of rotation is reversed, it can cause rough ride and vibration.

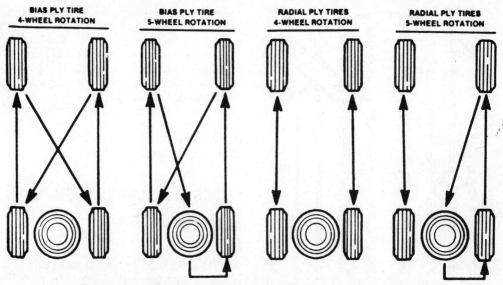

| BIAS PLY TIRE 4-WHEEL ROTATION | BIAS PLY TIRE 5-WHEEL ROTATION | RADIAL PLY TIRES 4-WHEEL ROTATION | RADIAL PLY TIRES 5-WHEEL ROTATION |

Tire rotation diagrams; note that radials should not be cross-switched

NOTE: *When radials or studded snows are taken off the vehicle, mark them, so you can maintain the same direction of rotation.*

TIRE INFLATION

The inflation is the most ignored item of auto maintenance. Gasoline mileage can drop as much as 0.8% for every 1 pound/square inch (psi) of under inflation.

Two items should be a permanent fixture in every glove compartment: a tire pressure gauge and a tread depth gauge. Check the tire air pressure (including the spare) regularly with a pocket type gauge. Kicking the tires won't tell you a thing and the gauge on the service station air hose is notoriously inaccurate.

The tire pressures recommended for your vehicle are usually found on the glove box door or in the owner's manual. Ideally, inflation pressure should be checked when the tires are cool. When the air becomes heated it expands and the pressure increases. Every 10° rise (or drop) in temperature means a difference of 1 psi, which also explains why the tire appears to lose air on a very cold night. When it is impossible to check the tires cold, allow for pressure build-up due to heat. If the hot pressure exceeds the cold pressure by more than 15 psi, reduce your speed, load or both. Otherwise internal heat is created in the tire. When the heat approaches the temperature at which the tire was cured, during manufacture, the tread can separate from the body.

CAUTION: *Never counteract excessive pressure build-up by bleeding off air pressure (letting some air out). This will only further raise the tire operating temperature.*

Before starting a long trip with lots of lug-gage, you can add about 2–4 psi to the tires to make them run cooler but never exceed the maximum inflation pressure on the side of the tire.

TREAD DEPTH

All tires have 8 built-in tread wear indicator bars that show up as ½″ (12.7mm) wide smooth bands across the tire when 1/16″ (1.5mm) of

Tread depth can be checked with an inexpensive gauge

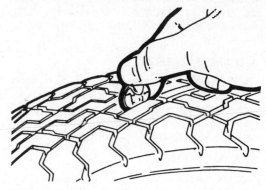

A penny works as well as anything for checking tire tread depth; when you can see the top of Lincoln's head, it's time for a new tire

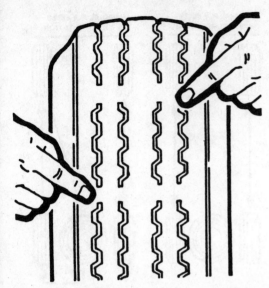

Tread wear indicators will appear when the tire is worn out

tread remains. The appearance of tread wear indicators means that the tires should be replaced. In fact, many states have laws prohibiting the use of tires with less than $\frac{1}{16}''$ (1.5mm) tread.

You can check your own tread depth with an inexpensive gauge or by using a Lincoln head penny. Slip the Lincoln penny into several into several tread grooves. If you can see the top of Lincoln's head in 2 adjacent grooves, the tires have less than $\frac{1}{16}''$ (1.5mm) tread left and should be replaced. You can measure snow tires in the same manner by using the tails side of the Lincoln penny. If you can see the top of the Lincoln memorial, it's time to replace the snow tires.

TIRE STORAGE

Store the tires at proper inflation pressures if they are mounted on wheels. All tires should be kept in a cool, dry place. If they are stored in the garage or basement, DO NOT let them stand on a concrete floor, set them on strips of wood.

ALUMINUM WHEELS

CAUTION: *If your vehicle has aluminum wheels, be very careful when using any type of cleaner on either the wheels or the tires. Read the label on the package of the cleaner to make sure that it will not damage aluminum.*

TIRE INFLATION

Factory installed wheels and tires are designed to handle loads up to and including their rated load capacity when inflated to the recommended inflation pressures. Correct tire

pressures and driving techniques have an important influence on tire life. Heavy cornering, excessively rapid acceleration and unnecessary braking increase tire wear. Underinflated tires can cause handling problems, poor fuel economy, shortened tire life and tire overloading.

Maximum axle load must never exceed the value shown on the side of the tire. The inflation pressure should never exceed 35 psi (standard tires) or 60 psi (compact tire).

FLUIDS AND LUBRICANTS

Engine Oil and Fuel

OIL

Use ONLY SF/CC or SF/CD rated oils of the recommended viscosity. Under the classification system developed by the American Petroleum Institute, the SF rating designates the highest quality oil for use in passenger vehicles. In addition, Chevrolet recommends the use of an SF/Energy Conserving oil. Oils labeled Energy Conserving (or Saving), Fuel (Gas or Gasoline) Saving, etc. are recommended due to their superior lubricating qualities (less friction—easier engine operation) and fuel saving characteristics. Pick your oil viscosity with regard to the anticipated temperatures during the period before your next oil change. Using the accompanying chart, choose the oil viscosity for the lowest expected temperature. You will be assured of easy cold starting and sufficient engine protection.

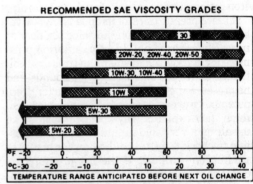

RECOMMENDED SAE VISCOSITY GRADES

NOTICE: Do not use SAE 5W-20 oils for continuous high-speed driving.

Oil viscosity chart; multi-viscosity oils offer greater temperature latitude

FUEL

NOTE: *Some fuel additives contain chemicals that can damage the catalytic converter and/or oxygen sensor. Read all of the labels carefully before using any additive in the engine or fuel system.*

Fuel should be selected for the brand and octane which performs best with your engine. Judge a gasoline by its ability to prevent pinging, it's engine starting capabilities (cold and hot) and general all weather performance. As far as the octane rating is concerned, refer to the General Engine Specifications chart in Chapter 3 to find your engine and its compression ratio.

If the compression ratio is 9.0:1 or lower, in most cases a regular unleaded grade of gasoline can be used. If the compression ratio is 9.0:1–9.3:1, use a premium grade of unleaded fuel.

NOTE: *Your van's engine fuel requirement can change with time, due to carbon buildup, which changes the compression ratio. If your van's engine knocks, pings or runs on, switch to a higher grade of fuel (if possible) and check the ignition timing. Sometimes changing brands of gasoline will cure the problem. If it is necessary to retard the timing from specifications, don't change it more than a few degrees. Retarded timing will reduce the power output and the fuel mileage, plus it will increase the engine temperature.*

Engine

The mileage figures given in your owner's manual are the Chevrolet recommended intervals for oil and filter changes assuming average driving. If your Astro Van is being used under dusty, polluted or off-road conditions, change the oil and filter sooner than specified. The same thing goes for vehicles driven in stop-and-go traffic or only for short distances.

Always drain the oil after the engine has been running long enough to bring it to operating temperature. Hot oil will flow easier and more contaminants will be removed along with the oil than if it were drained cold. You will need a large capacity drain pan, which you can purchase at any store that sells automotive parts. Another necessity is a container for the used oil. You will find that plastic bottles, such as those used for bleach or fabric softener, make excellent storage jugs. One ecologically desirable solution to the used oil disposal problem is to find a cooperative gas station owner who will allow you to dump your used oil into his tank. Another is to keep the oil for use around the house as a preservative on fences, railroad tie borders, etc.

Chevrolet recommends changing both the oil and filter during the first oil change and the filter every other oil change thereafter. For the small price of an oil filter, it's cheap insurance to replace the filter at every oil change. One of the larger filter manufacturers points out in it's advertisements that not changing the filter leaves one quart of dirty oil in the engine. This claim is true and should be kept in mind when changing your oil.

OIL LEVEL CHECK

The engine oil level is checked with the dipstick.

NOTE: *The oil should be checked before the engine is started or 5 minutes after the engine has been shut OFF. This gives the oil time to drain back to the oil pan and prevents an inaccurate oil level reading.*

Remove the dipstick from its tube, wipe it clean and insert it back into the tube. Remove it again and observe the oil level. It should be maintained between the Full and Add marks without going above Full or below Add.

The oil level is checked with the dipstick

The oil level should be between the "ADD" and "Full" marks on the dipstick

CAUTION: *DO NOT overfill the crankcase. It may result in oil-fouled spark plugs, oil leaks caused by oil seal failure or engine damage due to foaming of the oil.*

OIL AND FILTER CHANGE

1. Operate the engine until it reaches normal operating temperature.

2. Raise and support the front of the vehicle jackstands.

3. Slide a drain pan of at least 6 quarts capacity under the oil pan.

4. Loosen the drain plug. Turn it out by hand by keeping an inward pressure on the plug as you unscrew it. Oil won't escape past the threads and you can remove it without being burned by hot oil.

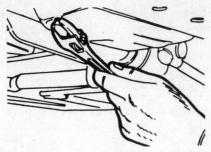

The oil drain plug is located at the lowest point of the oil pan

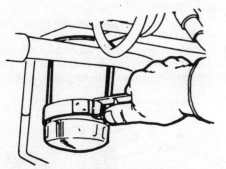

Use an oil filter strap wrench to remove the oil filter; install the new filter by hand

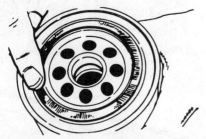

Apply a thin film of clean oil to the new gasket to prevent it from tearing upon installation

NOTE: *Dispose of the waste oil properly. Don't pollute the environment. Avoid prolonged skin contact with used oil directly or from oil-saturated clothing.*

5. Allow the oil to drain completely and then install the drain plug. Don't overtighten the plug or you'll be buying a new pan or a trick replacement plug for damaged threads.

6. Using a strap wrench, remove the oil filter. Keep in mind that it's holding about one quart of dirty, hot oil.

7. Empty the old filter into the drain pan and dispose of the filter.

8. Using a clean rag, wipe off the filter adapter on the engine block. Be sure that the rag doesn't leave any lint which could clog an oil passage.

9. Coat the rubber gasket on the filter with fresh oil. Spin it onto the engine by hand. When the gasket touches the adapter surface give it another 1/2–3/4 turn; no more or you'll squash the gasket and cause it to leak.

10. Refill the engine with the correct amount of new oil. See the Capacities chart.

11. Crank the engine over several times and then start it. If the oil pressure gauge shows zero, shut the engine Off and find out what's wrong.

12. If the oil pressure is OK and there are no leaks, shut the engine Off and lower the vehicle.

13. Wait a few minutes and check the oil level. Add oil, as necessary, to bring the level up to the Full mark.

Manual Transmission
FLUID RECOMMENDATIONS

Fill the main transmission housing with API GL5 SAE-80W90 (4-speed) multipurpose gear lubricant or Dexron®II (5-speed) automatic transmission fluid.

LEVEL CHECK

Remove the filler plug from the passenger's side of the transmission (the upper plug if the transmission has two plugs). The oil should be level with the bottom edge of the filler hole. This should be checked at least once every 6,000 miles and more often if any leakage or seepage is observed.

DRAIN AND REFILL

Under normal conditions, the transmission fluid should not be changed.

1. Raise and support the vehicle on jackstands.

2. Place a fluid catch pan under the transmission.

3. Remove the bottom plug and drain the fluid.

4. Install the bottom plug and refill the transmission housing.

Automatic Transmission
FLUID RECOMMENDATIONS

When adding fluid or refilling the transmission, use Dexron®II automatic transmission fluid.

LEVEL CHECK

Before checking the fluid level of the transmission, drive the vehicle for at least 15 miles to warm the fluid.

1. Place the vehicle on a level surface, apply the parking brake and block the front wheels.

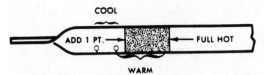

Automatic transmission dipstick marks; the proper level is within the shaded area

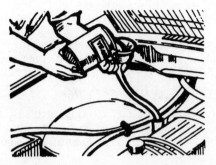

Add automatic transmission fluid through the dipstick tube

2. Start the engine and move the selector through each range, then place it in Park.

NOTE: *When moving the selector through each range, DO NOT race the engine.*

3. With the engine running at a low idle, remove the transmission's dipstick to check the fluid level.

4. The level should be at the Full Hot mark of the dipstick. If not, add fluid.

CAUTION: *DO NOT overfill the transmission, damage to the seals could occur. Use Dexron®II automatic transmission fluid. One pint raises the level from Add to Full.*

DRAIN AND REFILL

The vehicle should be driven 15 miles to warm the transmission fluid before the pan is removed.

NOTE: *The fluid should be drained while the transmission is warm.*

1. Raise and support the front of vehicle on jackstands.

2. Place a drain pan under the transmission pan.

3. Remove the pan bolts from the front and the sides, then loosen the rear bolts 4 turns.

4. Using a small pry bar, pry the pan from the transmission. This will allow the pan to partially drain. Remove the remaining pan bolts and lower the pan from the transmission.

NOTE: *If the transmission fluid is dark or has a burnt smell, transmission damage is indicated. Have the transmission checked professionally.*

5. Empty the pan, remove the gasket material and clean with a solvent.

6. Using a putty knife, clean gasket mounting surfaces.

7. To install the oil pan, use a new gasket and sealant, then reverse the removal procedures. Torque the pan bolts to 8 ft.lb. in a criss-cross pattern.

8. Using Dexron®II automatic transmission fluid, add it through the filler tube. See the Capacities Chart to determine the proper amount of fluid to be added.

CAUTION: *DO NOT OVERFILL the transmission. Foaming of the fluid and subsequent transmission damage due to slippage will result.*

9. With the gearshift lever in PARK, start the engine and let it idle. DO NOT race the engine.

10. Apply the parking brake and move the gearshift lever through each position. Return the lever to Park and check the fluid level with the engine idling. The level should be between the two dimples on the dipstick, about ¼" (6mm) below the ADD mark. Add fluid, if necessary.

11. Check the fluid level after the vehicle has been driven enough to thoroughly warm the transmission.

PAN AND FILTER SERVICE

1. Refer to the Drain and Refill procedures in this section and remove the oil pan.

2. Remove the screen and the filter from the valve body.

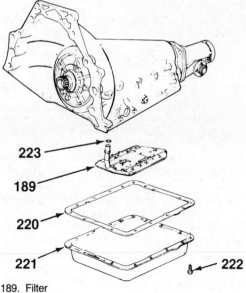

223
189
220
221
222

189. Filter
220. Gasket
221. Pan
222. Screw
223. Seal

Exploded view of the transmission oil and and filter

3. Install a new filter using a new gasket or O-ring.

NOTE: *If the transmission uses a filter having a fully exposed screen, it may be cleaned and reused.*

4. To install the oil pan, use a new gasket and sealant, then reverse the removal procedures. Torque the pan bolts to 8 ft.lb. in a criss-cross pattern. Refill the transmission.

Drive Axle

Several axle ratios are available, with the 7½″ (190.5mm) ring gear rear axle, to be used with various powertrain applications.

FLUID RECOMMENDATIONS

Standard Axle

Always use SAE-80W or SAE 80W-90 GL5. Drain and refill the differential at first oil fill, then at every other oil fill.

Locking Axle

CAUTION: *Never use standard differential lubricant in a positraction differential.*

Always use GM Rear Axle Fluid No. 1052271. Before refilling the rear axle, add 4 ounces of GM Fluid No. 1052358. Drain and refill the differential at first oil fill, then at every other oil fill.

LEVEL CHECK

The lubricant level should be checked at each chassis lubrication and maintained at the bottom of the filler plug hole.

1. Raise and support the vehicle on jackstands; be sure that the vehicle is level.

2. Remove the filler plug, located at the side of the differential carrier.

3. Check the fluid level, it should be level with the bottom of the filler plug hole, add fluid (if necessary).

4. Replace the filler plug.

DRAIN AND REFILL

Refer to Fluid Recommendations in this section for information on when to change the fluid.

1. Run the vehicle until the lubricant reaches operating temperature.

2. Raise and support the rear of the vehicle on jackstands; be sure that the vehicle is level.

3. Using a floor jack, support the drive axle. Position a drain pan under the rear axle.

4. Remove the cover from the rear of the drive axle and drain the lubricant.

5. Using a putty knife, clean the gasket mounting surfaces.

6. To install, use a new gasket, sealant and reverse the removal procedures.

7. Torque the cover-to-rear axle bolts in a criss-cross pattern to 20 ft.lb. Using a suction gun or a squeeze bulb, install the fluids through the filler plug hole. Install the filler plug.

Cooling System

At least once every 2 years or 30,000 miles, the engine cooling system should be inspected, flushed and refilled with fresh coolant. If the coolant is left in the system too long, it loses its ability to prevent rust and corrosion. If the coolant has too much water, it won't protect against freezing.

FLUID RECOMMENDATIONS

Using a good quality of ethylene glycol antifreeze (one that will not effect aluminum), mix it with water until a 50–50 antifreeze solution is attained.

LEVEL CHECK

NOTE: *When checking the coolant level, the radiator need not be removed, simply check the coolant tank.*

Check the coolant recovery bottle (see through plastic bottle). With the engine Cold, the coolant should be at the ADD mark (recovery tank ¼ full). With the engine warm, the coolant should be at the FULL mark (recovery tank ½ full). If necessary, add fluid to the recovery bottle.

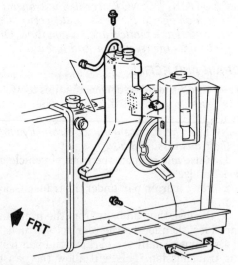

View of the radiator recovery tank

DRAIN AND REFILL

CAUTION: *To avoid injuries from scalding fluid and steam, DO NOT remove the radiator cap while the engine and radiator are still HOT.*

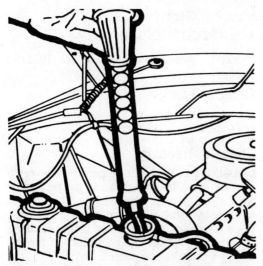

You can use an inexpensive tester to check anti-freeze protection

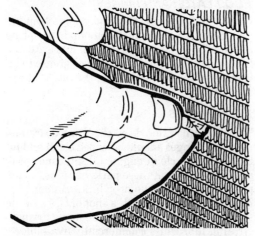

Clean the front of the radiator of any bugs, leaves, or other debris at every yearly coolant change

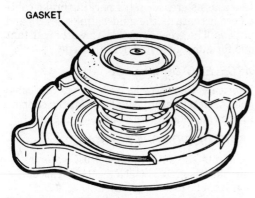

GASKET

Check the condition of the radiator cap gasket

1. When the engine is cool, remove the radiator cap using the following procedures.

    a. Slowly rotate the cap counterclockwise to the detent.

    b. If any residual pressure is present, WAIT until the hissing noise stops.

    c. After the hissing noise has ceased, press down on the cap and continue rotating it counterclockwise to remove it.

2. Place a fluid catch pan under the radiator, open the radiator drain valve and the engine drain plugs, then drain the coolant.

3. Close the drain valve and install the engine drain plugs.

4. Empty the coolant reservoir and flush it.

5. Using the correct mixture of antifreeze, fill the radiator to the bottom of the filler neck and the coolant tank to the FULL mark.

6. Install the radiator cap (make sure that the arrows align with the overflow tube).

7. Run the engine until it reaches the operating temperatures, allow it to cool, then check the fluid level and add fluid (if necessary).

FLUSHING AND CLEANING THE SYSTEM

1. Refer to the Drain and Refill procedures in this section, then drain the cooling system.

2. Close the drain valve and install the engine drain plugs, then add sufficient water to the cooling system.

3. Run the engine, then drain and refill the system. Perform this procedure several times, until the fluid (drained from the system) is clear.

4. Empty the coolant reservoir and flush it.

5. Using the correct mixture of antifreeze, fill the radiator to the bottom of the filler neck and the coolant tank to the FULL mark.

6. Install the radiator cap (make sure that the arrows align with the overflow tube).

Master Cylinder

FLUID RECOMMENDATIONS

Use only heavy-duty Delco Supreme 11 or DOT-3 brake fluid.

LEVEL CHECK

The brake fluid level should be inspected every 6 months.

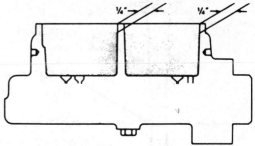

The fluid level in the master cylinder reservoir should be within ¼ in. of the top edge

1. Remove the master cylinder reservoir caps.

2. The fluid should be ¼" (6mm) from top of the reservoir, if necessary, add fluid.

3. Replace the reservoir caps.

Hydraulic Clutch

NOTE: *The clutch master cylinder is mounted on the firewall next to the brake master cylinder.*

FLUID RECOMMENDATIONS

Use only heavy duty Delco Supreme 11 or DOT-3 brake fluid.

LEVEL CHECK

The hydraulic clutch reservoir should be checked at least every 6 months. Fill to the line on the reservoir.

Power Steering Pump

The power steering pump reservoir is located at the front left side of the engine.

FLUID RECOMMENDATIONS

Use GM Power Steering Fluid No. 1050017 or equivalent.

NOTE: *Avoid using automatic transmission fluid in the power steering unit, except in an emergency.*

LEVEL CHECK

The power steering fluid should be checked at least every 6 months. There is a Cold and a Hot mark on the dipstick. The fluid should be checked when the engine is warm and turned OFF. If necessary, add fluid to the power steering pump reservoir.

NOTE: *On models equipped with a remote reservoir, the fluid level should be ½–1" (25.4mm) from the top when the wheels are turned to the extreme left position.*

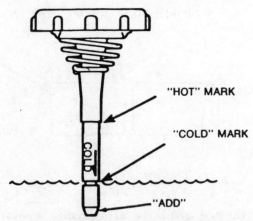

"HOT" MARK

"COLD" MARK

"ADD"

Use the dipstick to check the power steering fluid

Steering Gear

FLUID RECOMMENDATIONS

Use GM steering gear lubricant No. 1052182 or equivalent.

LEVEL CHECK

The steering lubricant should be checked every 6 months or 7,500 miles.

Chassis Greasing

Chassis greasing should be performed every 6 months or 7,500 miles, it can be performed with a commercial pressurized grease gun or at home by using a hand operated grease gun. Wipe the grease fittings clean before greasing in order to prevent the possibility of forcing any dirt into the component.

Body Lubrication

HOOD LATCH AND HINGES

Clean the latch surfaces and apply clean engine oil to the latch pilot bolts and the spring anchor. Use the engine oil to lubricate the hood hinges as well. Use a chassis grease to lubricate all the pivot points in the latch release mechanism.

DOOR HINGES

The gas tank filler door, the front doors and rear door hinges should be wiped clean and lubricated with clean engine oil. Silicone spray also works well on these parts but must be applied more often. The door lock cylinders can be lubricated easily with a shot of GM silicone spray No. 1052276 or one of the many dry penetrating lubricants commercially available.

PARKING BRAKE LINKAGE

Use chassis grease on the parking brake cable where it contacts the guides, links, levers and pulleys. The grease should be a water resistant one for durability under the vehicle.

ACCELERATOR LINKAGE

Lubricate the throttle body lever, the cable and the accelerator pedal lever (at the support inside the vehicle) with clean engine oil.

TRANSMISSION SHIFT LINKAGE

Lubricate the shift linkage with water resistant chassis grease which meets GM specification No. 6031M or equivalent.

Wheel Bearings

Once every 30,000 miles, clean and repack wheel bearings with a GM Wheel Bearing Grease No. 1051344 or equivalent. Use only enough grease to completely coat the rollers.

Remove any excess grease from the exposed surface of the hub and seal.

REMOVAL, PACKING AND INSTALLATION

NOTE: *The following procedures require the use of GM tools No. J-29117, J-8092, J-8850, J-8457 and J-9746-02 or equivalent.*

1. Raise and support the front of the vehicle on jackstands.
2. Remove the tire/wheel assembly.
3. Remove the caliper-to-steering knuckle bolts and the caliper from the steering knuckle. Using a wire, support the caliper from the vehicle; DO NOT disconnect the brake line.
4. From the hub/disc assembly, remove the dust cap, the cotter pin, the spindle nut, the thrust washer and the outer bearing.
5. Grasping the hub/disc assembly firmly, pull the assembly from the axle spindle.
6. Using a small pry bar, pry the grease seal from the rear of the hub/disc assembly, then remove the inner bearing.

NOTE: *DO NOT remove the bearing races from the hub, unless they show signs of damage.*

7. If it is necessary to remove the wheel bearing races, use the GM front bearing race removal tool No. J-29117 to drive the races from the hub/disc assembly.
8. Using solvent, clean the grease from all of the parts, then blow them dry with compressed air.
9. Inspect all of the parts for scoring, pitting or cracking, replace the parts (if necessary).
10. If the bearing races were removed, perform the following procedures to the install the them:

   a. Using grease, lightly lubricate the inside of the hub/disc assembly.

   b. Using the GM seal installation tools No. J-8092 and J-8850, drive the inner bearing race into the hub/disc assembly until it seats.

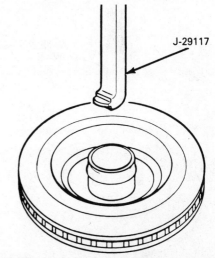

Removing the front wheel bearing races from the hub/disc assembly

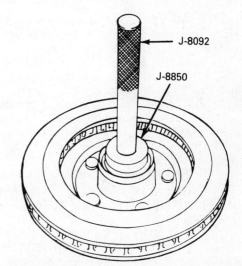

Installing the inner wheel bearing race to the hub/disc assembly

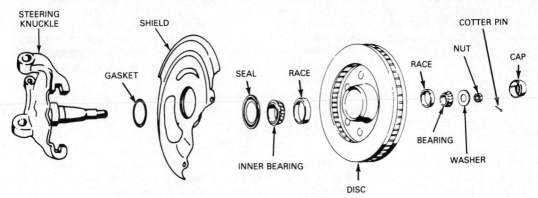

Exploded view of the front wheel hub/bearing assembly

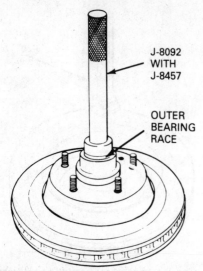

J-8092
WITH
J-8457

OUTER
BEARING
RACE

Installing the outer wheel bearing race to the hub/disc assembly

NOTE: *When installing the bearing races, be sure to support the hub/disc assembly with GM tool No. J-9746-02.*

c. Using the GM seal installation tools No. J-8092 and J-8457, drive the outer race into the hub/disc assembly until it seats.

11. Using wheel bearing grease, lubricate the bearings, the races and the spindle; be sure to place a gob of grease (inside the hub/disc assembly) between the races to provide an ample supply of lubricant.

NOTE: *To lubricate each bearing, place a gob of grease in the palm of the hand, then roll the bearing through the grease until it is well lubricated.*

12. Place the inner wheel bearing into the hub/disc assembly. Using a flat plate, drive the new grease seal into the rear of the hub/disc assembly until it is flush with the outer surface.

13. Onto the spindle, install the hub/disc assembly, the thrust washer and the hub nut. While turning the wheel, torque the hub nut to 16 ft.lb. until the bearings seat. Loosen the nut, retighten it and back it off until the nearest nut slot aligns with a spindle hole (not more than a ½ turn).

14. Install a new cotter pin through the nut and the spindle, then bend the ends and cut off the excess pin. Install the grease cap.

15. If necessary, use a dial indicator to the check the rotor endplay. The endplay should be 0.001–0.005″ (0.025–0.127mm); if not, readjust the hub/disc assembly.

16. Install the caliper onto the steering knuckle and torque the bolts to 37 ft.lb. Road test the vehicle.

TRAILER TOWING

Astro vans are popular as trailer towing vehicles. Their strong construction and variety of power train combinations make them ideal for towing campers, boat trailers and utility trailers.

Factory trailer towing packages are available on most vans. However, if you are installing a trailer hitch and wiring on your vehicle, there are a few things you ought to know.

General Recommendations

Wiring

Wiring the vehicle for towing is fairly easy. There are a number of good wiring kits available and these should be used, rather than trying to design your own. All trailers will need brake lights, turn signals, tail lights and side marker lights. Most states require extra marker lights for overwide trailers. Also, most states have recently required back-up lights for trailers, and most trailer manufacturers have been building trailers with back-up lights for several years.

Additionally, some Class I, most Class II and just about all Class III trailers will have electric brakes.

Add to this number an accessories wire, to operate the trailer internal equipment or to charge the trailer's battery, and you can have as many as seven wires in the harness.

Determine the equipment on your trailer and buy the wiring kit necessary. The kit will contain all the wires needed, plus a plug adapter set which included the female plug, mounted on the bumper or hitch, and the male plug, wired into, or plugged into the trailer harness.

When installing the kit, follow the manufacturer's instructions. The color coding of the wires is standard throughout the industry.

One point to note: some domestic vehicles and most imported vehicles, have separate turn signals. On most domestic vehicles, the brake lights and rear turn signals operate with the same bulb. For those vehicles with separate turn signals, you can purchase an isolation unit so that the brake lights won't blink whenever the turn signals are operated, or, you can go to your local electronics supply house and buy four diodes to wire in series with the brake and turn signal bulbs. Diodes will isolate the brake and turn signals. The choice is yours. The isolation units are simple and quick to install, but far more expensive than the diodes. The diodes, however, require more work to install properly, since they require the cutting of each bulb's wire and soldering in place of the diode.

One, final point, the best kits are those with a spring loaded cover on the vehicle mounted socket. This cover prevents dirt and moisture from corroding the terminals. Never let the vehicle socket hang loosely; always mount it securely to the bumper or hitch.

Cooling

ENGINE

One of the most common, if not THE most common, problems associated with trailer towing is engine overheating.

With factory installed trailer towing packages, a heavy duty cooling system is usually included. Heavy duty cooling systems are available as optional equipment on most vans, with or without a trailer package. If you have one of these extra capacity systems, you shouldn't have overheating problems.

If you have a standard cooling system, without an expansion tank, you'll definitely need to get an aftermarket expansion tank kit, preferably one with at least a 2 quart capacity. These kits are easily installed on the radiator's overflow hose, and come with a pressure cap designed for expansion tanks.

Another helpful accessory is a Flex Fan. These fan are large diameter units are designed to provide more airflow at low speeds, with blades that have deeply cupped surfaces. The blades then flex, or flatten out, at high speed, when less cooling air is needed. These fans are far lighter in weight than stock fans, requiring less horsepower to drive them. Also, they are far quieter than stock fans.

If you do decide to replace your stock fan with a flex fan, note that if your vehicle has a fan clutch, a spacer between the flex fan and water pump hub will be needed.

Aftermarket engine oil coolers are helpful for prolonging engine oil life and reducing overall engine temperatures. Both of these factors increase engine life.

While not absolutely necessary in towing Class I and some Class II trailers, they are recommended for heavier Class II and all Class III towing.

Engine oil cooler systems consist of an adapter, screwed on in place of the oil filter, a remote filter mounting and a multi-tube, a finned heat exchanger, which is mounted in front of the radiator or air conditioning condenser.

TRANSMISSION

An automatic transmission is usually recommended for trailer towing. Modern automatics have proven reliable and, of course, easy to operate, in trailer towing.

The increased load of a trailer, however, causes an increase in the temperature of the automatic transmission fluid. Heat is the worst enemy of an automatic transmission. As the temperature of the fluid increases, the life of the fluid decreases.

It is essential, therefore, that you install an automatic transmission cooler.

The cooler, which consists of a multi-tube, finned heat exchanger, is usually installed in front of the radiator or air conditioning compressor, and hooked inline with the transmission cooler tank inlet line. Follow the cooler manufacturer's installation instructions.

Select a cooler of at least adequate capacity, based upon the combined gross weights of the van and trailer.

Cooler manufacturers recommend that you use an aftermarket cooler in addition to, and not instead of, the present cooling tank in your vans radiator. If you do want to use it in place of the radiator cooling tank, get a cooler at least two sizes larger than normally necessary.

One note: transmission cooler can, sometimes, cause slow or harsh shifting in the transmission during cold weather, until the fluid has a chance to come up to normal operating temperature. Some coolers can be purchased with or retrofitted with a temperature bypass valve which will allow fluid flow through the cooler only when the fluid has reached operating temperature, or above.

Trailer and Hitch Weight Limits

Trailer Weight

Trailer weight is the first, and most important, factor in determining whether or not your vehicle is suitable for towing the trailer you have in mind. The horsepower-to-weight ratio should be calculated. The basic standard is a ratio of 35:1. That is, 35 lbs. of GVW for every horsepower.

To calculate this ratio, multiply you engine's rated horsepower by 35, then subtract the weight of the vehicle, including passengers and luggage. The resulting figure is the ideal maximum trailer weight that you can tow. One point to consider: a numerically higher axle ratio can offset what appears to be a low trailer weight. If the weight of the trailer that you have in mind is somewhat higher than the weight you just calculated, you might consider changing your rear axle ratio to compensate.

Hitch Weight

There are three kinds of hitches: bumper mounted, frame mounted and load equalizing.

Bumper mounted hitches are those which attach solely to the vehicle's bumper. Many states prohibit towing with this type of hitch, when it attaches to the vehicle's stock bumper, since it subjects the bumper to stresses for which it was not designed. Aftermarket rear step bumpers, designed for trailer towing, are acceptable for use with bumper mounted hitches.

Frame mounted hitches can be of the type which bolts to two or more points on the frame, plus the bumper, or just to several points on the frame. Frame mounted hitches can also be of the tongue type, for Class I towing, or, of the receiver type, for classes II and III.

Load equalizing hitches are usually used for large trailers. Most equalizing hitches are welded in place, they use equalizing bars and chains to level the vehicle after the trailer is connected.

The bolt-on hitches are the most common, since they are relatively easy to install.

Check the gross weight rating of your trailer. Tongue weight is usually figured as 10% of gross trailer weight. Therefore, a trailer with a maximum gross weight of 2,000 lbs. will have a maximum tongue weight of 200 lbs. Class I trailers fall into this category. Class II trailers are those with a gross weight rating of 2,000–3,500 lbs., while Class III trailers fall into the 3,500–6,000 lbs. category. Class IV trailers are those over 6,000 lbs. and are for use with fifth wheel trucks, only.

When you've determined the hitch that you'll need, follow the manufacturer's installation instructions, exactly, especially when it comes to fastener torques. The hitch will subjected to a lot of stress and good hitches come with hardened bolts. Never substitute an inferior bolt for a hardened bolt.

PUSHING AND TOWING

DO NOT push or tow your Astro Van to start it. Unusually high catalytic converter and exhaust system temperatures may result, which under extreme conditions may ignite the interior floor covering material above the converter.

Astro Vans may be towed at speeds up to 35 mph and distances not over 50 miles with the driveshaft in place, if no engine/driveline damage is present. If engine/driveline damage is known or suspected, the driveshaft should be disconnected before towing.

To be sure that no damage will occur to your vehicle, consult any GM dealer or professional tow truck service for towing instructions.

NOTE: *To avoid damage to the fiberglass*

springs when raising the vehicle, DO NOT allow the lifting equipment to come into contact with the springs.

JUMP STARTING

The following procedure is recommended by the manufacturer. Be sure that the booster battery is a 12 volt with a negative ground.

CAUTION: *DO NOT attempt this procedure on a frozen battery, it will probably explode. DO NOT attempt it on a sealed Delco Freedom battery showing a light color in the charge indicator. Be certain to observe the correct polarity connections. Failure to do so will result in almost immediate alternator and regulator destruction. Never allow the jumper cable ends to touch each other.*

1. Position the 2 vehicles so that they are not touching. Set the parking brake and place the transmission in Park (AT) or in Neutral (MT). Turn Off the lights, heater and other electrical loads.
2. Remove the vent caps from both the booster and discharged battery. Lay a cloth over the open vent cells of each battery. This is not necessary on batteries equipped with sponge type flame arrestor caps and it is not possible on sealed Freedom batteries.
3. Attach one cable to the positive (+) terminal of the booster battery and the other end to the positive terminal of the discharged battery.
4. Attach one end of the remaining cable to the negative (–) terminal of the booster battery and the other end to the alternator bracket (about 18″ [457mm] from the discharged battery). DO NOT attach to the negative terminal of discharged batteries.
5. Start the engine of the vehicle with the booster battery. Start the engine of the vehicle with the discharged battery. If the engine will no start, disconnect the batteries as soon as possible. If this is not done, the two batteries will soon reach a state of equilibrium, with both too weak to start any engine. This will not be a problem if the engine of the booster vehicle is kept running fast enough. Lengthy cranking can overheat and damage the starter.
6. Reverse the above steps to disconnect the booster and discharged batteries. Be certain to remove the negative connections first.
7. Dispose of the cloths, for they may have battery acid on them.

CAUTION: *The use of any "hot shot" type of jumper system in excess of 12 volts can damage the electronic control units or cause the discharged battery to explode.*

JUMP STARTING A DEAD BATTERY

The chemical reaction in a battery produces explosive hydrogen gas. This is the safe way to jump start a dead battery, reducing the chances of an accidental spark that could cause an explosion.

Jump Starting Precautions

1. Be sure both batteries are of the same voltage.
2. Be sure both batteries are of the same polarity (have the same grounded terminal).
3. Be sure the vehicles are not touching.
4. Be sure the vent cap holes are not obstructed.
5. Do not smoke or allow sparks around the battery.
6. In cold weather, check for frozen electrolyte in the battery. Do not jump start a frozen battery.
7. Do not allow electrolyte on your skin or clothing.
8. Be sure the electrolyte is not frozen.

CAUTION: *Make certain that the ignition key, in the vehicle with the dead battery, is in the OFF position. Connecting cables to vehicles with on-board computers will result in computer destruction if the key is not in the OFF position.*

Jump Starting Procedure

1. Determine voltages of the two batteries; they must be the same.
2. Bring the starting vehicle close (they must not touch) so that the batteries can be reached easily.
3. Turn off all accessories and both engines. Put both cars in Neutral or Park and set the handbrake.
4. Cover the cell caps with a rag—do not cover terminals.
5. If the terminals on the run-down battery are heavily corroded, clean them.
6. Identify the positive and negative posts on both batteries and connect the cables in the order shown.
7. Start the engine of the starting vehicle and run it at fast idle. Try to start the car with the dead battery. Crank it for no more than 10 seconds at a time and let it cool off for 20 seconds in between tries.
8. If it doesn't start in 3 tries, there is something else wrong.
9. Disconnect the cables in the reverse order.
10. Replace the cell covers and dispose of the rags.

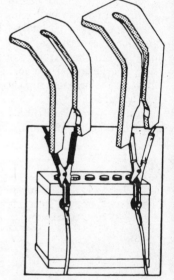

Side terminal batteries occasionally pose a problem when connecting jumper cables. There frequently isn't enough room to clamp the cables without touching sheet metal. Side terminal adaptors are available to alleviate this problem and should be removed after use.

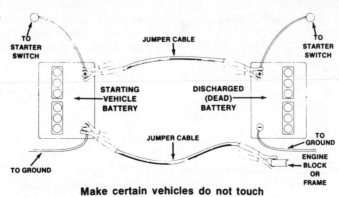

TO STARTER SWITCH

JUMPER CABLE

TO STARTER SWITCH

STARTING VEHICLE BATTERY

DISCHARGED (DEAD) BATTERY

JUMPER CABLE

TO GROUND

TO GROUND

ENGINE BLOCK OR FRAME

Make certain vehicles do not touch

This hook-up for negative ground cars only

JACKING

The jack supplied with the Astro Van is meant for changing tires; it is not meant to support a vehicle while you crawl under it and work. Whenever it is necessary to get under a vehicle to perform service operations, always be sure that it is adequately supported, preferably by jackstands at the proper points. Always block the wheels when changing tires.

If the Van is equipped with a positraction rear axle, DO NOT run the engine for any reason with one rear wheel off the ground. Power will be transmitted through the rear wheel remaining on the ground, possibly causing the vehicle to drive itself off the jack.

Some of the service operations in this book require that one or both ends of the vehicle be raised and supported safely. The best arrangement for this, of course, is a grease pit or a vehicle lift but these items are seldom found in the home garage. However, small hydraulic, screw or scissors jacks are satisfactory for raising the vehicle.

Heavy wooden blocks or adjustable jackstands should be used to support the vehi-

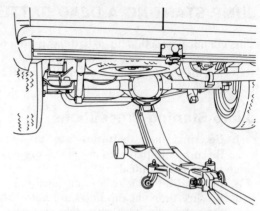

Using the rear axle to lift the rear of the vehicle

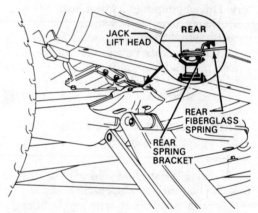

Using the rear spring bracket to lift the side of the vehicle

cle while it is being worked on. Drive-on trestles or ramps are also a handy and a safe way to raise the vehicle, assuming their capacity is adequate. These can be bought or constructed from suitable heavy timbers or steel.

In any case, it is always best to spend a little extra time to make sure that your Van is lifted and supported safely.

CAUTION: *Concrete blocks are not recommended. They may crumble if the load is not evenly distributed. Boxes and milk crates of any description must not be used. Shake the vehicle a few times to make sure the jackstands are securely supporting the weight before crawling under.*

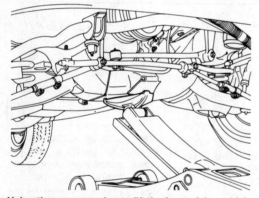

Using the crossmember to lift the front of the vehicle

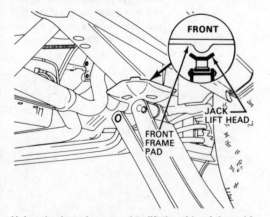

Using the front frame pad to lift the side of the vehicle

HOW TO BUY A USED VAN

Many people believe that a 2–3 year old used vehicle is a better buy than a new one. This may be true. The new vehicle suffers the heaviest depreciation in the first two years but is not old enough to present a lot of costly re-

Maintenance Intervals
Schedule I ①

The services shown in this schedule up to 48,000 miles are to be performed after 48,000 miles at the same intervals

Item No.	To Be Serviced	When to Perform Miles or Months, Whichever Occurs First Miles (000)	3	6	9	12	15	18	21	24	27	30	33	36	39	42	45	48
1	Engine Oil and Oil filter Change	Every 3,000 Miles or 3 Months	•	•	•	•	•	•	•	•	•	•	•	•	•	•	•	•
2	Chassis Lubrication	Every oil change	•	•	•	•	•	•	•	•	•	•	•	•	•	•	•	•
3	Carburetor Choke and Hose Inspection	At 6,000 Miles, then at 30,000 Miles		•								•					•	
4	Carburetor or T.B.I. Mounting Bolt Torque Check			•														
5	Engine Idle Speed Adjustment			•														
6	Engine Accessory Drive Belts Inspection	Every 12 Months or 15,000 Miles					•					•					•	
7	Cooling System Service	Every 24 Months or 30,000 Miles										•						
8	Front Wheel Bearing Repack	Every 15,000 Miles					•					•					•	
9	Transmission Service	15,000 Miles					•					•						
10	Vacuum Advance System Inspection	Check at 6,000 Miles, then at 30,000 Miles, and at 45,000 Miles		•								•					•	
11	Spark Plugs and Wire Service	Every 30,000 Miles										•						
12	PCV System Inspection	Every 30,000 Miles										•						
13	EGR System Check	Every 30,000 Miles										•						
14	Air Cleaner and PCV Filter Replacement	Every 30,000 Miles										•						
15	Engine Timing Check	Every 30,000 Miles										•						
16	Fuel Tank, Cap and Lines Inspection	Every 12 Months or 15,000 Miles					•					•					•	
17	Early Fuel Evaporation System Inspection	At 6,000 Miles then at 30,000 Miles		•								•						
18	Evaporative Control System Inspection	At 30,000 Miles										•						
19	Fuel Filter Replacement	Every 15,000 Miles					•					•					•	
20	Valve Lash Adjustment	Every 15,000 Miles					•					•					•	
21	Thermostatically Controlled Air Cleaner Inspection	Every 30,000 Miles										•						

Maintenance Intervals (cont.)
Schedule II ②

The services shown in this schedule up to 60,000 miles are to be performed after 60,000 miles at the same intervals

Item No.	To Be Serviced	When to Perform Miles or Months, Whichever Occurs First Miles (000)	7.5	15	22.5	30	37.5	45	52.5	60
1	Engine Oil Change	Every 7,500 Miles or 12 Months	•	•	•	•	•	•	•	•
	Oil Filter Change	At First and Every Other Oil Change or 12 Months	•		•		•		•	
2	Chassis Lubrication	Every oil change	•	•	•	•	•	•	•	•
3	Carburetor Choke and Hoses Inspection	At 6 Months or 7,500 Miles and at 60,000 Miles	•							•
4	Carburetor or T.B.I. Mounting Bolt Torque Check	At 6 Months or 7,500 Miles and at 60,000 Miles	•							•
5	Engine Idle Speed Adjustment	At 6 Months or 7,500 Miles and at 60,000 Miles	•							•
6	Engine Accessory Drive Belts Inspection	Every 24 Months or 30,000 Miles				•				•
7	Cooling System Service	Every 24 Months or 30,000 Miles				•				•
8	Front Wheel Bearing Repack	Every 30,000 Miles				•				•
9	Transmission Service	30,000 miles				•				•
10	Vacuum Advance System Inspection	Check at 6 Months or 7,500 Miles, then at 30,000 Miles, and then at 15,000 Mile intervals.	•			•		•		•
11	Spark Plugs and Wire Service	Every 30,000 Miles				•				•
12	PCV System Inspection	Every 30,000 Miles				•				•
13	EGR System Check	Every 30,000 Miles				•				•
14	Air Cleaner and PCV Filter Replacement	Every 30,000 Miles				•				•
15	Engine Timing Check	Every 30,000 Miles				•				•
16	Fuel Tank, Cap and Lines Inspection	Every 24 Months 30,000 Miles				•				•
17	Early Fuel Evaporation System Inspection	At 7,500 Miles and at 30,000 Miles than at 30,000 Mile intervals.	•			•				•
18	Evaporative Control System Inspection	Every 30,000 Miles				•				•
19	Fuel Filter Replacement	Every 30,000 Miles				•				•
20	Valve Lash Adjustment	Every 15,000 Miles		•				•		
21	Thermostatically Controlled Air Cleaner Inspection	Every 30,000 Miles				•				•

① Severe service   ② Normal service

Capacities Chart

Years	VIN	Engine No. Cyl. (cu. in.)	Crankcase Includes Filter (qt)	Transmission (pts)			Drive Axle (pts)	Fuel Tank (gal)	Cooling ① System (qt)	
				4-sp	5-sp	Auto			w/AC	wo/AC
1985	N	6-262	5.0	3.0	5.0	10.0	4.0	17/27	13.5	13.5
1985–87	E	4-151	3.0	3.0	5.0	10.0	4.0	17/27	10.0	10.0
1986–87	Z	6-262	5.0	3.0	5.0	10.0	4.0	17/27	13.5	13.5

① If equipped with a rear heater, add 2.84 qts.

pair problems. Whatever the age of the used vehicle you might want to buy, this section and a little patience will help you select one that should be safe and dependable.

TIPS

1. First decide what model you want and how much you want to spend.

2. Check the used car lots and your local newspaper ads. Privately owned vehicles are usually less expensive, however you will not get a warranty that, in most cases, comes with a used vehicle purchased from a lot.

3. Never shop at night. The glare of the lights make is easy to miss faults on the body caused by accident or rust repair.

4. Try to get the name and phone number of the previous owner. Contact him/her and ask about the vehicle. If the owner of the lot refuses this information, look for a vehicle somewhere else.

NOTE: *A private seller can tell you about the vehicle and maintenance. Remember, however, there's no law requiring honesty from private citizens selling used vehicles. There is a law that forbids the tampering with or turning back the odometer mileage. This includes both the private citizen and the lot owner. The law also requires that the seller or anyone transferring ownership of the vehicle must provide the buyer with a signed statement indicating the mileage on the odometer at the time of transfer.*

5. Write down the year, model and serial number before you buy any used vehicle. Then dial 1-800-424-9393, the toll free number of the National Highway Traffic Safety Administration, and ask if the vehicle has ever been included on any manufacturer's recall list. If so, make sure the needed repairs were made.

6. Use the Used Van Checklist in this section and check all the items on the used vehicle you are considering. Some items are more important than others. You know how much money you can afford for repairs, and, depending on the price of the vehicle, may consider doing any needed work yourself. Beware, however, of trouble in areas that will affect opera-

tion, safety or emission. Problems in the Used Van Checklist break down as follows:

1–8: Two or more problems in these areas indicate a lack of maintenance. You should beware.

9–13: Indicates a lack of proper care, however, these can usually be corrected with a tune-up or relatively simple parts replacement.

14–17: Problems in the engine or transmission can be very expensive. Walk away from any vehicle with problems in both of these areas.

7. If you are satisfied with the apparent condition of the vehicle, take it to an independent diagnostic center or mechanic for a complete check. If you have a state inspection program, have it inspected immediately before purchase or specify on the bill of sale that the sale is conditional on passing the state inspection.

8. Road test the vehicle – refer to the Road Test Checklist in this section If your original evaluation and the road test agree – the rest is up to you.

USED VAN CHECKLIST

1. *Mileage:* Average mileage is about 12,000 miles per year. More than average mileage may indicate hard usage. The catalytic converter may need converter service at 50,000 miles.

2. *Paint:* Check around the tail pipe, molding and windows for overspray indicating that the vehicle has been repainted.

3. *Rust:* Check the fenders, doors, rocker panels, window molding, wheelwells, floorboards, under the floormats and in the trunk for any signs of rust. Any rust at all will be a problem. There is no way to check the spread of rust, except to replace the part of panel.

4. *Body Appearance:* Check the moldings, the bumpers, grille, vinyl roof, glass, doors, trunk lid and body panels for general overall condition. Check for misalignment, loose hold down clips, ripples, scratches in the glass, rips or patches in the top. Mismatched paint, welding in the trunk, severe misalignment of the body panels or ripples may indicate crash work.

5. *Leaks:* Get down and look under the vehicle. There should be no normal leaks, other than water from the air conditioning condenser.

6. *Tires:* Check the tire air pressure. A common trick is to pump the tire pressure up to make the vehicle roll easier. Check the tread wear, open the trunk and check the spare too. Uneven wear is a clue that the front end needs alignment. See the troubleshooting chapter for clues to the causes of tire wear.

7. *Shock Absorbers:* Check the shock absorbers by forcing downward sharply on each corner of the vehicle. Good shocks will not allow the vehicle to bounce more than twice after you let go.

8. *Interior:* Check the entire interior. You're looking for an interior condition that agrees with the overall condition of the vehicle. Reasonable wear is expected but be suspicious of the new seat covers on sagging seats, new pedal pads and worn armrests. These indicate an attempt to cover up hard use. Pull back the carpets and look for evidence of water leaks or flooding. Look for missing hardware, door handles, control knobs and etc. Check the lights and signal operations. Make sure all of the accessories (air conditioner, heater, radio and etc.) work. Check the windshield wiper operation.

9. *Belts and Hoses:* Open the hood and check all the belts and hoses for wear, cracks or weak spots.

10. *Battery:* Low electrolyte level, corroded terminals and/or cracked case indicate a lack of maintenance.

11. *Radiator:* Look for corrosion or rust in the coolant indicating a lack of maintenance.

12. *Air Filter:* A dirty air filter usually means a lack of maintenance.

13. *Ignition Wires:* Check the ignition wires for cracks, burned spots or wear. Worn wires will have to be replaced.

14. *Oil Level:* If the oil level is low, chances are the engine uses oil or leaks. Beware of water in the oil (cracked block), excessively thick oil (used to quiet a noisy engine) or thin, dirty oil with a distinct gasoline smell (internal engine problems).

15. *Automatic Transmissions:* Pull the transmission dipstick out when the engine is running. The level should read Full and the fluid should be clear or bright red. Dark brown or black fluid that has distinct brunt odor, signals a transmission in need of repair or overhaul.

16. *Exhaust:* Check the color of the exhaust smoke. Blue smoke indicates, among other problems, worn rings. Black smoke can indicate burnt valves or fuel injection problems. Check the exhaust system for leaks. It can be expensive to replace.

17. *Spark Plugs:* Remove one of the spark plugs (the most accessible will do). An engine in good condition will show plugs with a light tan or gray deposit on the firing tip. See the color Tune-Up tips section for spark plug conditions.

ROAD TEST CHECKLIST

1. *Engine Performance:* The vehicle should be peppy whether cold or warm, with adequate power and good pickup. It should respond smoothly through the gears.

2. *Brakes:* They should provide quick, firm stops with no noise, pulling or brake fade.

3. *Steering:* Sure control with no binding, harshness or looseness and no shimmy in the wheel should be expected. Noise or vibration from the steering wheel when turning the vehicle means trouble.

4. *Clutch (Manual Transmission):* Clutch action should give quick, smooth response with easy shifting. The clutch pedal should have about 1–1½" (25–38mm) of free-play before it disengages the clutch. Start the engine, set the parking brake, place the transmission in first gear and slowly release the clutch pedal. The engine should begin to stall when the pedal is ½–¾ of the way up.

5. *Automatic Transmission:* The transmission should shift rapidly and smoothly, with no noise, hesitation or slipping.

6. *Differential:* No noise of thumps should be present. Differentials have no normal leaks.

7. *Driveshaft, Universal Joints:* Vibration and noise could mean driveshaft problems. Clicking at low speed or coast conditions means worn U-joints.

8. *Suspension:* Try hitting bumps at different speeds. A vehicle that bounces has weak shock absorbers. Clunks mean worn bushings or ball joints.

9. *Frame:* Wet the tires and drive in a straight line. Tracks should show two straight lines, not four. Four tire tracks indicate a frame bent by collision damage. If the tires can not be wet for this purpose, have a friend drive along behind you to see if the vehicle appears to be traveling in a straight line.

TUNE-UP PROCEDURES

In order to extract the full measure of performance and economy from your engine it is essential that it is properly tuned at regular intervals. A regular tune-up will keep your Van's engine running smoothly and will prevent the annoying breakdowns and poor performance associated with an untuned engine.

A complete tune-up should be performed every 30,000 miles. This interval should be halved if the vehicle is operated under severe conditions such as trailer towing, prolonged idling, start-and-stop driving, or if starting or running problems are noticed. It is assumed that the routine maintenance described in Chapter 1 has been kept up, as this will have a decided effect on the results of a tune-up. All of the applicable steps of a tune-up should be followed in order, as the result is a cumulative one.

If the specifications on the underhood tune-up sticker in the engine compartment disagree with the Tune-Up Specifications chart in this chapter, the figures on the sticker must be used. The sticker often reflects changes made during the production run.

Spark Plugs

Normally, a set of spark plugs requires replacement about every 20,000–30,000 miles on vehicles equipped with an High Energy Ignition (HEI) system. Any vehicle which is subjected to severe conditions will need more frequent plug replacement.

Under normal operation, the plug gap increases about 0.001 in. for every 1,000–2,000 miles. As the gap increases, the plug's voltage requirement also increases. It requires a greater voltage to jump the wider gap and about 2–3 times as much voltage to fire a plug at high speeds than at idle.

When you are removing the spark plugs, work on one at a time. Don't start by removing the plug wires all at once, for unless you number them, they may become mixed up. Take a minute before you begin and number the wires with tape. The best location for numbering the wires is near the distributor cap.

REMOVAL

When removing the spark plugs, work on one at a time. Don't start by removing the plug wire all at once because unless you number

Tune-Up Specifications

Years	VIN	Engine No. Cyl. (cu. in.)	Spark Plugs		Distributor		Ignition Timing (deg.)		Idle Speed		Valve Clearance	
			Type	Gap (in.)	Point Gap (in.)	Dwell (deg.)	Man. Trans.	Auto. Trans.	Man. Trans.	Auto. Trans.	In.	Exh.
1985–87	E	4-151	R43TSX	0.060	N.A.	N.A.	②	②	②	②	0	0
1985	N	6-262	R43CTS	②	N.A.	N.A.	②	②	②	②	①	①
1986–87	Z	6-262	R43CTS	②	N.A.	N.A.	②	②	②	②	①	①

N.A.—Not applicable
① One turn down from zero lash.
② Refer to underhood specifications.

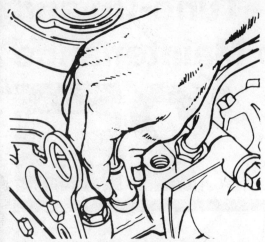

Twist and pull on the rubber boot to remove the spark plug wires; never pull on the wire itself

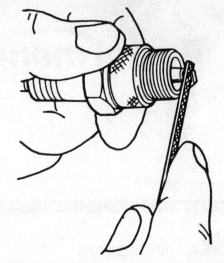

Plugs that are in good condition can be filed and re-used

them, they're going to get mixed up. On some models though, it will be more convenient for you to remove all of the wires before you start to work on the plugs. If this is necessary, take a minute before you begin and number the wires with tape before you take them off. The time you spend here will pay off later on.

1. Twist the spark plug boot ½ turn and remove the boot from the plug. You may also use a plug wire removal tool designed especially for this purpose. *DO NOT pull on the wire itself.* When the wire has been removed, take a wire brush and clean the area around the plug. Make sure that all the grime is removed so that none will enter the cylinder after the plug has been removed.

2. Remove the plug using the proper size socket, extensions and universals as necessary.

3. If removing the plug is difficult, drip some penetrating oil (Liquid Wrench®, WD-40® or etc.) on the plug threads, allow it to work, then remove the plug. Also, be sure that the socket is straight on the plug, especially on those hard to reach plugs.

Always use a wire gauge to check the electrode gap

INSPECTION

NOTE: *Once the plug is out, check it against the plugs shown on the Color Insert on Spark Plug Analysis to determine the engine condition.*

Check the plugs for deposits and wear. If they are not going to be replaced, clean the plugs thoroughly. Remember that any kind of deposit will decrease the efficiency of the plug. Plugs can be cleaned on a spark plug cleaning machine, which can sometimes be found in service stations or you can do an acceptable job of cleaning with a stiff brush. If the plugs are cleaned, the electrodes must be filed flat. Use

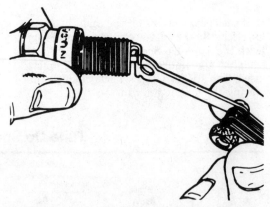

Adjust the electrode gap by bending the side electrode

an ignition points file, not an emery board or the like, which will leave deposits. The electrodes must be filed perfectly flat with sharp edges; rounded edges reduce the spark plug voltage by as much as 50%.

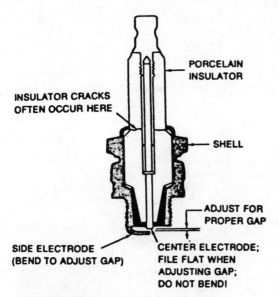

Cross section of a spark plug

PORCELAIN
INSULATOR

INSULATOR CRACKS
OFTEN OCCUR HERE

SHELL

ADJUST FOR
PROPER GAP

SIDE ELECTRODE
(BEND TO ADJUST GAP)

CENTER ELECTRODE;
FILE FLAT WHEN
ADJUSTING GAP;
DO NOT BEND!

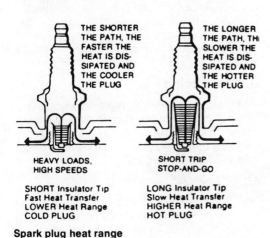

THE SHORTER
THE PATH, THE
FASTER THE
HEAT IS DIS-
SIPATED AND
THE COOLER
THE PLUG

THE LONGER
THE PATH, THE
SLOWER THE
HEAT IS DIS-
SIPATED AND
THE HOTTER
THE PLUG

HEAVY LOADS,
HIGH SPEEDS

SHORT TRIP
STOP-AND-GO

SHORT Insulator Tip
Fast Heat Transfer
LOWER Heat Range
COLD PLUG

LONG Insulator Tip
Slow Heat Transfer
HIGHER Heat Range
HOT PLUG

Spark plug heat range

Check the spark plug gap before installation. The ground electrode (the L-shaped one connected to the body of the plug) must be parallel to the center electrode and the specified size wire gauge (see Tune-Up Specifications) should pass through the gap with a slight drag. Always check the gap on the new plugs, they are not always set correctly at the factory. DO NOT use a flat feeler gauge when measuring the gap, because the reading will be inaccurate.

Wire gapping tools usually have a bending tool attached. Use that to adjust the side electrode until the proper distance is obtained. **Absolutely, never bend the center electrode.** Also, be careful not to bend the side electrode too far or too often; it may weaken and break off within the engine, requiring removal of the cylinder head to retrieve it.

INSTALLATION

1. Lubricate the threads of the spark plugs with a drop of oil. Install the plugs and tighten them hand tight. Take care not to crossthread them.

2. Tighten the spark plugs with the socket. DO NOT apply the same amount of force you would use for a bolt; just snug them in. If a torque wrench is available, tighten to 11–15 ft. lbs.

3. Install the wire on their respective plugs. Make sure the wires are firmly connected, you will be able to feel them click into place.

Spark Plug Wires

NOTE: *Please refer to the Color Insert on Spark Plug Analysis to determine the wire condition.*

Every 15,000 miles, visually inspect the spark plug cables for burns, cuts or breaks in the insulation. Check the spark plug boots and the nipples on the distributor cap and coil. Replace any damaged wiring.

Every 30,000 miles or so, the resistance of the wires should be checked with an ohmmeter. Wires with excessive resistance will cause misfiring and may make the engine difficult to start in damp weather. Generally, the useful life of the cables is 30,000–45,000 miles.

To check the resistance, remove the distributor cap, leaving the wires in place. Connect one lead of an ohmmeter to an electrode within the cap; connect the other lead to the corresponding spark plug terminal (remove it from the spark plug for this test). Replace any wire which shows a resistance over $30,000\Omega$. Generally speaking, however, resistance should not be over $25,000\Omega$, and $30,000\Omega$ must be considered the outer limit of acceptability.

It should be remembered that resistance is also a function of length; the longer the wire the greater the resistance. Thus, if the wires on your van are longer than the factory originals, resistance will be higher, quite possibly outside these limits.

When installing a new set of spark plug wires, replace the wires one at a time so there will be no mixup. Start by replacing the longest cable first. Install the boot firmly over the spark plug. Route the wire exactly the same as

HEI Plug Wire Resistance Chart

Wire Length	Minimum	Maximum
0–15 inches	3000 ohms	10,000 ohms
15–25 inches	4000 ohms	15,000 ohms
25–35 inches	6000 ohms	20,000 ohms
Over 35 inches		25,000 ohms

the original. Insert the distributor end of the wire firmly into the distributor cap tower, then seat the boot over the tower. Repeat the process for each wire.

Firing Orders

NOTE: *To avoid confusion, remove and tag the wires one at a time, for replacement.*

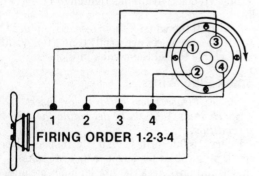

Pontiac-built (2.5L) 151-4 cylinder engine; Engine firing order: 1-3-4-2; Distributor rotation: clockwise

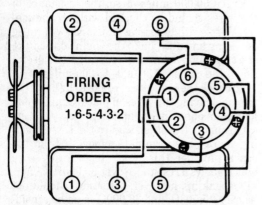

Chevrolet-built (4.3L) 262-V6 engine; Engine firing order: 1-6-5-4-3-2; Distributor rotation: clockwise

Electronic Ignition

NOTE: *This book contains simple testing procedures for your Vans's electronic ignition. More comprehensive testing on this system and other electronic control systems on your Van can be found in CHILTON'S GUIDE TO ELECTRONIC ENGINE CONTROLS, book part number 7535, available at your local retailer.*

SERVICE PRECAUTIONS

NOTE: *Some electronic diagnostic equipment and service tachometers may not be compatible with the HEI system, consult your manufacturer before using such equipment.*

1. Before making compression checks, disconnect the engine control switch feed wire at the distributor. To disconnect the connector from the distributor, release the locking tab and pull the connector body downward; NEVER use a metal tool to release the locking tab, for the tab may break off.

2. The distributor needs no periodic lubrication, for the engine lubrication system lubricates the lower bushing and an oil reservoir lubricates the upper bushing.

3. The tachometer (TACH) terminal is located next to the engine control switch (BAT) connector on the distributor cap.

NOTE: *NEVER allow the tachometer terminal to touch ground, for damage to the module and/or the coil may result.*

4. Since there are no points in the ignition system, NO manual dwell adjustment is necessary or possible.

5. The material used in the construction of the spark plug wires is very soft and pliable. These wires can withstand high heat and carry a higher voltage. It is very important that the wires be routed correctly, for they are highly susceptible to scuffing and/or cutting.

NOTE: *When removing a spark plug wire, be sure to twist the boot and then pull on it to remove it.*

Ignition Timing

NOTE: *The following procedure requires the use of a distributor wrench and a timing light. When using a timing light, be sure to consult the manufacturer's recommendations for installation and usage.*

ADJUSTMENT

1. Refer to the ignition timing specifications, listed on the Vehicle Emissions Control Information label, located on the radiator support panel and follow the instructions.

2. Using a timing light, connect it to the engine by performing the following procedures:

   a. If using a non-inductive type, connect an adapter between the No. 1 spark plug and the spark plug wire; DO NOT puncture the spark plug wire, for this will cause a voltage leak.

   b. If using an inductive type, clamp it around the No. 1 spark plug wire.

   c. If using a magnetic type, place the probe in the connector located near the damper pulley; this type must be used with special electronic timing equipment.

3. At the 4-terminal EST connector of the distributor, disconnect the black/tan wire connector (about 6 in. from the distributor).

4. Start the engine aim the timing light at the timing mark on the damper pulley; a line on the damper pulley will align the timing mark. If necessary (to adjust the timing), loos-

A view of a typical timing mark

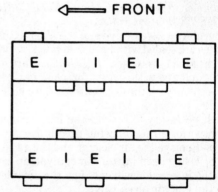

Valve arrangement of the 4.3L, V6 Chevrolet-built engine (E-exhaust; I-intake)

en the distributor holddown clamp and slowly turn the distributor slightly to align the marks. When the alignment is correct, tighten the holddown bolt.

5. Turn the engine Off, remove the timing light and reconnect the black/tan wire (if disconnected) of the distributor.

Valve Lash

The engines described in this book utilize a hydraulic valve lifter system to obtain zero lash. No adjustment is necessary. An initial adjustment is required anytime that the lifters are removed or the valve train is disturbed.

ADJUSTMENT

1. Refer to the Rocker Arm Cover, Removal and Installation procedures in Chapter 3 and remove the rocker arm cover.

2. Rotate the crankshaft until the mark on the damper pulley aligns with the 0° mark on the timing plate and the No. 1 cylinder is on the compression stroke.

NOTE: *To determine if the No. 1 cylinder is on the compression stroke, shake the rocker arms of the No. 1 cylinder, if they move the cylinder is on the compression stroke, if they don't move the cylinder is on the exhaust stroke. If the cylinder is on the exhaust stroke, it will be necessary to rotate the crankshaft one full revolution.*

← FRONT

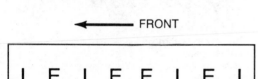

Valve arrangement of the 2.5L, 4-cyl Pontiac-built engine (E-exhaust; I-intake)

3. With the engine on the compression stroke, adjust the exhaust valves of cylinders No. 1 & 3 (2.5L) or No. 1, 5 & 6 (4.3L) and the intake valves of cylinders No. 1 & 2 (2.5L) or No. 1, 2 & 3 (4.3L).

4. To adjust the valves, perform the following procedures:

   a. Back out the adjusting nut until lash can be felt at the pushrod.

   b. While rotating the pushrod, turn the adjusting nut inward until all of the lash is removed.

   c. When the play has disappeared, turn the adjusting nut inward 1½ (2.5L) or 1 (4.3L) additional turns.

5. Rotate the crankshaft one complete revolution and align the mark on the damper pulley with the 0° mark on the timing plate.

6. With the engine on the compression stroke, adjust the exhaust valves of cylinders No. 2 & 4 (2.5L) or No. 2, 3 & 4 (4.3L) and the intake valves of cylinders No. 3 & 4 (2.5L) or No. 4, 5 & 6 (4.3L).

7. To adjust the valves, perform the following procedures:

   a. Back out the adjusting nut until lash can be felt at the pushrod.

   b. While rotating the pushrod, turn the adjusting nut inward until all of the lash is removed.

   c. When the play has disappeared, turn the adjusting nut inward 1½ (2.5L) or 1 (4.3L) additional turns.

8. To complete the installation, use new valve cover gaskets and reverse the removal procedures.

Idle Speed and Mixture Adjustments

4.3L Engine w/4-bbl.

NOTE: *The following procedure requires the use of a dwell meter, GM tool No. J-29030-B, BT-7610-B or equivalent, a center punch, a hammer, a hacksaw, GM tool No. J-33815, BT-8253-B or equivalent.*

The idle air bleed valve and the idle mixture needles are sealed with hardened plugs, to protect the factory settings. These settings are not to be tampered with, except for, cleaning, part replacement or if the carburetor is the cause of trouble.

1. If necessary to remove the idle air bleed cover, perform the following procedures:

   a. Remove the air cleaner and the gasket.

   b. Using masking tape or equivalent, cover the internal bowl vents and the air inlets to the idle air bleed valve.

   c. Carefully drill out the idle air bleed cover pop rivet heads.

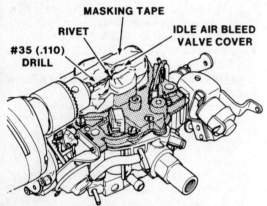

Removing the idle air bleed cover—4.3L 4-bbl carburetor

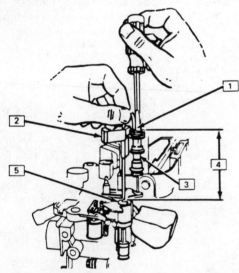

1. Tool contacting valve
2. Guide
3. Idle air bleed valve
4. Gaging tool—J-33815-2/BT8253B (1.756″ high)
5. Plunger against stop

Positioning the idle air valve—4.3L 4-bbl carburetor

   d. Using a drift and a small hammer, drive out the remaining portions of the rivet shanks.

   e. Remove/discard the idle air bleed cover and the masking tape used to cover the vents and the air passages.

2. To set the idle air bleed valve, perform the following procedures:

   a. Using the GM tool No. J-33815, BT-8253-B or equivalent, position it in the throttle side D-shaped hole in the air horn casting. The tool's upper end should be positioned over the open cavity next to the idle air bleed valve.

   b. Holding the gauging tool down slightly, so that the solenoid plunger is against the solenoid stop, adjust the idle air bleed valve so that the gauging tool will pivot over and just contact the top of the valve.

3. Using a new idle air bleed cover and pop rivets, install the cover to the air horn casting.

4. If necessary to adjust the idle mixture needle screws, perform the following procedures to remove the hardened steel plugs:

   a. Refer to the Carburetor, Removal and Installation procedures in Chapter 4 and remove the carburetor from the engine.

   b. Invert the carburetor and drain the fuel from the float bowl.

   c. Position the carburetor, in the inverted position, in a holding fixture to gain access to the idle mixture needle plugs.

NOTE: *When positioning the carburetor, be careful not to damage the linkage, the tubes and other parts protruding from the air horn.*

   d. Using a hacksaw, make two parallel cuts into the throttle body; cut on each side

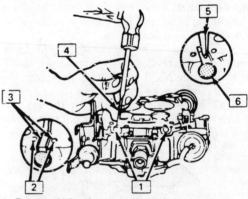

1. Recessed idle mixture needle and plug locations
2. Locator points
3. Hacksaw slots
4. Flat punch
5. Center punch
6. Plug

Removing the idle needle plugs—4.3L 4-bbl carburetor

of the locator points beneath the idle mixture needle plugs.

e. Using a punch and a hammer, drive the casting segment toward the hardened plug, be sure to drive out the plug.

f. Repeat this process for the other plug.

5. Using the GM tool No. J-29030-B, BT-7610-B or equivalent, turn the idle mixture needle screws clockwise until they are lightly seated, then turn them counterclockwise 3 turns.

6. Using a new carburetor-to-intake manifold gasket, install the carburetor onto the engine, DO NOT install the air cleaner or gasket.

7. Disconnect the vacuum hose-to-canister purge valve and plug it. At the carburetor, disconnect the electrical connector from the Mixture Control (M/C) solenoid.

8. Using a dwell meter, connect it to the M/C solenoid electrical connector and set it on the 6-cyl scale.

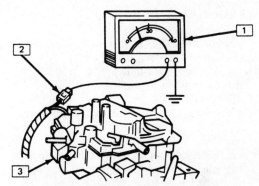

1. Dwell meter (set on 6-cyl scale)
2. M/C solenoid dwell connector
3. Carburetor

Connecting the dwell meter to the M/C electical connector—4.3L 4-bbl carburetor

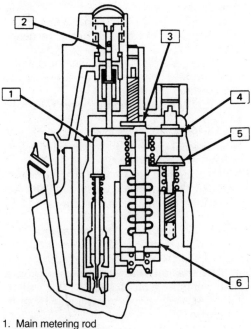

1. Main metering rod
2. Idle air bleed valve
3. Rich stop
4. Paddle
5. Lean stop
6. M/C solenoid

Cross-sectional view of the mixture control solenoid—4.3L 4-bbl carburetor

9. Start the engine and allow it to reach normal operating temperatures.

10. Place the transmission in Drive (AT) or Neutral (MT), then adjust the idle mixture needle screws, in 1/8 turn increments, until the dwell reading varies within the 25°–35° range (be as close to 30° as possible). If the reading is too low, turn the idle mixture needle screws counterclockwise. If the reading is too high, turn the idle mixture needle screws clockwise.

NOTE: *Be sure to allow the engine to stabilize between adjustments.*

11. After the adjustment is complete, seal the idle mixture screw openings with silicone sealant, this will prevent any further adjustment of the idle mixture screws and prevent any fuel vapor loss.

12. Adjust the curb idle speed, if necessary.

13. Check and/or adjust the fast idle speed by referring information on the Vehicle Emission Control Information Label in the engine compartment.

2.5L EFI Engine

NOTE: *The following procedures require the use a tachometer, GM tool No. J-33047 or equivalent, GM Torx Bit No. 20, silicone sealant, a $\frac{5}{32}$" drill bit, a prick punch and a $\frac{1}{16}$" pin punch.*

The throttle stop screw, used in regulating the minimum idle speed, is adjusted at the factory and is not necessary to perform. This adjustment should be performed ONLY when the throttle body has been replaced.

NOTE: *The replacement of the complete throttle body assembly will have the minimum idle adjusted at the factory.*

1. Remove the air cleaner and the gasket. Be sure to plug the THERMAC vacuum port (air cleaner vacuum line-to-throttle body) on the throttle body.

2. Remove the throttle valve cable from the throttle control bracket to provide access to the minimum air adjustment screw.

3. Using the manufacturer's instructions, connect a tachometer to the engine.

4. Remove the electrical connector from the

Idle Air Control (IAC) valve, located on the throttle body.

5. To remove the throttle stop screw cover, perform the following procedures:

a. Using a prick punch, mark the housing at the top over the center line of the throttle stop screw.

b. Using a $5/32''$ drill bit, drill (on an angle) a hole thru the casting to the hardened cover.

c. Using a $1/16''$ pin punch, place it thru the hole and drive out the cover to expose the throttle stop screw.

6. Place the transmission in Park (AT) or Neutral (MT), start the engine and allow the idle speed to stabilize.

7. Using the GM tool No. J-33047 or equivalent, install it into the idle air passage of the throttle body; be sure that the tool is fully seated in the opening and no air leaks exist.

8. Using the GM Torx Bit No. 20, turn the throttle stop screw until the engine speed is

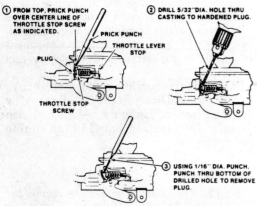

① FROM TOP, PRICK PUNCH OVER CENTER LINE OF THROTTLE STOP SCREW AS INDICATED.

PRICK PUNCH

THROTTLE LEVER STOP

PLUG

THROTTLE STOP SCREW

② DRILL 5/32"DIA. HOLE THRU CASTING TO HARDENED PLUG.

③ USING 1/16" DIA. PUNCH. PUNCH THRU BOTTOM OF DRILLED HOLE TO REMOVE PLUG.

Removing the throttle stop screw cover from the throttle body

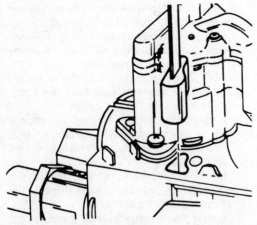

Using the GM tool No. J-33047 to plug the idle air passage of the throttle body

475–525 rpm (AT in Park or Neutral) or 750–800 rpm (MT in Neutral).

9. With the idle speed adjusted, stop the engine, remove the tool No. J-33047 from the throttle body.

10. Reconnect the Idle Air Control (IAC) electrical connector.

11. Using silicone sealant or equivalent, cover the throttle stop screw.

12. Reinstall the gasket and the air cleaner assembly.

4.3L EFI Engine

NOTE: *The following procedure requires the use of a tachometer, a prick punch, a $5/32''$ drill bit, a $1/16''$ pin punch, a grounding wire and silicone sealant.*

1. Remove the air cleaner and the gasket.

2. Remove the throttle stop screw cover by performing the following procedures:

a. Using a prick punch, mark the housing at the top over the center line of the throttle stop screw.

b. Using a $5/32''$ drill bit, drill (on an angle) a hole through the casting to the hardened cover.

c. Using a $1/16''$ pin punch, place it through the hole and drive out the cover to expose the throttle stop screw.

NOTE: *The following adjustment should be performed ONLY when the throttle body assembly has been replaced; the engine should be at normal operating temperatures before making this adjustment.*

3. With the Idle Air Control (IAC) connected, ground the diagnostic terminal of the Assembly Line Communications Link (ALCL) connector.

NOTE: *The Assembly Line Communications Link (ALCL) connector is located in the engine compartment on the left side firewall.*

4. Turn the ignition switch On but DO NOT start the engine. Wait 30 seconds, this will allow the IAC valve pintle to extend and seat in the throttle body.

5. With the ignition switch turned On, disconnect the Idle Air Control (IAC) valve electrical connector.

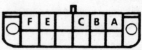

A. Ground
B. Diagnostic terminal
C. A.I.R. (if used)
E. Serial data (see special tools)
F. T.C.C. (if used)

Terminal identification of the Assembly Line Communications Link (ALCL) connector

6. Remove the ground from the Diagnostic Terminal ALCL connector and start the engine.

7. Adjust the idle stop screw to obtain 400–450 rpm (AT in Drive).

8. Turn the ignition Off and reconnect the IAC valve electrical connector.

9. Using silicone sealant or equivalent, cover the throttle stop screw.

10. Reinstall the gasket and the air cleaner assembly.

TROUBLESHOOTING

All GM dealerships are equipped with a testing tool, known as SCAN (it connects to the ALCL diagnostic connector), which performs quick checks of the sensors and switches that provide information to the Electronic Control Module (ECM). Due to the cost factor, it is not advisable for the do-it-yourselfer to purchase one. Since these troubleshooting procedures will be limited to NON-SCAN procedures, it is advisable to schedule an appointment with a dealership to have the vehicle thoroughly checked.

Understanding the diagnostic checks and using it correctly will reduce the diagnostic time and prevent unnecessary replacement of parts.

NOTE: *This book contains simple testing procedures for your Vans's electronic ignition and fuel injection system. More comprehensive testing on your Van's systems can be found in CHILTON'S GUIDE TO ELECTRONIC ENGINE CONTROLS, book part number 7535, and CHILTON'S GUIDE TO FUEL INJECTION AND FEEDBACK CARBURETORS, book part number 7488, available at your local retailer.*

CAUTION: *If attempting to do any checking or repair of the electrical system, be very careful, for these systems are VERY delicate and major damage can occur. All work of this nature should be referred to a qualified technician.*

Non-Scan Diagnostic Checks

The following is an explanation of the NON-SCAN diagnostic circuit check:

1. With engine stopped, the ignition turned On and a steady SERVICE ENGINE SOON light On, at the instrument panel, indicates that there is battery and ignition voltage to the ECM.

2. Connect a jumper wire between the terminals **A** to **B** of the ALCL diagnostic connector (located beneath the instrument panel), the following instrument panel display will occur:

a. The ECM will cause the SERVICE ENGINE SOON lamp to flash a Code 12, which indicates that the ECM diagnostics are working.

b. The Code 12 will flash three times, followed by any other trouble codes that are stored in its memory.

c. Each additional code will flash three times, starting with the lowest code, then the cycle will start over again with the Code 12.

d. If there are no other codes, the Code 12 will flash continuously until the jumper wire is disconnected or the engine is started.

3. Record all of the stored codes, except Code 12, then consult the service shop.

4. The Field Service Mode may be helpful in the diagnosis, depending on the severity of the problem. With the diagnostic terminal grounded and the engine running, the ECM will respond to the O_2 sensor signal voltage and use the SERVICE ENGINE SOON light to display the following information:

a. CLOSED LOOP – confirms that the O_2 sensor signal is being used by the ECM to control the fuel delivery and that the system is working normally; the signal voltage will quickly change from 0.35–0.55V.

b. OPEN LOOP – indicates that the O_2 sensor voltage signal is not usable to the ECM; the signal is at a constant value between 0.35–0.55V.

NOTE: *The system will flash Open Loop for $1/2$–2 min. after the engine starts or until the sensor reaches normal operating temperature; if the system fails to go to Closed Loop.*

c. SERVICE ENGINE SOON – with this light Off, the exhaust is lean; the O_2 sensor signal voltage will remain under 0.35V and steady.

d. SERVICE ENGINE SOON – with this light On and steady (not flashing), the exhaust is rich; the O_2 sensor voltage will be over 0.55V and steady.

5. Road test the vehicle, at steady speeds, using the Field Service Mode.

Because the vehicle operations are different in the Field Service Mode the following conditions may be observed and should be considered normal:

• Acceleration – The light may be On too long due to acceleration enrichment.

• Deceleration – The light may be Off too long due to deceleration enleanment or fuel cut-off.

• Idle – The light may be On too long with the idle below 1200 rpm.

6. To clear the codes, turn the ignition Off and disconnect the battery terminal or the ECM **B** fuse for ten seconds.

ECM CODE DESCRIPTIONS

2.5L EFI Engines

- Code 12 – No reference code.
- Code 13 – Oxygen sensor circuit open.
- Code 14 – Coolant sensor circuit indicating low signal voltage.
- Code 15 – Coolant sensor circuit indicating high signal voltage.
- Code 21 – Throttle Position Sensor (TPS) indicating high signal voltage.
- Code 22 – Throttle Position Sensor (TPS) indicating low signal voltage.
- Code 24 – Vehicle Speed Sensor (VSS) defective.
- Code 33 – Manifold Absolute Pressure (MAP) sensor indicating high signal voltage.
- Code 34 – Manifold Absolute Pressure (MAP) sensor indicating low signal voltage.
- Code 35 – Idle Air Control (IAC) valve defective.
- Code 42 – Electronic Spark Timing (EST) circuit indicating an open or short in the EST or bypass circuits.
- Code 44 – Lean exhaust indicating open oxygen sensor circuit.
- Code 45 – Rich exhaust indicating open oxygen sensor circuit.
- Code 51 – Programmable Read Only Memory (PROM) unit defective or loose terminals.
- Code 55 – Electronic Control Module (ECM) unit defective.

4.3L Engines

CARBURETOR (1985)

- Code 12 – No reference code.
- Code 13 – Oxygen sensor circuit open.
- Code 14 – Coolant sensor circuit indicating low signal voltage.
- Code 15 – Coolant sensor circuit indicating high signal voltage.
- Code 21 – Throttle Position Sensor (TPS) indicating high signal voltage.
- Code 22 – Throttle Position Sensor (TPS) indicating low signal voltage.
- Code 23 – M/C solenoid circuit open or grounded.
- Code 24 – Vehicle Speed Sensor (VSS) circuit defective.
- Code 32 – Barometric Pressure Sensor (BARO) circuit indicating low voltage.
- Code 34 – Manifold Absolute Pressure (MAP) sensor indicating low signal voltage.
- Code 35 – Idle Speed Control (ISC) switch short circuited.
- Code 41 – Distributor-to-ECM circuit open.
- Code 42 – Electronic Spark Timing (EST) circuit indicating an open or short in the EST or bypass circuits.

- Code 43 – Electronic Spark Control (ESC) system defective.
- Code 44 – Lean exhaust indicating open oxygen sensor circuit.
- Code 45 – Rich exhaust indicating open oxygen sensor circuit.
- Code 51 – Programmable Read Only Memory (PROM) unit defective or loose terminals.
- Code 53 – Exhaust Gas Recirculation (EGR) system defective
- Code 54 – M/C Solenoid shorted and/or faulty ECM.
- Code 55 – Electronic Control Module (ECM) unit defective.

THROTTLE BODY (1986–87)

- Code 12 – No reference code.
- Code 13 – Oxygen sensor circuit open.
- Code 14 – Coolant sensor circuit indicating low signal voltage.
- Code 15 – Coolant sensor circuit indicating high signal voltage.
- Code 21 – Throttle Position Sensor (TPS) indicating high signal voltage.
- Code 22 – Throttle Position Sensor (TPS) indicating low signal voltage.
- Code 24 – Vehicle Speed Sensor (VSS) defective.
- Code 32 – Exhaust Gas Recirculation (EGR) system failure.
- Code 33 – Manifold Absolute Pressure (MAP) sensor indicating high signal voltage.
- Code 34 – Manifold Absolute Pressure (MAP) sensor indicating low signal voltage.
- Code 42 – Electronic Spark Timing (EST) circuit indicating an open or short in the EST or bypass circuits.
- Code 43 – Electronic Spark Control (ESC) system defective.
- Code 44 – Lean exhaust indicating open oxygen sensor circuit.
- Code 45 – Rich exhaust indicating open oxygen sensor circuit.
- Code 51 – Programmable Read Only Memory (PROM) unit defective or loose terminals.
- Code 52 – CALPAK unit defective.
- Code 55 – Electronic Control Module (ECM) unit defective.

DIAGNOSTIC INSPECTION

Initial Checks

The importance of these procedures can save valuable time by preventing any further inspections.

1. Check the hoses for splits, kinks and proper connections (see the Vehicle Emission Control Information label).

2. Inspect for air leaks at the throttle body or carburetor and the intake manifold.

3. Check the ignition wires for cracking, hardening, routing and carbon tracking.

4. Check the wiring for pinches, cuts and proper connections.

Intermittent Problems

NOTE: *These problems may or may not turn On the SERVICE ENGINE SOON light or store a code. DO NOT use the trouble codes in this section. If a fault is present, locate it and repair it.*

1. Most intermittent problems are caused by faulty electrical connections or wiring. Perform careful visual checks of the suspected circuits for:

• BACKED OUT CONNECTORS – Terminals not fully seated in the connector or poor mating of the connector halves.

• DAMAGED CONNECTORS – Improperly formed connectors. Reform the connectors to increase the contact tension.

• POOR TERMINAL TO WIRE CONNECTION – Remove the terminal from the connector and check the condition of the wire to the terminal.

2. Connect a voltmeter to the suspected circuit and drive it around. An abnormal voltage reading in the circuit may indicate the problem is in that circuit.

3. The trouble memory code may be lost. Disconnect the Throttle Position Sensor (TPS) and curb idle the engine until the SERVICE ENGINE SOON light turns On. Code 22 should be stored and kept in the memory when the ignition is turned Off (for at least 10 seconds); if not, the ECM is faulty.

4. If the problem still exists, perform the following checks:

• A sharp electrical surge occurs, usually when a faulty component is operated, such as: a relay, an Electronic Control Module (ECM) driven solenoid or a switch.

• The improper installation of optional equipment, such as: A two-way radio, lights or etc.

• Electronic Spark Timing (EST) wires may be too close to the spark plug wires, the distributor wires, the distributor housing, the coil and/or the alternator. Be sure that the distributor ground wire is grounded well.

• The secondary ignition may be shorted to ground.

• The Electronic Control Module (ECM) power wire may be grounded.

Hard Starting

The engine cranks OK but will not start for a long period of time, it eventually runs or it may start and immediately dies.

1. Check the fuel system for:
• Water in the fuel.
• Poor fuel pressure.
• A sticking or binding Throttle Position Sensor (TPS).
• A bad fuel pump relay.
• A poor in-tank fuel pump check valve.

2. Check the ignition system for:
• Ignition coil output.
• A worn distributor shaft.
• Bare and/or shorted wires.
• Poor pickup coil resistance and connections.
• Loose ignition coil ground.
• Moisture in the distributor cap.
• Defective spark plugs.

3. If the engine starts, then immediately stalls, open the distributor by-pass line. If it then starts and runs OK, replace the distributor pickup coil.

4. If the engine is hard to start, at normal operating temperature, check the ECM.

Surge and/or Chuggle

At normal speed, with no change in the accelerator pedal position, the engine speeds up and slows down, inspect the following:

• Vehicle Speed Sensor (VSS) using the ALCL diagnostic connector.
• Exhaust Gas Recirculation (EGR) system if the problem is intermittent at idle.
• Ignition timing (see the Vehicle Emission Control Information label).
• Inline fuel filter for restrictions.
• Fuel pressure.
• Alternator output voltage, it must between 9–16V.
• Oxygen sensor.
• Spark plugs, distributor cap and ignition wire condition.
• Transmission Convertor Clutch (TCC) operation.

Lack of Power (Sluggish)

When the accelerator is pushed part way down, there is little or no increase in speed or power.

1. Compare your vehicles performance with a similar one.

2. Check and/or replace the air cleaner.

3. Check the following equipment:
• Ignition timing (see Vehicle Emission Control Information label).
• Fuel system for a plugged fuel filter, poor fuel pressure and/or contaminated fuel.
• Poor Electronic Control Module (ECM) grounds.

• Exhaust Gas Recirculation (EGR) valve being open or partly open all of the time.

• Alternator output voltage, it must be between 9–16V.

• Valve timing.

• Engine compression.

• Worn camshaft lobes.

4. To inspect the exhaust system, perform the following procedures with the engine at normal operating temperatures:

a. Using a vacuum gauge, connect it to an intake manifold port.

b. Disconnect the EGR solenoid electrical connector or connect the EGR valve directly to a vacuum source bypassing any switches or solenoids.

c. Operate the engine at 1000 rpm and record the vacuum reading.

d. Slowly increase the engine speed to 2500 rpm, hold the speed at 2500 rpm and record the vacuum reading.

NOTE: *If the vacuum reading, taken at 2500 rpm, decreases more than 3 inches from the one taken at 1000 rpm, the exhaust system should be inspected for restrictions*

e. Disconnect the exhaust pipe from the engine and repeat the Steps 4c and 4d.

NOTE: *If the reading still drops more than 3 inches, check the valve timing.*

Detonation/Spark Knock

The engine makes a sharp metallic knocks, which range from mild to severe pings, usually worse under acceleration.

1. If a heating problem is noticed, check for:

a. Low engine coolant.

b. A loose water pump drive belt.

c. Restricted air or water flow through the radiator.

2. For other than heating problems, check for:

a. Poor quality fuel (low octane rating).

b. Correct Progammable Read Only Memory (PROM) unit.

c. THERMAC may be staying closed.

d. Ignition timing (see the Vehicle Emission Control Information label).

e. Low fuel pressure.

f. Exhaust Gas Recirculation (EGR) valve may be closed.

g. Transmission for proper shifting points and operation of the Transmission Convertor Clutch (TCC).

h. Incorrect engine parts, such as: camshaft, cylinder head(s), pistons and etc.

3. If the problem persists, obtain a can of engine (carbon) cleaner and follow the instructions on the can.

Hesitation or Stumble

This condition is a momentary lack of response when accelerating, which can occur at all speeds but usually when trying to make the vehicle move from a stop sign; it may cause the vehicle to stall, if severe enough.

To check the systems, perform the following checks:

• Low fuel pressure.

• Water in fuel.

• Binding or sticking Throttle Position Sensor (TPS).

• Ignition timing (see Vehicle Emission Control Information label).

• Alternator output, it must be between 9–16V.

• An ungrounded in the High Energy Ignition (HEI) system.

• Non-working emissions canister purge.

• Non-working Exhaust Gas Recirculation (EGR) valve.

Misses or Cuts Out

This condition is a steady pulsation or jerking which follows the engine speed, it is usually more pronounced as the engine increases speed. At low speed or idle, the exhaust has a steady spitting sound.

1. To check for a missing cylinder, perform the following procedures:

a. Disconnect the electrical connector from the Idle Air Control (IAC) motor.

b. Start the engine.

c. Using insulated pliers, remove one spark plug wire at a time and check for an rpm drop. If no drop is noticed, check the spark plugs for cracks, wear, improper gap, burned electrodes and/or heavy deposits.

NOTE: *If a drop of 50 rpm is recorded between the cylinders, replace the IAC electrical connector and proceed to the Rough, Unstable or Incorrect Idle, Stalling section.*

2. Using an ohmmeter, over 30,000Ω, check the spark plug wires and replace them, if necessary.

3. Using the Spark Tester tool No. J-26792 or equivalent, check the ignition coil's primary and secondary voltages.

4. Check the fuel system for a plugged fuel filter, water in the fuel and/or low fuel pump pressure.

5. Inspect the ignition timing (see the Vehicle Emission Control Information label).

6. Perform a compression check on the engine; if the compression is low, repair as necessary.

7. Inspect the distributor cap and rotor for dust, cracks, burns, moisture and etc. Using a

fine water mist, spray the cap and plug wires to check for shorts.

8. Remove the rocker arm covers and inspect for bent pushrods, worn rocker arms, broken valve springs and/or worn camshaft lobes.

Poor Fuel Economy

By performing an actual road test, it is determined that the fuel economy is lower than some other actual road test on the same vehicle.

To determine the reason for the poor fuel economy, inspect the following items:

1. The engine thermostat for the wrong heat range or a faulty (always open) part.

2. The fuel system for low fuel pressure.

3. The ignition timing (see the Vehicle Emission Control Information label).

4. The Transmission Convertor Clutch (TCC) for proper operation.

Rough, Unstable or Incorrect Idle, Stalling

In this condition, the engine idles unevenly, it may shake (if bad enough) and/or may stall.

To determine the reason(s) for poor operation, inspect the following items:

1. The ignition timing (see the Vehicle Emission Control Informations label).

2. The Park/Neutral (P/N) switch, if equipped with an AT.

3. A leaking fuel injector.

4. A fuel injector operating too rich or lean.

If rough idle occurs ONLY when the engine is Hot, perform the additional checks:

1. To check for vacuum leaks, perform the following checks:

   a. Using the GM Plug tool No. J-33047 or equivalent, block the idle air passage.

   b. If the engine speed is higher than 650 rpm with the throttle closed, locate and correct the vacuum leak, such as: A disconnected thermac or cruise control hose.

2. The Park/Neutral (P/N) switch, if equipped with an AT.

3. The Throttle Position Switch (TPS) may be sticking or binding, causing the throttle to remain open.

4. Exhaust Gas Recirculation (EGR) system—if it is on while the engine is idling, roughness, stalling and hard starting will occur.

5. Battery cables and ground straps—dirty and loose battery connections will cause erratic voltage, which will cause the Idle Air Control (IAC) valve to change its position, resulting in poor idle quality. The IAC valve will not move if the system voltage is below 9V or greater than 17.8V.

6. Power Steering system—the ECM should compensate for power steering loads; if the signal is lost, the vehicle will be difficult to park and steer with heavy loads.

7. Manifold Absolute Pressure (MAP) sensor—idle the engine and disconnect the electrical connector from the sensor, if the idle improves, substitute a known GOOD sensor and recheck.

8. The Air Conditioning (A/C) compressor and relay, also, the refrigerant pressure may be too high or have a faulty cycling switch.

9. The Positive Crankcase Ventilation (PCV) valve—place your finger over the end and release it several times, if the valve does not snap back, replace it.

10. Perform a cylinder compression check and compare the results, then repair as necessary.

11. Oxygen sensor—inspect it for sensor contamination (white, powdery coating) and high electrical conductivity; as a result, the ECM will reduce the amount of fuel to the engine.

12. Air Management system—check for intermittent air to the ports while in the Closed Loop operation (4.3L engines).

Abnormal Emissions (Odors)

To correct abnormal emissions, inspect or test the following items, for:

1. Excessive CO and HC emissions (odors), plus, any thing that will make the engine run rich.

2. Incorrect ignition timing (see the Vehicle Emission Control Information label).

3. Loading of the fuel emissions canister.

4. Stuck or blocked Positive Crankcase Ventilation (PCV) valve.

5. Condition of the spark plugs, ignition wires and distributor cap.

6. Lead contamination of the Catalytic Converter.

Dieseling

This condition exists when the ignition key is turned Off and the engine continues to run roughly. If the engine runs smoothly, check and/or adjust the ignition switch.

NOTE: *The only way to prevent the engine from dieseling is to eliminate fuel leakage to the cylinders.*

To remedy this situation, turn the ignition switch On, to energize the fuel pump, then check the fuel injector(s) and the throttle body for fuel leakage. If necessary, repair or replace the leaking items.

Backfire

This condition exists when fuel ignites in the intake or exhaust manifold, making a loud popping noise.

To correct this situation, inspect and/or replace the following items:

• Exhaust Gas Recirculation (EGR) system, it must not be open all of the time.

• Output voltage of the ignition coil.

• Crossfire between the spark plugs (distributor cap, ignition wires).

• Intermittent condition in the primary ignition system.

• Ignition timing (see the Vehicle Emission Control Information label).

• Faulty spark plugs and/or ignition wires.

• Valve timing.

• Compression check – look for leaking or sticking valves.

ENGINE ELECTRICAL

The engine electrical system can be broken down into three separate and distinct systems—(1) the ignition system; (2) the charging system; (3) the starting system.

High Energy Ignition (HEI) System

The HEI system operates in basically the same manner as the conventional ignition system, with the exception of the type of switching device used. A toothed iron timer core is mounted on the distributor shaft which rotates inside of an electronic pole piece. The pole piece has internal teeth (corresponding to those on the timer core) which contains a permanent magnet and pick-up coil (not to be confused with the ignition coil). The pole piece senses the magnetic field of the timer core teeth and sends a signal to the ignition module which electronically controls the primary coil voltage. The ignition coil operates in basically the same manner as a conventional ignition coil (though the ignition coils DO NOT interchange).

NOTE: *The HEI systems uses a capacitor within the distributor which is primarily used for radio interference purposes.*

None of the electrical components used in the HEI systems are adjustable. If a component is found to be defective, it must be replaced.

PRECAUTIONS

Before troubleshooting the systems, it might be a good idea to take note of the following precautions:

Timing Light Use

Inductive pick-up timing lights are the best kind to use. Timing lights which connect between the spark plug and the spark plug wire occasionally give false readings.

Some engines incorporate a magnetic timing probe terminal (at the damper pulley) for use of special electronic timing equipment. Refer to the manufacturer's instructions when using this equipment.

Spark Plug Wires

The plug wires are of a different construction than conventional wires. When replacing them, make sure to use the correct wires, since conventional wires won't carry the higher voltage. Also, handle them carefully to avoid cracking or splitting them and never pierce them.

Tachometer Use

Not all tachometers will operate or indicate correctly. While some tachometers may give a reading, this does not necessarily mean the reading is correct. In addition, some tachometers connect differently than others. If you can't figure out whether or not your tachometer will work on your vehicle, check with the tachometer manufacturer.

System Testers

Instruments designed specifically for testing the HEI system are available from several tool manufacturers. Some of these will even test the module.

The Charging System

The charging system provides electrical power for operation of the vehicle's ignition, starting system and all of the electrical accessories. The battery serves as an electrical surge or storage tank, storing (in chemical form) the energy originally produced by the alternator. The system also provides a means of regulating the alternator output to protect the battery from being overcharged and the accessories from being destroyed.

The storage battery is a chemical device incorporating parallel lead plates in a tank containing a sulfuric acid-water solution. Adjacent plates are slightly dissimilar and the chemical reaction of the two dissimilar plates produces electrical energy when the battery is connected to a load such as the starter motor. The chemical reaction is reversible, so that when the alternator is producing a voltage (electrical pressure) greater than that produced by the battery, electricity is forced into the battery and it is returned to it's fully charged state.

Alternators are used on the modern vehicle for they are lighter, more efficient, rotate at higher speeds and have fewer brush problems. In an alternator, the field rotates while all of the current produced passes only through the stator windings. The brushes bear against the continuous slip rings; this causes the current produced to periodically reverse the direction of it's flow. Diodes (electrical one-way switches) block the flow of current from traveling in the wrong direction. A series of diodes are wired together to permit the alternating flow of the stator to be converted to a pulsating but unidirectional flow at the alternator output. The alternator's field is wired in series with the voltage regulator.

Battery and Starting System

The battery is the first link in the chain of mechanisms which work together to provide cranking of the engine. In most modern vehicles, the battery is a lead-acid electrochemical device consisting of six 2 volt (2V) subsections connected in series so the unit is capable of producing approximately 12V of electrical pressure. Each subsection (cell) consists of a series of positive and negative plates held a short distance apart in a solution of sulfuric acid and water. The two types of plates are of dissimilar metals. A chemical reaction takes place which produces current flow from the battery, when it's positive and negative terminals are connected to an electrical appliance such as a lamp or motor. The continued transfer of electrons would eventually convert the sulfuric acid in the electrolyte to water and make the two plates identical in chemical composition. As electrical energy is removed from the battery, it's voltage output tends to drop. Thus, measuring battery voltage and battery electrolyte composition are two ways of checking the ability of the unit to supply power. During the starting of the engine, electrical energy is removed from the battery. However, if the charging circuit is in good condition and the operating conditions are normal, the power removed from the battery will be replaced by the alternator which will force electrons back into the battery, reversing the normal flow and restoring the battery to it's original chemical state.

The battery and starting motor are linked by very heavy electrical cables designed to minimize resistance to the flow of current. Generally, the major power supply cable that leaves the battery goes directly to the starter, while other electrical system needs are supplied by a smaller cable. During the starter operation, power flows from the battery to the starter, then is grounded through the vehicle's frame and the battery's negative ground strap.

The starting motor is a specially designed, direct current electric motor capable of producing a very great amount of power for it's size. One thing that allows the motor to produce a great deal of power is it's tremendous rotating speed. It drives the engine through a tiny pinion gear (attached to the starter's armature), which drives the very large flywheel ring gear at a greatly reduced speed. Another factor allowing it to produce so much power is that only intermittent operation is required of it. Thus, little allowance for air circulation is required and the windings can be built into a very small space.

The starter solenoid is a magnetic device which employs the small current supplied by the starting switch circuit of the ignition switch. This magnetic action moves a plunger, which mechanically engages the starter and electrically closes the heavy switch which connects it to the battery. The starting switch circuit consists of the starting switch (contained within the ignition switch), a transmission neutral safety switch or clutch pedal switch and wiring necessary to connect these with the starter solenoid or relay.

The pinion (small gear) is mounted to a one-way drive clutch. This clutch is splined to the starter armature shaft. When the ignition switch is moved to the Start position, the solenoid plunger slides the pinion toward the flywheel ring rear via a collar and spring. If the teeth on the pinion and flywheel match properly, the pinion will engage the flywheel immediately. If the gear teeth butt one another, the spring will be compressed and will force the gears to mesh as soon as the starter turns far enough to allow them to do so. As the solenoid plunger reaches the end of its travel, it closes the contacts that connect the battery to the starter, then the engine is cranked.

As soon as the engine starts, the flywheel ring gear begins turning fast enough to drive the pinion at an extremely high rate of speed. At this point, the one-way clutch allows the pinion to spin faster than the starter shaft so that the starter will not operate at excessive speed(s). When the ignition switch is released from the starter position, the solenoid is de-energized, the spring (contained within the solenoid assembly) pulls the pinion out of mesh and interrupts the current flow to the starter.

Ignition Coil

The ignition coil on the 2.5L engine, is located on the right rear side of the engine; on the 4.3L (1985) engine, it is located on top of the distributor cap; on the 4.3L (1986–87) engine, it is located on intake manifold to the right side of the distributor.

TESTING

NOTE: *The following procedures require the use of an ohmmeter.*

2.5L Engine

For this procedure, the ignition coil may be removed from the engine or simply remove the electrical connectors and test it on the engine.

1. Using an ohmmeter (on the high scale), connect the probes between the primary (low voltage) terminal and coil ground; the reading should be very high or infinity, if not, replace the coil.

2. Using an ohmmeter (on the low scale), connect the probes between both primary (low voltage) terminals; the reading should be very low or zero, if not, replace the coil.

3. Using an ohmmeter (on the high scale), connect the probes between a primary (low voltage) terminal and the secondary (high voltage) terminal; the reading should be high (not infinite), if not, replace the coil.

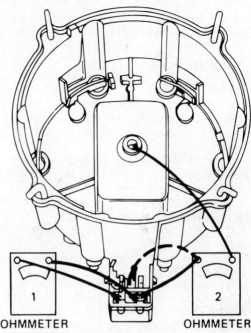
Testing the internal ignition coil—4.3L 4-bbl engine

4.3L Carbureted Engine – 1985

To test the ignition coil, the distributor cap must be removed from the distributor.

1. Remove the electrical connector from the distributor cap and the distributor cap from the distributor. Place the distributor cap on a workbench in the inverted position.

2. Using an ohmmeter (on the low scale), connect the probes between the primary (low voltage) terminals; the reading should be low or nearly zero, if not, replace the coil.

3. Using an ohmmeter (on the high scale), connect the probes between a primary (low voltage) terminal and the secondary (center terminal or high voltage) terminal; the reading should be high (not infinite), if not, replace the coil.

4.3L TBI Engine – 1986–87

For this procedure, the ignition coil may be removed from the engine or simply remove the electrical connectors and test it on the engine.

1. Using an ohmmeter (on the high scale), connect the probes between the primary (low voltage) terminal and coil ground; the reading should be very high or infinity, if not, replace the coil.

2. Using an ohmmeter (on the low scale), connect the probes between both primary (low voltage) terminals; the reading should be very low or zero, if not, replace the coil.

3. Using an ohmmeter (on the high scale), connect the probes between a primary (low voltage) terminal and the secondary (high

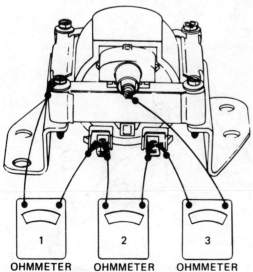
Testing the external ignition coil from the 2.5L TBI engine—4.3L TBI engine is similar.

voltage) terminal; the reading should be high (not infinite), if not, replace the coil.

REMOVAL AND INSTALLATION

2.5L Engine

The ignition coil is located near the cylinder head at the right rear side of the engine.

1. Disconnect the negative battery terminal.

2. At the ignition coil, disconnect the ignition switch-to-coil wire and the distributor-to-coil wires.

3. Remove the coil-to-engine nuts/bolts and the coil from the engine.

4. If necessary, test or replace the ignition coil.

5. To install, reverse the removal procedures.

4.3L Carbureted Engine—1985

The ignition coil is located in the top of the distributor which is positioned at the top rear of the engine.

1. Disconnect the negative battery terminal.

2. At the ignition coil, on top of the distributor, disconnect the electrical connector.

3. Remove the coil cover-to-distributor cap screws and the cover.

4. Remove the coil-to-distributor cap screws and the coil from the cap.

5. If necessary, test or replace the coil.

6. To install, reverse the removal procedures.

4.3L TBI Engine—1986–87

The ignition coil is located, on top of the intake manifold, next to the distributor.

1. Disconnect the negative battery terminal.

2. Disconnect the engine control switch and tachometer terminals from the ignition coil.

3. Disconnect the ignition coil-to-distributor lead wire from the coil.

4. Remove the coil bracket/coil assembly-to-engine bracket nuts and the assembly from the engine.

5. If necessary, test or replace the coil.

6. If necessary to remove the coil from the bracket, perform the following procedures:

   a. Using a drill, drill out the coil-to-bracket rivets.

   b. Using a center punch, drive the rivets from the coil-to-bracket assembly.

   c. Remove the coil from the coil bracket.

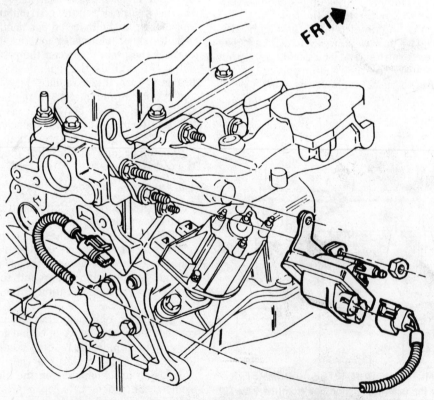

Removing the external ignition coil—2.5L TBI engine—4.3L TBI engine is similar

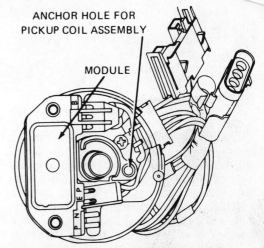

Replacing the ignition module—2.5L distributor

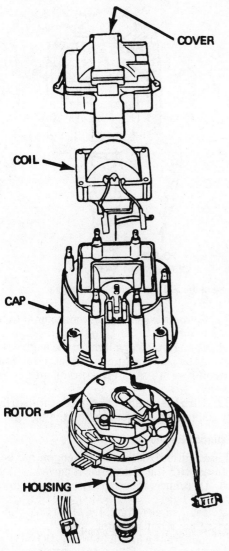

Removing the internal ignition coil—4.3L 4-bbl engine

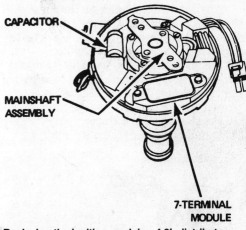

Replacing the ignition module—4.3L distributor

7. To install, reverse the removal procedures.

Ignition Module

The ignition modules are located inside the distributor; they may be replaced without removing the distributor from the engine.

REMOVAL AND INSTALLATION

1. Disconnect the negative battery terminal.

2. Remove the distributor cap and the rotor.

3. If the flange, of the distributor shaft, is positioned above the module, place a socket on the crankshaft pulley bolt and rotate the crankshaft (turning the distributor shaft) to provide clearance to the ignition module.

4. Remove the ignition module-to-distributor bolts, lift the module and disconnect the electrical connectors from it.

5. If the module is suspected as being defective, take it to a module testing machine and have it tested.

NOTE: *When replacing the module, sure to coat the module-to-distributor surface with silicone lubricant that will provide heat dissipation.*

6. To install, apply silicone lubricant to the module mounting area of the distributor and reverse the removal procedures. Install the rotor, the distributor cap and the negative battery terminal.

Distributor

REMOVAL AND INSTALLATION

Undisturbed Engine

This condition exists if the engine has not been rotated with the distributor removed.

1. Disconnect the negative battery terminal from the battery.

2. Tag and disconnect the electrical connector(s) from the distributor.

3. Remove the distributor cap (DO NOT remove the ignition wires) from the distributor and move it aside.

4. Using a crayon or chalk, make locating marks (for installation purposes) on the rotor, the ignition module, the distributor housing and the engine.

5. Loosen and remove the distributor clamp bolt and clamp, then lift the distributor from the engine.

NOTE: *Noting the relative position of the rotor and the module alignment marks, make a second mark on the rotor to align it with the one mark on the module.*

6. Install a new O-ring on the distributor housing.

7. Align the second mark on the rotor with the mark on the module, then install the distributor, taking care to align the mark on the housing with the one on the engine.

NOTE: *It may be necessary to lift the distributor and turn the rotor slightly to align the gears and the oil pump driveshaft.*

8. With the respective marks aligned, install the clamp and bolt finger tight.

9. Install and secure the distributor cap.

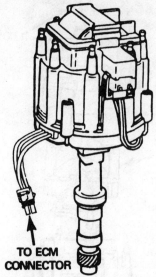

TO ECM CONNECTOR

View of the HEI distributor—4.3L engine

10. Connect the electrical connector(s) to the distributor.

11. Connect a timing light to the engine (following the manufacturer's instructions). Start the engine, then check and/or adjust the timing.

12. Turn the engine Off, tighten the distributor clamp bolt and remove the timing light.

Disturbed Engine

This condition exists when the engine has been rotated with the distributor removed.

1. Disconnect the negative battery terminal from the battery.

2. Tag and disconnect the electrical connector(s) from the distributor.

3. Remove the distributor cap (DO NOT remove the ignition wires) from the distributor and move it aside.

4. Using a crayon or chalk, make locating marks (for installation purposes) on the rotor, the ignition module, the distributor housing and the engine.

5. Loosen and remove the distributor clamp bolt and clamp, then lift the distributor from the engine.

NOTE: *Noting the relative position of the rotor and the module alignment marks, make a second mark on the rotor to align it with the one mark on the module.*

6. Install a new O-ring on the distributor housing.

7. Rotate the crankshaft to position the No. 1 cylinder on the TDC of it's compression stroke. This may be determined by inserting a rag into the No. 1 spark plug hole and slowly turn the engine crankshaft. When the timing mark on the crankshaft pulley aligns with the

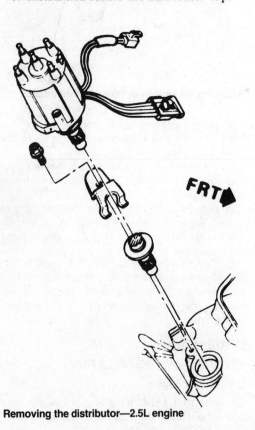

FRT

Removing the distributor—2.5L engine

0° mark on the timing scale and the rag is blown out by the compression, the No. 1 piston is at top-dead-center (TDC).

8. Turn the rotor so that it will point to the No. 1 terminal of the distributor cap.

9. Install the distributor into the engine block. It may be necessary to turn the rotor, a little in either direction, in order to engage the gears.

10. Tap the starter a few times to ensure that the oil pump shaft is mated to the distributor shaft.

11. Bring the engine to No. 1 TDC again and check to see that the rotor is indeed pointing toward the No. 1 terminal of the cap.

12. With the respective marks aligned, install the clamp and bolt finger tight.

13. Install and secure the distributor cap.

14. Connect the electrical connector(s) to the distributor.

15. Connect a timing light to the engine (following the manufacturer's instructions). Start the engine, then check and/or adjust the timing.

16. Turn the engine Off, tighten the distributor clamp bolt and remove the timing light.

Alternator

The alternating current generator (alternator) supplies a continuous output of electrical energy at all engine speeds. The alternator generates electrical energy and recharges the battery by supplying it with electrical current. This unit consists of four main assemblies: two

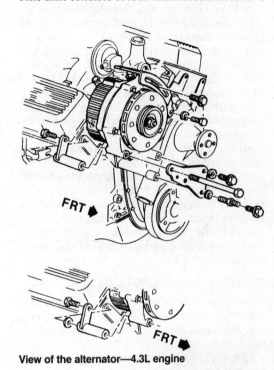

View of the alternator—4.3L engine

ENGINE ASSEMBLY · BRACKET ASSEMBLY (ENGINE ASSEMBLY) · BOLT/STUD (ENGINE ASSEMBLY) · BRACKET ASSEMBLY (ENGINE ASSEMBLY) · VIEW A · BRACE · FRT · SUPPORT

View of the alternator—2.5L engine

end-frame assemblies, a rotor assembly and a stator assembly. The rotor assembly is supported in the drive end-frame by a roller bearing. These bearings are lubricated during assembly and require no maintenance. There are six diodes in the end-frame assembly. These diodes are electrical check valves that also change the alternating current developed within the stator windings to a direct current (DC) at the output (BAT) terminal. Three of these diodes are negative and are mounted flush with the end-frame, while the other three are positive and are mounted into a strip called a heat sink. The positive diodes are easily identified as the ones within the small cavities or depressions.

In 1986, the alternators experienced engineering changes, which are: The elimination of the diode trio and the reduction of the external wiring connectors from three-to-two wires.

NOTE: *The new alternators are not serviceable and no periodic maintenance is required.*

ALTERNATOR PRECAUTIONS

Observing these precautions will ensure safe handling of the electrical system components and will avoid damage to the vehicle's electrical system:

1. Be absolutely sure of the polarity of a booster battery before making connections. Connect the cables positive-to-positive and negative-to-negative. If jump starting, connect the positive cables first and the last connection to a ground on the body of the booster vehicle, so that arcing cannot ignite the hydrogen gas that may have accumulated near the battery. Even a momentary connection of a booster battery with polarity reserved may damage the alternator diodes.

2. Disconnect both vehicle battery cables before attempting to charge the battery.

3. Never ground the alternator output or battery terminal. Be cautious when using metal tools around a battery to avoid creating a short circuit between the terminals.

4. Never run an alternator without a load unless the field circuit (1985) is disconnected.

5. Never attempt to polarize an alternator.

6. Never disconnect any electrical components with the ignition switch turned **On.**

REMOVAL AND INSTALLATION

NOTE: *The following procedures require the use of GM Belt Tension Gauge No. BT-33-95-ACBN (regular V-belts) or BT-33-97M (poly V-belts). The belt should deflect about ¼" (6mm) over a 7–10" (178–254mm) span, or ½" (12.7mm) over a 13–16" (330–406mm) span at this point.*

1. Disconnect the negative battery terminal from the battery.

2. Remove the top radiator hose bracket from the radiator.

3. Remove the wiring harness that is clamped to the radiator core support.

4. Remove the upper fan support-to-radiator support bolts and the fan support.

5. Label and disconnect the alternator's electrical connectors.

6. Remove the alternator brace bolt and the drive belt.

7. Support the alternator, then remove the mounting bolts and the unit from the vehicle.

8. To install, reverse the removal procedures and adjust the drive belt tension. Torque the top mounting bolt to 20 ft.lb. (2.5L) or 18.4 ft.lb. (4.3L) and the lower mounting bolt to 37 ft.lb. (2.5L) or 35 ft.lb. (4.3L). Reconnect the negative battery terminal.

9. To adjust the drive belt, perform the following procedures:

    a. If the belt is cold, operate the engine (at idle speed) for 15 minutes; the belt will seat itself in the pulleys allowing the belt fibers to relax or stretch. If the belt is hot, allow it to cool, until it is warm to the touch.

NOTE: *A used belt is one that has been rotated at least one complete revolution on the pulleys. This begins the belt seating process and it must never be tensioned to the new belt specifications.*

    b. Loosen the component-to-mounting bracket bolts.

    c. Using a GM Belt Tension Gauge No. BT-33-95-ACBN (standard V-belts) or BT-33-97M (poly V-belts), place the tension gauge at the center of the belt between the longest span.

    d. Applying belt tension pressure on the component, adjust the drive belt tension to the correct specifications.

    e. While holding the correct tension on the component, tighten the component-to-mounting bracket bolt.

    f. When the belt tension is correct, remove the tension gauge.

Regulator

The voltage regulators are sealed units mounted within the alternator body and are nonadjustable.

REMOVAL AND INSTALLATION

1985 Models

NOTE: *This procedure is to be performed with the alternator removed from the vehicle. The new alternators, 1986 and later models, are nonservicable.*

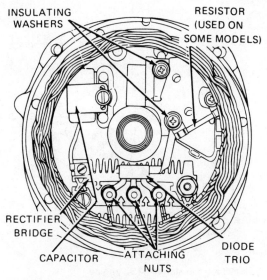

View of the alternator end frame

INSULATING WASHERS

RESISTOR (USED ON SOME MODELS)

RECTIFIER BRIDGE

CAPACITOR

ATTACHING NUTS

DIODE TRIO

1. Mark scribe lines on the end-frames to make the reassembly easier.

2. Remove the 4 through-bolts and separate the drive end-frame assembly from the rectifier end-frame assembly.

3. Remove the 3 diode trio attaching nuts and the 3 regulator attaching screws.

4. Remove the diode trio and the regulator from the end frame.

NOTE: *Before installing the regulator, push the brushes into the brush holder and install*

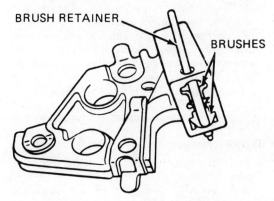

BRUSH RETAINER

BRUSHES

Voltage regulator with the brushes depressed

a brush retainer or a tooth pick to hold the brushes in place.

5. To install the regulator, reverse the removal procedures. After the alternator is assembled, remove the brush retainer.

VOLTAGE ADJUSTMENT

The voltage regulator is electronic and is housed within the alternator. Adjustment of the regulator is not possible. Should replacement of the regulator become necessary, the alternator must be disassembled.

Battery

The battery is mounted in front, left side of the engine compartment. It is a non-tamperable type with side mounted terminals.

REMOVAL AND INSTALLATION

1. Disconnect the negative battery terminal, then the positive battery terminal.

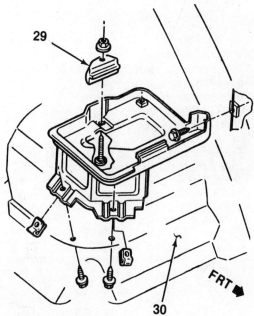

29. Battery retainer
30. Front wheelhouse panel

Exploded view of the battery tray

Alternator and Regulator Specifications

Years	Engine No. Cyl. (cu. in.)	Alternator Field Current @ 12v (amps)	Output (amps)	Regulated Volts @ 75° F	Series	Rotation	Type
1985–87	4-151	5.4–6.4	85 ①	12	CS 130	CW	100
	6-262	5.4–6.4	85 ①	12	CS 130	CW	100

① Heavy duty—100 amps.

2. Remove the battery holddown retainer.

3. Remove the battery from the vehicle.

4. Inspect the battery, the cables and the battery carrier for damage.

5. To install, reverse the removal procedures. Torque the battery retainer to 11 ft.lb. and the top bar to 8 ft.lb.

ADJUSTMENTS

No adjustments are necessary or possible. If the battery is determined to be defective (other than charging), discard it.

Starter

The starter is located on the left side (2.5L) or right side (4.3L) of the engine.

REMOVAL AND INSTALLATION

1. Disconnect the negative battery cable.

2. Raise and support the front of the vehicle on jackstands.

3. If equipped, remove any starter braces or shields that may be in the way.

4. Disconnect the electrical connectors from the starter solenoid.

5. Remove the starter-to-engine bolts, nuts, washers and shims. Allow the starter to drop, then remove it from the engine.

NOTE: *Be sure to keep the shims in order so that they may be reinstalled in the same order.*

6. To install, reverse the removal procedures. Torque the starter-to-engine bolts to 31 ft.lb. (2.5L) or 28 ft.lb. (4.3L). Connect the wires to the starter solenoid and the negative battery cable.

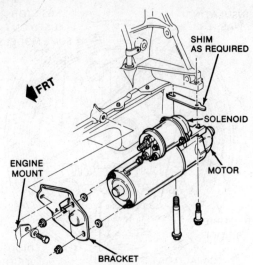

Replacing the starter—2.5L engine

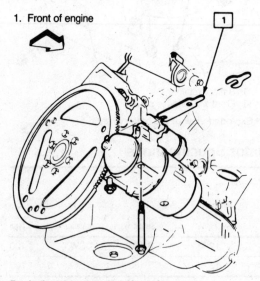

1. Front of engine

Replacing the starter—4.3L engine

SOLENOID REPLACEMENT

1. Refer to the Starter, Removal and Installation procedures in this section and remove the starter, then place it on a workbench.

2. Remove the screw and the washer from the motor connector strap terminal.

3. Remove the two solenoid retaining screws.

4. Twist the solenoid housing clockwise to remove the flange key from the keyway in the housing, then remove the housing.

5. To install the unit, place the return spring on the plunger and place the solenoid body on the drive housing. Turn it counterclockwise to engage the flange key. Place the two retaining screws in position, then install the screw and washer which secures the strap terminal. Install the unit on the starter.

OVERHAUL

Drive Replacement

1. Disconnect the field coil straps from the solenoid.

2. Remove the through-bolts, then separate the commutator end-frame, the field frame assembly, the drive housing and the armature assembly, from each other.

3. Slide the two piece thrust collar off the end of the armature shaft.

4. Slide a suitably sized metal cylinder, such as a standard ½" (12.7mm) pipe coupling or an old pinion, onto the shaft so that the end of the coupling or pinion butts against the edge of the pinion retainer.

5. Support the lower end of the armature securely on a soft surface, such as a wooden block and tap the end of the coupling or pinion, driv-

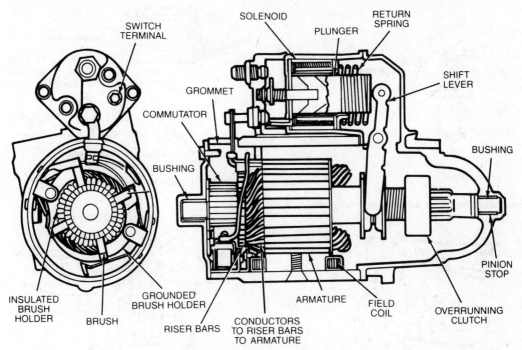

Cross-sectional view—5MT starter

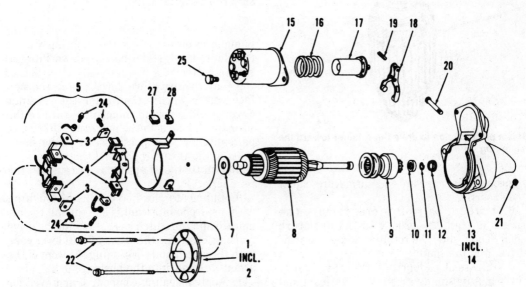

1. Frame—commutator end
2. Brush and holder pkg.
3. Brush
4. Brush holder
5. Housing—drive end
6. Frame and field asm.
7. Solenoid switch
8. Armature
9. Drive asm.
10. Plunger
11. Shift lever
12. Plunger return springer
13. Shift lever shaft
14. Lock washer
15. Screw—brush attaching
16. Screw—field lead to switch
17. Screw—switch attaching
18. Washer—brake
19. Thru bolt
20. Bushing—commutator end
21. Bushing—drive end
22. Pinion stop collar
23. Thrust collar
24. Grommet
25. Grommet
26. Plunger pin
27. Pinion stop retainer ring
28. Lever shaft retaining ring

Exploded view of the starter

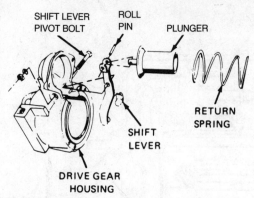

Removing shaft lever and plunger from starter

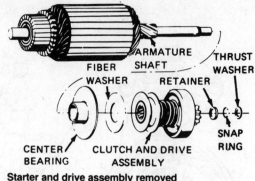

Starter and drive assembly removed

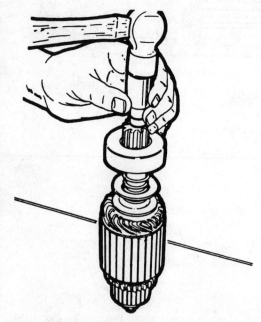

Use a piece of pipe to drive the retainer toward the snap-ring

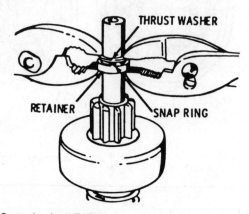

Snap ring installation

ing the retainer towards the armature end of the snapring.

6. Using a pair of pliers, remove the snapring from the groove in the armature shaft. Then, slide the retainer and the starter drive from the shaft.

7. To assemble, lubricate the drive end of the armature shaft with silicone lubricant and slide the starter drive onto the shaft *with the pinion facing outward.* Slide the retainer onto the shaft *with the cupped surface facing outward.*

8. Again, support the armature on a soft surface, with the pinion at the upper end. Center the snapring on top of the shaft (use a new snapring if the original was damaged during removal). Gently place a block of wood flat on top of the snapring , so as not to move it from a centered position. Tap the wooden block with a

hammer in order to force the snapring around the shaft. Then, slide the ring down into the snapring groove.

9. Lay the armature down flat on the surface you're working on. Slide the retainer close, up on the shaft, then position it and the thrust collar next to the snapring. Using two pairs of pliers, on opposite sides of the shaft, squeeze the thrust collar and the retainer together until the snapring is forced into the retainer.

10. Lubricate the drive housing bushing with a silicone lubricant. Then, install the armature and the clutch assembly into the drive housing, engaging the solenoid shift lever yoke with the clutch and positioning the front of the armature shaft into the bushing.

11. Apply a sealing compound, approved for this application onto the drive housing, then, position the field frame around the armature's shaft and against the drive housing. *Work slowly and carefully to prevent damaging the starter brushes.*

12. Lubricate the bushing in the commutator end-frame with a silicone lubricant, place the leather brake washer onto the armature shaft and then slide the commutator end-frame over the shaft and into position against the field

frame. Line up the bolt holes, then install and tighten the through-bolts.

13. Reconnect the field coil straps to the **Motor** terminal of the solenoid.

NOTE: *If replacement of the starter drive fails to cure the improper engagement of the starter pinion to flywheel, there are probably defective parts in the solenoid and/or the shift lever. The best procedure would probably be to take the assembly to a shop where a pinion clearance check can be made by energizing the solenoid on a test bench. If the pinion clearance is incorrect, disassemble the solenoid and the shift lever, then inspect and replace the worn parts.*

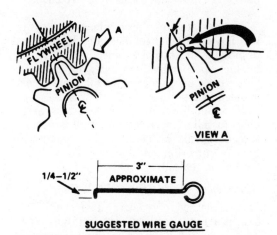

VIEW A

SUGGESTED WIRE GAUGE

Flywheel-to-pinion clearance

Brush Replacement

1. Disassemble the starter by following Steps 1 and 2 of the Drive Replacement procedure, above.

2. Replace the brushes, one at a time, to avoid having to mark the wiring. For each brush, remove the brush holding screw and the old brush, then position the new brush in the same direction (large end toward the center of the field frame), position the wire connector on top of the brush, line up the holes and reinstall the screw. Make sure the screw is snug enough to ensure good contact.

3. Reassemble the starter according to Steps 10–13, above.

ENGINE MECHANICAL

Description

Two engines and three fuel systems are used to power your Astro Van, they are: Pontiac built 2.5L (151 cu. in.) EFI for 1985–87, Chevy built 4.3L (262 cu. in.) 4-bbl for 1985 and 4.3L (262 cu. in.) EFI for 1986–87.

On the 1985, 2.5L EFI engine, the cylinder head and engine block are both constructed of cast iron. The valve guides are integral with the cylinder head and the rocker arms are retained by individual threaded shoulder bolts. Hydraulic roller lifters are incorporated to reduce the friction between the valve lifters and the camshaft lobes.

On the 1986–87, 2.5L EFI engine, a few changes appeared, such as: (1) the pistons were replaced with hypereutectic types (pistons embedded with silicone nodules in the walls to reduce the cylinder wall friction), (2) a reduced weight, high efficiency alternator and (3) a variable ratio A/C compressor.

The 4.3L engine, utilizes a 4-bbl (for 1985) or an EFI system (for 1986–87) and the use of swirl chamber heads (to increase power and fuel efficiency). The engine block and cylinder heads are constructed of cast iron. Other major features are: a wider oil pan flange, raised rails inside the cylinder heads (to improve oil return control), machined rocker cover seal surfaces, a trough along the rocker cover rails (to channel oil away from the gasket) and even distribution of the clamping loads, to make this engine one of the most leak-resistant on the road today.

In 1986, the 4.3L EFI engine began using a new one-piece rear crankshaft seal, lighter engine oil, remachined camshaft lobes and new poly-vee alternator drive belts.

Engine Overhaul Tips

Most engine overhaul procedures are fairly standard. In addition to specific parts replacement procedures and complete specifications for your individual engine, this chapter also is a guide to accept rebuilding procedures. Examples of standard rebuilding practice are shown and should be used along with specific details concerning your particular engine.

Starter Specifications

Years	Engine No. Cyl. (cu. in.)	Series	Type	No-Load Test		
				Amps	Volts	RPM
1985–87	4-151	5 MT	101	50–75	10	6,000–11,900
	6-262	10 MT	101	70–110	10	6,500–11,700

Competent and accurate machine shop services will ensure maximum performance, reliability and engine life.

On most instances it is more profitable for the do-it-yourself mechanic to remove, clean and inspect the component(s), buy the necessary parts and deliver these to a shop for actual machine work.

On the other hand, much of the rebuilding work (crankshaft, block, bearings, piston rods, and other components) is well within the scope of the do-it-yourself mechanic.

TOOLS

The tools required for an engine overhaul or parts replacement will depend on the depth of your involvement. With a few exceptions, they will be the tools found in a mechanic's tool kit (see Chapter 1). More in-depth work will require any or all of the following:

• A dial indicator (reading in thousandths) mounted on a universal base
• Micrometers and telescope gauges
• Jaw and screw-type pullers
• Scraper
• Valve spring compressor
• Ring groove cleaner
• Piston ring expander and compressor
• Ridge reamer
• Cylinder hone or glaze breaker
• Plastigage®
• Engine stand

Use of most of these tools is illustrated in this chapter. Many can be rented for a one-time use from a local parts jobber or tool supply house specializing in automotive work.

Occasionally, the use of special tools is called for. See the information on Special Tools and Safety Notice in the front of this book before substituting another tool.

INSPECTION TECHNIQUES

Procedures and specifications are given in this chapter for inspecting, cleaning and assessing the wear limits of most major components. Other procedures such as Magnaflux® and Zyglo® can be used to locate material flaws and stress cracks. Magnaflux® is a magnetic process applicable only to ferrous materials. The Zyglo® process coats the material with a fluorescent dye penetrant and can be used on any material. Check for suspected surface cracks can be more readily made using spot check dye. The dye is sprayed onto the suspected area, wiped off and the area sprayed with a developer. Cracks will show up brightly.

OVERHAUL TIPS

Aluminum has become extremely popular for use in engines, due to its low weight. Observe the following precautions when handling aluminum parts:

• Never hot tank aluminum parts (the caustic hot tank solution will eat the aluminum.
• Remove all aluminum parts (identification tag, etc.) from engine parts prior to the tanking.
• Always coat threads lightly with engine oil or anti-seize compounds before installation, to prevent seizure.
• Never over-torque bolts or spark plugs especially in aluminum for you may strip the threads.

Stripped threads in any component can be repaired using any of several commercial repair kits (Heli-Coil®, Microdot®, Keenserts®, etc.).

When assembling the engine, any parts that will have frictional contact must be prelubed to provide lubrication at initial start-up. Any product specifically formulated for this purpose can be used, but engine oil is not recommended as a prelube.

When semi-permanent (locked, but removable) installation of bolts or nuts is desired, threads should be cleaned and coated with Loctite® or other similar, commercial non-hardening sealant.

REPAIRING DAMAGED THREADS

Several methods of repairing damaged threads are available. Heli-Coil® (shown here), Keenserts® and Microdot® are among the most widely used. All involve basically the same principle—drilling out stripped threads, tapping the hole and installing a prewound insert—making welding, plugging and oversize fasteners unnecessary.

Two types of thread repair inserts are usually supplied—a standard type for most Inch Coarse, Inch Fine, Metric Course and Metric Fine thread sizes and a spark lug type to fit most spark plug port sizes. Consult the individual manufacturer's catalog to determine exact applications. Typical thread repair kits will contain a selection of prewound threaded inserts, a tap (corresponding to the outside diameter threads of the insert) and an installation tool. Spark plug inserts usually differ because they require a tap equipped with pilot threads and a combined reamer/tap section. Most manufacturers also supply blister-packed thread repair inserts separately in addition to a master kit containing a variety of taps and inserts plus installation tools.

Before effecting a repair to a threaded hole, remove any snapped, broken or damaged bolts or studs. Penetrating oil can be used to free frozen threads; the offending item can be removed with locking pliers or with a screw or stud ex-

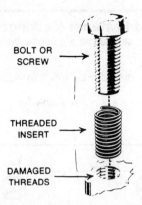

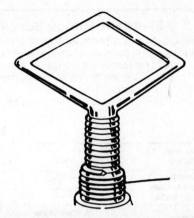

Screw the threaded insert onto the installation tool until the tang engages the slot. Screw the insert into the tapped hole until it is ¼–½ turn below the top surface. After installation break off the tang with a hammer and punch

Damaged bolt holes can be repaired with thread repair inserts

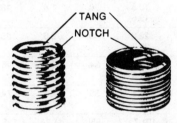

Standard thread repair insert (left) and spark plug thread insert (right)

Drill out the damaged threads with specified drill. Drill completely through the hole or to the bottom of a blind hole

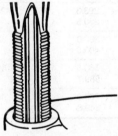

With the tap supplied, tap the hole to receive the thread insert. Keep the tap well oiled and back it out frequently to avoid clogging the threads

tractor. After the hole is clear, the thread can be repaired, as follows:

Checking Engine Compression

A noticeable lack of engine power, excessive oil consumption and/or poor fuel mileage measured over an extended period are all indicators of internal engine wear. Worn piston rings, scored or worn cylinder bores, blown head gaskets, sticking or burnt valves and worn valve seats are all possible culprits here. A check of each cylinder's compression will help you locate the problems.

As mentioned in the Tools and Equipment section of Chapter 1, a screw-in type compression gauge is more accurate that the type you

simply hold against the spark plug hole, although it takes slightly longer to use. It's worth it to obtain a more accurate reading. Follow the procedures below.

1. Warm up the engine to normal operating temperature.

2. Remove all spark plugs.

3. Disconnect the high tension lead from the ignition coil.

4. Fully open the throttle, either by operating the carburetor throttle linkage by hand or by having an assistant floor the accelerator pedal.

5. Screw the compression gauge into the No. 1 spark plug hole until the fitting is snug. NOTE: *Be careful not to crossthread the plug hole. On aluminum cylinder heads use extra care, as the threads in these heads are easily ruined.*

6. Ask an assistant to depress the accelerator pedal fully on both carbureted and fuel injected vehicles. Then, while reading the compression gauge, ask the assistant to crank the engine two or three times in short bursts using the ignition switch.

Standard Torque Specifications and Fastener Markings

In the absence of specific torques, the following chart can be used as a guide to the maximum safe torque of a particular size/grade of fastener.
- There is no torque difference for fine or coarse threads.
- Torque values are based on clean, dry threads. Reduce the value by 10% if threads are oiled prior to assembly.
- The torque required for aluminum components or fasteners is considerably less.

U.S. Bolts

SAE Grade Number	1 or 2			5			6 or 7		
Number of lines always 2 less than the grade number.									
Bolt Size (Inches)—(Thread)	Maximum Torque			Maximum Torque			Maximum Torque		
	Ft./Lbs.	Kgm	Nm	Ft./Lbs.	Kgm	Nm	Ft./Lbs.	Kgm	Nm
¼ — 20	5	0.7	6.8	8	1.1	10.8	10	1.4	13.5
— 28	6	0.8	8.1	10	1.4	13.6			
⁵⁄₁₆ — 18	11	1.5	14.9	17	2.3	23.0	19	2.6	25.8
— 24	13	1.8	17.6	19	2.6	25.7			
⅜ — 16	18	2.5	24.4	31	4.3	42.0	34	4.7	46.0
— 24	20	2.75	27.1	35	4.8	47.5			
⁷⁄₁₆ — 14	28	3.8	37.0	49	6.8	66.4	55	7.6	74.5
— 20	30	4.2	40.7	55	7.6	74.5			
½ — 13	39	5.4	52.8	75	10.4	101.7	85	11.75	115.2
— 20	41	5.7	55.6	85	11.7	115.2			
⁹⁄₁₆ — 12	51	7.0	69.2	110	15.2	149.1	120	16.6	162.7
— 18	55	7.6	74.5	120	16.6	162.7			
⅝ — 11	83	11.5	112.5	150	20.7	203.3	167	23.0	226.5
— 18	95	13.1	128.8	170	23.5	230.5			
¾ — 10	105	14.5	142.3	270	37.3	366.0	280	38.7	379.6
— 16	115	15.9	155.9	295	40.8	400.0			
⅞ — 9	160	22.1	216.9	395	54.6	535.5	440	60.9	596.5
— 14	175	24.2	237.2	435	60.1	589.7			
1 — 8	236	32.5	318.6	590	81.6	799.9	660	91.3	894.8
— 14	250	34.6	338.9	660	91.3	849.8			

Metric Bolts

Relative Strength Marking	4.6, 4.8			8.8		
Bolt Markings						
Bolt Size Thread Size x Pitch (mm)	Maximum Torque			Maximum Torque		
	Ft./Lbs.	Kgm	Nm	Ft./Lbs.	Kgm	Nm
6 x 1.0	2–3	.2–.4	3–4	3–6	.4–.8	5–8
8 x 1.25	6–8	.8–1	8–12	9–14	1.2–1.9	13–19
10 x 1.25	12–17	1.5–2.3	16–23	20–29	2.7–4.0	27–39
12 x 1.25	21–32	2.9–4.4	29–43	35–53	4.8–7.3	47–72
14 x 1.5	35–52	4.8–7.1	48–70	57–85	7.8–11.7	77–110
16 x 1.5	51–77	7.0–10.6	67–100	90–120	12.4–16.5	130–160
18 x 1.5	74–110	10.2–15.1	100–150	130–170	17.9–23.4	180–230
20 x 1.5	110–140	15.1–19.3	150–190	190–240	26.2–46.9	160–320
22 x 1.5	150–190	22.0–26.2	200–260	250–320	34.5–44.1	340–430
24 x 1.5	190–240	26.2–46.9	260–320	310–410	42.7–56.5	420–550

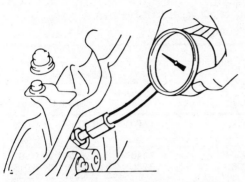

The screw-in type compression gauge is more accurate

7. Read the compression gauge at the end of each series of cranks, and record the highest of these readings. Repeat this procedure for each of the engine's cylinders. Compare the highest reading of each cylinder to the compression pressure specification in the Tune-Up Specifications chart in Chapter 2. The specs in this chart are maximum values.

NOTE: *A cylinder's compression pressure is usually acceptable if it is not less than 80% of maximum. The difference between each cylinder should be no more than 12–14 pounds.*

8. If a cylinder is unusually low, pour a tablespoon of clean engine oil into the cylinder

General Engine Specifications

Years	VIN	Engine No. Cyl. (cu. in.)	Fuel System Type	SAE Net Horsepower @ rpm	SAE Net Torque ft. lb. @ rpm	Bore x Stroke	Comp. Ratio	Oil Press. (psi.) @ 2000 rpm
1985–87	E	4-151	TBI	98 @ 4400	134 @ 3200	4.000 x 3.000	9.0:1	36–41
1985	N	6-262	4-bbl.	150 @ 4000	225 @ 2400	4.000 x 3.480	9.3:1	30–35
1986–87	Z	6-262	TBI	150 @ 4000	230 @ 2400	4.000 x 3.480	9.3:1	30–35

Valve Specifications

Year	VIN	Engine No. Cyl. (cu. in.)	Seat Angle (deg)	Face Angle (deg)	Spring Test Pressure (lbs. @ in.)	Spring Installed Height (in.)	Stem to Guide Clearance (in.) Intake	Stem to Guide Clearance (in.) Exhaust	Stem Diameter (in.) Intake	Stem Diameter (in.) Exhaust
1985–87	E	4-151	46	45	①	1.69	0.0010–0.0027	②	0.342–0.343	0.342–0.343
1985	N	6-262	46	45	③	1.72④	0.0010–0.0027	0.0010–0.0027	—	—
1986–87	Z	6-262	46	45	③	1.72④	0.0010–0.0027	0.0010–0.0027	—	—

① 78–86 @ 1.66—Closed
170–180 @ 1.26—Open
② 0.0010–0.0027—Top
0.0020–0.0037—Bottom
③ 76–84 @ 1.70—Closed
194–206 @ 1.25—Open
④ ± 1/32

Camshaft Specifications
All Specifications in inches

Years	VIN	Engine No. Cyl. (cu. in.)	Journal Diameter 1	2	3	4	5	Bearing Clearance	Elevation Int.	Elevation Exh.	End Play
1985–87	E	4-151	1.869	1.869	1.869	—	—	0.0007–0.0027	0.398	0.398	0.0015–0.0050
1985	N	6-262	1.868–1.869	1.868–1.869	1.868–1.869	1.868–1.869	—	N.A.	0.355–0.359	0.388–0.392	0.004–0.012
1986–87	Z	6-262	1.868–1.869	1.868–1.869	1.868–1.869	1.868–1.869	—	N.A.	0.355–0.359	0.388–0.392	0.004–0.012

N.A.—Not available

Crankshaft and Connecting Rod Specifications
All Specifications in inches

Years	VIN	Engine No. Cyl. (cu. in.)	Crankshaft					Connecting Rod		
			Main Bearing Journal Dia.	Main Bearing Oil Clearance	Shaft End Play	Thrust on No.		Journal Dia.	Oil Clearance	Side Clearance
1985–87	E	4-151	2.300	0.0005–0.0022	0.0035–0.0085	5		2.000	0.0005–0.0026	0.006–0.022
1985	N	6-262	①	②	0.002–0.006	4		2.2487–2.2497	0.0010–0.0032	0.007–0.015
1986–87	Z	6-262	①	②	0.002–0.006	4		2.2487–2.2497	0.0013–0.0035	0.006–0.014

① No. 1—2.4484–2.4493
   No. 2 & 3—2.4481–2.4490
   No. 4—2.4479–2.4488
② No. 1—0.0008–0.0020
   No. 2 & 3—0.0011–0.0023
   No. 4—0.0017–0.0032

Piston and Ring Specifications
All Specifications in inches

Years	VIN	Engine No. Cyl. (cu. in.)	Ring Gap			Ring Side Clearance			Piston Clearance
			#1 Compr.	#2 Compr.	Oil Control	#1 Compr.	#2 Compr.	Oil Control	
1985	E	4-151	0.010–0.022	0.010–0.027	0.015–0.055	0.0015–0.0030	0.0015–0.0030	—	①
1986–87	E	4-151	0.010–0.020	0.010–0.020	0.020–0.060	0.002–0.003	0.001–0.003	0.002–0.006	0.0014–0.0022 ②
1985	N	6-262	0.010–0.020	0.010–0.025	0.015–0.055	0.0012–0.0032	0.0012–0.0032	0.002–0.007	0.00025–0.00035
1986–87	Z	6-262	0.010–0.020	0.010–0.025	0.015–0.055	0.0012–0.0032	0.0012–0.0032	0.002–0.007	0.00025–0.00035

① 0.0025–0.0033 (Top)
   0.0017–0.0041 (Bottom)
② Measured 1.8 inch down from top of piston

Torque Specifications
Piston Engines

Years	VIN	Engine No. Cyl. (cu. in.)	Cyl. Head	Conn. Rod	Main Bearing	Crankshaft Damper	Flywheel	Manifold	
								Intake	Exhaust
1985	E	4-151	92	32	70	160	44	29	44
1986–87	E	4-151	90	32	70	160	①	②	②
1985	N	6-262	65	45	70	60	55–75	30	20
1986–87	Z	6-262	65	45	75	70	75	36	③

① 55 ft. lbs.—Automatic
   65 ft. lbs.—Manual
② Refer to the Manifold Installation procedures for the correct torquing procedures.
③ 26 ft. lbs.—Center two bolts
   20 ft. lbs.—All other bolts

through the spark plug hole and repeat the compression test. If the compression rises after adding the oil, it appears that the cylinder's piston rings or bore are damaged or worn. If the pressure remains low, the valves may not be seating properly (a valve job is needed), or the head gasket may be blown near that cylinder. If compression in any two adjacent cylinders is low and if the addition of oil doesn't help the compression, there is leakage past the head gasket. Oil and coolant water in the combustion chamber can result from this problem. There may be evidence of water droplets on the engine dipstick when a head gasket has blown.

Engine

REMOVAL AND INSTALLATION

2.5L Engine

CAUTION: *Relieve the pressure on the fuel system before disconnecting any fuel line connection.*

1. Disconnect the negative battery cable from the battery.
2. From inside the vehicle, remove the engine cover.
3. Place a drain pan under the radiator, open the drain cock and drain the cooling system; be sure to save the cooling fluid for reuse.
4. Remove the headlight bezel and grille.
5. Remove the lower radiator close out panel and the radiator support brace.
6. Remove the lower tie bar, the cross braces and the hood latch assembly.
7. Remove the radiator hoses, then disconnect and plug the transmission-to-radiator oil cooler lines (if equipped).
8. Remove the radiator filler panels, then the radiator and the fan shroud as an assembly.
9. At the bulkhead connector, disconnect the engine electrical harness. Disconnect the electrical harness from the Electronic Control Module (ECM) and pull it through the bulkhead.
10. Remove the heater hoses from the heater core.
11. Disconnect the accelerator, the cruise control and the detent (if equipped) cables. Disconnect the ground cable from the cylinder head.
12. Remove the oil filler neck and the thermostat housing from the engine.
13. Remove the purge hose from the charcoal canister, then the air cleaner and adapter from the carburetor or throttle body. Disconnect the fuel hoses from the throttle body.
14. Raise and support the front of the vehicle on jackstands.

15. Disconnect the exhaust pipe from the exhaust manifold. Remove the flywheel cover from the bellhousing.
16. Disconnect the electrical harness from the transmission and the frame, then the electrical connectors from the starter.
17. Remove the starter-to-engine bolts and the starter from the engine.
18. Remove the through bolts from the engine mounts and install an engine lifting device to the engine.
19. Remove the bellhousing-to-engine bolts, then lower the vehicle. Using a floor jack, support the transmission.
20. Using an engine lifting device, lift the engine, separate it from the transmission and remove it from the vehicle.
21. To install, reverse the removal procedures. Torque the engine-to-frame (through mount) bolts to 50 ft.lb. or nuts to 31 ft.lb. Refill the cooling system. Start the engine and check for leaks.

NOTE: *All engine fasteners are important parts that may affect the performance of the components and systems, they could result in major repair expense. If replacement becomes necessary, they MUST BE replaced with the same part number or equivalent part. Use specific torque values when assembling the parts, to assure proper retention.*

4.3L Engine

CAUTION: *Relieve the pressure on the fuel system before disconnecting any fuel line connection.*

1. Disconnect the negative battery cable from the battery.
2. Place a pan under the radiator, open the drain cock and drain the engine coolant.
3. Raise and support the front of the vehicle on jackstands.
4. Disconnect the exhaust pipes from the exhaust manifolds.
5. At the flywheel cover, remove the strut rods, then the flywheel cover from the bellhousing. If equipped with an AT, mark the torque converter-to-flywheel position, then disconnect the torque converter from the flywheel.
6. Disconnect the electrical connectors from the starter, then remove the starter from the engine. Disconnect the electrical harness and connectors from the transmission and the frame.
7. Remove the oil filter and the lower fan shroud bolts. Disconnect the fuel hoses from the frame.
8. From the radiator, disconnect the lower transmission oil cooler line (if used) and the lower engine oil cooler line (if used).

9. Remove the through bolts of the engine-to-frame mounts, then remove the jackstands and lower the vehicle.

10. Remove the headlight bezels and the grille. At the radiator, remove the lower close-out panel, the support brace and the core support cross brace, then remove the lower tie-bar and the hood latch mechanism.

11. At the firewall, remove the master cylinder.

12. From the radiator, remove the upper fan shroud, the upper radiator core support, the filler panels and the radiator.

NOTE: *Before removing the radiator, be sure to discharge the A/C system (if equipped).*

13. From inside the vehicle, remove the engine cover and the right side kick panel.

14. From the A/C system, remove the rear compressor brace, the hose from the accumulator, then the compressor (with the bracket) and the accumulator.

15. Remove the power steering pump (DO NOT disconnect the pressure hoses) and move it aside.

16. Disconnect the vacuum hoses from the intake manifold. Disconnect the electrical harness connector from the bulkhead and the Electronic Control Module (ECM); push the electrical harness connector through the bulkhead.

17. Remove the distributor cap, the fuel line(s) from the carburetor or throttle body and the diverter valve (if equipped).

18. Remove the transmission dipstick tube, the heater hose(s) from the heater core, the horn and the Air Injector Reactor (AIR) check valves.

19. Using and engine lifting device, attach it to the engine.

20. Using a floor jack, raise and support the transmission, then remove the bellhousing-to-engine bolts.

21. Raise the engine, disconnect it from the bellhousing and remove it from the vehicle.

22. To install, reverse the removal procedures. Torque the engine-to-frame (through mount) bolts to 75 ft.lb. or nuts to 50 ft.lb. Refill the cooling system, the engine and transmission lubrication systems. Recharge the A/C system (if equipped). Bleed the brake system. Start the engine and check for leaks.

NOTE: *All engine fasteners are important parts that may affect the performance of the components and systems, they could result in major repair expense. If replacement becomes necessary, they MUST BE replaced with the same part number or equivalent part. Use specific torque values when assembling the parts, to assure proper retention.*

Pushrod Side Cover – 2.5L Engine

The pushrod side cover is located on the right side of the engine and must be removed to service the valve lifters.

REMOVAL AND INSTALLATION

1. Disconnect the negative battery cable from the battery.

2. Remove the alternator and the bracket from the engine.

3. Place a pan under the radiator, open the drain cock and drain the cooling system. Remove the intake manifold-to-engine brace.

4. Remove the lower radiator and heater hoses.

5. Disconnect the electrical connector from the oil sender and the wiring harness from around the pushrod side cover. Remove the wiring harness brackets from the pushrod cover.

6. Remove the side cover-to-engine nuts and the side cover.

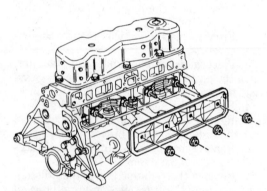

Replacing the side cover—2.5L engine

7. Using a putty knife, clean the gasket mounting surfaces.

NOTE: *Use a solvent to clean the oil and grease from the gasket mounting surfaces.*

8. To install, use a new cover gasket, a bead of $3/16''$ (4.7mm) RTV sealant and reverse the removal procedures. Torque the pushrod side cover-to-engine nuts to 90 inch lbs. Refill the cooling system.

Rocker Arm Cover

REMOVAL AND INSTALLATION

2.5L Engine

1. Disconnect the negative battery cable from the battery.

2. Remove the air cleaner.

3. Disconnect the Positive Crankcase Ventilation (PCV) valve hose, the ignition wires from the rocker arm cover.

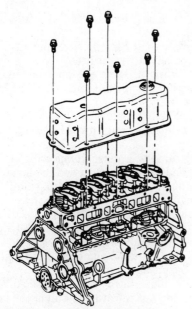

Removing the valve cover—2.5L engine

4. Remove the Exhaust Gas Recirculation (EGR) valve.

5. From the intake stud, label and disconnect the vacuum hoses.

6. Remove the rocker arm cover-to-cylinder head bolts and the cover.

7. Using a putty knife, clean the gasket mounting surface.

NOTE: *Be sure to use solvent to remove any oil or grease that may remain on the sealing surfaces.*

8. To install, use a new gasket, a $^3/_{16}''$ (4.7mm) continuous bead of RTV sealant and

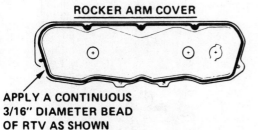

ROCKER ARM COVER

**APPLY A CONTINUOUS
3/16" DIAMETER BEAD
OF RTV AS SHOWN**

PUSH ROD COVER

**APPLY A CONTINUOUS
3/16" DIAMETER BEAD
OF RTV AS SHOWN**

Applying RTV sealant to the valve and the push rod side cover gaskets—2.5L engine

reverse the removal procedures. Torque the valve cover-to-cylinder head bolts to 7 ft.lb.

4.3L Engine
RIGHT SIDE

1. Disconnect the negative battery cable from the battery.

2. Remove the air cleaner. Disconnect the Air Injection Reaction (AIR) hoses from the diverter valve, then the diverter valve bracket from the intake manifold.

3. From the alternator bracket, remove the engine oil filler tube and the transmission (if equipped with an AT) oil filler tube.

4. From the valve cover, remove the Positive Crankcase Ventilation (PCV) valve.

5. From the back side of the right cylinder head, remove the AIR pipe-to-cylinder head bolts and move the pipe (hose) out of the way.

6. Remove the ignition wires from the valve cover and the distributor cap (with the wires attached), then move the cap out of the way.

7. Remove the valve cover-to-cylinder head bolts and the cover.

8. Using a putty knife, clean the gasket mounting surfaces.

9. To install, use a new gasket and reverse the removal procedures. Torque the valve cover-to-cylinder head bolts to 7 ft.lb. Start the engine and check for oil leaks.

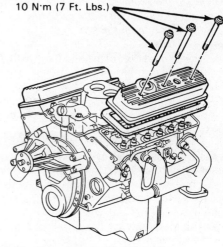

10 N·m (7 Ft. Lbs.)

Installing the valve cover—4.3L engine

LEFT SIDE

1. Disconnect the negative battery cable from the battery.

2. Remove the air cleaner.

NOTE: *If equipped with a carburetor, remove the vacuum pipe from the carburetor.*

3. Disconnect the electrical harness from

the rocker arm cover and any vacuum hoses (if necessary).

4. Disconnect the accelerator and the detent cables from the carburetor/throttle body, then remove the mounting brackets from the intake manifold.

5. Remove the valve cover-to-cylinder head bolts and the cover.

6. Using a putty knife, clean the gasket mounting surfaces.

7. To install, use a new gasket and reverse the removal procedures. Torque the valve cover-to-cylinder head bolts to 7 ft.lb. Start the engine and check for oil leaks.

Rocker Arms

The rocker arm opens and closes the valves through a very simple ball pivot type operation.

REMOVAL AND INSTALLATION

2.5L Engine

1. Refer to the Valve Cover, Removal and Installation procedures in this section and remove the valve cover.

2. Using a socket wrench, remove the rocker arm bolts, the ball washer and the rocker arm.

NOTE: *If only the pushrod is to be removed, back off the rocker arm bolt, swing the rocker arm aside and remove the pushrod. When removing more than assembly, at the same time, be sure to keep them in order for reassembly purposes.*

3. Inspect the rocker arms and ball washers for scoring and/or other damage, replace them (if necessary).

NOTE: *If replacing worn components with new ones, be sure to coat the new parts with Molykote*[X] *before installation.*

4. To install, reverse the removal procedures. Torque the rocker arm-to-cylinder head bolts to 20 ft.lb.; DO NOT overtighten.

5. To prepare the engine for valve adjustment, rotate the crankshaft until the mark on the damper pulley aligns with the 0° mark on the timing plate and the No. 1 cylinder is on the compression stroke.

NOTE: *To determine if the No. 1 cylinder is on the compression stroke, shake the rocker arms of the No. 1 cylinder, if they move, the cylinder is on the compression stroke; if they don't move, the cylinder is on the exhaust stroke. If the cylinder is on the exhaust stroke, it will be necessary to rotate the crankshaft one full revolution.*

6. With the engine on the compression stroke, adjust the exhaust valves of cylinders No. 1 & 3 and the intake valves of cylinders No. 1 & 2 by performing the following procedures:

   a. Back out the adjusting nut until lash can be felt at the pushrod.

   b. While rotating the pushrod, turn the adjusting nut inward until all of the lash is removed.

   c. When the play has disappeared, turn the adjusting nut inward 1½ additional turns.

7. Rotate the crankshaft one complete revolution and align the mark on the damper pulley with the 0° mark on the timing plate. With the engine on the compression stroke, adjust the exhaust valves of cylinders No. 2 & 4 and the intake valves of cylinders No. 3 & 4, by performing the following procedures:

   a. Back out the adjusting nut until lash can be felt at the pushrod.

   b. While rotating the pushrod, turn the adjusting nut inward until all of the lash is removed.

   c. When the play has disappeared, turn the adjusting nut inward 1½ additional turns.

8. To complete the installation, reverse the removal procedures. Start the engine, the check for oil leaks and engine operation.

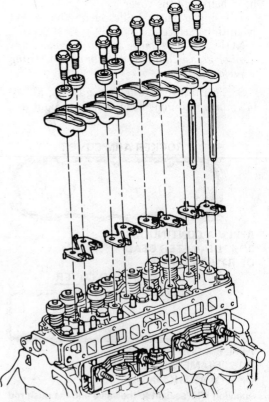

Exploded view of the rocker arm assembly—2.5L engine

4.3L Engine

1. Refer to the Valve Cover, Removal and Installation procedures in this section and remove the valve covers.

2. Using a socket wrench remove the rocker arm-to-cylinder head nuts, the ball washers, the rocker arms and the pushrods (if necessary).

Removing the rocker arm assemblies—4.3L engine

3. Inspect the parts for excessive wear and/or damage, then replace any parts (if necessary).

NOTE: *If replacing any parts with new ones, coat the new parts with Molykote*.

4. To install valve assembly, reverse the removal procedures.

5. To prepare the engine for valve adjustment, rotate the crankshaft until the mark on the damper pulley aligns with the 0° mark on the timing plate and the No. 1 cylinder is on the compression stroke.

NOTE: *To determine if the No. 1 cylinder is on the compression stroke, shake the rocker arms of the No. 1 cylinder, if they move, the cylinder is on the compression stroke; if they don't move, the cylinder is on the exhaust stroke. If the cylinder is on the exhaust stroke, it will be necessary to rotate the crankshaft one full revolution.*

6. With the engine on the compression stroke, adjust the exhaust valves of cylinders No. 1, 5 & 6 and the intake valves of cylinders No. 1, 2 & 3, by performing the following procedures:

a. Back out the adjusting nut until lash can be felt at the pushrod.

b. While rotating the pushrod, turn the adjusting nut inward until all of the lash is removed.

c. When the play has disappeared, turn the adjusting nut inward one additional turn.

7. Rotate the crankshaft one complete revolution and align the mark on the damper pulley with the 0° mark on the timing plate.

8. With the engine on the compression stroke, adjust the exhaust valves of cylinders No. 2, 3 & 4 and the intake valves of cylinders No. 4, 5 & 6, by performing the following procedures:

a. Back out the adjusting nut until lash can be felt at the pushrod.

b. While rotating the pushrod, turn the adjusting nut inward until all of the lash is removed.

c. When the play has disappeared, turn

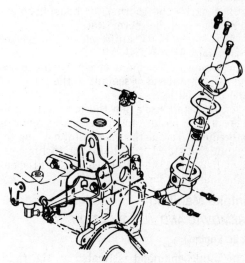

Exploded view of the thermostat and housing—2.5L engine

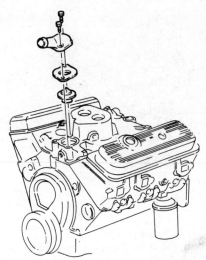

Exploded view of the thermostat and housing—4.3L engine

the adjusting nut inward one additional turn.

9. To complete the installation, reverse the removal procedures. Start the engine, then check for oil leaks and engine operation.

Thermostat

The thermostat is located inside the thermostat housing, which is attached to the front of the cylinder head (2.5L) or to the front of the intake manifold (4.3L).

REMOVAL AND INSTALLATION

1. Disconnect the negative battery cable from the battery.

2. Place a catch pan under the radiator, open the drain cock and drain the cooling system.

3. Remove the thermostat housing-to-engine bolts and the thermostat.

4. Using a putty knife, clean the gasket mounting surfaces.

5. Using RTV sealant or equivalent, place an 1/8" (3mm) bead of sealant in the groove of the water outlet.

6. To install, use a new thermostat (if possible), a new gasket and reverse the removal procedures. Torque the thermostat housing-to-engine bolts to 21 ft.lb. Refill the cooling system. Reconnect the battery cable, start the engine and check for leaks.

Intake Manifold

REMOVAL AND INSTALLATION

2.5L Engine

The intake manifold is located on the right side of the cylinder head.

CAUTION: *Relieve the pressure on the fuel system before disconnecting any fuel line connection.*

1. Disconnect the negative battery cable from the battery.

2. Place a catch pan under the radiator, open the drain cock and drain the cooling fluid.

3. Remove the air cleaner assembly. Label and disconnect the vacuum hoses from the exhaust manifold, thermostat housing and etc.

4. Label and disconnect the electrical connectors that may be in the way. Disconnect the accelerator, the cruise control and TV cables.

5. Remove the coolant hoses from the intake manifold. Remove and plug the fuel line at the throttle body.

6. Remove the alternator bracket-to-engine bolts and move the alternator/bracket aside.

7. Remove the ignition coil-to-cylinder head/intake manifold bolts and the coil from the engine.

8. Remove the intake manifold-to-engine bolts and the manifold from the engine.

9. Using a putty knife, clean the gasket mounting surfaces.

10. To install, use a new gasket, sealant (for some bolts) and reverse the removal procedures. Torque the intake manifold-to-engine bolts to 25–37 ft.lb. Refill the cooling system. Start the engine and check for leaks.

4.3L Engine

The intake manifold is located between the cylinder heads.

CAUTION: *If equipped with an EFI system, relieve the pressure on the fuel system before disconnecting any fuel line connection.*

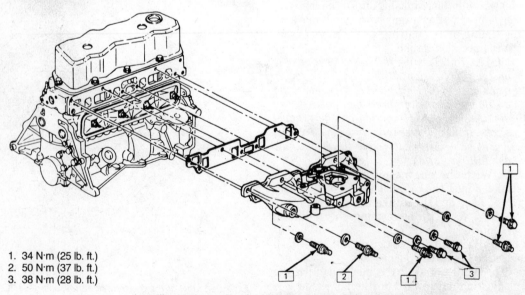

1. 34 N·m (25 lb. ft.)
2. 50 N·m (37 lb. ft.)
3. 38 N·m (28 lb. ft.)

Installing and torquing the intake manifold—2.5L engine

1. Disconnect the negative battery cable from the battery.

2. Remove the air cleaner. Disconnect the Electronic Spark Control (ESC) electrical connector. Remove the distributor.

3. Place a catch pan under the radiator, open the drain cock and drain the cooling fluid.

4. Disconnect the accelerator and the transmission detent (if equipped) cables.

5. Remove the rear brace from the A/C compressor, then the engine and the transmission oil filler (if equipped) tube(s) from the alternator bracket.

6. Remove the A/C compressor belt idler (if equipped) from the alternator bracket, then the alternator bracket.

7. From the carburetor or throttle body, remove the fuel hoses, the vacuum lines and the electrical connectors.

8. Remove the Air Injection Reactor (AIR) hoses and brackets.

9. Remove the heater hose from the intake manifold.

10. Remove the intake manifold-to-cylinder head bolts and the intake manifold from the engine.

11. Using a putty knife, clean the gasket mounting surfaces, the carbon deposits from the exhaust/EGR passages and the scale/deposits from the coolant passages.

12. Using the Magnaflux™ or equivalent process, inspect the intake manifold for cracks.

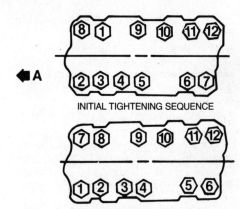

A. Front of engine

Torquing sequence for the intake manifold—4.3L engine

13. To install, use new gaskets, RTV sealant (apply a $^{3}/_{16}''$ (4.7mm) bead to the front and rear manifold seals) and reverse the removal procedures. Torque the intake manifold-to-cylinder head bolts/studs (in sequence) to 36 ft.lb.

Exhaust Manifold

REMOVAL AND INSTALLATION

2.5L Engine

The exhaust manifold is located on the left side of the engine.

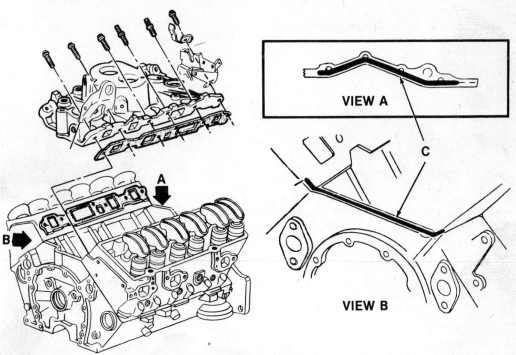

C. RTV sealant

Installing the intake manifold and applying sealant—4.3L engine

1. Disconnect the negative battery cable from the battery.

2. If equipped, remove the thermac heat stove pipe from the exhaust manifold.

3. At the A/C compressor, remove the drive belt, the compressor (lay it aside) and the rear adjusting bracket.

4. Raise and support the front of the vehicle on jackstands.

5. Disconnect the exhaust pipe from the exhaust manifold, then lower the vehicle.

6. Remove the air cleaner and disconnect the electrical connector from the oxygen sensor.

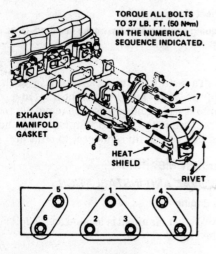

BOLT LOCATIONS

Torquing sequence for the exhaust manifold—2.5L engine (1985)

7. Remove the exhaust manifold-to-engine bolts and the manifold from the engine.

8. Using a putty knife, clean the gasket mounting surfaces.

9. To install, use a new gasket and reverse the removal procedures. Torque the exhaust manifold-to-engine bolts to 37 ft.lb. (1985) or 44 ft.lb. (1986–87).

4.3L Engine

RIGHT SIDE

1. Disconnect the negative battery cable from the battery.

2. Raise and support the front of the vehicle on jackstands.

3. Disconnect the right exhaust pipe from the exhaust manifold.

4. Remove the jackstands and lower the vehicle.

5. Disconnect the Air Injection Reactor (AIR) hose from the check valve and the diverter valve.

6. Remove the exhaust manifold-to-engine bolts, the washers, the tab washers and the manifold from the engine.

7. Using a putty knife, clean the gasket mounting surfaces.

8. To install, use a new gasket and reverse the removal procedures. Torque the outer manifold (pipe) bolts to 20 ft.lb. and the inner manifold (pipe) bolts to 26 ft.lb.

LEFT SIDE

1. Disconnect the negative battery cable from the battery.

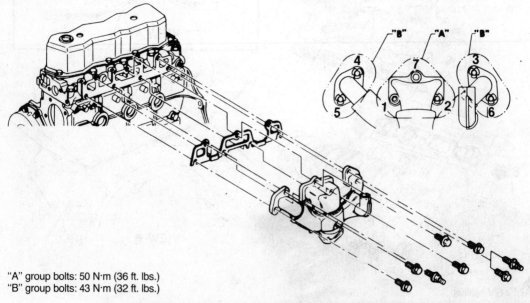

"A" group bolts: 50 N·m (36 ft. lbs.)
"B" group bolts: 43 N·m (32 ft. lbs.)

Torquing sequence for the exhaust manifold—2.5L engine (1986–87)

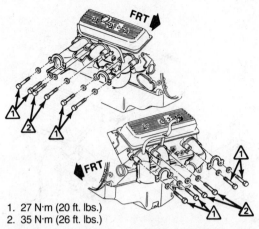

1. 27 N·m (20 ft. lbs.)
2. 35 N·m (26 ft. lbs.)

Torquing sequence for the exhaust manifold—4.3L engine

2. Raise and support the front of the vehicle on jackstands.

3. Disconnect the left exhaust pipe from the exhaust manifold.

4. Remove the jackstands and lower the vehicle.

5. Disconnect the Air Injection Reactor (AIR) pipe bracket from the cylinder head.

6. Remove the exhaust manifold-to-engine bolts, the washers, the tab washers and the manifold from the engine.

NOTE: *If equipped with a heat shield, remove it.*

7. Using a putty knife, clean the gasket mounting surfaces.

8. To install, use a new gasket and reverse

the removal procedures. Torque the outer manifold (pipe) bolts to 20 ft.lb. and the inner manifold (pipe) bolts to 26 ft.lb.

Air Conditioning Compressor

REMOVAL AND INSTALLATION

2.5L Engine

1. Refer to, Discharging The A/C System in Chapter 1 and discharge the A/C system.

2. Disconnect the negative battery cable from the battery.

3. Disconnect the electrical connectors from the compressor.

4. At the rear of the compressor, remove the bracket from the exhaust manifold.

5. Remove the compressor-to-front bracket bolts, the drive belt and the compressor from the vehicle.

6. To install, reverse the removal procedures. Torque the compressor-to-front bracket bolts to 22 ft.lb. and the compressor-to-rear bracket bolts to 18 ft.lb.

7. Refer to the, Drive Belt Adjusting procedures in Chap. 1 and adjust the A/C drive belt.

8. Refer to, Charging The A/C System in Chap. 1 and charge the A/C system.

4.3L Engine

1. Refer to, Discharging The A/C System in Chap. 1 and discharge the A/C system.

2. Disconnect the negative battery cable from the battery.

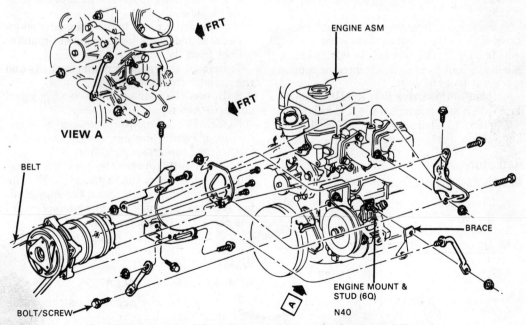

Exploded view of the A/C compressor and mounting brackets—2.5L engine

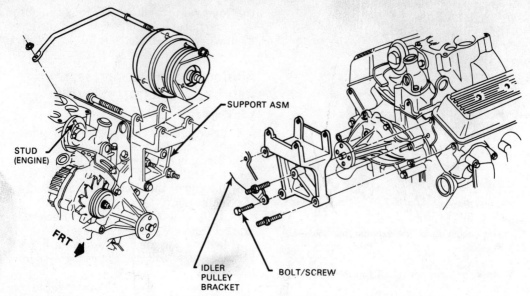

STUD (ENGINE)

FRT

SUPPORT ASM

IDLER PULLEY BRACKET

BOLT/SCREW

Exploded view of the A/C compressor and mounting brackets—4.3L engine

3. Disconnect the electrical connectors from the compressor.

4. From the rear of the compressor, remove the intake manifold-to-compressor support bracket.

NOTE: *If the engine is equipped with a carburetor, disconnect the vacuum brake from the carburetor for access.*

5. Remove the drive belt idler bracket-to-intake manifold bolts, the drive belt and the bracket from the vehicle.

6. Remove the compressor-to-mounting bracket bolts and the compressor from the vehicle.

7. To install, reverse the removal procedures. Torque the compressor-to-front bracket bolts to 25 ft.lb., the idler belt-to-engine bracket bolts to 16 ft.lb. and the compressor support bracket bolts to 61 ft.lb.

8. Refer to the, Drive Belt Adjusting procedures in Chap. 1 and adjust the A/C drive belt.

9. Refer to, Charging The A/C System in Chap. 1 and charge the A/C system.

Radiator

REMOVAL AND INSTALLATION

1. Disconnect the negative battery cable from the battery.

2. Place a catch pan under the radiator, open the drain cock and drain the cooling system.

3. Remove the brake master cylinder from the firewall (non-power brakes) or the power booster (power brakes) and move it aside.

NOTE: *DO NOT disconnect the brake lines from the master cylinder, unless there is not enough room to move the master cylinder to provide enough room.*

4. Separate and remove the upper fan shield from the bottom shield.

5. Remove the radiator hoses and the coolant overflow hose from the radiator.

6. If equipped with transmission and/or engine oil cooler lines, perform the following procedures:

   a. Disconnect the upper transmission-to-radiator and/or the upper engine-to-radiator lines from the radiator.

   b. Raise and support the front of the vehicle on jackstands.

   c. Disconnect the lower transmission-to-radiator and/or the lower engine-to-radiator lines from the radiator.

7. Remove the radiator mounting bolts and the radiator from the vehicle.

8. Inspect the radiator for leaks or physical damage, then repair (if necessary).

NOTE: *The radiator is constructed of aluminum, if repairs are necessary, it should be taken to a radiator repair shop.*

9. To install, reverse the removal procedures. Torque all of the fasteners to 18 ft.lb. Refill the cooling system. Start the engine, allow it to reach normal operating temperature and check the system for leaks.

Water Pump

REMOVAL AND INSTALLATION

1. Disconnect the negative battery cable from the battery.

2. Place a catch pan under the radiator,

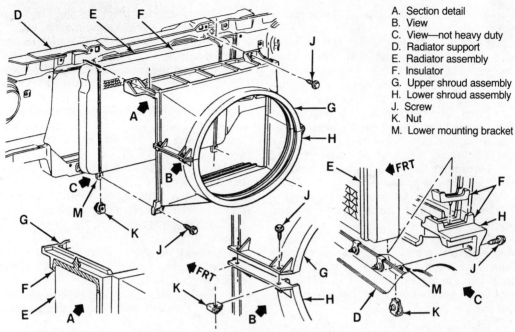

A. Section detail
B. View
C. View—not heavy duty
D. Radiator support
E. Radiator assembly
F. Insulator
G. Upper shroud assembly
H. Lower shroud assembly
J. Screw
K. Nut
M. Lower mounting bracket

Exploded view of the radiator and fan shroud assembly—2.5L engine shown, 4.3L engine is similar

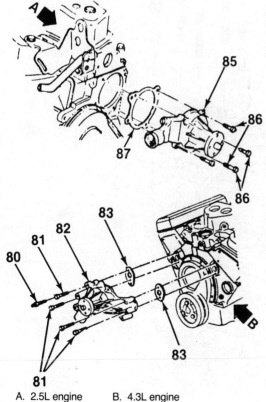

A. 2.5L engine
85. Water pump
86. Bolt
87. Gasket
88. Hose

B. 4.3L engine
80. Stud
81. Bolt
82. Water pump
83. Gasket

Exploded view of the water pump installation—2.5L and 4.3L engines

open the drain cock and drain the cooling system.

3. At the front of the engine, loosen the accessory drive belt adjustments and remove the belts.

4. Remove the upper fan shroud. Remove the fan/clutch assembly-to-water pump bolts and the fan/clutch assembly from the water pump pulley.

5. Remove the drive belt pulley from the water pump.

6. Remove the clamps and the hoses from the water pump.

7. Remove the water pump-to-engine bolts and the water pump from the engine.

8. Using a putty knife, clean the gasket mounting surfaces.

9. To install, use new gasket(s), coat the bolt threads with sealant and reverse the removal procedures. Torque the water pump-to-engine bolts to 17 ft.lb. (2.5L) or 22 ft.lb. (4.3L). Refill the cooling system. Start the engine and check for leaks.

Cylinder Head

REMOVAL AND INSTALLATION

2.5L Engine

NOTE: *Before disassembling the engine, make sure that it is overnight cold.*
CAUTION: *Relieve the pressure on the fuel system before disconnecting any fuel line connection.*

1. Refer to the Rocker Arm Cover, Removal

and Installation in this section and remove the rocker arm cover.

2. Place a catch pan under the radiator, open the drain cock and drain the cooling system.

3. Disconnect the accelerator, the cruise control and the TVS cables, if equipped.

4. From the intake manifold, remove the water pump bypass and heater hoses.

5. From the alternator, remove the front and rear braces, then move it aside.

6. Disconnect the A/C compressor brackets and move the compressor aside.

7. Remove the thermostat housing-to-cylinder head bolts and the housing from the engine.

8. Remove the ground cable and any necessary electrical connectors from the cylinder head. Disconnect the wires from the spark plugs and the oxygen sensor. Disconnect and remove the ignition coil from the intake manifold and the cylinder head.

9. Remove the vacuum lines and fuel hoses from the intake manifold and the TBI unit.

10. Disconnect the exhaust pipe from the exhaust manifold.

11. Remove the rocker arm nuts, the washers, the rocker arms and the pushrods from the cylinder head.

12. Remove the cylinder head-to-engine bolts and the cylinder head from the engine (with the manifolds attached), then place the assembly on a workbench. If necessary, remove the intake and the exhaust manifolds from the cylinder head.

13. Using a putty knife, clean the gasket mounting surfaces. Using a wire brush, clean the carbon deposits from the combustion chambers.

14. Inspect the cylinder head and block for cracks, nicks, heavy scratches or other damage.

15. To install, use new gaskets, sealant (where necessary) and reverse the removal

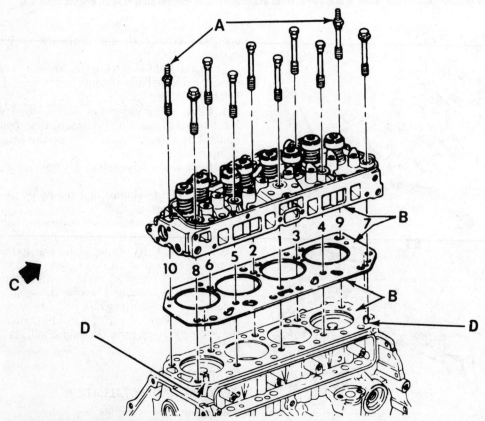

A. Apply sealing compound to threads on these bolts
B. Mounting surfaces of block asm., head asm. and both sides of gasket must be free of oil and foreign material
C. Forward
D. Dowel pins

Cylinder head installation and torquing sequence—2.5L engine

procedures. Torque the cylinder head bolts (in sequence) to 90 ft.lb. (in 3 steps). Adjust the rocker arms. Refill the cooling system, start the engine and check for leaks.

4.3L Engine

CAUTION: *If equipped with an EFI system, relieve the pressure on the fuel system before disconnecting any fuel line connection.*

1. Refer to the Rocker Arm, Removal and Installation, the Intake Manifold, Removal and Installation and the Exhaust Manifold, Removal and Installation procedures in this section, then remove the rocker arms, the intake manifold and the exhaust manifold (depending on which cylinder head is being removed) from the engine.

2. Remove the cylinder head bolts, the cylinder head(s) and the gasket(s) (discard the gasket).

3. Using a putty knife, clean the gasket mounting surfaces.

4. Inspect the cylinder head and block for cracks, nicks, heavy scratches or other damage.

5. To install, use new gasket(s), sealant (where necessary) and reverse the removal procedures. The head gasket is installed with the bead up.

NOTE: *If a steel head gasket is used, coat both sides of the gasket (thinly and evenly) with sealer. Clean the bolt threads, apply sealing compound No. 1052080 or equivalent and install the bolts finger tight.*

6. Torque the head bolts a little at a time, in the sequence, to 67 ft.lb. Adjust the valves. Refill the cooling system, start the engine and check for leaks.

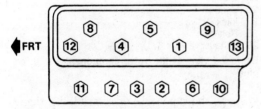

Cylinder head torquing sequence—4.3L engine

CLEANING AND INSPECTION

1. Refer to the Valves, Removal and Installation procedures in this section and remove the valve assemblies from the cylinder head.

2. Using a small wire power brush, clean the carbon from the combustion chambers and the valve ports.

3. Inspect the cylinder head for cracks in the exhaust ports, combustion chambers or external cracks to the water chamber.

4. Thoroughly clean the valve guides using a suitable wire bore brush.

NOTE: *Excessive valve stem-to-bore clearance will cause excessive oil consumption and may cause valve breakage. Insufficient clearance will result in noisy and sticky functioning of the valve and disturb engine smoothness.*

5. Measure the valve stem clearance as follows:

   a. Clamp a dial indicator on one side of the cylinder head rocker arm cover gasket rail.

   b. Locate the indicator so that movement of the valve stem from side to side (crosswise to the head) will cause a direct movement of the indicator stem. The indicator stem must contact the side of the valve stem just above the valve guide.

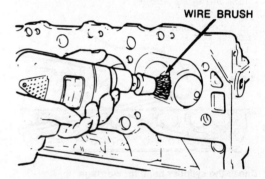

WIRE BRUSH

Remove the carbon from the cylinder head with a wire brush and electric drill

   c. Prop the valve head about $\frac{1}{16}$" (1.5mm) off the valve seat.

   d. Move the stem of the valve from side to side using light pressure to obtain a clearance reading. If the clearance exceeds specifications, it will be necessary to ream (for oversize valves) or knurl (raise the bore for original valves) the valve guides.

Measuring the valve stem clearances

6. Inspect the rocker arm studs for wear or damage.

7. Install a dial micrometer into the valve guide and check the valve seat for concentricity.

RESURFACING

1. Using a straightedge, check the cylinder head for warpage.

2. If warpage exceeds 0.003″ (0.076mm) in a 6″ (152mm) span, or 0.006″ (0.152mm) over the total length, the cylinder head must be resurfaced. Resurfacing can be performed at most machine shops.

NOTE: *When resurfacing the cylinder head(s), the intake manifold mounting position is altered and must be corrected by machining a proportionate amount from the intake manifold flange.*

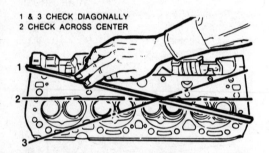

Check the cylinder head for warpage

Valves

REMOVAL AND INSTALLATION

1. Refer to the Cylinder Head, Removal and Installation procedures in this section and remove the cylinder head.

2. Using a C-Type spring compressor, compress the valve springs, then remove the valve

Compressing valve spring—typical

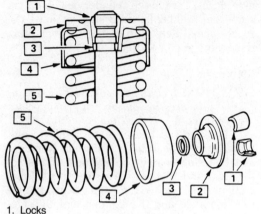

1. Locks
2. Cap
3. Seal
4. Shield
5. Spring

Exploded view of the valve components—2.5L engine

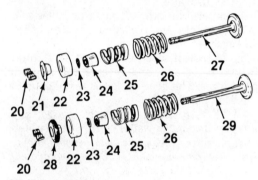

20. Valve keeper
21. Cap
22. Shield
23. O-ring seal
24. Seal
25. Damper
26. Spring
27. Intake valve
28. Rotator
29. Exhaust valve

Exploded view of the valve components—4.3L engine

keepers, the cap (2.5L) or rotor (4.3L), the O-ring seal, the shield, damper (4.3L), valve stem seal (4.3L) and the spring.

3. Remove the valve(s) from the cylinder head.

NOTE: *If removing all of the valves at one time, be sure to keep them in order for reinstallation purposes.*

4. Using a bench mounted wire brush, clean all of the deposits from the valve faces and stems. Using a small drill mounted wire brush, clean the deposits from the combustion chambers.

5. Inspect the valves, the valve seats and

the valve guides for damage or wear; replace or remachine the damaged parts or items. Reface the valve(s) and valve seat(s) or lap the valve into the cylinder head.

6. To install, lubricate the parts being installed, use new seals on the valves, new gaskets and reverse the removal procedures. Adjust the valves. Refill the cooling system. Start the engine and check the timing. Inspect the cooling system and the fuel system for leaks.

INSPECTION

Inspect the valve faces and seats (in the head) for pits, burned spots and other evidence of poor seating. If a valve face is in such bad shape that the head of the valve must be ground, in order to true up the face, discard the valve, because the sharp edge will run too hot. The correct angle for valve faces are 45°. We recommend the refacing be performed by a reputable machine shop.

Check the valve stem for scoring and burned spots. If not noticeably scored or damaged, clean the valve stem with solvent to remove all gum and varnish. Clean the valve guides using solvent and an expanding wire-type valve guide cleaner. If you have access to a dial indicator for measuring valve stem-to-guide clear-

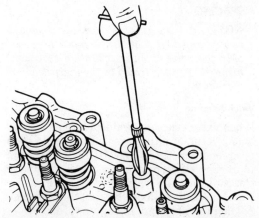

Using an expandable wire type cleaner to clean the valve guides

ance, mount it so that the stem of the indicator is at 90° to the valve stem and as close to the valve guide as possible. Move the valve off its seat, then measure the valve guide-to-stem clearance by rocking the stem back and forth to actuate the dial indicator. Measure the valve stem diameter using a micrometer, and compare to specifications to determine whether the stem or guide wear is responsible for the excess clearance. If a dial indicator and micrometer are not available to you, take the cylinder head and valves to a reputable machine shop for inspection.

Some of the engines covered in this guide are equipped with valve rotators, which double as valve spring caps. In normal operation the rotators put a certain degree of wear on the tip of the valve stem; this wear appears as concentric rings on the stem tip. However, if the rotator is not working properly, the wear may appear as straight notches or **X** patterns across the valve stem tip. Whenever the valves are removed from the cylinder head, the tips should be inspected for improper pattern, which could indicate valve rotator problems. Valve stem tips will have to be ground flat if the rotator problems are severe.

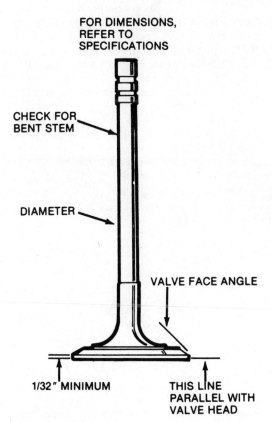

FOR DIMENSIONS, REFER TO SPECIFICATIONS

CHECK FOR BENT STEM

DIAMETER

VALVE FACE ANGLE

1/32" MINIMUM

THIS LINE PARALLEL WITH VALVE HEAD

Critical valve dimensions

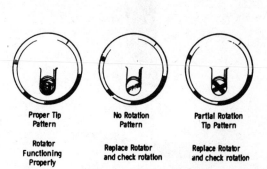

Proper Tip Pattern	No Rotation Pattern	Partial Rotation Tip Pattern
Rotator Functioning Properly	Replace Rotator and check rotation	Replace Rotator and check rotation

Using an "X" to check the valve stem wear

REFACING

NOTE: *All valve grinding operations should be performed by a qualified machine shop; only the valve lapping operation is recommended to be performed by the inexperienced mechanic.*

Valve Lapping

When valve faces and seats have been refaced and/or recut, or if they are determined to be in good condition, the valves MUST BE lapped in to ensure efficient sealing when the valve closes against the seat.

1. Invert the cylinder head so that the combustion chambers are facing upward.

2. Lightly lubricate the valve stems with clean engine oil and coat the valve seats with valve grinding compound. Install the valves in the cylinder head as numbered.

3. Attach the suction cup of a valve lapping tool to a valve head. *You will probably have to moisten the cup to securely attach the tool to the valve.*

Lapping the valves by hand

HAND DRILL

ROD

SUCTION CUP

Home made valve lapping tool

4. Rotate the tool between the palms, changing position and lifting the tool often to prevent grooving. Lap the valve until a smooth polished seat is evident (you may have to add a bit more compound after some lapping is done).

5. Remove the valve and tool, then remove ALL traces of the grinding compound with a solvent-soaked rag or rinse the head with solvent.

NOTE: *Valve lapping can also be done by fastening a suction cup to a piece of drill rod in a hand egg-beater type drill. Proceed as above, using the drill as a lapping tool. Due to the higher speeds involved when using the hand drill, care must be exercised to avoid grooving the seat. Lift the tool and change direction of rotation often.*

Valve Springs

REMOVAL AND INSTALLATION

If the cylinder head is removed from the engine, refer to the Valve, Removal and Installation procedures in this section and remove the valve spring.

NOTE: *The following procedures requires the use of GM Air Adapter tool No. J-23590 or equivalent, and Spring Compressor tool No. J-5892 or equivalent.*

1. Refer to the Rocker Arm, Removal and Installation procedures in this section and remove the rocker arm bolts (2.5L) or nuts (4.3L), the washers and the rocker arms.

2. Remove the spark plugs from the cylinders being worked on.

3. To remove the valve keepers, perform the following procedures:

    a. Using the GM Air Adapter tool No. J-23590 or equivalent, install it into the spark plug hole.

    b. Apply compressed air to the cylinder to hold the valves in place.

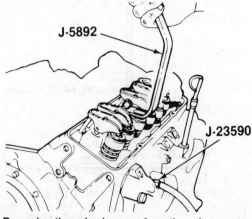

J-5892

J-23590

Removing the valve keepers from the valve assemblies

c. Install a rocker arm bolt (2.5L) or nut (4.3L) into the cylinder head.

d. Using the GM Spring Compressor tool No. J-5892 or equivalent, compress the valve spring and remove the valve keepers.

e. Carefully release the spring pressure and remove the compressor tool.

4. Remove the valve cap or rotor (4.3L), the shield and the spring and/or the damper (4.3L).

5. Remove the O-ring seal and valve stem seal (4.3L).

6. Inspect the valve spring, replace as necessary.

7. Lubricate the parts with engine oil, then install a new O-ring seal and valve stem seal (4.3L) onto each valve stem.

8. To complete the installation, adjust the valves and reverse the removal procedures. Start the engine, then check and/or adjust the timing.

INSPECTION

1. Position the valve spring on a flat, clean surface next to a square.

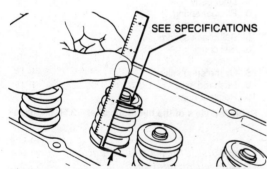

Measuring the installed height of the valve spring

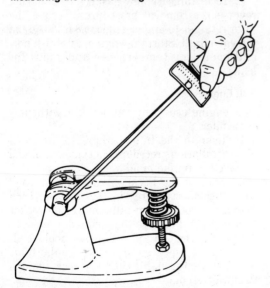

Checking the pressure of the valve spring

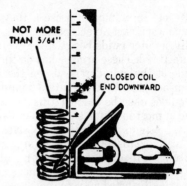

Check the valve spring free length and squareness

2. Measure the height of the spring and rotate it against the engine of the square to measure the distortion (out-of-roundness). If the spring height varies between the springs by more than $\frac{1}{16}''$ (0.0762mm), replace the spring.

3. Using a valve spring tester, check the spring pressure at the installed and compressed height.

Valve Seats

The valve seats are cast into the cylinder head(s) and cannot be replaced; the seats can be machined during a valve job to provide optimum sealing between the valve and the seat.

The seating services should be performed by a professional machine shop which has the specialized knowledge and tools necessary to perform the service.

Have the valve seat concentricity checked at a machine shop

Valve Guides

The engines covered in this guide use integral valves guides; that is, they are a part of the cylinder head and cannot be replaced. The guides can, however, be reamed oversize if they are found to be worn past an acceptable limit. Occasionally, a valve guide bore will be oversize as manufactured. These are marked on the inboard side of the cylinder heads on the machined surface just above the intake manifold.

If the guides must be reamed (this service is available at most machine shops), then valves with oversize stems must be fitted. Valves are usually available in 0.001" (0.0254mm), 0.003" (0.0762mm) and 0.005" (0.127mm) stem oversizes. Valve guides which are not excessively worn or distorted may, in some cases, be knurled rather than reamed. Knurling is a process in which the metal on the valve guide bore is displaced and raised, thereby reducing clearance. Knurling also provides excellent oil control. The option of knurling rather than reaming valve guides should be discussed with a reputable machinist or engine specialist.

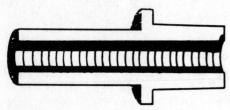

Cutaway of a knurled valve guide

Valve Lifters

REMOVAL AND INSTALLATION

NOTE: *Valve lifters and pushrods should be kept in order so they can be reinstalled in their original position.*

2.5L Engine

This engine uses a hydraulic lifter with equipped with a roller to reduce engine friction.

1. Refer to the Rocker Arm, Removal and Installation procedures in this section, then loosen the rocker arms bolts, move the rocker arms aside and remove the pushrods.
2. Refer to the Pushrod Cover, Removal and Installation procedures in this section and remove the pushrod cover.
3. Remove the hydraulic lifter retainer studs, the retainer(s) and the guides. Lift the hydraulic lifter from the engine block.
4. Inspect the hydraulic lifter for:
• Wear or scuffing.
• Wear or scuffing in the engine bore.
• Freedom of the roller movement.
• Flat spots or pitting on the roller surface.
NOTE: *If the hydraulic lifter is found to be defective, replace it. If installing a new lifter, be sure to remove all of the protective sealant*

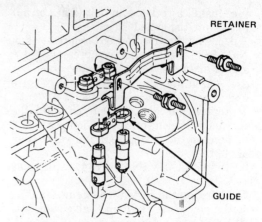

Exploded view of the hydraulic lifter-to-engine assembly—2.5L engine

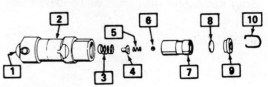

1. Roller
2. Lifter body
3. Plunger spring
4. Ball check retainer
5. Ball check spring
6. Ball check
7. Plunger
8. Oil metering valve
9. Push rod seat
10. Retainer ring

Exploded view of the hydraulic lifter—2.5L engine

from inside the body, then lubricate it and the roller with engine oil.
5. To install, use new gaskets, sealant and reverse the removal procedures. Torque the lifter retainer-to-engine studs to 8 ft.lb. Adjust the valve lash. Start the engine, establish normal operating temperature and check for leaks.

4.3L Engine

This engine uses a hydraulic lifter without a cam roller.

1. Refer to the Intake Manifold, Removal and Installation procedures in this section and remove the intake manifold.
2. Refer to the Rocker Arm, Removal and Installation procedures in this section, then loosen the rocker arm nuts, move the rocker arm aside and remove the pushrods.
3. Using the GM Lifter Remover tool No. J-3049 (pliers type), grasp the hydraulic lifter and remove it from the cylinder block, using a twisting action.
4. If the lifters are sticking in the cylinder

Using GM tool No. J-3049 to remove the hydraulic lifters—4.3L engine

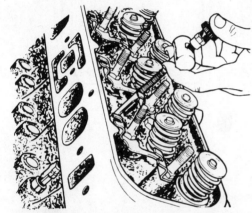

Using GM tool No. J-9290-01 to remove the hydraulic lifters—4.3L engine

block, use the GM Lifter Removal tool No. J-9290-01 (slide hammer type) to pull the hydraulic lifter from the cylinder block.

NOTE: *When removing the hydraulic lifters, be sure to place them in an organizer rack so that they may be reinstalled in the same engine bore from which they were removed.*

5. Inspect the lifters for:
• Wear or scuffing.
• Wear or scuffing in the engine bore.
• Lifter to bore clearance; if the clearance is excessive, replace the lifter.
• Worn spots, pitting or damage on the lifter surface; the lifter foot must be smooth and slightly convex.

NOTE: *If a new camshaft has been installed, install all new hydraulic lifters. If a new camshaft or new lifter(s) have been installed, add engine oil supplement to the crankcase.*

6. To install, use new gaskets, sealant and reverse the removal procedures. Adjust the valves. Start the engine, establish normal operating temperature and check for leaks.

Oil Pan

REMOVAL AND INSTALLATION

1. Disconnect the negative battery cable from the battery.
2. Raise and support the front of the vehicle on jackstands.
3. Position a catch pan under the crankcase and drain the oil from the engine.
4. Remove the strut rods. Remove the flywheel/torque convertor dust cover from the bellhousing.
5. Disconnect the electrical connectors from the starter, then remove the starter-to-engine bolts, the brace and the starter from the vehicle.
6. Disconnect the exhaust pipe(s) from the exhaust manifold(s) and the exhaust pipe-to-catalytic converter hanger(s).
7. If necessary, remove the engine mount through bolts, then using an engine lifting device, raise the engine (enough) in order to make room for the oil pan removal.
8. Remove the oil pan-to-engine bolts and the oil pan from the engine.
9. Using a putty knife, clean the gasket

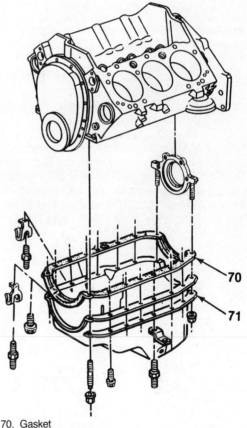

70. Gasket
71. Reinforcement

Exploded view of the oil pan assembly—4.3L engine

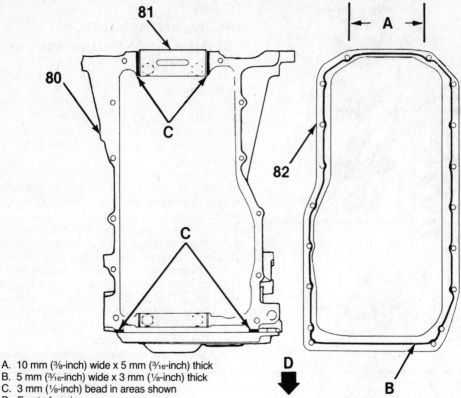

A. 10 mm (⅜-inch) wide x 5 mm (³⁄₁₆-inch) thick
B. 5 mm (³⁄₁₆-inch) wide x 3 mm (⅛-inch) thick
C. 3 mm (⅛-inch) bead in areas shown
D. Front of engine
80. Block
81. Rear main bearing cap
82. Oil pan

Applying RTV sealant to the oil pan—2.5L engine

mounting surfaces. Using solvent, clean the excess oil from the mounting surfaces.

10. On the 2.5L engine, apply a $\frac{3}{16}$" (4.7mm) bead of RTV sealant to the oil pan flange (keep the bead inside the bolt holes), the rear main bearing, the timing gear cover and the engine block sealing surface. On the 4.3L engine, apply a small amount of RTV sealant to the front and rear corners of the oil pan; too much sealant may prevent sealing of the gasket.

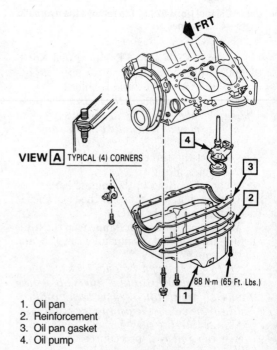

VIEW **A** TYPICAL (4) CORNERS

4. 88 N·m (65 Ft. Lbs.)

1. Oil pan
2. Reinforcement
3. Oil pan gasket
4. Oil pump

View of the oil pump—4.3L engine

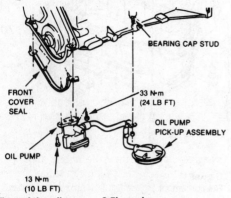

BEARING CAP STUD

FRONT COVER SEAL

33 N·m (24 LB FT)

OIL PUMP PICK-UP ASSEMBLY

OIL PUMP

13 N·m (10 LB FT)

View of the oil pump—2.5L engine

NOTE: *The 4.3L engine uses a one piece oil pan gasket.*

11. To install, use a new gasket (4.3L), RTV sealant and reverse the removal procedures. Torque the oil pan-to-engine bolts to 8 ft.lb. and the oil pan-to-engine nuts to 14 ft.lb. (4.3L). Fill the crankcase with fresh oil. Start the engine, establish normal operating temperatures and check for leaks.

Oil Pump

REMOVAL AND INSTALLATION

1. Refer to the Oil Pan, Removal and Installation procedures in this section and remove the oil pan.
2. Remove the oil pump-to-rear main bearing cap bolts, the pump and the extension shaft.
3. To install, assemble the oil pump and the extension shaft into the rear main bearing cap; be sure to align the slot (on top of the extension shaft) with the drive tang (on the lower end of the distributor driveshaft).
4. Torque the oil pump-to-bearing cap bolts to 22 ft.lb. (2.5L) or 65 ft.lb. (4.3L). Refill the crankcase with fresh oil. Start the engine, establish normal operating temperatures and check for leaks.

OVERHAUL

1. Remove the pump cover-to-pump screws and the cover.
2. Mark the gear teeth so that they may be reassembled in the same position.

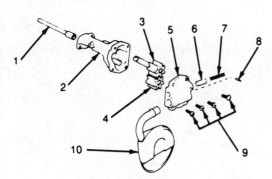

1. Shaft extension
2. Pump body
3. Drive gear and shaft
4. Idler gear
5. Pump cover
6. Pressure regulator valve
7. Pressure regulator spring
8. Retaining pin
9. Screws
10. Pickup screen and pipe

Exploded view of the oil pump

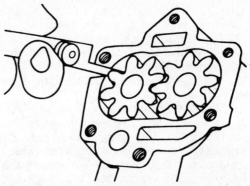

Measuring the clearance between the oil pump gears and the oil pump body

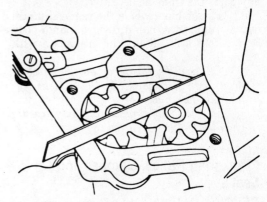

Measure the oil pump end clearance with a feeler gauge and straightedge

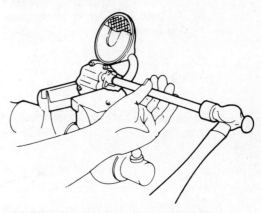

Install the oil pump screen by tapping lightly

3. Separate the idler gear, the drive gear and the shaft from the pump body.
4. Remove the retaining pin from the pressure valve, then separate the valve and the related parts.
5. If the pickup screen and the pipe assembly need replacing, place the pump in a soft-jawed vise and remove the pipe from the pump. Do not disturb the pickup screen on the pipe; it is serviced as an assembly.

NOTE: *If the pickup screen and pipe assembly have been removed from the pump, it should be replaced with a new one.*

6. Wash all of the parts in solvent, blow dry with compressed air.

7. Inspect the parts for cracks, damage or excessive wear.

NOTE: *If the pump gears or body are damaged, replace the entire pump assembly.*

8. Check the drive gear shaft-to-body for looseness, the pump cover for wear (which would permit leaks past the end gears), the pickup screen/pipe assembly for damage and the pressure regulator for fit.

9. If any of the parts are defective, replace any parts that may be defective.

10. To assemble, reverse the removal procedures. Torque the pump cover-to-pump body screws to 7 ft.lb. Refill the crankcase with fresh oil.

NOTE: *Pack the inside of the pump completely with petroleum jelly. DO NOT use engine oil. The pump MUST be primed this way or it will not produce any oil pressure when the engine is started.*

Crankshaft Pulley, Damper and Oil Seal

REMOVAL AND INSTALLATION

2.5L Engine

NOTE: *The following procedure requires the use of the GM Seal Installer/Centering tool No. J-34995 or equivalent.*

1. Disconnect the negative battery cable from the battery.

2. If equipped, remove the power steering fluid reservoir from the radiator shroud.

3. Remove the upper fan shroud. Loosen and remove the accessory-to-damper pulley drive belts.

4. Remove the damper pulley/hub assembly-to-crankshaft bolt and washer, then the pulley/hub assembly from the crankshaft.

NOTE: *The damper pulley is connected to the damper pulley hub by three bolts; if necessary, remove the pulley-to-hub bolts and separate the pulley from the hub. When it becomes necessary to remove the damper pulley/hub assembly, ALWAYS replace the front oil seal with a new one.*

5. Inspect the damper hub (oil seal surface) for rust or burrs; remove the roughness with fine emery cloth.

NOTE: *When installing the damper pulley hub to the crankshaft, be careful not to damage the front oil seal.*

6. To replace the timing cover oil seal, perform the following procedures:

a. Using a medium pry bar, pry the oil seal from the timing cover.

b. Using the GM Seal Installer/Centering tool No. J-34995 or equivalent, install the new oil seal into the timing cover, then remove the tool from the timing cover.

7. To install the damper hub, lubricate the it with engine oil, align it onto the keyway and reverse the removal procedures. Torque the damper pulley hub-to-crankshaft bolt to 160

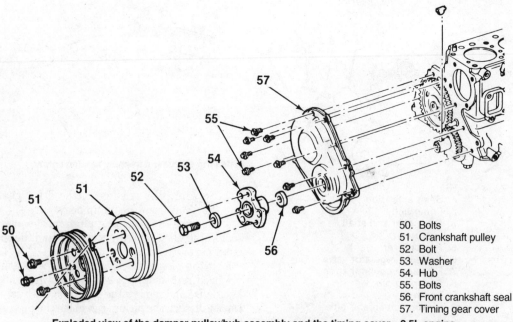

50. Bolts
51. Crankshaft pulley
52. Bolt
53. Washer
54. Hub
55. Bolts
56. Front crankshaft seal
57. Timing gear cover

Exploded view of the damper pulley/hub assembly and the timing cover—2.5L engine

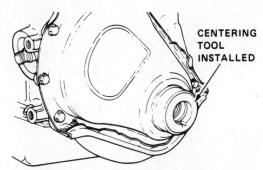

Using GM tool No. J-34995 to install the oil seal into the timing cover—2.5L engine

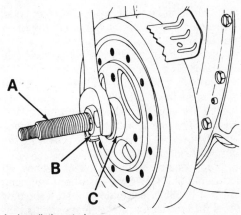

A. Installation stud
B. Nut
C. Washer and bearing

Using GM tool No. J-23523 to press the damper onto the crankshaft—4.3L engine

ft.lb. Install the drive belts and adjust the belt tension.

4.3L Engine

NOTE: *The following procedure requires the use of GM Torsional Damper Puller/Installer tool No. J-23523-E or equivalent, and the GM Seal Installer tool No. J-23042 or equivalent.*

1. Disconnect the negative battery cable from the battery.

2. Loosen and remove the accessory-to-damper pulley drive belts.

3. Remove the drive belt pulley-to-damper bolts and the pulley from the damper. Remove the damper-to-crankshaft bolt.

4. Using the GM Torsional Damper Puller/Installer tool No. J-23523-E or equivalent, connect it to the damper and remove it from the crankshaft.

NOTE: *When performing this operation, ALWAYS replace the front oil seal with a new one.*

5. To replace the oil seal to the timing cover, perform the following procedures:

   a. Using a medium pry bar, pry the oil seal from the timing cover.

Using GM tool No. J-23523 to remove the damper from the crankshaft—4.3L engine

   b. Coat the lips of the new seal with engine oil.

   c. Using the GM Seal Installer tool No. J-23042 or equivalent, install the new oil seal into the timing cover, then remove the tool from the timing cover.

6. Inspect the damper (oil seal surface) for rust or burrs; remove the roughness with fine emery cloth.

NOTE: *When installing the damper onto the crankshaft, be careful not to damage the front oil seal.*

7. To install, lubricate the hub with engine oil, align it with the keyway and install it onto the crankshaft. Using the GM Torsional Damper Puller/Installer tool No. J-23523-E or equivalent, connect it to the damper and press it onto the crankshaft.

8. To complete the installation, reverse the removal procedures. Torque the damper pulley hub-to-crankshaft bolt to 70 ft.lb. Install the drive belts and adjust the belt tension.

Timing Cover and Oil Seal
REMOVAL AND INSTALLATION

2.5L Engine

NOTE: *The following procedure requires the use of the GM Seal Installer/Centering tool No. J-34995 or equivalent.*

1. Refer to the Crankshaft Pulley, Damper and Oil Seal, Removal and Installation procedures in this section and remove the damper from the crankshaft.

2. Remove the fan and the pulley.

3. Remove the alternator and the brackets from the front of the engine.

4. Remove the lower radiator hose clamp at the water pump.

5. Remove the timing cover-to-oil pan bolts, the timing cover-to-engine bolts and the cover from the engine.

6. Using a medium pry bar, pry the oil seal from the timing cover.

7. Using a putty knife, clean the gasket mounting surfaces. The clean the surface with solvent to remove all traces of oil and grease.

NOTE: *The timing cover can become distorted very easily, so be careful when cleaning the gasket surface.*

8. Apply engine oil to the lips of the new oil seal. Using the GM Seal Installer/Centering tool No. J-34995 or equivalent, install the new oil seal into the timing cover; leave the tool installed in the timing cover.

9. Using RTV sealant or equivalent, apply a ¼" (6mm) wide bead to the timing cover mounting surface and a ⅜" (9.5mm) wide bead to the oil pan at the timing cover sealing surface.

10. Install the timing cover onto the engine and partially tighten the bolts.

11. First, torque the timing cover-to-engine bolts to 90 inch lbs.; secondly, torque the timing cover-to-oil pan bolts to 90 inch lbs. Remove the Seal Installer/Centering tool No. J-34995 or equivalent, from the timing cover.

12. To complete the installation, reverse the removal procedures. Torque the damper pulley hub-to-crankshaft bolt to 160 ft.lb. Adjust the drive belt(s) tension. Refill the cooling system (if necessary) and the power steering reservoir (if equipped).

4.3L Engine

NOTE: *The following procedure requires the use of GM Torsional Damper Puller/Installer tool No. J-23523-E or equivalent, and the GM Seal Installer tool No. J-23042 or equivalent.*

1. Refer to the Crankshaft Pulley, Damper and Oil Seal, Removal and Installation procedures in this section and remove the damper from the crankshaft.

2. Place a catch pan under the radiator, open the drain cock and drain the cooling system.

3. Remove the timing cover-to-engine bolts and the cover from the engine.

4. Using a putty knife, clean the gasket mounting surfaces. Using solvent and a rag, clean the oil and grease from the gasket mounting surfaces.

5. Inspect the timing cover for distortion and damage, if necessary, replace it.

6. To replace the oil seal in the timing cover, perform the following procedures:

   a. Using a medium pry bar, pry the oil seal from the timing cover.

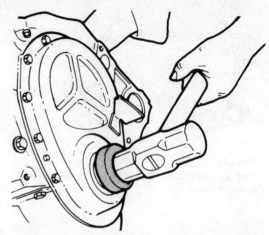

Using GM tool No. J-23042 to install the oil seal into the timing cover, either installed or removed from the engine—4.3L engine

   b. Coat the lips of the new oil seal with engine oil.

NOTE: *The oil seal is installed with the open end of the seal lips facing toward the inside of the engine.*

   c. Using the GM Seal Installer tool No. J-23042 or equivalent, drive the new oil seal into the timing cover.

7. To install, use a new gasket, apply an ⅛" (3mm) bead of sealant (to hold the gasket in place), then align the cover with the dowels and install the cover finger tight. Torque the timing cover-to-engine bolts to 92 inch lbs.

NOTE: *When torquing the timing cover bolts, tighten them alternately and evenly, while evenly pressing on the cover.*

8. To complete the installation, reverse the removal procedures. Using the GM Torsional Damper Puller/Installer tool No. J-23523-E or equivalent, torque the damper pulley hub-to-crankshaft bolt to 70 ft.lb. Install the drive belts and adjust the belt tension. Refill the cooling system.

Timing Chain
REMOVAL AND INSTALLATION
4.3L Engine

NOTE: *The following procedure requires the use of GM Crankshaft Sprocket Puller tool No. J-5825 or equivalent, and GM Crankshaft Sprocket Installer tool No. J-5590 or equivalent.*

1. Refer to the Timing Cover, Removal and Installation procedures in this section and remove the timing cover.

2. Rotate the crankshaft until the marks on the timing chain sprockets are facing each other.

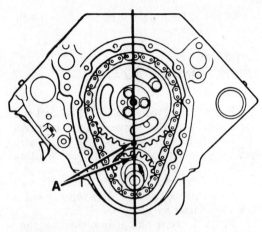

A. Align marks as shown
Aligning the timing gear sprockets—4.3L engine

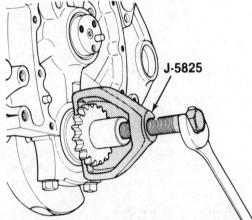

Removing the crankshaft sprocket—4.3L engine

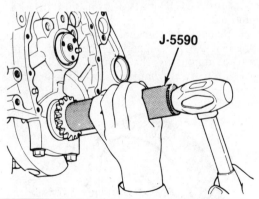

Installing the crankshaft sprocket—4.3L engine

3. Remove the camshaft sprocket-to-camshaft bolts, the camshaft sprocket and timing chain from the camshaft.

NOTE: *If difficulty is experienced in removing the camshaft sprocket, tap it at the lower edge with a mallet.*

4. Inspect the timing chain, the camshaft sprocket and the crankshaft sprocket for wear, then replace them (if necessary).

5. If necessary to remove and install the crankshaft sprocket, perform the following procedures:

a. Using the GM Crankshaft Sprocket Puller tool No. J-5825 or equivalent, pull the crankshaft sprocket from the crankshaft. Remove the the woodruff key.

b. To install, place the woodruff key into the crankshaft groove and align the crankshaft sprocket with the key.

c. Using the GM Crankshaft Sprocket Installer tool No. J-5590 or equivalent, and a hammer, drive the crankshaft sprocket onto the crankshaft until it seats.

6. To install the camshaft sprocket, position the timing chain onto the sprockets, align the sprockets (timing marks facing one another), then the camshaft sprocket onto the camshaft and the camshaft sprocket bolts. Torque the camshaft sprocket-to-camshaft bolts to 18 ft.lb.

7. To complete the installation, reverse the removal procedures. Refill the cooling system, start the engine and check for leaks.

Timing Gears

REMOVAL AND INSTALLATION

2.5L Engine

The timing gear is pressed onto the camshaft. To remove or install the timing gear, an arbor press must be used.

NOTE: *The following procedure requires the use of an arbor press, a press plate, the GM Gear Removal tool No. J-971 or equivalent,*

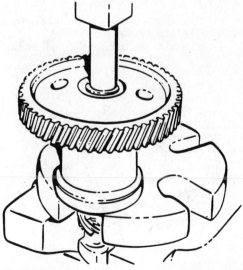

Removing the timing gear from the camshaft—2.5L engine

1. Arber press
2. J-21474-13 or
   J-21795-1

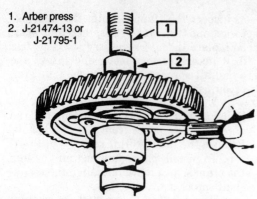

Installing the timing gear onto the camshaft—2.5L engine

the GM Gear Installation tool No. J-21474-13, J-21795-1 or equivalent.

1. Refer to the Camshaft, Removal and Installation procedures in this section and remove the camshaft from the engine.

2. Using an arbor press, a press plate and the GM Gear Removal tool No. J-971 or equivalent, press the timing gear from the camshaft.

NOTE: *When pressing the timing gear from the camshaft, be certain that the position of the press plate does not contact the woodruff key.*

3. To assembly, position the press plate to support the camshaft at the back of the front journal. Place the gear spacer ring and the thrust plate over the end of the camshaft, then install the woodruff key. Press the timing gear onto the camshaft, until it bottoms against the gear spacer ring.

NOTE: *The end clearance of the thrust plate should be 0.0015–0.005" (0.038–0.127mm). If less than 0.0015" (0.038mm), replace the spacer ring; if more than 0.005" (0.127mm), replace the thrust plate.*

4. To complete the installation, align the marks on the timing gears and reverse the removal procedures.

Camshaft

REMOVAL AND INSTALLATION

2.5L Engine

1. Refer to the Pushrod Cover, Removal and Installation and the Valve Lifters, Removal and Installation procedures in this section, then remove the pushrods and the valve lifters from the engine.

NOTE: *When removing the pushrods and the valve lifters, be sure to keep them in order for reassembly purposes.*

2. Place a catch pan under the radiator, open the drain cock and drain the cooling system.

3. Remove the power steering reservoir from the fan shroud, then the upper fan shroud, the radiator. Remove the grille, the headlight bezel and the bumper filler panel.

4. Remove the accessory drive belts, the cooling fan and the water pump pulley.

5. If equipped with A/C, disconnect the condenser baffles and the condenser, then raise the condenser and block it aside.

6. Remove the crankshaft drive belt pulley and the damper hub. Remove the timing gear cover-to-engine bolts and the cover.

7. Label and disconnect the distributor electrical connectors, then the holddown bolt and the distributor from the engine. Remove the oil pump driveshaft.

8. Label and disconnect the vacuum lines from the intake manifold and the thermostat housing, then remove the Exhaust Gas Recirculation (EGR) valve from the intake manifold.

9. Remove the camshaft thrust plate-to-engine bolts. While supporting the camshaft (to prevent damaging the bearing or lobe surfaces), remove it from the front of the engine.

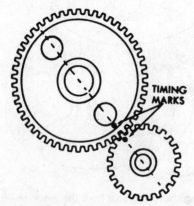

Aligning the timing gear marks—2.5L engine

Removing the camshaft-to-engine thrust plate bolts—2.5L engine

10. Inspect the camshaft for scratches, pitting and/or wear on the bearing and lobe surfaces. Check the timing gear teeth for damage.

11. To install, lubricate all of the parts with engine oil and reverse the removal procedures. Torque the camshaft thrust plate-to-engine bolts to 90 inch lbs. Refill the cooling system, start the engine, allow it to reach operating temperatures and check for leaks.

4.3L Engine

NOTE: *The following procedure requires the use of the GM Torsional Damper Puller/Installer tool No. J-23523-E or equivalent.*

1. Refer to the Valve Lifters, Removal and Installation procedures in this section and remove the valve lifters from the engine.

NOTE: *When removing the pushrods and the valve lifters, be sure to keep them in order for reassembly purposes.*

2. Place a catch pan under the radiator, open the drain cock and drain the cooling system. Remove the radiator.

3. Loosen and remove the accessory drive belts from the crankshaft pulley.

4. If equipped, remove the power steering pump and move it aside; DO NOT disconnect the pressure hoses.

5. Remove the Air Injection Reactor (AIR) pump/bracket, the fan and the water pump pulley.

6. Disconnect the electrical connectors, then remove the alternator mounting bracket from the water pump.

7. Remove the water pump-to-engine bolts and the pump from the engine.

8. To remove the damper hub, perform the following procedures:

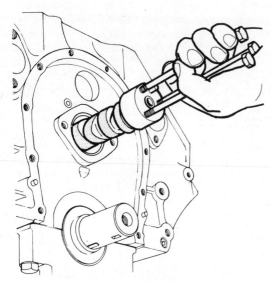

Replacing the camshaft—4.3L engine

a. Remove the drive belt pulley-to-damper bolts and the pulley from the damper.

b. Remove the damper-to-crankshaft bolt.

c. Using the GM Torsional Damper Puller/Installer tool No. J-23523-E or equivalent, connect it to the damper and remove it from the crankshaft.

9. Remove the timing cover-to-engine bolts and the cover from the engine.

10. Rotate the crankshaft until the marks on the timing sprockets align (face each other). Remove the camshaft sprocket-to-camshaft bolts, then the sprocket and the timing chain from the camshaft and the crankshaft sprocket.

11. Using two or three, $^{5}/_{16}$" bolts, 4–5" long, install them into the camshaft holes. Using these camshaft bolts as handles, support the camshaft and pull the camshaft from the front of the engine block; be careful not to damage the camshaft bearing or lobe surfaces.

12. Inspect the camshaft for scratches, pitting and/or wear on the bearing and lobe surfaces. Check the timing sprockets teeth and timing chain for damage and/or wear, replace the damaged parts (if necessary).

13. To install, lubricate the parts with engine oil and reverse the removal procedures. With the timing chain installed on the sprockets, realign the timing mark (on the sprockets) and install the camshaft sprocket to the camshaft. Torque the camshaft sprocket-to-camshaft bolts to 18 ft.lb.

14. To complete the installation, use new gaskets, sealant (if necessary) and reverse the removal procedures. Adjust the drive belt tensions. Refill the cooling system, start the engine, allow it to reach normal operating temperatures and check for leaks. Check and/or adjust the engine timing.

INSPECTION

Using solvent, degrease the camshaft and clean out all of the oil holes. Visually inspect the cam lobes and bearing journals for excessive wear. If a lobe is questionable, check all of the lobes as indicated. If a journal or lobe is worn, the camshaft MUST BE reground or replaced.

NOTE: *If a journal is worn, there is a good chance that the bushings are worn and need replacement.*

If the lobes and journals appear intact, place the front and rear journals in V-blocks and rest a dial indicator on the center journal. Rotate the camshaft to check the straightness. If deviation exceeds 0.001" (0.0254mm), replace the camshaft.

Check the camshaft lobes with a micrometer, by measuring the lobes from the nose to

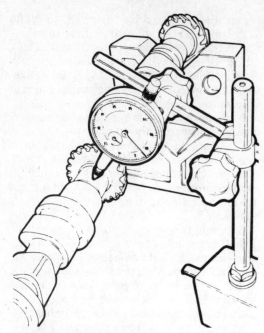

Check the camshaft for straightness

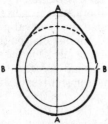

Camshaft lobe measurement

the base and again at 90° (see illustration). The lobe lift is determined by subtracting the second measurement from the first. If all of the exhaust and intake lobes are not identical, the camshaft must be reground or replace.

Camshaft Bearings

REMOVAL AND INSTALLATION

2.5L Engine

NOTE: *The following procedure requires the use of the GM Camshaft Bushing Removal/Installation Adapter tool No. J-21437-1 or equivalent, and GM Camshaft Bushing Removal/Installation Handle tool No. J-21054-1 or equivalent.*

1. Refer to the Engine, Removal and Installation procedures in this section and remove the engine from the vehicle and secure it onto a work stand.

2. Refer to the Camshaft, Removal and Installation and the Oil Pan, Removal and Installation procedures in this section and re-

move the camshaft and the oil pan from the engine.

3. Remove the flywheel-to-crankshaft bolts and the flywheel from the engine.

4. Using a blunt tool, drive the camshaft expansion plug from the rear of the engine.

5. Using the GM Camshaft Bushing Removal/Installation Adapter tool No. J-21437-1 or equivalent and a hammer, drive the front camshaft bearing toward the rear and the rear camshaft bearing toward the front of the engine.

6. Install the GM Camshaft Bushing Removal/Installation Handle tool No. J-21054-1 or equivalent, onto the GM Camshaft Bushing Removal/Installation Adapter tool No. J-21437-1 or equivalent, and drive the center camshaft bearing toward the rear of the engine.

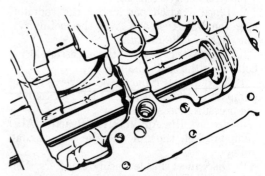

Replacing the camshaft bearings—2.5L engine

7. To install the new camshaft bearings, position them on the tool(s) and reverse the removal procedures.

NOTE: *The front bearing MUST BE driven to approximately 1/8" (3mm) behind the front of the cylinder block; BE SURE that the oil hole-to-timing gear oil nozzle is uncovered.*

8. To complete the installation, reverse the removal procedures. Adjust the valves. Refill the cooling system and the crankcase. Start the engine, allow it to reach normal operating temperatures and check for leaks.

4.3L Engine

To perform this procedure, it is recommended to remove the engine from the vehicle.

NOTE: *The following procedure requires the use of the GM Camshaft Bearing Remover/Installer tool No. J-6098 or equivalent.*

1. Refer to the Camshaft, Removal and Installation and the Crankshaft, Removal and Installation procedures in this section and remove the camshaft and the crankshaft from the engine; leave the cylinder heads attached and the pistons in place.

NOTE: *Before removing the crankshaft, tape the threads of the connecting rod bolts to prevent damage to the crankshaft. Fasten the connecting rods against the sides of the engine, so that they will not be in the way while replacing the camshaft bearings.*

2. Drive the camshaft rear plug from the block.

3. Assemble the GM Camshaft Bearing Remover/Installer tool No. J-6098 or equivalent, using it's shoulder, on the bearing to be removed.

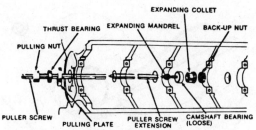

Replacing the camshaft bearings, using GM tool No. J-6098—4.3L engine

4. Gradually, tighten the puller nut until the bearing is removed. Remove the remaining bearings, leaving the front and the rear for last.

5. To remove the front and rear bearing, reverse the position of the tool, so as to press the bearings toward the center of the block.

6. To install the new bearings, leave the tool in this position, pilot the new front and rear bearings on the installer, then press them into position.

7. Return the tool to it's original position and press the remaining bearings into position.

NOTE: *Ensure that the oil holes align when installing the bearings.*

8. Replace the camshaft rear plug and stake it into position to aid retention.

9. To complete the installation, reverse the removal procedures.

Pistons and Connecting Rods

REMOVAL

1. Refer to the Engine, Removal and Installation procedures in this section and remove the engine from the vehicle.

2. Remove the intake manifold and the cylinder head(s).

3. Remove the oil pan and the oil pump assembly.

4. Stamp the cylinder number on the machined surfaces of the bolt bosses of the connecting rod and cap for identification when reinstalling. If the pistons are to be removed

from the connecting rod, mark the cylinder number on the piston with a silver pencil or quick drying paint for proper cylinder identification and cap to rod location. The 2.5L (4-cyl) engine is numbered 1-2-3-4 (front-to-rear); on the 4.3L (V6) engine, is numbered 1-3-5 (front-to-rear) on the right side and 2-4-6 (front-to-rear) on the left side.

5. Examine the cylinder bore above the ring travel. If a ridge exists, remove it with a ridge reamer before attempting to remove the piston and rod assembly.

6. Remove the rod bearing cap and bearing.

7. Install a guide hose over the rod bolt threads; this will prevent damage to the bearing journal and rod bolt threads.

8. Remove the rod and piston assembly through the top of the cylinder bore; remove the other rod and piston assemblies in the same manner.

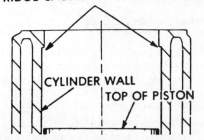

RIDGE CAUSED BY CYLINDER WEAR

CYLINDER WALL

TOP OF PISTON

Remove the ridge from the cylinder bore

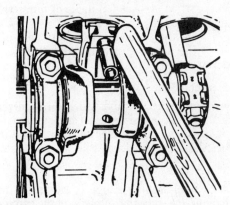

Push the piston out with a hammer handle

CLEANING AND INSPECTION

Using a piston ring expanding tool, remove the piston rings from the pistons; any other method (screwdriver blades, pliers, etc.) usually results in the rings being bent, scratched or distorted and/or the piston itself being damaged.

Pistons

Clean the varnish from the piston skirts and pins with a cleaning solvent. DO NOT WIRE

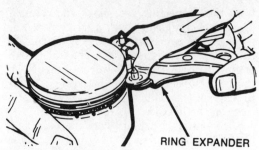

Remove the piston rings

RING EXPANDER

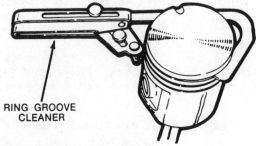

RING GROOVE CLEANER

Clean the piston ring grooves

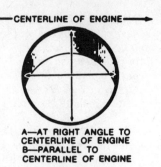

CENTERLINE OF ENGINE

A—AT RIGHT ANGLE TO CENTERLINE OF ENGINE
B—PARALLEL TO CENTERLINE OF ENGINE

Cylinder bore measuring points

Measuring the cylinder bore with a dial gauge

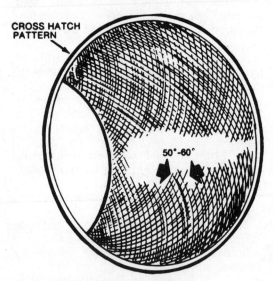

CROSS HATCH PATTERN

50°-60°

Correct cylinder bore honing pattern

BRUSH ANY PART OF THE PISTION. Clean the ring grooves with a groove cleaner and make sure that the oil ring holes and slots are clean.

Inspect the piston for cracked ring lands, scuffed or damaged skirts, eroded areas at the top of the piston. Replace the pistons that are damaged or show signs of excessive wear.

Inspect the grooves for nicks of burrs that might cause the rings to hang up.

Measure the piston skirt (across the center line of the piston pin) and check the piston clearance.

Connecting Rods

Wash the connecting rods in cleaning solvent and dry with compressed air. Check for twisted or bent rods and inspect for nicks or cracks. Replace the connecting rods that are damaged.

Cylinder Bores

Using a telescoping gauge or an inside micrometer, measure the diameter of the cylinder bore, perpendicular (90°) to the piston pin, at 2½" (63.5mm) below the surface of the cylinder block. The difference between the two measurements is the piston clearance.

If the clearance is within specifications or slightly below (after the cylinders have been bored or honed), finish honing is all that is necessary, If the clearance is excessive, try to obtain a slightly larger piston to bring the clearance within specifications. If this is not possible obtain the first oversize piston and hone the cylinder or (if necessary) bore the cylinder

to size. Generally, if the cylinder bore is tapered more than 0.005" (0.127mm) or is out-of-round more than 0.003" (0.0762mm), it is advisable to rebore for the smallest possible oversize piston and rings. After measuring, mark the pistons with a felt-tip pen for reference and for assembly.

NOTE: *Boring of the cylinder block should be performed by a reputable machine shop with the proper equipment. In some cases, clean-up honing can be done with the cylinder block in the vehicle, but most excessive honing and all cylinder boring MUST BE done with the block stripped and removed from the vehicle.*

PISTON PIN REPLACEMENT

NOTE: *The following procedure requires the use of the GM Fixture/Support Assembly tool No. J-24086-20 or equivalent, the GM Piston Pin Removal tool No. J-24086-8 or equivalent, and the GM Piston Pin Installation tool No. J-24086-9 or equivalent.*

Use care at all times when handling and servicing the connecting rods and pistons. To prevent possible damage to these units, DO NOT clamp the rod or piston in a vise since they may become distorted. DO NOT allow the pistons to strike one another, against hard objects or bench surfaces, since distortion of the piston contour or nicks in the soft aluminum material may result.

1. Using an arbor press, the GM Fixture/Support Assembly tool No. J-24086-20 or equivalent, and the GM Piston Pin Removal tool No. J-24086-8 or equivalent, place the piston assembly in the fixture/support tool and press the pin from the piston assembly.

NOTE: *The piston and the piston pin are a matched set which are not serviced separately.*

2. Using solvent, wash the varnish and oil from the parts, then inspect the parts for scuffing or wear.

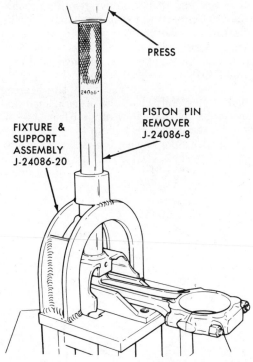

Removing the piston pin from the piston assembly

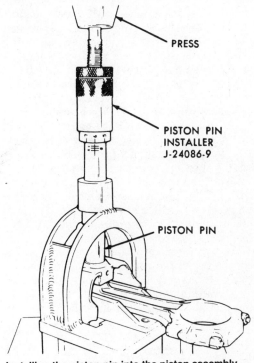

Installing the piston pin into the piston assembly

3. Using a micrometer, measure the diameter of the piston pin. Using a inside micrometer or a dial bore gauge, measure the diameter of the piston bore.

NOTE: *If the piston pin-to-piston clearance is in excess of 0.001" (0.0254mm), replace the piston and piston pin assembly.*

4. Before installation, lubricate the piston pin and the piston bore with engine oil.

5. To install the piston pin into the piston assembly, use an arbor press, the GM Fixture/Support Assembly tool No. J-24086-20 or equivalent, and the GM Piston Pin Installation tool No. J-24086-9 or equivalent, then press the piston pin into the piston/connecting rod assembly.

NOTE: *When installing the piston pin into the piston/connecting rod assembly and the installation tool bottoms onto the support assembly, DO NOT exceed 5000 lbs. of pressure for structural damage may occur to the tool.*

6. After installing the piston pin, make sure that the piston has freedom of movement with the piston pin. The piston/connecting rod assembly is ready for installation into the engine block.

PISTON RING REPLACEMENT AND SIDE CLEARANCE MEASUREMENT

Check the pistons to see that the ring grooves and oil return holes have been properly cleaned. Slide a piston ring into its groove and check the side clearance with a feeler gauge. Make sure the feeler gauge is inserted between the ring and its lower land (lower edge of the groove), because any wear that occurs forms a step at the inner portion of the lower land. If the piston grooves have been worn to the extent that relatively high steps exist on the lower land, the piston should be replaced, because these will interfere with the operation of the new rings and ring clearances will be excessive. Piston rings are not furnished in oversize widths to compensate for ring groove wear.

Install the rings on the piston, bottom ring first, using a piston ring expander. There is a high risk of breaking or distorting the rings and/or scratching the piston, if the rings are installed by hand or other means.

Position the rings on the piston as illustrated; spacing of the various piston ring gaps is crucial to the proper oil retention and cylinder wear. When installing the new rings, refer to the installation diagram furnished with the new parts.

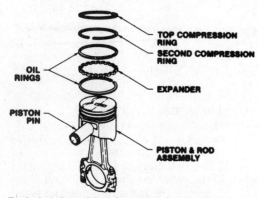

Exploded view of the piston and ring assembly

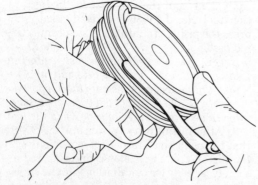

Using a feeler gauge to check the ring side clearances

CHECKING RING END GAP

The piston ring end gap should be checked while the rings are removed from the pistons.

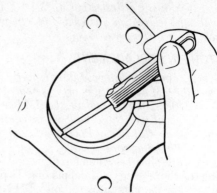

Check the piston ring end gap

Incorrect end gap indicates that the wrong size rings are being used; *ring breakage could result*.

1. Compress the new piston ring into a cylinder (one at a time).

2. Squirt some clean oil into the cylinder so that the ring and the top 2" (51mm) of the cylinder wall are coated.

3. Using an inverted piston, push the ring approximately 1" (25.4mm) below the top of the cylinder.

4. Using a feeler gauge, measure the ring gap and compare it to the Ring Gap chart in this chapter. Carefully remove the ring from the cylinder.

ROD BEARING REPLACEMENT

Replacement bearings are available in standard size and undersize (for reground crankshafts). Connecting rod-to-crankshaft bearing clearance is checked using Plastigage® at either the top or the bottom of each crank journal. The Plastigage® has a range of 0.001–0.003" (0.0254–0.0762mm).

1. Remove the rod cap with the bearing shell. Completely clean the bearing shell and the crank journal, blow any oil from the oil hole in the crankshaft; place the Plastigage® lengthwise along the bottom center of the lower bearing shell, then install the cap with the shell and torque the bolt or nuts to specifica-

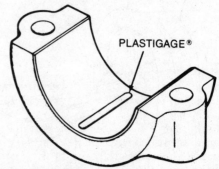

Plastigage® installed on the lower bearing shell

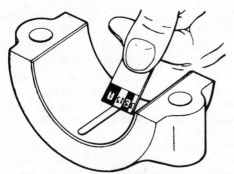

Measure Plastigage® to determine bearing (rod or main) clearance

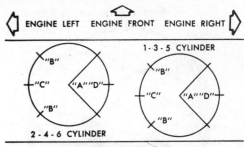

"A" OIL RING SPACER GAP
(Tang in Hole or Slot within Arc)
"B" OIL RING RAIL GAPS
"C" 2ND COMPRESSION RING GAP
"D" TOP COMPRESSION RING GAP

Locating the ring gaps on the 4.3L engine—the 2.5L engine is similar

tion. DO NOT turn the crankshaft with the Plastigage® on the bearing.

2. Remove the bearing cap with the shell. The flattened Plastigage® will be found sticking to either the bearing shell or the crank journal. DO NOT remove it yet.

3. Use the scale printed on the Plastigage® envelope to measure the flattened material at its widest point. The number within the scale which most closely corresponds to the width of the Plastigage® indicates the bearing clearance in thousandths of an inch.

4. Check the specifications chart in this chapter for the desired clearance. It is advisable to install a new bearing if the clearance exceeds 0.003″ (0.0762mm); however, if the bearing is in good condition and is not being checked because of bearing noise, bearing replacement is not necessary.

5. If you are installing new bearings, try a standard size, then each undersize in order until one is found that is within the specified limits when checked for clearance with Plastigage®; each undersize shell has its size stamped on it.

6. When the proper size shell is found, clean off the Plastigage®, oil the bearing thoroughly, reinstall the cap with its shell and torque the rod bolt nuts to specifications.

NOTE: *With the proper bearing selected and the nuts torqued, it should be possible to move the connecting rod back and forth freely on the crank journal as allowed by the specified connecting rod end clearance. If the rod cannot be moved, either the rod bearing is too far undersize or the rod is misaligned.*

INSTALLATION

Position the rings on the piston as illustrated; *spacing of the various piston ring gaps is crucial to proper oil retention and even cylinder wear.* When installing new rings, refer to the installation diagram furnished with the new parts.

Install the connecting rod to the piston, making sure that the piston installation notches and marks (if any) on the connecting rod are in proper relation to one another.

1. Make sure that the connecting rod big-end bearings (including the end cap) are of the correct size and properly installed.

2. Fit rubber hoses over the connecting rod bolts to protect the crankshaft journals, as in the Piston Removal procedure. Lubricate the connecting rod bearings with clean engine oil.

3. Using the ring compressor, compress the rings around the piston head. Insert the piston assembly into the cylinder, so that the notch (on top of the piston) faces the front of the engine.

4. From beneath the engine, coat each crank journal with clean oil. Using a hammer handle, drive the connecting rod/piston assembly into the cylinder bore. Align the connecting rod (with bearing shell) onto the crankshaft journal.

5. Remove the rubber hoses from the studs. Install the bearing cap (with bearing shell) onto the connecting rod and the cap nuts. Torque the connecting rod cap nuts to 32 ft.lb. (2.5L engine) or 45 ft.lb. (4.3L engine).

NOTE: *When more than one connecting rod/piston assembly are being installed, the con-*

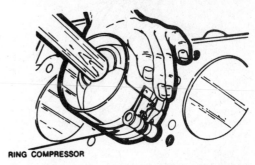

RING COMPRESSOR

Install piston ring compressor, then tap the piston into the cylinder bore. Make sure that the piston front marks are correctly positioned when installing

Install the pistons with the notch facing the front of the engine

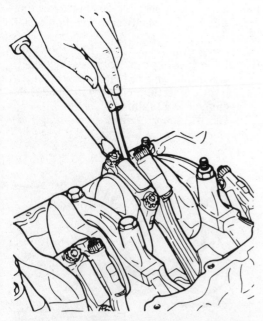

Check the connecting rod side clearance with a feeler gauge. Use a small pry bar to carefully spread the rods to specified clearance

necting rod cap nuts should only be tightened enough to keep each rod in position until the all have been installed. This will ease the installation of the remaining piston assemblies.

6. Check the clearance between the sides of the connecting rods and the crankshaft using a feeler gauge. Spread the rods slightly with a small pry bar to insert the feeler gauge. If the clearance is below the minimum tolerance, the rod may be machined to provide adequate clearance. If the clearance is excessive, substitute an unworn rod and recheck. If clearance is still outside specifications, the crankshaft must be welded and reground or replaced.

7. To complete the installation, reverse the removal procedures. Refill the cooling system. Refill the engine crankcase. Start the engine, allow it to reach normal operating temperatures and check for leaks.

Rear Main Oil Seal

REMOVAL AND INSTALLATION

2.5L Engine

The rear main oil seal is a one piece unit. It can be removed or installed without removing the oil pan or the crankshaft.

NOTE: *The following procedure requires the use of the GM Oil Seal Installation tool No. J-34924 or equivalent.*

1. Refer to the Transmission, Removal and Installation procedures in Chapter 6 and remove the transmission from the vehicle.

2. If equipped with an MT, remove the clutch assembly, the flywheel-to-crankshaft bolts and the flywheel from the crankshaft.

3. Using a small prybar, pry the oil seal from the rear of the crankshaft.

NOTE: *When removing the oil seal, be careful not to damage the crankshaft sealing surface.*

4. To install the new oil seal into the rear retainer, perform the following procedures:

   a. Using new engine oil, lubricate the inner and outer diameter of the seal.

   b. Using the GM Oil Seal Installation tool No. J-34924 or equivalent, install the new oil seal onto it, position the assembly against the crankshaft.

   c. Align the dowel with the alignment hole in the crankshaft and thread the attaching screws into the tapped holes in the crankshaft.

   d. Using a screwdriver, tighten the screws securely; this will ensure that the seal is installed squarely over the crankshaft.

   e. Turn the handle until it bottoms and remove the installation tool.

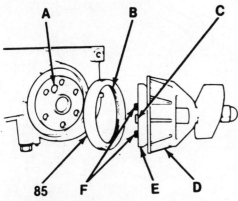

A. Alignment hole in crankshaft
B. Dust lip
C. Dowel pin
D. Collar
E. Mandrel
F. Screws
85. Crankshaft rear oil seal

Using GM tool No. J-34924 or equivalent, to install the rear oil seal—2.5L engine

5. To complete the installation, install the flywheel, the clutch assembly and the transmission. Torque the flywheel-to-crankshaft bolts to 55 ft.lb. and the bellhousing-to-engine bolts to 46 ft.lb.

4.3L Engine – 1985

1. Refer to the Oil Pan, Removal and Installation procedures in this section and remove the oil pan from the engine.
2. Remove the oil pump and the rear main bearing cap.
3. Using a small pry bar, pry the oil seal from the rear main bearing cap.
4. Using a small hammer and a brass pin

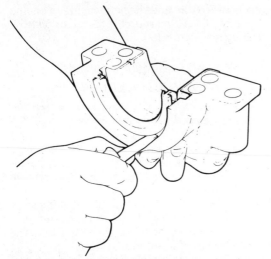

Removing the lower half of the rear main oil seal from the rear bearing cap—4.3L engine (1985)

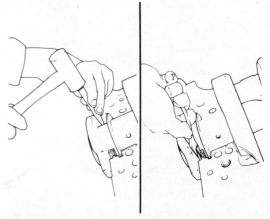

Removing the upper half of the rear main oil seal from the engine block—4.3L engine (1985)

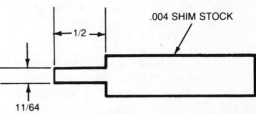

Dimensions for making a rear main oil seal installation tool—4.3L engine (1985)

punch, drive the top half of the oil seal from the rear main bearing. Drive it out far enough, so it may be removed with a pair of pliers.
5. Using a non-abrasive cleaner, clean the rear main bearing cap and the crankshaft.
6. Fabricate an oil seal installation tool from 0.004″ (0.01mm) shim stock, shape the end to ½″ (12.7mm) long by $^{11}/_{64}$″ (4.4mm) wide.
7. Coat the new oil seal with engine oil; DO NOT coat the mating ends of the seal.
8. Position the fabricated tool between the crankshaft and seal seat in the cylinder case.
9. Position the new half seal between the crankshaft and the tip of the tool, so that the seal bead contacts the tip of the tool.
   NOTE: *Make sure that the seal lip is positioned toward the front of the engine.*
10. Using the fabricated tool as a shoe horn, to protect the seal's bead from the sharp edge of the seal seat surface in the cylinder case, roll the seal around the crankshaft. When the seal's ends are flush with the engine block, remove the installation tool.
11. Using the same manner of installation, install the lower seal half onto the lower half of the rear main bearing cap.
12. Apply sealant to the cap-to-case mating surfaces and install the lower rear main bear-

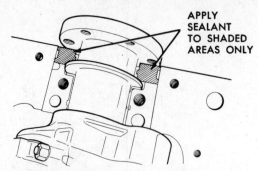

APPLY SEALANT TO SHADED AREAS ONLY

Applying sealant to the rear main oil seal halves—4.3L engine (1985)

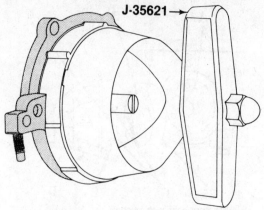

J-35621 →

Using the oil seal installation tool J-35621 to install the new oil seal—4.3L engine

ing half to the engine; keep the sealant off of the seal's mating line.

13. Install the rear main bearing cap bolts and torque to 75 ft.lb. Using a lead hammer, tap the crankshaft forward and rearward, to align the thrust bearing surfaces.

14. To complete the installation, use a new oil pan gasket, sealant (if necessary) and reverse the removal procedures. Refill the crankcase with clean engine oil. Start the engine, allow it to reach normal operating temperatures and check for leaks.

4.3L Engine – 1986 and Later

NOTE: *The following procedure requires the use of the GM Oil Seal Installation tool No. J-35621 or equivalent.*

1. Refer to the Transmission, Removal and Installation procedures in Chapter 6 and remove the transmission from the vehicle.

2. If equipped with an MT, remove the clutch assembly, the flywheel-to-crankshaft bolts and the flywheel from the crankshaft.

3. Using a small prybar, insert it into the

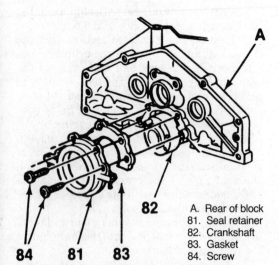

A

82

84   81   83

A. Rear of block
81. Seal retainer
82. Crankshaft
83. Gasket
84. Screw

Exploded view of the rear oil seal—4.3L engine

notches provided in the oil seal retainer and pry the oil seal from the retainer.

NOTE: *When removing the oil seal from the retainer, be careful not to nick the crankshaft sealing surface.*

4. To install the new oil seal into the rear retainer, perform the following procedures:

a. Using engine oil, lubricate the inner and outer diameter of the seal.

b. Using the GM Oil Seal Installation tool No. J-35621, install the new oil seal onto it, position the assembly against the crankshaft and thread the attaching screws into the tapped holes in the crankshaft.

c. Using a screwdriver, tighten the screws securely; this will ensure that the seal is installed squarely over the crankshaft.

d. Turn the handle until it bottoms and remove the installation tool.

5. To complete the installation, install the flywheel, the clutch assembly and the transmission. Torque the flywheel-to-crankshaft bolts to 75 ft.lb. and the bellhousing-to-engine bolts to 46 ft.lb. (carburetor model) or 55 ft.lb. (throttle body model).

Crankshaft and Main Bearings
REMOVAL AND INSTALLATION

NOTE: *The following procedure requires the use of the GM Guide Tool Set No. J-6305-11 (2.5L engine), J-5239 (4.3L engine) or equivalent.*

1. Refer to the Engine, Removal and Installation procedures in this section and remove the engine from the vehicle.

2. If equipped with a flywheel, remove it and mount the engine onto a workstand.

3. Disconnect the spark plug wires from the plugs, then remove the spark plugs.

4. Remove the drive belt pulley from the damper hub, the damper hub-to-crankshaft

bolt, the damper hub from the crankshaft and the timing cover from the engine.

NOTE: *After removing the damper hub from the crankshaft, be sure to remove the wood-ruff key from the crankshaft. When removing the damper hub from the crankshaft, the oil seal should be replaced.*

5. Rotate the crankshaft, until the timing marks on the timing gears (2.5L engine) or sprockets (4.3L engine) align with each other, then remove the timing gear (2.5L) or timing chain/sprocket (4.3L) from the crankshaft.

NOTE: *After removing the timing gear or sprocket from the crankshaft, be sure to re-move the woodruff key from the crankshaft.*

6. Place a catch pan under the engine, re-move the oil pan plug and drain the oil into the pan. Invert the engine and remove the oil pan from the engine.

NOTE: *If working on the 4.3L engine, re-move the oil pump.*

7. Inspect the connecting rods and bearing caps for identification marks (numbers); if there are none, mark them for reassembly purposes.

8. Remove the connecting rod nuts and caps, then store them in the order of removal. Using the GM Guide Tool Set No. J-6305-11 (2.5L en-gine), J-5239 (4.3L engine) or equivalent, in-stall them on the connecting rod studs and push the connecting rods into the block. Re-move the bearing shells from the connecting rod and the bearing cap.

NOTE: *When installing the guide tool set onto the connecting rod studs, position the long tool so that it may be used to push the connecting rod up into the bore.*

9. Check the main bearing caps for identifi-cation marks (if not identified, mark them).

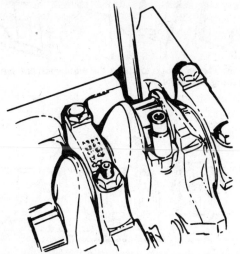
View of the connecting rod studs with the stud pro-tectors installed

Remove the main bearing caps and store them in order, for reassembly purposes; the caps must be reinstalled in their original position.

10. Remove the crankshaft, the main bear-ing inserts and the rear main oil seal (2.5L), the rear main oil shell sections (4.3L, 1985) or the rear main oil seal/retainer (4.3L, 1986 and later).

NOTE: *When removing the bearing shells, it is recommended to replace them with new ones.*

11. Using solvent, clean all of the parts for inspection purposes. If necessary, replace any part that may be questionable.

12. To install, use new bearing shell inserts and check the bearing clearances using the Plastigage® method.

NOTE: *If necessary, deliver the crankshaft to an automotive machine shop, have the crank-shaft journals ground and new bearing shells matched.*

13. Lubricate all of the parts and oil seals with clean engine oil.

14. To complete the installation, use new gaskets (sealant if necessary) and reverse the removal procedures. Torque the main bearing cap-to-engine bolts to 70 ft.lb. (2.5L) or 75 ft.lb. (4.3L). Refill the cooling system (with the saved coolant) and the crankcase (with new oil). Start the engine, allow it to reach normal operating temperatures and check for leaks.

CLEANING AND INSPECTION

1. Remove the bearing cap and wipe the oil from the crankshaft journal and outer/inner surfaces of the bearing shell.

2. Place a piece of Plastigage® material in the center of the bearing.

3. Reinstall the bearing cap and bearing. Lubricate the main bearing bolts with engine oil, install the bolts and torque them to specifications.

4. Remove the bearing caps and determine the bearing clearance by comparing the width

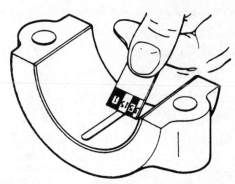
Measure the main bearing clearance by comparing the flattened strip to the Plasticgage scale as shown

of the flattened Plastigage⸌ material at its widest point with the graduations on the gaging material conatainer. The number within the graduation on the envelope indicates the clearance in millimeters or thousandths of an inch. If the clearance is greater than allowed. REPLACE BOTH BEARING SHELLS AS A SET. Recheck the clearance after replacing the shells. Refer to the Main Bearing Replacement in this section.

MAIN BEARING REPLACEMENT

Main bearing clearances must be corrected by the use of selective upper and lower shells. UNDER NO CIRCUMSTANCES should the use of shims behind the shells to compensate for wear be attempted. To install the main bearing shells, proceed as follows:

1. Refer to the Oil Pan, Removal and Installation procedures in this section and remove the oil pan.

2. Loosen all of the main bearing cap bolts.

3. Remove the bearing cap bolts, the caps and the lower bearing shell.

4. Insert a flattened cotter pin or a roll out pin in the oil passage hole in the crankshaft, then rotate the crankshaft in the direction opposite to the cranking rotation. The pin will contact the upper shell and roll it out.

5. The main bearing journals should be checked for roughness and wear. Slight roughness may be removed with a fine grit polishing cloth, saturated with engine oil. Burrs may be removed with a fine oil stone. If the journals

are scored or ridged, the crankshaft must be replaced.

NOTE: *The journals can be measured for out-of-round with the crankshaft installed by using a crankshaft caliper and inside micrometer or a main bearing micrometer. The upper bearing shell must be removed when measuring the crankshaft journals. Maximum out-of-round of the crankshaft journal must not exceed 0.0015" (0.038mm).*

6. Clean the crankshaft journals and bearing caps thoroughly before installing the new main bearings.

7. Apply special lubricant, GM No. 1050169 or equivalent, to the thrust flanges of the bearing shells.

8. Place the new upper shell on the crankshaft journal with the locating tang in the correct position and rotate the shaft to turn it into place using a cotter pin or a roll out pin as during removal.

9. Place a new bearing shell in the bearing cap.

10. Lubricate the new bearings and the main bearing cap bolts with engine oil. Install the main bearing shells, the crankshaft and the main bearing caps. Using the Plastigage⸌ method, check the bearing clearances. Using a feeler gauge, pry the crankshaft forward and rearward, then check for the crankshaft (thrust bearing) end play.

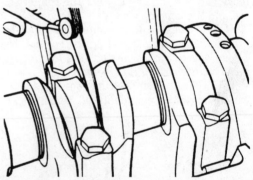

Use a feeler gauge to check the crankshaft end play during assembly

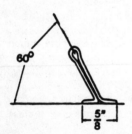

Fabricate a roll-out pin as illustrated, if necessary

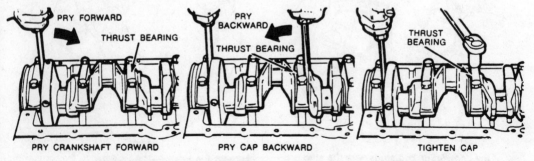

Align the thrust bearing as illustrated. Torque the caps to specifications

NOTE: *In order to prevent the possibility of cylinder block and/or main bearing cap damage, the main bearing caps are to be tapped into their cylinder block cavity, using a brass or leather mallet before the bolts are installed. Do not use the bolts to pull the main bearing caps into their seats. Failure to observe this procedure may damage the cylinder block or bearing cap.*

11. To complete the installation, use new oil seals, gaskets (sealant, if necessary) and reverse the removal procedures. Torque the main bearing cap-to-engine bolts to 70 ft.lb. (2.5L) or 75 ft.lb. (4.3L).

Flywheel

The flywheel and the ring gear are machined from one piece of metal and cannot be separated.

REMOVAL AND INSTALLATION

NOTE: *The following procedure requires the use of the GM Clutch Disc Aligner tool No. J-33169 or equivalent.*

1. Refer to the Manual Transmission, Removal and Installation procedures in Chapter 6 and remove the transmission from the bellhousing.

2. Remove the slave cylinder-to-bellhousing bolts and move the slave cylinder aside; DO NOT disconnect the hydraulic line from the cylinder.

3. Remove the bellhousing-to-engine bolts and the bellhousing from the engine. When removing the bellhousing, slide the clutch fork from the ball stud.

NOTE: *The clutch fork ball stud is threaded into the bellhousing and can easily be replaced, if necessary.*

4. Using the GM Clutch Disc Aligner tool No. J-33169 or equivalent, position it in the pilot bushing (to support the clutch disc).

5. Inspect the flywheel/pressure plate assembly for match marks (a stamped or a painted **X** mark); if no mark exists, mark the flywheel and the pressure plate.

6. Loosen the clutch-to-flywheel bolts, evenly (one turn at a time), until the spring tension is relieved, then remove the retaining bolts, the pressure plate and the clutch assembly.

7. Remove the flywheel-to-crankshaft bolts and the flywheel from the engine.

8. Clean the clutch disc (use a stiff brush), the pressure plate and the flywheel of all dirt, oil and grease. Inspect the flywheel, the pressure plate and the clutch disc for scoring, cracks, heat checking and/or other defects.

NOTE: *When the flywheel is removed, it is a good idea to replace the rear main oil seal, the pilot bushing and/or the clutch plate (if necessary).*

9. To install, align flywheel with the crankshaft, then torque the flywheel-to-crankshaft bolts to 55–75 ft.lb. (2.5L) or 48–62 ft.lb. (4.3L).

10. Using the GM Clutch Disc Aligner tool No. J-33169 or equivalent, position it in the pilot bushing (to support the clutch disc), then assemble the clutch disc (the damper springs

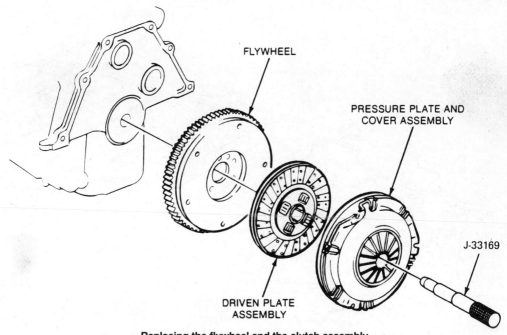

FLYWHEEL

PRESSURE PLATE AND COVER ASSEMBLY

J-33169

DRIVEN PLATE ASSEMBLY

Replacing the flywheel and the clutch assembly

facing the transmission), the pressure plate and the retaining bolts onto the flywheel.

NOTE: *When installing the pressure plate onto the flywheel, be sure to align the* **X** *marks.*

11. Tighten the pressure plate-to-flywheel bolts gradually and evenly (to prevent clutch plate distortion) to 15–22 ft.lb. (2.5L) or 25–35 ft.lb. (4.3L), then remove the alignment tool.

12. To complete the installation, lubricate the pilot bushing and the clutch release lever, then reverse the removal procedures. Torque the bellhousing-to-engine bolts to 11–15 ft.lb., the transmission-to-bellhousing bolts to 25 ft. and the clutch slave cylinder-to-bellhousing bolts to 10–15 ft.lb.

EXHAUST SYSTEM

Two types of pipe connections are used on the exhaust system, they are: the ball joint (to allow angular movement for alignment purposes) and the slip joint. No gaskets are used in the entire system.

The system is supported by free hanging rubber mountings which permit some movement of the exhaust system but do not allow the transfer of noise and vibration into the passenger compartment. Any noise vibrations or rattles in the exhaust system are usually caused by misalignment of the parts.

CAUTION: *Before performing any operation on the exhaust system, be sure to allow it to cool down.*

Front Pipe
REMOVAL AND INSTALLATION

1. Raise and support the front of the vehicle on jackstands.

2. Remove the front pipe(s)-to-manifold(s) nuts and separate (pry, if necessary) the front pipe (ball joint) from the exhaust manifold(s).

3. At the catalytic converter, loosen the front pipe-to-converter clamp nuts, slide the clamp away from converter and separate the front pipe from the converter.

NOTE: *Use a twisting motion to separate the front pipe-to-converter slip joint connection. If the front pipe cannot be removed from the catalytic converter, use a hammer (to loosen the connection) or wedge tool separate the connection.*

4. Inspect the pipe for holes, damage or deterioration; if necessary, replace the front pipe.

5. To install, lubricate the front pipe-to-manifold(s) studs/nuts and the front pipe-to-converter clamp threads, then reverse the removal procedures.

6. Start the engine and check for exhaust leaks.

Catalytic Converter

The catalytic converter is an emission control device added to the exhaust system to reduce the emission of hydrocarbon and carbon monoxide pollutants.

REMOVAL AND INSTALLATION

1. Raise and support the front of the vehicle on jackstands.

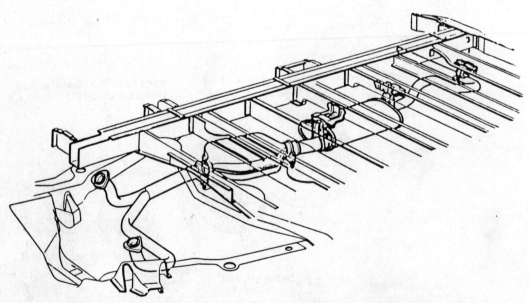

View of the exhaust system with 4.3L engine—2.5L engine equipped vehicle, is similar

2. Remove the catalytic converter-to-muffler stud nuts and separate the muffler from the converter.

NOTE: *The connection between the converter and the muffler is a ball joint type, which can be easily separated.*

3. Remove the catalytic converter-to-front pipe clamp nuts and move the clamp forward.

4. Remove the converter-to-mounting bracket bolts (if equipped), then twist the converter to separate it from the front pipe.

5. Inspect the condition of the catalytic converter for physical damage, replace it, if necessary.

NOTE: *When installing the catalytic converter, be sure that it is installed with adequate clearance from the floor pan, to prevent overheating of the vehicle floor.*

6. To install, align the components and reverse the removal procedures; be careful not to damage the pipe sealing surfaces when tightening the retaining clamps.

7. Start the engine and check for exhaust leaks.

Muffler

NOTE: *The following procedure requires the use of GM Sealing Compound No. 1051249 or equivalent. When replacing the muffler, always replace the tail pipe.*

REMOVAL AND INSTALLATION

1. Refer to the Tail Pipe, Removal and Installation procedures in this section and remove the tail pipe from the vehicle.

2. Loosen and move the catalytic converter-to-muffler clamp or remove the catalytic converter-to-muffler flange bolts and separate the items.

3. Remove the muffler-to-mounting bracket bolts and lower the muffler from the vehicle.

4. To install, coat the slip joints with GM Sealing Compound No. 1051249 or equivalent and loosely install the components onto the vehicle.

5. After aligning the components, tighten the connecting bolts and clamps.

NOTE: *When torquing the exhaust system connectors, be careful not to tighten the pipe clamps too tight, for deformation of the pipes may occur.*

6. Start the engine and check for exhaust leaks.

Tail Pipe

NOTE: *The following procedure requires the use of GM Sealing Compound No. 1051249 or equivalent.*

REMOVAL AND INSTALLATION

NOTE: *Normally, when the tail pipe requires replacement, the muffler should be replaced also.*

1. Raise and support the rear of the vehicle on jackstands.

2. Remove the tail pipe-to-muffler clamp, then slide the clamp rearward.

3. Remove the tail pipe-to-mounting bracket clamp.

4. Using a twisting motion, remove the tail pipe from the muffler.

NOTE: *If removal of the tail pipe difficult, use a hammer to free the pipe from the muffler.*

5. Inspect the tail pipe for holes of physical damage.

6. To install, use a new tail pipe (if necessary), a new muffler (if necessary), apply GM Sealing Compound No. 1051249 or equivalent to the slip joint(s), lubricate the pipe clamp threads with engine oil, loosely assemble the exhaust system, then final torque the components.

7. Start the engine and check for exhaust leaks.

TROUBLESHOOTING

Engine Speed Oscillates at Idle

When the engine idle speed will not remain constant, replace or repair the following items or systems, as necessary:

• A faulty fuel pump.
• A leaky Exhaust Gas Recirculation (EGR) valve.
• A blown head gasket.
• A worn camshaft.
• Worn timing gears, chain or sprockets.
• Leaking intake manifold-to-engine gasket.
• A blocked Positive Crankcase Ventilation (PCV) valve.
• Overheating of the cooling system.

Low Power Output of Engine

When the engine power output is below normal, replace or repair the following items or systems, as necessary:

• Overheating of the cooling system.
• Leaks in the vacuum system.
• Leaking of the fuel pump or hoses.
• Unadjusted valve timing.
• A blown head gasket.
• A slipping clutch disc or unadjustment pedal.
• Excessive piston-to-bore clearance.
• Worn piston rings.
• A worn camshaft.
• Sticking valve(s) or weak valve spring(s).
• A poorly operating diverter valve.

- A faulty pressure regulator valve (Auto. Trans.).
- Low fluid level (Auto. Trans.).

Poor High Speed Operation

When the engine cannot maintain high speed operations, replace or repair the following items or systems, as necessary:
- A faulty fuel pump producing low fuel volume.
- A restriction in the intake manifold.
- A worn distributor shaft.
- Unadjusted valve timing.
- Leaking valves or worn valve springs.

Poor Acceleration

When the engine experiences poor acceleration characteristics, replace or repair the following items or systems, as necessary:
- Incorrect ignition timing.
- Poorly seated valves.
- Improperly adjusted accelerator pump stroke (carburetor equipped).
- Worn accelerator pump diaphragm or piston (carburetor equipped).

Backfire – Intake Manifold

When the engine backfires through the intake manifold, replace or repair the following items or systems, as necessary:
- Incorrect ignition timing.
- Incorrect operation of the choke (carburetor equipped).
- Choke setting (initial clearance) too large (carburetor equipped).
- Defective Exhaust Gas Recirculation (EGR) valve.
- A very lean air/fuel mixture (carburetor equipped).

Backfire – Exhaust Manifold

When the engine backfires through the exhaust manifold, replace or repair the following items or systems, as necessary:
- Leaks in the vacuum hose system.
- Leaks in the exhaust sytem.
- Faulty choke adjustments or operation (carburetor equipped).
- Faulty vacuum diverter valve.

Engine Detonation (Dieseling)

When the engine operates beyond the controlled limits, replace or repair the following items or systems, as necessary:
- Faulty ignition electrical system components.
- The ignition timing may be too far advanced.
- Inoperative Exhaust Gas Recirculation (EGR) valve.
- Inoperative Positive Crankcase Ventilation (PCV) valve.
- Faulty or loose spark plugs.
- Clogged fuel delivery system.
- Sticking, leaking or broken valves.
- Excessive deposits in the combustion chambers.
- Leaks in the vacuum system.

Excessive Oil Leakage

When large amounts of oil are noticed under the engine after each operation, replace or repair the following items or systems, as necessary:
- Damaged or broken oil filter gasket.
- Leaking oil pressure sending switch.
- Worn rear main oil seal gasket.
- Worn front main oil seal gasket.
- Damaged or broken fuel pump gasket (mechanical pump).
- Damaged or loose valve cover gasket.
- Damaged oil pan gasket or bent oil pan.
- Improperly seated oil pan drain plug.
- Broken timing chain cover gasket.
- Blocked camshaft bearing drain hole.

Heavy Oil Consumption

When the engine is burning large amounts of oil, replace or repair the following items or systems, as necessary:
- The engine oil level may be to high.
- The engine oil may be to thin.
- Wrong size of piston rings.
- Clogged piston ring grooves or oil return slots.
- Insufficient tension of the piston rings.
- Piston rings may be sticking in the grooves.
- Excessively worn piston ring grooves.
- Reversed (upsidedown) compression rings.
- Non-staggered piston ring gaps.
- Improper Positive Crankcase Ventilation (PCV) valve operation.
- Damaged valve O-ring seals.
- Restricted oil drain back holes.
- Worn valve stem or guides.
- Damaged valve stem oil deflectors.
- Too long intake gasket dowels.
- Mismatched rail and expander of the oil ring.
- Excessive clearance of the main and connecting rods.
- Scored or worn cylinder walls.

Negative Oil Pressure

When the engine presents no oil pressure, replace or repair the following items or systems, as necessary:
- Low oil level in the crankcase.
- Broken oil pressure gauge or sender.

- Blocked oil pump passages.
- Blocked oil pickup screen or tube.
- Malfunctioning oil pump.
- Sticking oil pressure relief valve.
- Leakage of the internal oil passages.
- Worn (loose) camshaft bearings.

Low Oil Pressure

When the engine presents low oil pressure, replace or repair the following items or systems, as necessary:
- Low oil level in the crankcase.
- Blocked oil pickup screen or tube.
- Malfunctioning or excessive clearance of the oil pump.
- Sticking oil pressure relief valve.
- Very thin engine oil.
- Worn (loose) main, rod or camshaft bearings.

High Oil Pressure

When the engine presents high oil pressure, replace or repair the following items or systems, as necessary:
- Sticking (closed) oil pressure relief valve.
- Wrong grade of oil.
- Faulty oil pressure gauge or sender.

Knocking Main Bearings

When the main bearings are constantly making noise, replace or repair the following items or systems, as necessary:
- Oval shaped crankshaft journals.
- Loose torque converter or flywheel mounting bolts.
- Loose damper pulley hub.
- Excessive clearance of the main bearings.
- Excessive belt tension.
- Low oil supply to the main bearings.
- Extreme crankshaft end play.

Knocking Connecting Rods

When the connecting rod bearings are constantly making noise, replace or repair the following items or systems, as necessary:
- Misaligned connecting rod or cap.
- Missing bearing shell or excessive bearing clearance.
- Incorrectly torqued connecting rod bolts.
- Connecting rod journal of the crankshaft is out-of-round.

Knocking Pistons and Rings

When the pistons and/rings are constantly making noise, replace or repair the following items or systems, as necessary:
- Misaligned connecting rods.
- Out-of-round or tapered cylinder bore.
- Loose or tight ring side clearance.
- Build-up of carbon on the piston(s).
- Piston-to-cylinder bore clearance is excessive.
- Broken piston rings.
- Loose or seized piston pin(s).

Knocking Valve Train

When the valve train is constantly making noise, replace or repair the following items or systems, as necessary:
- Retighten any loose rocker arms.
- Remove any dirt or chips in the valve lifters.
- Excessive valve stem-to-guide clearance.
- Remove restrictions from valve lifter oil holes.
- Incorrect valve lifter may be installed in the engine.
- Valve lock(s) may be missing.
- Valve lifter check ball may be faulty.
- Valve lifter leak down may be excessive.
- Rocker arm nut may be reversed (installed upsidedown).
- Camshaft lobes may be excessively worn.
- Bent or worn pushrods.
- Excessively worn bridged pivots or rocker arms.
- Cocked or broken valve springs.
- Bent valve(s).
- Worn valve lifter face(s).
- Damaged lifter plunger or pushrod seat.

Knocking Valves

When the valves are constantly noisy, replace or repair the following items or systems, as necessary:
- Unadjusted valve lash.
- Valve springs may be broken.
- Pushrods may be bent.
- Camshaft lobes may be excessively worn.
- Dirty or worn valve lifters.
- Valve guides may be worn.
- Valve seat or face runout may be excessive.
- Loose rocker arm studs.

Emission Controls and Fuel System

EMISSION CONTROLS

Due to the complex nature of modern electronic engine control systems comprehensive diagnosis and testing procedures fall outside the confines of this repair manual. For complete information on diagnosis testing and repair procedures concerning all modern engine and emission control systems, please refer to **CHILTON'S GUIDE TO ELECTRONIC ENGINE CONTROLS**.

Crankcase Ventilation System

OPERATION

The crankcase vapors are drawn into the intake manifold to be burned in the combustion chambers, instead of merely venting the crankcase vapors into the atmosphere. An added benefit to engines equipped with this system is that the engine oil will tend to stay cleaner for a longer period of time; therefore, if you notice that the oil in your engine becomes dirty very easily, check the functioning of the PCV valve. Engines which use a PCV system are calibrated to run richer, to compensate for the added air which accompanies the crankcase vapors to the combustion chambers. If the PCV valve or line is clogged, the engine idle will tend to be rough due to the excessively rich mixture. Maintenance is covered in Chapter 1.

TESTING

NOTE: *Inspect the PCV system hose(s) and connections at each tune-up and replace any*

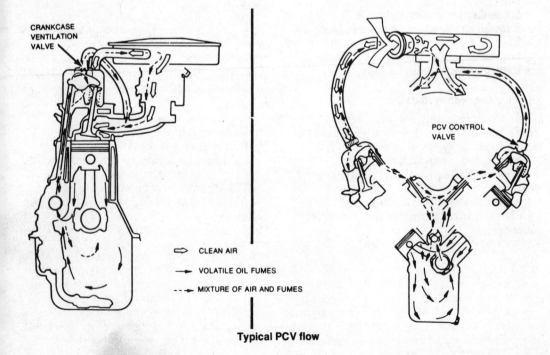

CRANKCASE VENTILATION VALVE

PCV CONTROL VALVE

⇨ CLEAN AIR

→ VOLATILE OIL FUMES

--→ MIXTURE OF AIR AND FUMES

Typical PCV flow

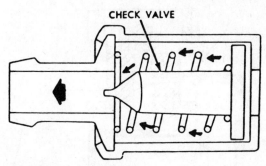

Cross section of a PCV valve

deteriorated hoses. Check the PCV valve at every tune-up and replace it at 30,000 mile intervals.

1. Remove the PCV valve from the rocker arm cover.
2. Operate the engine at idle speed.
3. Place your thumb over the end of the valve to check for vacuum. If no vacuum exists, check the valve, the hoses or the manifold port for a plugged condition.
4. Remove the valve from the hose(s), then shake it and listen for a rattling of the check needle (inside the valve); the rattle means the valve is working. If no rattle is heard, replace the valve.

REMOVAL AND INSTALLATION

1. Pull the PCV valve from the rocker arm cover grommet.
2. Remove the hose(s) from the PCV valve.
3. Shake the valve to make sure that it is not plugged.
4. To install, reverse the removal procedures.

Evaporative Emission Controls (EEC)

OPERATION

The EEC system is designed to reduce the amount of escaping gasoline vapors into the atmosphere. Fuel vapors are directed through lines to a canister containing an activated charcoal filter; unburned fuel vapor is trapped here until the engine is started. When the engine is started, the canister is purged by air drawn in by the manifold vacuum. The air/fuel vapor mixture is drawn into the engine and burned.

On the 4.3L carburetor models (Calif.), depending upon various conditions of operation, the ECM will either energize or de-energize the solenoid. When the solenoid is energized, vacuum is not available to draw fuel vapors from the canister; when de-energized, vacuum

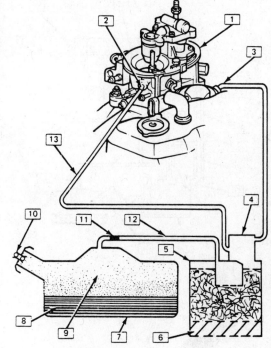

1. TBI
2. Canister purge port
3. Vacuum signal
4. Purge valve
5. Vapor storage canister
6. Purge air
7. Fuel tank
8. Fuel
9. Vapor
10. Pressure-vacuum relief gas cap
11. Vent restricter
12. Fuel tank vent
13. Purge line

Evaporative Emission Control (EEC) System—2.5L engine

draws the canister vapors into the intake tract of the engine.

TESTING

Charcoal Canister

2.5L AND 4.3L (1985)

1. Remove the lower tube of the canister (purge valve) and install a short length of tube, then try to blow through it (little or no air should pass).
2. Using a vacuum source, apply 15 in.Hg to the upper tube of the canister (purge valve). The diaphragm should hold the vacuum for at least 20 seconds, if not replace the canister.
3. While holding the vacuum on the upper tube, blow through the lower tube (air should now pass); if not, replace the canister.

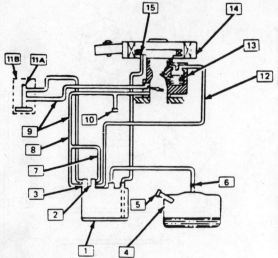

1. Canister
2. Vapor vent control valve
3. Canister purge control valve
4. Fuel tank
5. Fuel cap
6. Fuel tank vent line restriction
7. Vacuum signal for bowl vent valve
8. Vapor purge line (full manifold vacuum)
9. Ported manifold vacuum
10. PCV valve
11A. TVS-federal application
11B. Electric purge solenoid-California application
12. Carburetor bowl vent line
13. Carburetor
14. Air cleaner
15. Fuel vapor canister vent

Cross-sectional view of the evaporative emission control system—4.3L carbureted engine (1985)

REMOVAL AND INSTALLATION

Charcoal Canister

1. Label and disconnect the hoses from the canister.
2. Loosen the retaining bolt and remove the canister from the vehicle.
NOTE: *If necessary to replace the canister filter, simply pull the filter from the bottom of the charcoal filter and install a new one.*
3. To install, reverse the removal procedures.

Purge Solenoid

1. Disconnect the negative battery cable.
2. Remove the solenoid cover bolt, the cover and the solenoid.
3. Disconnect the electrical connector and the hoses from the solenoid.
4. To install, reverse the removal procedures.

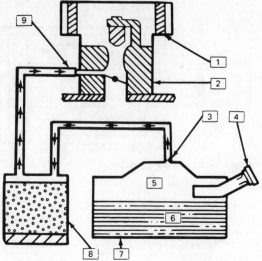

1. Air cleaner
2. T.B.I. unit
3. Restrictor
4. Press-vacuum relief gas cap
5. Vapor
6. Fuel
7. Fuel tank
8. Charcoal canister
9. Purge

Cross-sectional view of the evaporative emission control system—4.3L TBI engine (1986–87)

Exhaust Gas Recirculation (EGR) System

OPERATION

All engines are equipped with an exhaust gas recirculation (EGR) system. This system consists of a metering valve, a vacuum line to the intake manifold and cast-in exhaust gas passages in the intake manifold.

On the 2.5L engine, the EGR is controlled by

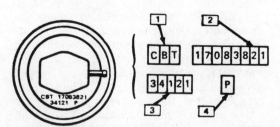

1. Assembly plant code
2. Part number
3. Date built
4. Look here for letter
   P = postive back pressure
   N = negative back pressure
   Blank = ported valve

Explanation of the EGR valve serial numbers

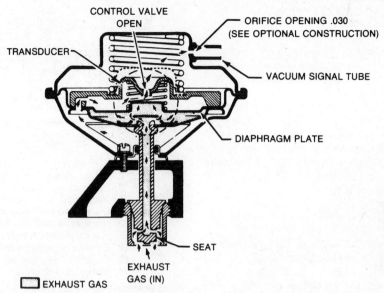

CONTROL VALVE OPEN

ORIFICE OPENING .030 (SEE OPTIONAL CONSTRUCTION)

TRANSDUCER

VACUUM SIGNAL TUBE

DIAPHRAGM PLATE

SEAT

EXHAUST GAS (IN)

□ EXHAUST GAS

Cross-sectional view of the positive backpressure EGR valve used—2.5L engine

manifold vacuum which accordingly opens and closes to admit exhaust gases into the fuel/air mixture. The exhaust gases lower the combustion temperature and reduce the amount of oxides of nitrogen (NOx) produced. The valve is closed at idle between the two extreme throttle positions.

On the 4.3L engine, the vacuum to the EGR valve is controlled by EGR solenoid (controlled by the ECM) or a Thermal Vacuum Switch (TVS). Vacuum to the EGR valve is restricted until the engine is hot. This prevents the stall-

DIAPHRAGM IS SEATED WHEN ENGINE IS NOT RUNNING

VACUUM SIGNAL TUBE

DIAPHRAGM PLATE

ORIFICE OPENING .030 (SEE OPTIONAL CONSTRUCTION)

TRANSDUCER

ORIFICE OPENING .020

SEAT

INTAKE MANIFOLD VACUUM

EXHAUST

OPTIONAL CONSTRUCTION

Cross-sectional view of the negative backpressure EGR valve used—4.3L engine

ing and lumpy idle conditions which would result if the EGR occurred when the engine was cold.

TESTING

EGR Valve

1. Remove the vacuum hose from the EGR valve.
2. Using a vacuum source, connect it to the EGR valve hose fitting and apply 10 in.Hg; the valve should lift off of its seat, if not, replace the EGR valve.

EGR Solenoid

1. Disconnect the electrical connector from the solenoid.
2. Using an ohmmeter, measure the solenoid's resistance, it should be more than 20Ω. If less than 20Ω, replace the solenoid and/or possibly the ECM.

Thermostatic Vacuum Switch

If the thermostatic vacuum switch is not working, a Code 32 will store in the ECM memory and a "Service Engine Soon" lamp will light on the instrument panel.

1. Remove the TVS from the engine.
2. Using a vacuum gauge, connect it to one of the hose connections and apply 10 in.Hg
   NOTE: *A vacuum drop of 2 in.Hg in 2 minutes is allowable.*
3. Place the tip of the switch in boiling water. When the switch reaches 195°F (91°C), the valve should open and the vacuum will drop; if not, replace the switch.

REMOVAL AND INSTALLATION

EGR Valve

1. Remove the engine cover (from inside the vehicle) and the air cleaner.

2. Detach the vacuum hose from the EGR valve.

3. On the 4.3L EFI engine, disconnect the temperature switch from the EGR valve.

4. Remove the EGR valve-to-intake manifold bolts and the valve from the manifold.

5. To install, use a new gasket and reverse the removal procedures. Torque the EGR valve-to-manifold bolts to 14 ft.lb.

EGR Solenoid

1. Disconnect the negative battery cable.

2. Remove the engine cover (1986–87) and the air cleaner.

3. Disconnect the electrical connector and the vacuum hoses from the solenoid.

4. Remove the mounting nut and the solenoid.

5. To install, reverse the removal proce-

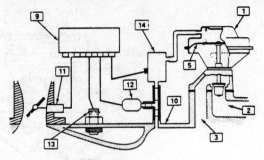

1. EGR valve
2. Exhaust gas
3. Intake air
5. Diaphragm
9. Electronic control module
10. Manifold vacuum
11. Throttle position sensor
12. Manifold pressure sensor
13. Coolant temperature sensor
14. EGR control solenoid

Electronic controlled EGR system—4.3L engine

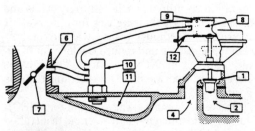

1. EGR valve
2. Exhaust gas
4. Intake flow
6. Vacuum port
7. Throttle valve
8. Vacuum chamber
9. Valve return spring
10. Thermal vacuum switch
11. Coolant
12. Diaphragm

Thermostatic Vacuum Switch controlled EGR system—4.3L carbureted engine

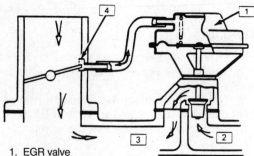

1. EGR valve
2. Exhaust gas
3. Intake manifold
4. Calibrated carb or TBI port

View of the EGR valve operation—2.5L engine

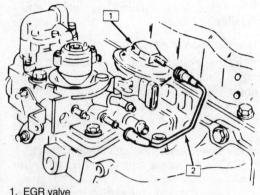

1. EGR valve
2. EGR valve tube

View of the EGR valve-to-throttle body hookup—2.5L engine

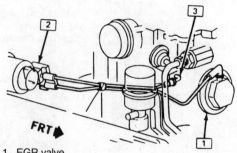

1. EGR valve
2. Vacuum solenoid
3. Carb port "J"

View of the EGR solenoid—4.3L carbureted engine

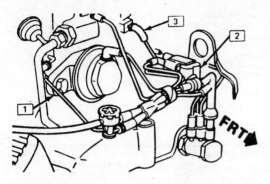

1. EGR valve
2. TVS
3. Carb port "H"

View of the EGR Thermostatic Vacuum Switch—4.3L engine

dures. Torque the solenoid mounting nut to 17 ft.lb.

Thermostatic Vacuum Switch (TVS)–4.3L Carbureted Engine

The thermostatic vacuum switch, is installed on the front left side of the intake manifold.

1. Drain the radiator to a level below the Thermostatic Vacuum Switch (TVS).

2. Disconnect the vacuum hoses from the switch.

3. Remove the switch from the engine.

4. To install, apply soft sealant to the threaded portion of the new switch and reverse the removal procedure. Torque the TVS to 10 ft.lb. Refill the cooling system, start the engine and check for leaks.

Resetting

To clear the codes stored in the ECM, turn the ignition Off and disconnect the negative battery terminal or the ECM **B** fuse for ten seconds.

Thermostatic Air Cleaner (THERMAC)
OPERATION

This system is designed to improve driveability and exhaust emissions when the engine is cold. Components added to the basic air cleaner assembly include a temperature sensor (connected to a manifold vacuum source), a vacuum diaphragm motor (connected to the temperature sensor) and an inlet damper door (installed in the air cleaner inlet snorkel). Additional components of the system include an exhaust manifold mounted heat stove and a hot air duct running from the heat source to the underside of the air cleaner snorkel.

When the engine is cold, the temperature sensor allows vacuum to pass through to the vacuum diaphragm motor. The vacuum acting on the vacuum motor causes the motor to close the damper door, which prohibits the introduction of cold, outside air to the air cleaner. The intake vacuum then pulls hot air, generated by the exhaust manifold, through the hot air duct and into the air cleaner. This heated air supply helps to more effectively vaporize the fuel mixture entering the engine. As the engine warms, the temperature sensor bleeds off vacuum to the vacuum motor, allowing the damper door to gradually open.

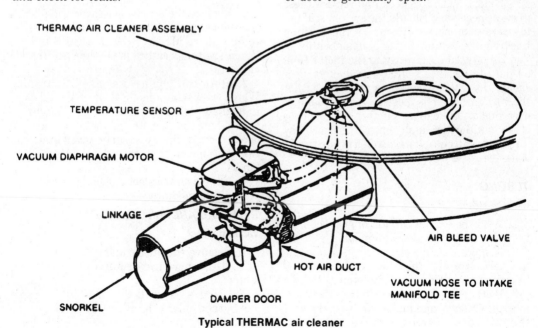

Typical THERMAC air cleaner

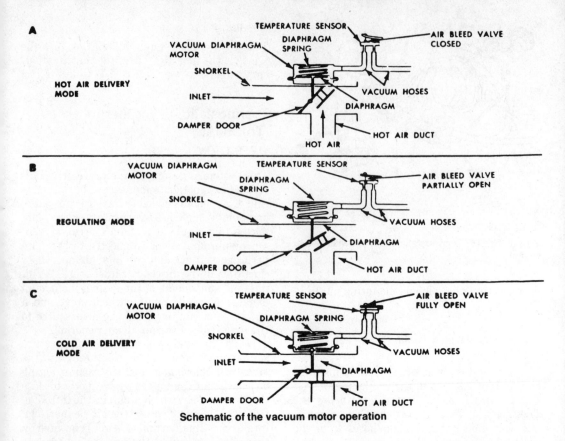

Schematic of the vacuum motor operation

The usual problems with this system are leaking vacuum lines (which prevent proper operation of the sensor and/or motor); torn or rusted through hot air ducts and/or rusted through heat stoves (either condition will allow the introduction of too much cold air to the air cleaner). Visually check and replace these items as necessary. Should the system still fail to operate properly, disconnect the vacuum line from the vacuum motor and apply at least 7 in.Hg of vacuum directly to the motor from an outside vacuum source; the damper door should close. If the door does not close, either the vacuum motor is defective or the damper door and/or linkage is binding. If the door closes, but then gradually opens (with a steady vacuum source), the vacuum motor is defective.

TESTING

Vacuum Motor

1. With the engine Off, disconnect the hose from the vacuum diaphragm motor.
2. Using a vacuum source, apply 7 in.Hg to the vacuum motor; the door should close and block off the outside air, completely.
3. Bend the vacuum hose (to trap the vacuum in the motor) and make sure that the door stays closed; if not, replace the vacuum motor.

NOTE: *Before replacing the vacuum motor (if defective), be sure to check the motor linkage, for binding.*
4. If the vacuum motor is OK and the problem still exists, check the temperature sensor.

Temperature Sensor

1. Remove the air cleaner cover and place a thermometer near the temperature sensor; the temperature MUST BE below 86°F (30°C). When the temperature is OK, replace the air cleaner.
2. Start the engine and allow it to idle. Watch the vacuum motor door, it should close immediately (if the engine is cool enough).
3. When the vacuum motor door starts to open, remove the air cleaner cover and read the thermometer, it should be about 131°F (55°C).
4. If the door does not respond correctly, replace the temperature sensor.

REMOVAL AND INSTALLATION

Vacuum Motor

1. Remove the air cleaner.
2. Disconnect the vacuum hose from the motor.
3. Using a ⅛″ drill bit, drill out the spot welds, then enlarge as necessary to remove the retaining strap.

4. Remove the retaining strap.

5. Lift up the motor and cock it to one side to unhook the motor linkage at the control damper assembly.

6. Install the new vacuum motor as follows:

a. Using a $^{7}/_{64}''$ drill bit, drill a hole in the snorkel tube at the center of the vacuum motor retaining strap.

b. Insert the vacuum motor linkage into the control damper assembly.

c. Use the motor retaining strap and a sheet metal screw to secure the retaining strap and motor to the snorkel tube.

NOTE: *Make sure the screw does not interfere with the operation of the damper assembly; shorten the screw, if necessary.*

Temperature Sensor

1. Remove the air cleaner.

2. Disconnect the hoses from the sensor.

3. Pry up the tabs on the sensor retaining clip and remove the clip and sensor from the air cleaner.

4. To install, reverse the removal procedures.

Air Injection Reactor (AIR)—4.3L Engine

OPERATION

The AIR system uses an air pump, a diverter valve (1985 Federal), an electric air control valve (1985–87 California), air check valves and a deceleration valve (1985).

On the Federal (1985) models, the diverter valve, directs the air flow from the AIR pump to the exhaust manifolds (during normal operation) and away from the exhaust manifolds (during engine deceleration).

On the California (1985–87) models, the Electronic Control Module (ECM) operates the electric air control valve which directs the air flow to the engine exhaust manifold ports or the the air cleaner. When the engine is cold or in wide-open throttle, the ECM energizes the solenoid to direct the air flow into the exhaust manifold check valves. When the engine warms, operating at high speeds or deceleration, the ECM de-energizes the electric air control valve, changing the air flow from the exhaust manifold to the air cleaner. The diversion of the air flow to the air cleaner acts as a silencer.

A check valve, on each side of the engine, prevents back flow of the exhaust gases into the air pump, if there is an exhaust backfire or pump drive belt failure.

The deceleration valve helps to prevent backfiring during periods of high vacuum (deceleration) by allowing large quantities of air to flow into the intake manifold.

TESTING

Air Injection Pump

1. Check for proper drive belt tension.

2. Make sure that the pump is not seized.

3. Remove the air hoses, accelerate the engine to 1,500 rpm and check for air flow from the hose outlets.

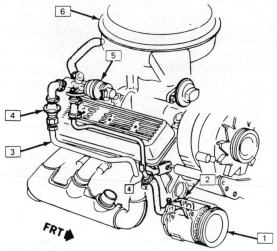
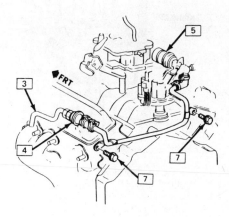

1. Air pump
2. Adapter and seal—tighten screws to 25 N·m (18 ft. lbs)
3. Air injection pipe—tighten nuts to 28 N·m (20 ft. lbs.)
4. Check valve—tighten to 85 N·m (26 ft. lbs.)
5. Diverter valve or EAC valve
6. Air cleaner
7. Bolt—tighten to 34 N·m (25 ft. lbs.)

View of the Air Injection Reaction System—4.3L engine

Check Valves

1. Disconnect the hose from the valve and unscrew the valve from the injection manifold assembly.

2. Blow into each side of the valve: air

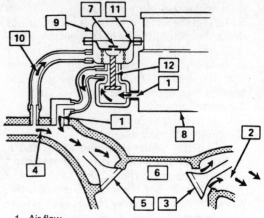

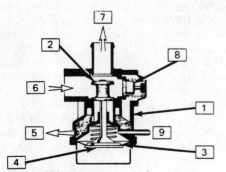

1. Standard diverter valve
2. Metering valve
3. Diaphragm
4. Timing valve
5. Vent
6. Pump air inlet
7. Exhaust port outlet
8. Relief valve
9. Vacuum signal tube

Cross-sectional view of the diverter valve—4.3L engine 1985

1. Air flow
2. Exhaust gas
3. Exhaust valve
4. Intake flow
5. Intake valve
6. Combustion chamber
7. Vacuum bleed valve
8. Air cleaner
9. Deceleration valve
10. Manifold vacuum
11. Diaphragm
12. Valve

Cross-sectional view of the deceleration valve—4.3L engine (185)

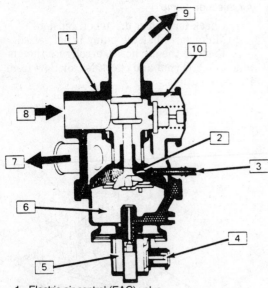

1. Electric air control (EAC) valve
2. Decel timing assembly
3. Manifold vacuum signal tube
4. Electrical terminal
5. EAC solenoid
6. Decel timing chamber
7. Air to air cleaner
8. Air from air pump
9. Air to exhaust ports or manifold
10. Pressure relief assembly

Cross-sectional view of the electric air control valve—4.3L engine (1986–87)

should pass only in one direction; if air passes through the valve in both directions, replace the valve. Check each valve in the same manner.

Diverter Valve

The diverter valve will act like the electric air control valve, except, that it is not controlled by an ECM. Air is directed to the exhaust ports, unless there is a sudden rise of manifold vacuum due to throttle deceleration.

Electric Air Control Valve

1. Perform the following inspection checks:
a. The engine coolant must be at operating temperatures.
b. Disconnect the air cleaner-to-electric air control valve hose.
c. Start the engine and operate it at idle (under 2000 rpm). Within the first 5 seconds, the air should be directed to the exhaust ports and then change to the air cleaner.
d. If the system checks OK, the electric air control valve is working.

2. If inspections in Step 1 were not satisfactory, perform the following procedures:
a. Turn the engine Off but allow the ignition switch to remain On.
b. Reconnect the air cleaner-to-electric air control valve hose.

c. Disconnect the electrical connector from the electric air control valve solenoid and connect a test light between the harness connector terminals.

d. If the test light is On, check for a ground between the solenoid-to-ECM wire (Circuit 436) or replace the ECM (if not grounded).

3. If the test light is Off, perform the following procedures:

a. Using a jumper wire, connect it between the ECM diagnostic (C2) terminal and ground.

b. If the test light turns On, replace the electric air control valve.

c. Remove the jumper wire.

4. If the test light still remains Off, perform the following procedures:

a. Connect one probe of the test light to terminal **A** of the solenoid's connector and the other probe to a ground.

b. If the light still remains Off, check for a blown fuse or an broken ignition (pink) wire.

5. If the light turns On, check for the following problems:

a. A broken solenoid-to-ECM (Circuit 436) wire or check the solenoid's resistance of the air control valve.

b. If the resistance of the solenoid is above 20Ω, replace the ECM.

c. If the resistance of the solenoid is below 20Ω, replace the electric air control valve and the ECM.

Deceleration Valve

1. Install a tachometer to the engine and allow the engine to establish normal operating temperatures.

2. Remove the air cleaner and plug the air cleaner vacuum hose(s).

3. Operate the engine at idle speed, then remove the deceleration valve-to-intake manifold (diaphragm) hose.

4. Reconnect the hose and listen for a noticeable air flow (hiss) through the air cleaner-to-deceleration valve hose; there should also be a noticeable drop in idle speed.

5. If the air flow does not continue for at least one second or the engine speed does not drop, check the hoses (of the deceleration valve) for restrictions or leaks.

6. If no restrictions are found, replace the deceleration valve.

REMOVAL AND INSTALLATION

Air Injection Pump

1. Compress the drive belt to keep the pump pulley from turning, then loosen the pump pulley bolts.

2. Loosen the pump-to-mounting brackets, release the tension on the drive belt and remove the drive belt.

3. Unscrew the mounting bolts and then remove the pump pulley.

4. If necessary, use a pair of needle nose pliers to pull the fan filter from the hub.

5. Remove the hoses, the vacuum lines, the electrical connectors (if equipped) and the air control or diverter valve.

6. Unscrew the pump mounting bolts and then remove the pump.

7. To install, reverse the removal procedures. Torque the pump pulley bolts to 90 in.lb. and the pump-to-bracket nuts/bolts to 25 ft.lb. Adjust the drive belt tension after installation.

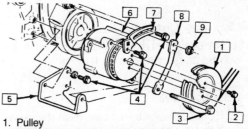

1. Pulley
2. Bolt—tighten to 10 N·m (90 in. lbs.)
3. Bolt—tighten to 45 N·m (32 ft. lbs.)
4. Bolt—tighten to 84 N·m (25 ft. lbs.)
5. Support
6. Air pump
7. Bracket
8. Brace
9. Nut—tighten to 34 N·m (25 ft. lbs.)

Exploded view of the air pump assembly—4.3L engine

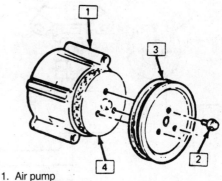

1. Air pump
2. Pulley bolt tighten to 10 N·m (90 in. lbs.)
3. Pulley
4. Filter fan

Removing the air filter from the air pump—4.3L engine

Check Valve(s)

1. Remove the clamp and disconnect the hose from the valve.

2. Unscrew the valve from the air injection pipe.

3. To test the valve(s), air should pass only in one direction.

4. To install, reverse the removal procedures.

Air Control Valve

1. Disconnect the negative battery cable.

2. Disconnect the air inlet and outlet hoses from the valve.

3. Disconnect the electrical connector (if equipped) and the vacuum hoses at the valve. Remove the electric air control or the diverter valve.

4. To install, reverse the removal procedures. For California models, check the system operation.

Air Switching Valve

The switching valve is replaced in basically the same manner as the control valve.

Deceleration Valve

1. Remove the vacuum hoses from the valve.

2. Remove the deceleration valve-to-engine bracket screws.

3. Remove the deceleration valve.

4. To install, reverse the removal procedures. Torque the deceleration valve-to-engine bracket screws to 30 in.lb.

1. Bracket
2. Deceleration valve
3. Bolt—tighten to 3.5 N·m (30 in. lbs.)

Removing the deceleration valve—4.3L engine

Electronic Spark Timing (EST) System

The EST system does not have vacuum or mechanical spark advance mechanisms, as these functions are controlled electronically by the distributor module assembly and the ECM of the computer emissions system.

The purpose of the EST system is to precisely adjust the spark timing according to specific engine operating conditions, as sensed by the various monitoring devices of the computer emissions system.

Because the EST system is directly tied into the computer emissions system, service, testing and repair should be performed by a qualified, professional technician.

For further EST system information, re-

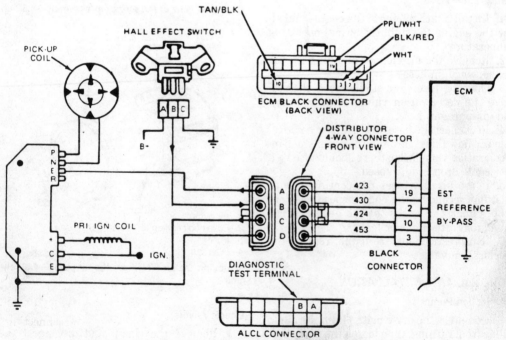

Schematic of the electronic spark timing system—2.5L engine (1985)

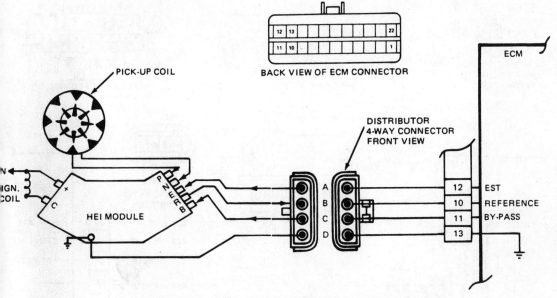

Schematic of the electronic spark timing system—4.3L engine (1985)

fer to the Electronic Spark Control (ESC) System in this section.

Electronic Spark Control (ESC) System

OPERATION

Since varying octane levels of gasoline can cause detonation (spark knock) in an engine, causing piston and ring rattle or vibration, the ESC system has been added to the engine to remedy the knocking situation by retarding the spark timing by as much as 20°; this allows the engine to maximize the spark advance to improve the fuel economy and driveability.

A sensor is mounted on the left side of the block (near the cylinders) to detect the knock and send the information to the Electronic

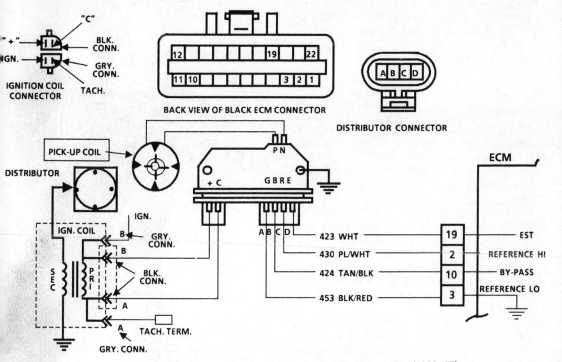

Schematic of the electronic spark timing system—2.5L engine (1986–87)

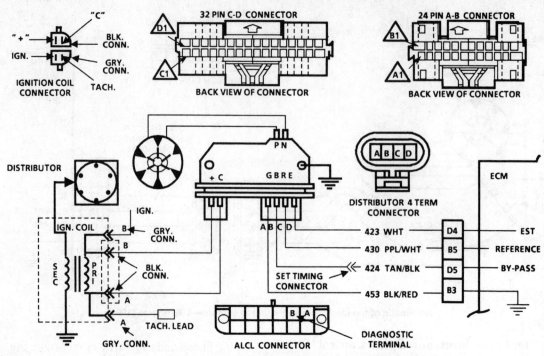

Schematic of the electronic spark timing system—4.3L engine (1986–87)

Spark Control (ESC) module. The ESC module sends a signal to the Electronic Control Module (ECM) which adjusts the Electronic Spark Timing (EST) to reduce the spark knock. If no signal is received from the ESC sensor, the ECM provides normal spark advance.

Loss of the signal, through a bad ESC sensor, ESC module or a poor ground, will cause the engine to operate sluggishly and cause a Code 43 (to be set).

View of the knock sensor—4.3L engine

TESTING

1. With the engine operating at 1,500 rpm, the transmission in Neutral or Park, tap on the engine block in the area of the knock sensor, the engine rpm should drop.

NOTE: *If the speed does not drop, the timing is not retarding or it is retarded all of the time.*

2. Disconnect the ESC module connector (the engine rpm should drop); after 4 seconds, the "CHECK ENGINE" light should turn ON and the Code 43 will be stored.

3. Using a digital voltmeter (set on the low AC scale), check the knock sensor voltage; low or no voltage will indicate an open circuit at terminal **E** or a bad sensor.

4. Check the CHECK ENGINE light and the Code 43 in the ESC system. If no light turns ON, the ECM is not retarding the engine spark for there may be voltage on the **L** (1985)

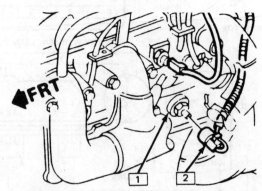

1. ESC knock sensor
2. Harness connector

Location of the knock sensor—4.3L engine

or **B7** (1986–87) terminal or the ECM may be faulty, replace the ECM.

5. Disconnect the electrical connector from the knock sensor; if the rpm increases with the

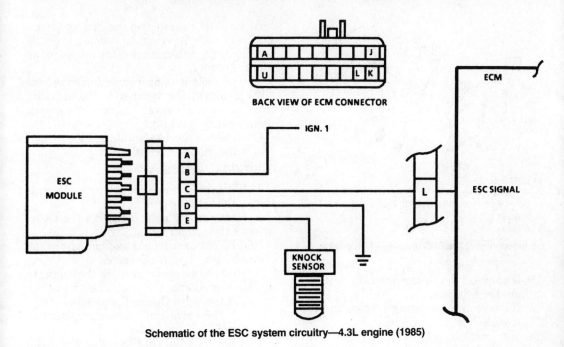

Schematic of the ESC system circuitry—4.3L engine (1985)

sensor disconnected, the sensor is bad and should be replaced.

REMOVAL AND INSTALLATION

Knock Sensor

1. Disconnect the negative battery cable.
2. Disconnect the electrical harness connector from the knock sensor.

3. Remove the knock sensor from the engine block.
4. To install, apply teflon tape to the threads and reverse the removal procedures.

ESC Module

The ESC module is located at the top rear of the engine.

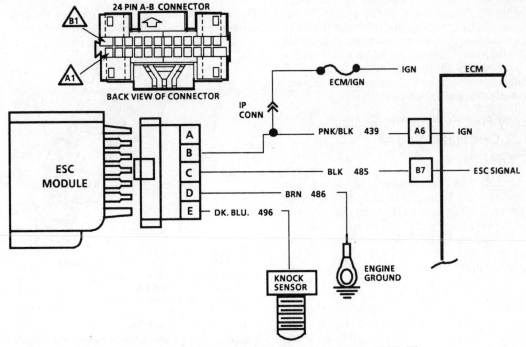

Schematic of the ESC system circuitry—4.3L engine (1986–87)

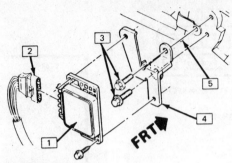

1. ESC module
2. Harness connector
3. Bolt—tighten to 34 N·m (25 ft. lbs.)
4. Bracket
5. Air pipe

Exploded view of the ESC module—4.3L engine

1. Disconnect the electrical harness connector from the ESC module.
2. Remove the mounting screws and the ESC module from the vehicle.
3. To install, reverse the removal procedures.

Transmission Converter Clutch (TCC) System

All vehicles equipped with an automatic transmission use the TCC system. The ECM controls the converter by means of a solenoid mounted in the outdrive housing of the transmission. When the vehicle speed reaches a certain level, the ECM energizes the solenoid and allows the torque converter to mechanically couple the transmission to the engine. When the operating conditions indicate that the transmission should operate as a normal fluid coupled transmission, the ECM will de-energize the solenoid. Depressing the brake pedal will also return the transmission to normal automatic operation.

Early Fuel Evaporation System— 4.3L Carbureted Engine

OPERATION

The early fuel evaporation system provides a rapid heating source to the engine induction system during cold driveaway conditions, thus, providing quick fuel evaporation and more uniform fuel distribution. When reducing the length of carburetor choking time, the exhaust emissions are also reduced.

The system consists of a valve and a vacuum actuator which increases the exhaust gas flow under the intake manifold during cold operation. The valve, located under the left exhaust manifold, is operated by a vacuum actuator which is controlled by a Thermal Vacuum

Switch (TVS), mounted on the front of the intake manifold. Applying vacuum to the actuator, closes the valve, causing the intake manifold to heat up.

As the coolant temperature increases, the TVS turns Off the vacuum to the actuator, thereby, causing the valve to open; the engine now operates normally.

Operational checks should be made at normal maintenance intervals.

TESTING

1. With the engine Cold, observe the position of the actuator arm.
2. Start the engine and observe the movement of the actuator arm.
NOTE: *The arm should move in toward the diaphragm, to close the valve.*
3. With the valve closed, allow the engine to warm, then observe the position of the valve:
    a. If the valve Opens, the system is OK.
    b. If the valve stays Closed, replace the Thermal Vacuum Switch (TVS).
4. If the valve did not Close, disconnect the vacuum hose from the valve, start the engine (engine running Cold) and check the vacuum:
    a. If no vacuum is felt, replace the TVS.
    b. If vacuum is felt, try to move the valve arm to check for freeness. If the arm moves freely, replace the actuator valve; if the arm does not move, lubricate it or replace the actuator valve.

REMOVAL AND INSTALLATION

Actuator Valve

The actuator valve is located between the left exhaust manifold and the exhaust pipe.

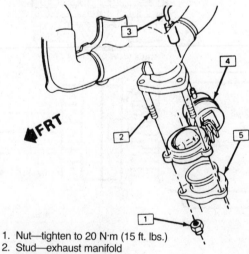

1. Nut—tighten to 20 N·m (15 ft. lbs.)
2. Stud—exhaust manifold
3. Manifold vacuum pipe
4. Valve and actuator
5. Left hand exhaust manifold

Exploded view of the actuator valve—4.3L engine (1985)

1. Remove the vacuum hose from the actuator of the valve.

2. Raise and support the vehicle on jackstands.

3. Remove the exhaust pipe-to-manifold nuts and the tension springs.

4. Remove the lower right hand exhaust (crossover) pipe and seal.

NOTE: *It may not be necessary to remove the crossover pipe entirely.*

5. Remove the actuator valve.

6. Inspect the actuator valve and replace it, if necessary.

7. To install, use new seals, gaskets and reverse the removal procedures. Torque the exhaust manifold-to-exhaust pipe nuts to 15 ft.lb.

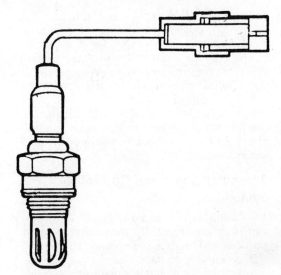

View of the oxygen sensor

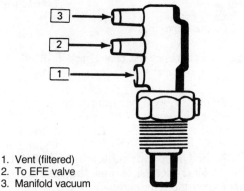

1. Vent (filtered)
2. To EFE valve
3. Manifold vacuum

View of the thermal vacuum switch—4.3L engine (1985)

Thermal Vacuum Switch (TVS)

The TVS is located on the front of the engine coolant outlet housing.

1. Place a catch pan under the radiator, open the drain cock and drain the coolant to a level below the engine coolant housing.

2. Remove the vacuum hoses from the TVS ports.

3. Remove the TVS from the engine coolant housing.

NOTE: *If replacing the TVS, refer to the calibration number stamped on the base.*

4. To install, apply soft setting sealant to the male threads of the TVS and reverse the removal procedures. Torque the TVS-to-engine coolant housing to 120 in.lb. Refill the cooling system. Start the engine, run the engine to normal operating temperatures and check the TVS operation.

NOTE: *When applying sealant to the TVS, be sure not to coat the sensor end.*

Oxygen Sensor

The oxygen sensor protrudes into the exhaust stream and monitors the oxygen content of the exhaust gases. The difference between the oxygen content of the exhaust gases and that of the outside air generates a voltage signal to the ECM. The ECM monitors this voltage and, depending upon the value of the signal received, issues a command to adjust for a rich or a lean condition.

No attempt should ever be made to measure the voltage output of the sensor. The current drain of any conventional voltmeter would be such that it would permanently damage the sensor. No jumpers, test leads or any other electrical connections should ever be made to the sensor. Use these tools ONLY on the ECM side of the wiring harness connector AFTER disconnecting it from the sensor.

REMOVAL AND INSTALLATION

The oxygen sensor must be replaced every 30,000 miles (48,000 km). The sensor may be difficult to remove when the engine temperature is below 120°F (48°C). Excessive removal force may damage the threads in the exhaust manifold or pipe; follow the removal procedure carefully.

1. Locate the oxygen sensor.

NOTE: *It protrudes from the exhaust manifold on the left side of engine or at the Y-intersection of the exhaust pipe (4.3L – 1985), it looks somewhat like a spark plug.*

2. Disconnect the electrical connector from the oxygen sensor.

3. Spray a commercial solvent onto the sensor threads and allow it to soak in for at least five minutes.

4. Carefully unscrew and remove the sensor.

5. To install, first coat the new sensor's

threads with GM anti-sieze compound No. 5613695 or equivalent. This is not a conventional anti-seize paste. The use of a regular compound may electrically insulate the sensor, rendering it inoperative. You must coat the threads with an electrically conductive anti-seize compound.

6. Torque the sensor to 30 ft.lb. (42 Nm). Be careful not to damage the electrical pigtail; check the sensor boot for proper fit and installation.

Computer Command Control (CCC) System

The Computer Command Control (CCC) System is an electronically controlled exhaust emission system that can monitor and control a large number of interrelated emission control systems. It can monitor many engine/vehicle operating conditions and then use the information to control the various engine related systems. The system is thereby making constant adjustments to maintain good vehicle performance under all normal driving conditions while at the same time allowing the catalytic converter to effectively control the emissions of HC, CO and NOx.

OPERATION

Electronic Control Module (ECM)

The Electronic Control Module (ECM) is the control center of the fuel control system. It con-

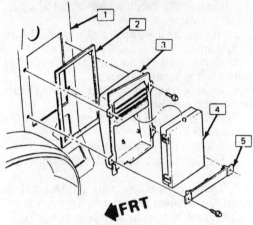

1. Right hand plenum side panel
2. Sealer
3. Housing assembly
4. Electronic control module
5. Retainer

Location of the electronic control module (ECM)

stantly monitors various information from the sensors and controls the systems that affect the vehicle performance. The ECM has two parts: A Controller (the ECM without the PROM) and a separate calibrator (the PROM). The ECM is located behind the instrument panel's console trim plate.

Programmable Read Only Memory (PROM)

To allow the Controller to be used in many different vehicles, a device called a Calibrator or Programmable Read Only Memory (PROM) is used. The PROM which is located inside the ECM, stores information such as: the vehicle's weight, engine, transmission, axle ratio and many other specifications. Since the PROM stores specific information, it is important that the correct one be used in the right vehicle.

NOTE: *Due to the intricacy of the system, it is advised to have a qualified mechanic perform any testing, adjusting or replacement of the system components.*

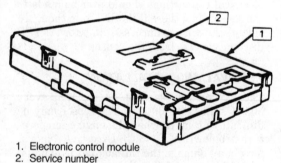

1. Electronic control module
2. Service number

View of the electronic control module (ECM)

Throttle Position Sensor (TPS)

The throttle position sensor is mounted on the throttle body or carburetor and is used to supply throttle position information to the ECM. The ECM memory stores an average of operating conditions with the ideal air/fuel ratios for each of these conditions. When the ECM receives a signal that indicates throttle position change, it immediately shifts to the last remembered set of operating conditions that resulted in an ideal air/fuel ratio control. The

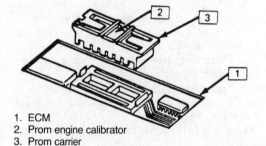

1. ECM
2. Prom engine calibrator
3. Prom carrier

Removing the PROM from the ECM

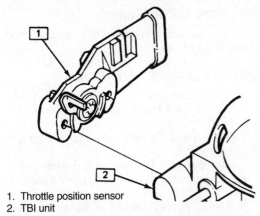

1. Throttle position sensor
2. TBI unit

View of the throttle position sensor (TPS)—2.5L engine

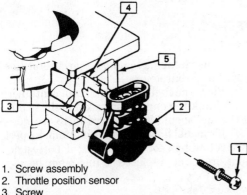

1. Screw assembly
2. Throttle position sensor
3. Screw
4. Lever
5. Throttle body assembly

View of the throttle position sensor (TPS)—4.3L engine

memory is continually being updated during normal operations.

TESTING

The throttle position sensor is non-adjustable but a test should be performed ONLY when throttle body parts have been replaced or AFTER the minimum idle speed has been adjusted.

NOTE: *The following procedure requires the use of the Digital Voltmeter tool No. J-29125-A or equivalent.*

1. Using the Digital Voltmeter tool No. J-29125-A or equivalent, set it on the 0–5.0V scale, then connect the probes to the center terminal **B** and the outside terminal **C** (2.5L engine) or **A** (4.3L engine).

NOTE: *To attach probes to the TPS electrical connector, disconnect the TPS electrical connector, install thin wires into the sockets and reconnect the connector.*

2. Turn the ignition switch On (engine stopped).

3. The output voltage should be 1.25V. If the voltage is more that 1.25V, replace the TPS.

4. Remove the voltmeter and the jumper wires.

REMOVAL AND INSTALLATION

1. Remove the air cleaner.

2. Disconnect the electrical connector from the throttle position sensor (TPS).

3. Remove the TPS mounting screws, the lockwashers and the retainers.

4. Remove the TPS sensor.

5. To install, make sure that the throttle valve is in the closed position, then install the TPS sensor.

NOTE: *Make sure that the TPS pickup lever is located ABOVE the tang on the throttle actuator lever.*

6. To complete the installation, lubricate the mounting screws with Loctite® (thread locking compound) No. 262 or equivalent, then reverse the removal procedures.

Manifold Pressure Sensor (MAP)

The manifold pressure sensors, used ONLY on fuel injected engines, are located on the air cleaner side.

OPERATION

The manifold pressure sensor measures the pressure (load and speed) changes in the intake manifold, then converts these changes into voltage output. The voltage changes are sent to the ECM, which analyzes the information to alter the fuel delivery and the ignition timing.

At closed throttle, the MAP sensor produces relatively low MAP output, while at wide-open throttle, it would produce high output. When the pressure inside the intake manifold is equal to the outside pressure, the MAP sensor will produce high output voltage.

NOTE: *The manifold absolute pressure is opposite what would measure on a vacuum gauge.*

This sensor is also used to measure the barometric pressure (under certain conditions) to adjust for differences in altitude.

The failure of the MAP sensor circuit should set a Code 33 or 34.

TESTING

NOTE: *The following procedure requires the use of a Voltmeter and a Vacuum pump.*

1. Turn the ignition switch On (engine stopped).

2. Using a voltmeter, set it on the 0–10.0V scale, then attach the probes to the MAP sen-

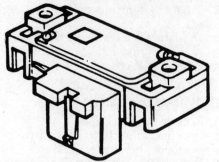

View of the manifold absolute pressure (MAP)–fuel injection

ALTITUDE	VOLTAGE RANGE
BELOW 1,000	3.8 - 5.5V
1,000 - 2000	3.6 - 5.3V
3,000 - 4,000	3.3 - 5.0V
4,000 - 5,000	3.2 - 4.8V
5,000 - 6,000	3.0 - 4.6V
6,000 - 7,000'	2.9 - 4.5V
7,000 - 8,000'	2.8 - 4.3V
8,000 - 9,000	2.6 - 4.2V
9,000 - 10,000'	2.5 - 4.0V

Manifold absolute pressure (MAP) chart

sor terminals **A** and **B**. Compare the acquired voltage to the voltage/altitude chart for the correct values; if not correct, replace the sensor.

3. Using a vacuum pump, apply 10 in.Hg to the MAP sensor and note the change; it should be 1.2–2.3V less than the initial voltage, (if not) replace the sensor.

4. If no trouble is found, check the vacuum hose for leakage or restriction. If replacing the hose, be sure to use one specifically for MAP sensor use.

REMOVAL AND INSTALLATION

1. Remove the sensor-to-throttle body vacuum hose.

2. Disconnect the sensor's electrical connector.

3. Remove the MAP sensor from the air cleaner mounting bracket.

4. To install, reverse the removal procedures.

CARBURETED FUEL SYSTEM

Only the 4.3L engine, for 1985, use a carburetor.

Mechanical Fuel Pump

The mechanical fuel pump is located on the right front of the engine.

REMOVAL AND INSTALLATION

1. Disconnect the fuel inlet hose from the fuel pump and the vapor return hose (if equipped).

2. Disconnect the fuel outlet hose from the fuel pump.

3. Remove the fuel pump-to-engine bolts, the fuel pump, the pushrod, the gasket and the mounting plate.

4. Using a putty knife, clean the gasket mounting surfaces.

5. To install, use a new gasket and reverse the removal procedures. Start the engine and check for fuel leaks.

TESTING

Flow Test

1. Remove the fuel pump-to-carburetor line from the carburetor.

2. Place the fuel line into a clean container.

3. Crank the engine; approximately ½ pint of the fuel should be delivered in 15 seconds.

4. If the fuel flow is below minimum, inspect the fuel system for restrictions; if no restrictions are found, replace the fuel pump.

Pressure Test

NOTE: *The following procedure requires the use of a GM Fuel Pressure Gauge tool No. J-29658-A or equivalent.*

1. Remove the air cleaner, then disconnect and plug the THERMAC vacuum port on the carburetor.

2. Place a rag (to catch excess fuel) under the fuel line-to-carburetor connection. Disconnect the fuel line from the carburetor.

NOTE: *When disconnecting the fuel line, use a back-up wrench to hold the fuel nut on the carburetor.*

3. Using a GM Fuel Pressure Gauge tool No. J-29658-A or equivalent, install it into the fuel line.

4. Start the engine and observe the fuel pressure, it should be 4–6.5 psi.

NOTE: *If the fuel pressure does not meet specifications, inspect the fuel system for restrictions or replace the fuel pump.*

5. Stop the engine, relieve the fuel pressure and remove the GM Fuel Pressure Gauge tool No. J-29658-A or equivalent.

6. Install a new fuel line-to-carburetor O-ring or washer and reverse the removal procedures. Unplug the THERMAC vacuum port. Start the engine and check for fuel leaks.

Carburetor

ADJUSTMENTS

Idle Speed and Mixture Adjustments

Refer to the Idle Speed and Mixture Adjustment procedures in Chapter 2 and adjust the idle speed and fuel mixture.

Float and Fuel Level Adjustment

NOTE: *The following procedure requires the use of the GM Float Gauge tool No. J-34935, BT-8420-A or equivalent.*

1. Remove the air cleaner from the carburetor.

2. With the engine idling and the choke plate in the Wide-Open position, insert the GM Float Gauge tool No. J-34935, BT-8420-A or equivalent, into the vent hole (slot) of the air horn; allow the gauge to float freely.

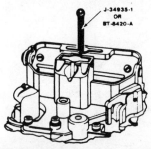

Using the GM Float Gauge tool No. J-34935-1, BT-8420-A or equivalent, to check the float level

NOTE: *DO NOT press down on the gauge, for flooding or float damage may occur.*

3. Observe the mark (on the gauge) that aligns with the top of the air horn; the float setting should be within ± $\frac{1}{16}$" (1.5mm) of the specifications.

NOTE: *Incorrect fuel pressure will adversely affect the fuel level.*

4. If the float level is not correct, perform the following procedures:

a. Turn the ignition switch Off.

b. Disconnect the fuel line, the throttle linkage and/or any electrical connectors from the top of the carburetor (air horn).

c. Remove the air horn-to-fuel bowl screws. Lift the air horn from the fuel bowl and discard the gasket.

d. Bend the float tang (at the needle valve) to the correct specifications.

e. To install the air horn, use a new fuel bowl gasket, install the air horn and the air horn-to-fuel bowl screws.

f. Install the throttle linkage and the fuel line.

5. To complete the installation, install the air cleaner. Start the engine and check for fuel leaks.

Air Valve Spring Adjustment

1. Using a $\frac{3}{32}$" Allen wrench, loosen the air valve spring lock screw.

2. Turning the tension adjusting screw counterclockwise, open the air valve part way.

3. Turning the tension adjusting screw clockwise, close the air valve, then turn it an additional number of specified turns (see carburetor chart).

4. Tighten the lock screw, then apply Lithium grease to the spring-to-lever contact area.

Choke Coil Lever Adjustment

1. Drill out and remove the choke coil housing cover rivets. Retain the choke housing cov-

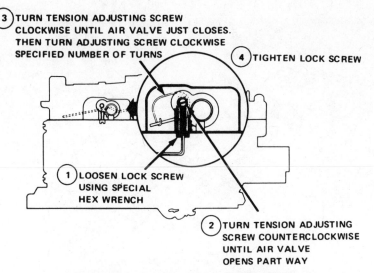

Adjusting the air valve spring—M4ME, E4ME

Exploded view of the E4ME carburetor

er, then remove the thermostatic cover and coil assembly from the choke housing.

2. Place the fast idle cam follower on the high step of the fast idle cam.

3. Close the choke valve by pushing up on the thermostatic coil tang (counterclockwise).

4. Insert a drill or gauge, of the specified size, into the hole in the choke housing. The lower edge of the choke lever should be just touching the side of the gauge.

5. If the choke lever is not touching the side

of the gauge, bend the choke rod until you see that it does.

Fast Idle Cam (Choke Rod) Adjustment

NOTE: *The following procedure requires the use of the GM Valve Angle Gauge tool No. J-26701, BT-7704 or equivalent.*

1. Using a rubber band, attach it between the green tang of the intermediate choke shaft and the air horn housing.

1. Gasket—air cleaner	236. Hinge pin—float
5. Gasket—flange	237. Float
10. Air horn assembly	238. Pull clip—float needle
11. Rivet—cover attaching	239. Needle—float
12. Cover—air bleed valve	240. Seat—float needle
15. Air bleed valve assembly	241. Gasket—float needle seat
16. O-ring—air bleed valve—lower	250. Plug—pump discharge (retainer)
17. O-ring—air bleed valve—upper	251. Ball—pump discharge
30. Screw—secondary metering rod holder attaching	252. Baffle—pump well
31. Holder—secondary metering rod	255. Primary metering jet assembly
32. Rod—secondary metering	315. Hose—secondary side (rear) vacuum break
35. Lever—choke	316. Tee—secondary side (rear) vacuum break
36. Screw—choke lever attaching	320. Vacuum break assembly—secondary side (rear)
40. Retainer—pump link	321. Screw—secondary side (rear) vacuum break assembly attaching
41. Lever—pump	322. Link—secondary side (rear) vacuum break to choke
42. Pin—pump lever hinge	330. Rivet—choke cover attaching
45. Screw assembly—air horn to throttle body	331. Retainer—choke cover
46. Screw assembly—air horn to float bowl	335. Electric choke cover and stat assembly
47. Screw—air horn to float bowl (countersunk)	340. Choke housing assembly
50. Baffle—air horn	341. Screw and washer assembly—choke housing to float bowl
55. Vacuum break assembly—primary side (front)	345. Screw—choke stat lever attaching
56. Screw—primary side (front) vacuum break assembly attaching	348. Lever—choke stat
57. Hose—primary side (front) vacuum break	350. Intermediate choke shaft, lever and link assembly
58. Link—primary side vacuum break—air valve lever	352. Fast idle cam assembly
60. Plunger—sensor actuator	354. Lever—intermediate choke
61. Plug—TPS adjusting screw	356. Link—choke
62. Screw—TPS adjusting	360. Lever—secondary throttle lockout
65. Retainer—TPS seal	364. Seal—intermediate choke shaft
66. Seal—TPS plunger	370. Nut—fuel inlet
67. Retainer—pump stem seal	372. Gasket—fuel inlet nut
68. Seal—pump stem	375. Filter—fuel inlet
70. Plug—solenoid adjusting screw	377. Spring—fuel filter
71. Plug—solenoid stop screw	380. Screw—throttle stop
72. Screw—solenoid stop (rich mixture)	381. Spring—throttle stop screw
73. Spring—rich authority adjusting	400. Throttle body assembly
201. Gasket—air horn to float bowl	401. Gasket—float bowl to throttle body
205. Pump assembly	405. Screw assembly—float bowl to throttle body
206. Spring—pump return	410. Link—pump
210. Sensor—throttle position (TPS)	420. Needle—idle mixture
211. Spring—sensor adjusting	421. Spring—idle mixture needle
213. Rod—primary metering	422. Plug—idle mixture needle
215. Plunger—solenoid	425. Screw—fast idle adjusting
217. Spring—primary metering rod	426. Spring—fast idle adjusting screw
221. Screw—solenoid connector attaching	500. Solenoid and bracket assembly
222. Gasket—solenoid connector to air horn	501. Screw—bracket attaching
225. Mixture control solenoid assembly	505. Bracket—solenoid
226. Screw—solenoid adjusting (lean mixture)	510. Throttle kicker assembly
227. Stop—rich limit	511. Bracket—throttle kicker
228. Spring—solenoid adjusting screw	512. Nut—throttle kicker assembly attaching
229. Spring—solenoid return	513. Washer—tab locking
234. Insert—aneroid cavity	515. Idle speed control assembly
235. Insert—float bowl	

Exploded view of the E4ME carburetor

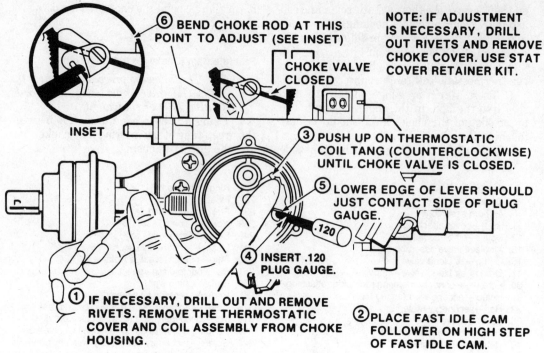

⑥ BEND CHOKE ROD AT THIS POINT TO ADJUST (SEE INSET)

INSET

NOTE: IF ADJUSTMENT IS NECESSARY, DRILL OUT RIVETS AND REMOVE CHOKE COVER. USE STAT COVER RETAINER KIT.

CHOKE VALVE CLOSED

③ PUSH UP ON THERMOSTATIC COIL TANG (COUNTERCLOCKWISE) UNTIL CHOKE VALVE IS CLOSED.

⑤ LOWER EDGE OF LEVER SHOULD JUST CONTACT SIDE OF PLUG GAUGE.

.120

④ INSERT .120 PLUG GAUGE.

① IF NECESSARY, DRILL OUT AND REMOVE RIVETS. REMOVE THE THERMOSTATIC COVER AND COIL ASSEMBLY FROM CHOKE HOUSING.

② PLACE FAST IDLE CAM FOLLOWER ON HIGH STEP OF FAST IDLE CAM.

Adjusting the choke coil lever—E4ME carburetor

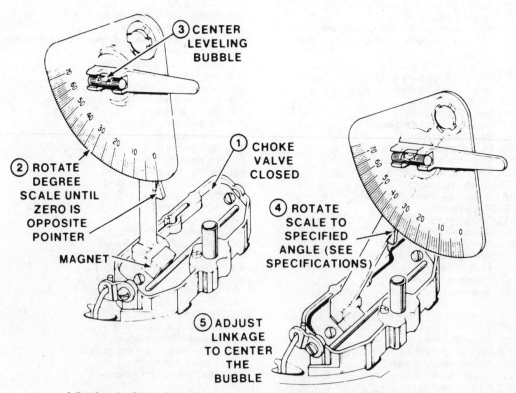

③ CENTER LEVELING BUBBLE

② ROTATE DEGREE SCALE UNTIL ZERO IS OPPOSITE POINTER

MAGNET

① CHOKE VALVE CLOSED

④ ROTATE SCALE TO SPECIFIED ANGLE (SEE SPECIFICATIONS)

⑤ ADJUST LINKAGE TO CENTER THE BUBBLE

Adjusting the Choke Valve Angle Gauge tool No. J-26701, BT-7704 or equivalent.

(1) ATTACH RUBBER BAND TO GREEN
TANG OF INTERMEDIATE CHOKE
SHAFT

(2) OPEN THROTTLE TO ALLOW CHOKE
VALVE TO CLOSE

(3) SET UP ANGLE GAGE AND SET
ANGLE TO SPECIFICATIONS

(4) PLACE CAM FOLLOWER ON
SECOND STEP OF CAM, AGAINST
RISE OF HIGH STEP. IF CAM
FOLLOWER DOES NOT CONTACT
CAM, TURN IN FAST IDLE SPEED
SCREW ADDITIONAL TURN(S).
NOTICE: FINAL FAST IDLE SPEED
ADJUSTMENT MUST BE PERFORMED
ACCORDING TO UNDER-HOOD
EMISSION CONTROL INFORMATION
LABEL.

(5) ADJUST BY BENDING TANG OF FAST
IDLE CAM UNTIL BUBBLE IS CEN-
TERED.

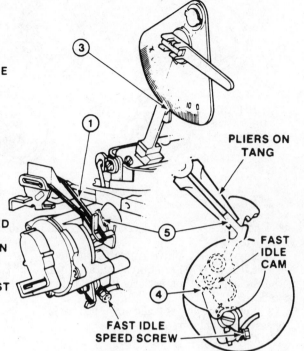

Fast idle cam (choke rod) adjustment—E4ME carburetor

(1) ATTACH RUBBER BAND TO GREEN
TANG OF INTERMEDIATE CHOKE
SHAFT

(2) OPEN THROTTLE TO ALLOW CHOKE
VALVE TO CLOSE

(3) SET UP ANGLE GAGE AND SET TO
SPECIFICATION

(4) RETRACT VACUUM BREAK PLUNGER
USING VACUUM SOURCE, AT LEAST
18" HG. PLUG AIR BLEED HOLES
WHERE APPLICABLE

ON QUADRAJETS, AIR VALVE ROD
MUST NOT RESTRICT PLUNGER
FROM RETRACTING FULLY. IF
NECESSARY, BEND ROD (SEE
ARROW) TO PERMIT FULL PLUNGER
TRAVEL. FINAL ROD CLEARANCE
MUST BE SET AFTER VACUUM
BREAK SETTING HAS BEEN MADE.

(5) WITH AT LEAST 18" HG STILL
APPLIED, ADJUST SCREW TO
CENTER BUBBLE

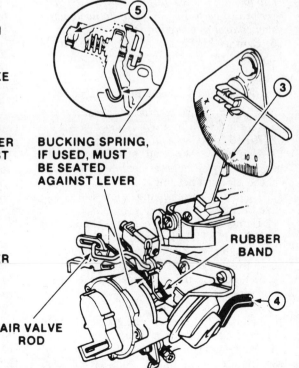

Front (primary-side) vacuum break adjustment—E4ME carburetor

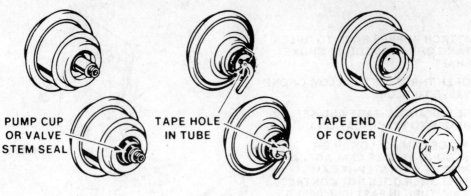

PUMP CUP
OR VALVE
STEM SEAL

TAPE HOLE
IN TUBE

TAPE END
OF COVER

Plugging the air bleed holes of the vacuum break—E4ME carburetor

2. Open the throttle and allow the choke valve to close.

3. Using the GM Valve Angle Gauge tool No. J-26701, BT-7704 or equivalent, attach it to the choke plate, then perform the following procedures:

    a. Rotate the degree scale until the zero is opposite the pointer.

    b. Center the leveling bubble.

    c. Rotate the scale to the specified angle degrees (see carburetor chart).

4. Position the cam follower on the 2nd step (against the rise of the high step) of the fast idle cam.

NOTE: *If the cam follower does not contact the cam, adjust the fast idle speed screw. Final fast idle speed adjustment MUST BE performed according to the underhood emission control information label.*

5. Center the bubble of the Valve Angle Gauge, by bending the fast idle cam tang.

Front (Primary Side) Vacuum Break Adjustment

NOTE: *The following procedure requires the use of the GM Valve Angle Gauge tool No. J-26701, BT-7704 or equivalent.*

1. Using a rubber band, attach it between the green tang of the intermediate choke shaft and the air horn housing.

2. Open the throttle and allow the choke valve to close.

3. Using the GM Valve Angle Gauge tool No. J-26701, BT-7704 or equivalent, attach it to the choke plate, then perform the following procedures:

    a. Rotate the degree scale until the zero is opposite the pointer.

    b. Center the leveling bubble.

    c. Rotate the scale to the specified angle degrees (see carburetor chart).

4. Apply a vacuum source (18 in.Hg) to retract the vacuum break and plug the air bleed holes.

5. Center the bubble of the Valve Angle Gauge, by turning the adjusting screw.

Rear (Secondary Side) Vacuum Break Adjustment

NOTE: *The following procedure requires the use of the GM Valve Angle Gauge tool No. J-26701, BT-7704 or equivalent.*

1. Using a rubber band, attach it between the green tang of the intermediate choke shaft and the air horn housing.

2. Open the throttle and allow the choke valve to close.

3. Using the GM Valve Angle Gauge tool No. J-26701, BT-7704 or equivalent, attach it to the choke plate, then perform the following procedures:

    a. Rotate the degree scale until the zero is opposite the pointer.

    b. Center the leveling bubble.

    c. Rotate the scale to the specified angle degrees (see carburetor chart).

4. Apply a vacuum source (18 in.Hg) to retract the vacuum break and plug the air bleed holes.

5. Center the bubble of the Valve Angle Gauge by performing one of the following procedures:

    a. Using a 1/8″ Allen wrench, turn the vacuum break adjusting screw.

    b. Using a rod bending tool, support the S-rod and bend the vacuum break rod.

Air Valve Rod Adjustment

NOTE: *The following procedure requires the use of an vacuum source (18 in.Hg) and a 0.025″ (0.6mm) plug gauge.*

1. Apply a vacuum source (18 in.Hg) to retract the vacuum break and plug the air bleed holes.

2. Open the throttle and allow the choke valve to close.

3. Using a 0.025″ (0.6mm) plug gauge, position it between the control rod and the slot in the choke valve cam.

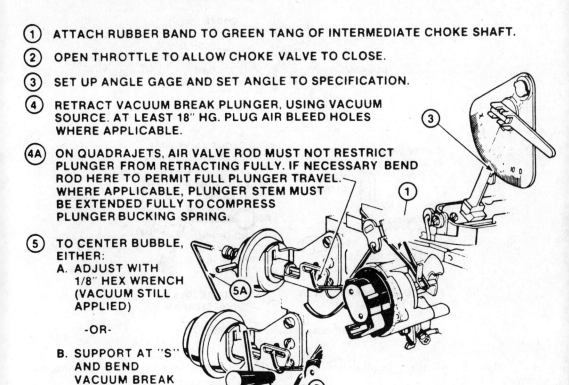

1. ATTACH RUBBER BAND TO GREEN TANG OF INTERMEDIATE CHOKE SHAFT.

2. OPEN THROTTLE TO ALLOW CHOKE VALVE TO CLOSE.

3. SET UP ANGLE GAGE AND SET ANGLE TO SPECIFICATION.

4. RETRACT VACUUM BREAK PLUNGER, USING VACUUM SOURCE. AT LEAST 18" HG. PLUG AIR BLEED HOLES WHERE APPLICABLE.

4A. ON QUADRAJETS, AIR VALVE ROD MUST NOT RESTRICT PLUNGER FROM RETRACTING FULLY. IF NECESSARY BEND ROD HERE TO PERMIT FULL PLUNGER TRAVEL. WHERE APPLICABLE, PLUNGER STEM MUST BE EXTENDED FULLY TO COMPRESS PLUNGER BUCKING SPRING.

5. TO CENTER BUBBLE, EITHER:
   A. ADJUST WITH 1/8" HEX WRENCH (VACUUM STILL APPLIED)

   -OR-

   B. SUPPORT AT "S" AND BEND VACUUM BREAK ROD (VACUUM STILL APPLIED)

Rear (secondary-side) vacuum break adjustment— E4ME carburetor

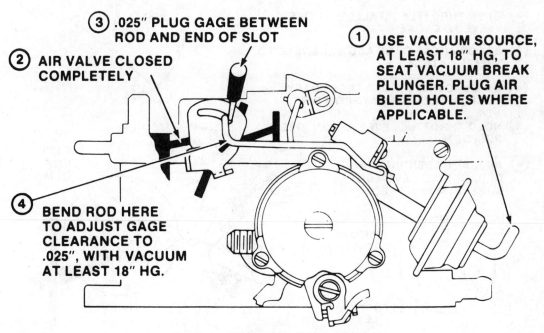

3. .025" PLUG GAGE BETWEEN ROD AND END OF SLOT

2. AIR VALVE CLOSED COMPLETELY

1. USE VACUUM SOURCE, AT LEAST 18" HG, TO SEAT VACUUM BREAK PLUNGER. PLUG AIR BLEED HOLES WHERE APPLICABLE.

4. BEND ROD HERE TO ADJUST GAGE CLEARANCE TO .025", WITH VACUUM AT LEAST 18" HG.

Air valve rod adjustment—E4ME carburetor

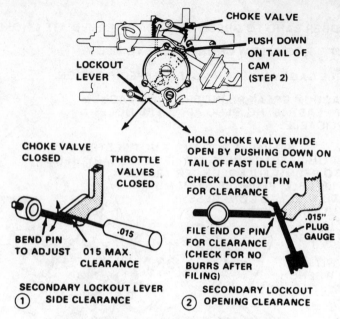

Secondary lockout adjustment—M4ME, E4ME

4. To adjust, bend (using a bending tool) the air valve rod.

Secondary Lockout Adjustment

NOTE: *The following procedure requires the use of a 0.015" (0.38mm) plug gauge and a rod bending tool.*

1. Pull the choke wide open by pushing out on the choke lever.

2. Open the throttle until the end of the secondary actuating lever is opposite the toe of the lockout lever.

3. Measure the clearance between the lockout lever and the secondary lever.

① ATTACH RUBBER BAND TO GREEN TANG OF INTERMEDIATE CHOKE SHAFT

② OPEN THROTTLE TO ALLOW CHOKE VALVE TO CLOSE

③ SET UP ANGLE GAGE AND SET ANGLE TO SPECIFICATION

④ ON QUADRAJET, HOLD SECONDARY LOCKOUT LEVER AWAY FROM PIN

⑤ HOLD THROTTLE LEVER IN WIDE OPEN POSITION

⑥ ADJUST BY BENDING TANG OF FAST IDLE LEVER UNTIL BUBBLE IS CENTERED

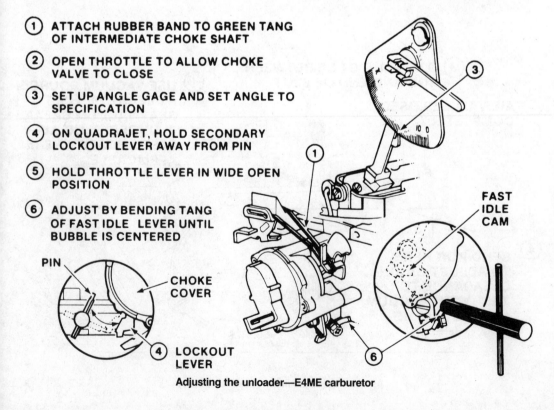

Adjusting the unloader—E4ME carburetor

4. Bend the lockout pin until the clearance is in accordance with the proper specifications.

Unloader Adjustment

NOTE: *The following procedure requires the use of the GM Valve Angle Gauge tool No. J-26701, BT-7704 or equivalent, a rubber band and a bending tool.*

1. Using a rubber band, attach it between the green tang of the intermediate choke shaft and the air horn housing.

2. Open the throttle and allow the choke valve to close.

3. Using the GM Valve Angle Gauge tool No. J-26701, BT-7704 or equivalent, attach it to the choke plate, then perform the following procedures:

    a. Rotate the degree scale until the zero is opposite the pointer.

    b. Center the leveling bubble.

    c. Rotate the scale to the specified angle degrees (see carburetor chart).

NOTE: *On a quadrajet, hold the secondary lockout lever away from the pin.*

4. Adjust and hold the throttle lever in the wide-open position.

5. Center the bubble of the Valve Angle Gauge, by bending the fast idle lever tang.

Throttle Position Sensor (TPS)

The throttle position sensor is a potentiometer, mounted on the carburetor; one end is connected to the ECM and the other to a ground. As the throttle plate opens, the output voltage increases; at wide-open throttle the output voltage is approx. 5V.

NOTE: *The following procedure requires the use of GM Adjustment tool No. J-28696 or equivalent, a digital voltmeter tool No. J-29125-A, a drill, a $\frac{5}{64}$" drill bit.*

1. Disconnect the negative battery cable from the battery.

2. Remove the air cleaner and stuff a clean rag into the intake bore to keep the carburetor clean.

3. To remove the throttle position plug cover, perform the following procedures:

    a. Using a $\frac{5}{64}$" drill bit, drill a hole in the aluminum plug covering TPS adjusting screw.

NOTE: *When drilling the hole in the aluminum plug, be careful not to damage the adjusting screw head.*

    b. Using a No. 8, $\frac{1}{2}$" self-tapping screw, install it into the drilled hole.

    c. Using a wide blade screwdriver, pry against the screw head to remove the plug, then discard the plug.

4. Using the GM adjusting tool No. J-28696,

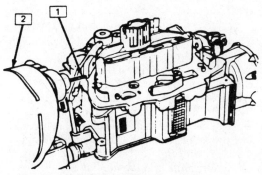

1. Plug (throttle position sensor adjustment screw)
2. Drill

Drilling a hole in the TPS screw cover plug

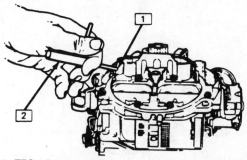

1. TPS adjustment screw
2. Tool—J28696/BT7967A

Using GM Adjusting tool No. J-28696, BT-7967-A or equivalent, to adjust the TPS screw

BT-7967-A or equivalent, remove the TPS adjusting screw.

5. Using the digital voltmeter tool No. J-29125-A or equivalent, connect one probe to the center terminal and the other to the bottom terminal of the TPS connector.

6. Turn the ignition switch On with the engine stopped. Install the TPS adjustment screw.

7. Using the GM adjusting tool No. J-28696, BT-7967-A or equivalent, install the TPS adjusting screw and turn it to obtain a voltage of 0.255V (A/C Off and at curb idle).

8. After the adjustment is complete, install a new TPS plug cover; drive the plug in until it flush with the raised pump lever boss on the casting.

NOTE: *If a TPS plug is not available, apply Delco Threadlock Adhesive X-10 or equivalent, to the screw threads and repeat the adjustment.*

9. After adjustment, clear the trouble code memory.

Mixture Control Solenoid (Plunger Travel)

If the dwell is off at 3000 rpm, perform this check and/or adjustment procedure.

CHECKING

NOTE: *The following procedure requires the use of the GM Float Gauge tool No. J-34935, BT-8420-A or equivalent.*

1. With the engine Off, remove the air cleaner from the carburetor.

2. Insert the GM Float Gauge tool No. J-34935-1, BT-8420-A or equivalent, into the vertical D-shaped vent hole of the air horn; allow the gauge to touch the solenoid plunger.

NOTE: *If difficulty is experienced in inserting the gauge into the hole, it may be necessary to grind some of the material from it.*

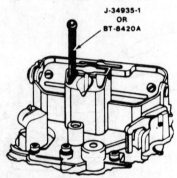

Checking the mixture control solenoid plunger travel—E4ME carburetor

3. With the gauge released (plunger in the Up position), observe and record the mark (on the gauge) that aligns with the top of the air horn.

4. Press down (lightly) on the gauge until it bottoms, then read and record the mark that aligns with the top of the air horn.

5. Subtract the Up position from the Down position; the difference is the total plunger travel:

a. If the plunger travel is $1/16$–$3/16$″ (1.5–4.8mm) and the dwell reading was OK at 3,000 rpm (10°–50°), refer to the Idle Air Bleed Valve Adjustment, located in the Idle Speed and Mixture Adjustment procedures in Chapter 2.

b. If the plunger travel is less than $1/16$″ (1.5mm) or greater than $3/16$″ (4.8mm) or the dwell reading was Off at 3,000 rpm, adjust the mixture control solenoid plunger travel.

ADJUSTMENT

NOTE: *The following procedure requires the use of the GM Mixture Solenoid Gauge tool No. J-33815-1, BT-8253-A or equivalent, and the GM Adjustment tool No. J-28696-10, BT-7928 or equivalent.*

1. Disconnect the negative battery terminal from the battery, then the M/C solenoid, the throttle position sensor and the idle speed solenoid connectors from the carburetor.

2. To remove the air horn, perform the following procedures:

a. Remove the idle speed solenoid-to-air horn screws and the solenoid.

b. Remove the choke lever-to-choke shaft screw, rotate the upper choke lever and remove the choke rod from the slot in the lever.

c. To remove the choke rod from the lower lever (inside the float bowl casting), use a small screwdriver to hold the lower lever outward and twist the rod counterclockwise.

d. Remove the fuel pump link from the pump lever; DO NOT remove the pump link from the air horn.

e. From the front of the float bowl, remove the front vacuum break hose from the tube.

f. Remove the air horn-to-fuel bowl screws and lift the air horn straight up from the float bowl; discard the gasket.

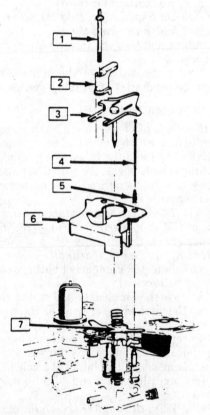

1. Screw—solenoid adjusting (lean mixture)
2. Stop—rich limit
3. Solenoid plunger
4. Rod—primary metering
5. Spring—primary metering rod
6. Insert—float bowl
7. M/C solenoid

Exploded view of the mixture control solenoid assembly—E4ME carburetor

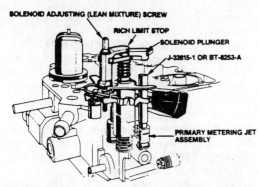

SOLENOID ADJUSTING (LEAN MIXTURE) SCREW

RICH LIMIT STOP

SOLENOID PLUNGER

J-33815-1 OR BT-8253-A

PRIMARY METERING JET ASSEMBLY

Positioning the mixture control solenoid gauging tool

NOTE: *When removing the air horn-to-float bowl screws, be sure to remove the 2 countersunk screws located next to the venturi.*

3. Remove the solenoid adjustment screw, the rich limit stop, the M/C solenoid plunger, the primary metering rods with the springs, the plastic filler block and the M/C solenoid.

4. Inspect the carburetor for the cause of an incorrect mixture:

   a. Inspect for a worn M/C solenoid bore or sticking plunger.

   b. Inspect the metering rods for an incorrect part number, sticking condition and improperly installed rods or springs.

   c. Inspect for dirt in the jets.

5. Using the GM Mixture Solenoid Gauging tool No. J-33815-1, BT-8253-A or equivalent, install it over the throttle side metering jet rod guide and temporarily reinstall the solenoid adjusting screw spring, the M/C solenoid, the plunger, the rich limit stop and the solenoid adjusting screw.

6. To adjust the solenoid plunger, perform the following procedures:

   a. Using light finger pressure, as close to the plunger shaft as possible, hold the solenoid plunger in the Down position.

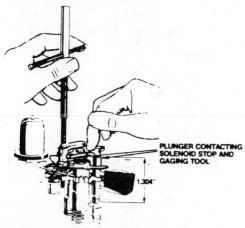

PLUNGER CONTACTING SOLENOID STOP AND GAGING TOOL

1.304"

Adjusting the mixture control solenoid screw

   b. Using the GM Adjustment tool No. J-28696-10, BT-7928 or equivalent, turn the solenoid adjusting screw clockwise until the plunger contacts the gauging tool.

   c. Turn the tool counterclockwise until the plunger breaks contact with the gauging tool.

NOTE: *When the solenoid plunger contacts both the Solenoid Stop and the Gauge tool, the adjustment is correct.*

7. Noting the position of the tool's tee handle, turn the solenoid's adjusting screw clockwise (counting and recording the number of turns) until the solenoid bottoms against the float bowl.

8. Remove the solenoid adjusting screw, the rich limit stop, the M/C solenoid, the plunger, the solenoid adjusting screw spring and the gauging tool.

9. Install the solenoid adjusting screw spring, the M/C solenoid, the plastic filler block, the primary metering rods/springs, the M/C solenoid plunger, the rich limit stop and the solenoid adjusting screw.

10. Using the GM Adjustment tool No. J-28696-10, BT-7928 or equivalent, turn the adjusting screw clockwise (counting the exact number of turns from Step 7) until the solenoid bottoms against the float bowl.

11. To install the air horn, use a new gasket and reverse the removal procedures. Start the engine and check the dwell at 3000 rpm.

12. To set the engine for dwell inspection, perform the following procedures:

   a. Disconnect and plug the vacuum line-to-canister purge valve.

   b. Ground the diagnostic test terminal.

   c. Attach a dwell meter to the engine.

   d. Operate the engine until normal operating temperature is established; the upper radiator hose is Hot.

13. To inspect the dwell, operate the engine at 3,000 rpm and check for the following conditions:

   a. If the dwell is 10°–50° the mixture control solenoid adjustment is complete.

   b. If the dwell is greater than 50°, check the carburetor for a rich condition.

   c. If the dwell is less than 10°, check for vacuum leaks or a lean operating carburetor.

REMOVAL AND INSTALLATION

Carburetor

1. Raise the hood. From inside the vehicle, remove the engine cover.

2. Disconnect the negative battery terminal from the battery.

3. Remove the air cleaner and the accelerator linkage.

4. If equipped with an AT, remove the detent cable from the carburetor.

5. Disconnect the cruise control, if equipped.

6. Label and disconnect all of the necessary vacuum lines.

7. Place a shop cloth under the fuel line-to-carburetor connection and disconnect the fuel line from the carburetor; the cloth will catch the excess fuel.

8. Label and disconnect all of the necessary electrical connections.

9. Remove the carburetor-to-intake manifold bolts, the carburetor and the gasket (discard it).

10. To install the carburetor, use a new carburetor-to-intake manifold gasket and reverse the removal procedures. Torque the carburetor-to-intake manifold bolts to 7 ft.lb. (long) or 11 ft.lb. (short). Start the engine and check for fuel leaks.

Throttle Position Sensor (TPS)

1. Disconnect the negative battery terminal from the battery, then the M/C solenoid, the throttle position sensor and the idle speed solenoid connectors from the carburetor.

2. At the air horn, remove the following items by performing the following procedures:

   a. Remove the idle speed solenoid-to-air horn screws and the solenoid.

   b. Remove the choke lever-to-choke shaft screw, rotate the upper choke lever and remove the choke rod from the slot in the lever.

   c. To remove the choke rod from the lower lever (inside the float bowl casting), use a small screwdriver to hold the lower lever outward and twist the rod counterclockwise.

   d. Remove the fuel pump link from the pump lever; DO NOT remove the pump link from the air horn.

   e. From the front of the float bowl, remove the front vacuum break hose from the tube.

   f. Remove the air horn-to-fuel bowl screws and lift the air horn straight up from the float bowl; discard the gasket.

NOTE: *When removing the air horn-to-float bowl screws, be sure to remove the 2 countersunk screws located next to the venturi.*

3. To remove the TPS from the float bowl, perform the following procedures:

   a. Using a flat tool or a piece of metal, lay it across the float bowl to protect the gasket sealing surface.

   b. Using a small prybar, lightly depress the TPS sensor and hold against the spring tension.

   c. Using a small chisel, pry upward (against the bowl staking) to remove the staking.

NOTE: *When removing the bowl staking, be sure to apply prying force against the metal piece and not the bowl casting.*

   d. Pushing up on the bottom of the TPS electrical connector, remove it and the connector assembly from the fuel bowl.

4. To install the TPS/connector assembly, align the groove in the electrical connector with the slot in the float bowl casting. Push down on the assembly so that the connector and wires are located below the bowl casting surface; be sure the green TPS actuator plunger is aligned in the air horn.

5. To install the air horn, hold the pump plunger assembly down against the return spring tension. Align the pump plunger stem with the hole in the gasket and the gasket over the TPS plunger, the solenoid plunger return spring, the metering rods, the solenoid mounting screws and the electrical connector. Use the two dowel locating pins (on the float bowl) to align the gasket.

6. While holding the solenoid metering rod plunger, the air horn gasket and the pump plunger assembly, align the slot in the end of the plunger with the solenoid mounting screw.

7. While lowering the air horn assembly

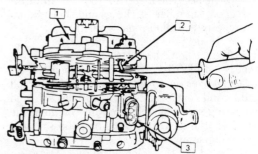

1. Air horn
2. TPS adjustment lever
3. TPS electrical connector

Using a screwdriver to install the air horn onto the float bowl—E4ME carburetor

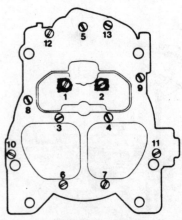

Air horn torquing sequence—E4ME carburetor

(carefully) onto the float bowl, position the TPS adjustment lever of the TPS sensor and guide the pump plunger stem through the air horn casting seal.

NOTE: *To ease the installation of the air horn onto the float bowl, insert a thin screwdriver between the air horn gasket and the float bowl to raise the TPS adjustment lever while positioning it over the TPS sensor.*

8. Install the air horn-to-float bowl screws and tighten all of the screws evenly, using the torquing sequence.

9. To complete the installation, reverse the removal procedures. Reconnect all of the vacuum and electrical connectors. Clear the trouble code from the ECM memory. Check and/or adjust the TPS voltage.

Mixture Control Solenoid

NOTE: *The following procedure requires the use of GM Solenoid Adjusting tool No. J-28696-1 or equivalent.*

1. Disconnect the negative battery terminal from the battery, then the M/C solenoid and the Throttle Position Sensor (TPS) electrical connectors from the carburetor.

2. Remove the air horn, by performing the following procedures:

a. Remove the choke lever-to-choke shaft screw, rotate the upper choke lever and remove the choke rod from the slot in the lever.

b. To remove the choke rod from the lower lever (inside the float bowl casting), use a small screwdriver to hold the lower lever outward and twist the rod counterclockwise.

c. Remove the fuel pump link from the pump lever; DO NOT remove the pump link from the air horn.

d. From the front of the float bowl, remove the front vacuum break hose from the tube.

e. Remove the air horn-to-fuel bowl screws and lift the air horn straight up from the float bowl; discard the gasket.

NOTE: *When removing the air horn-to-float bowl screws, be sure to remove the 2 countersunk screws located next to the venturi.*

f. Lift the air horn straight up from the float bowl.

3. Using the GM Solenoid Adjusting tool No. J-28696-1 or equivalent, remove the M/C solenoid adjusting screw.

4. Lift the air horn-to-float bowl gasket from the dowel locating pins and discard it.

5. Remove the plastic filler block from over the float bowl.

6. Lift (carefully) each metering rod from the guided metering jet; be sure to remove the return spring with each rod.

7. Remove the M/C solenoid-to-float bowl screw, then lift the solenoid and the connector assembly from the float bowl.

NOTE: *If a new mixture control solenoid package is being installed, the solenoid and the plunger MUST BE installed as a matched set.*

8. When installing the M/C solenoid, perform the following procedures:

a. Align the solenoid's pin with the hole in the raised boss at the bottom of the float bowl.

Rochester E4ME Specifications

Year	Carburetor Number	Float Level +1/16"	Lean Mixture Screw (Gauge)	Rich Mixture Screw +1/16"	Idle Mixture Needle (No. of Turns)	Idle Air Bleed Valve	Air Valve Spring (No. of Turns)	Choke Stat Lever (Gauge)	Choke Rod Cam +2.5°	Vacuum Break Front +2.5°	Vacuum Break Rear +3.5°	Air Valve Rod	Unloader +4°
1985	17085202	11/32	1.304	1/8	3 3/8	①	7/8	0.120	20°	27°	—	0.025	38°
	17085203	11/32	1.304	1/8	3 3/8	①	7/8	0.120	20°	27°	—	0.025	38°
	17085204	11/32	1.304	1/8	3 3/8	①	7/8	0.120	20°	27°	—	0.025	38°
	17085207	11/32	1.304	1/8	3 3/8	①	7/8	0.120	38°	27°	—	0.025	38°
	17085218	11/32	1.304	1/8	3 3/8	①	7/8	0.120	20°	27°	—	0.025	38°
	17085502	7/16	1.304	—	②	①	7/8	0.120	20°	26°	36°	0.025	39°
	17085503	7/16	1.304	—	②	①	7/8	0.120	20°	26°	36°	0.025	39°
	17085506	7/16	1.304	—	②	①	1	0.120	20°	27°	36°	0.025	36°
	17085508	7/16	1.304	—	②	①	1	0.120	20°	27°	36°	0.025	36°
	17085524	7/16	1.304	—	②	①	1	0.120	20°	25°	36°	0.025	36°
	17085526	7/16	1.304	—	②	①	1	0.120	20°	25°	36°	0.025	36°

① Preset with 1.756 gage, final adjustment on vehicle
② Preset 3 turns, final adjustment on vehicle

Rochester M4MC/M4ME Specifications

Year	Carburetor Part No.	Float Level Inches + 1/16″	Pump Rod Setting Inches	Pump Rod Location	Air Valve Spring (Turns)	Choke Coil Lever	Fast Idle Cam (Choke Rod) +2.5°	Vacuum Break Front +2.5°	Vacuum Break Rear +3.5°	Air Valve Rod Inches	Unloader +4°
1985	17085000	3/8	9/32	Inner	1	0.120	46°	23°	30°	0.025	40°
	17085001	3/8	9/32	Inner	7/8	0.120	46°	24°	30°	0.025	40°
	17085003	13/32	9/32	Inner	7/8	0.120	46°	23°	—	0.025	35°
	17085004	13/32	9/32	Inner	7/8	0.120	46°	23°	—	0.025	35°
	17085205	13/32	9/32	Inner	7/8	0.120	20°	26°	38°	0.025	39°
	17085206	13/32	9/32	Inner	7/8	0.120	46°	—	26°	0.025	39°
	17085208	13/32	9/32	Inner	7/8	0.120	20°	26°	38°	0.025	39°
	17085209	13/32	9/32	Inner	7/8	0.120	20°	26°	36°	0.025	39°
	17085210	13/32	9/32	Inner	7/8	0.120	20°	26°	38°	0.025	39°
	17085211	13/32	9/32	Inner	7/8	0.120	20°	26°	36°	0.025	39°
	17085212	13/32	9/32	Inner	7/8	0.120	46°	23°	—	0.025	35°
	17085213	13/32	9/32	Inner	7/8	0.120	20°	23°	—	0.025	35°
	17085215	13/32	9/32	Inner	7/8	0.120	46°	—	26°	0.025	39°
	17085216	13/32	9/32	Inner	7/8	0.120	20°	26°	38°	0.025	39°
	17085217	13/32	9/32	Inner	1/2	0.120	20°	26°	36°	0.025	39°
	17085219	13/32	9/32	Inner	1/2	0.120	20°	26°	36°	0.025	39°
	17085220	13/32	3/8	Outer	7/8	0.120	20°	—	26°	0.025	39°
	17085221	13/32	3/8	Outer	7/8	0.120	20°	—	26°	0.025	39°
	17085222	13/32	9/32	Inner	1/2	0.120	20°	26°	36°	0.025	39°
	17085223	13/32	3/8	Outer	1/2	0.120	20°	26°	36°	0.025	39°
	17085224	13/32	9/32	Inner	1/2	0.120	20°	26°	36°	0.025	39°
	17085225	13/32	3/8	Outer	1/2	0.120	20°	26°	36°	0.025	39°
	17085226	13/32	9/32	Inner	7/8	0.120	20°	—	24°	0.025	36°
	17085227	13/32	9/32	Inner	7/8	0.120	20°	—	24°	0.025	36°
	17085228	13/32	9/32	Inner	7/8	0.120	46°	—	24°	0.025	39°
	17085229	13/32	9/32	Inner	7/8	0.120	46°	—	24°	0.025	39°
	17085230	13/32	9/32	Inner	7/8	0.120	20°	—	26°	0.025	32°
	17085231	13/32	9/32	Inner	7/8	0.120	20°	—	26°	0.025	32°
	17085235	13/32	9/32	Inner	7/8	0.120	46°	—	26°	0.025	39°
	17085238	13/32	3/8	Outer	7/8	0.120	20°	—	26°	0.025	32°
	17085239	13/32	3/8	Outer	7/8	0.120	20°	—	26°	0.025	32°
	17085290	13/32	9/32	Inner	7/8	0.120	46°	—	24°	0.025	39°
	17085291	13/32	3/8	Outer	7/8	0.120	46°	—	26°	0.025	39°
	17085292	13/32	9/32	Inner	7/8	0.120	46°	—	24°	0.025	39°
	17085293	13/32	3/8	Outer	7/8	0.120	46°	—	26°	0.025	39°
	17085294	13/32	9/32	Inner	7/8	0.120	46°	—	26°	0.025	39°
	17085298	13/32	9/32	Inner	7/8	0.120	46°	—	26°	0.025	39°

b. Align the wires of the solenoid's connector in the bowl slot or the plastic insert (if used).

c. Install the solenoid-to-fuel bowl mounting screw and engage the first six screw threads (to assure proper thread engagement).

9. To complete the installation, use a new gasket and reverse the removal procedures. Calibrate the M/C solenoid plunger.

OVERHAUL

Efficient carburetion depends greatly on careful cleaning and inspection during overhaul, since dirt, gum, water or varnish in or on the carburetor parts are often responsible for poor performance.

Overhaul your carburetor in a clean, dust-free area. Carefully disassemble the carburetor, referring often to the exploded views and directions packaged with the rebuilding kit. Keep all similar and look-alike parts segregated during disassembly and cleaning to avoid accidental interchange during assembly. Make a note of all jet sizes.

When the carburetor is disassembled, wash all parts (except diaphragms, electric choke units, solenoids, pump plunger and any other plastic, leather, fiber or rubber parts) in clean carburetor solvent. DO NOT leave the parts in the solvent any longer than is necessary to sufficiently loosen the deposits. Excessive cleaning may remove the special finish from the float bowl and choke valve bodies, leaving these parts unfit for service. Rinse all parts in clean solvent and blow them dry with compressed air or allow them to air dry. Wipe clean all cork, plastic, leather and fiber parts with a clean, lint-free cloth.

Blow out all passages and jets with compressed air and be sure that there are no restrictions or blockages. Never use wire or similar tools to clean the jets, fuel passages or air bleeds. Clean all jets and valves separately to avoid accidental interchange.

Check all parts for wear or damage. If wear or damage is found, replace the defective parts. Especially check the following:

1. Check the float needle and seat for wear. If wear is found, replace the complete assembly.

2. Check the float hinge pin for wear and the float(s) for dents or distortion. Replace the float if fuel has leaked into it.

3. Check the throttle and choke shaft bores for wear or an out-of-round condition. Damage or wear to the throttle arm, shaft or shaft bore will often require replacement of the throttle body. These parts require a close fitting tolerance; wear may allow air leakage, which could affect starting and idling.

NOTE: *Throttle shafts and bushings are not included in overhaul kits. They can be purchased separately.*

4. Inspect the idle mixture adjusting needles for burrs or grooves. Any such condition requires replacement of the needle, since you will not be able to obtain a satisfactory idle.

5. Test the accelerator pump check valves. They should pass air one way but not the other. Test for proper seating by blowing and sucking on the valve. Replace the valve check ball and spring as necessary. If the valve is satisfactory, wash the valve parts again to remove breath moisture.

6. Check the bowl cover for warped surfaces with a straightedge.

7. Closely inspect the accelerator pump plunger for wear and damage, replacing as necessary.

8. After the carburetor is assembled, check the choke valve for freedom of operation.

Carburetor overhaul kits are recommended for each overhaul. These kits contain all gaskets and new parts to replace those which deteriorate most rapidly. Failure to replace all parts supplied with the kit (especially gaskets) can result in poor performance later.

Some carburetor manufacturers supply overhaul kits of three basic types: minor repair, major repair and gasket kits. Basically, they contain the following:

Minor Repair Kits:
- All gaskets
- Float needle valve
- All diagrams
- Spring for the pump diaphragm

Major Repair Kits:
- All jets and gaskets
- All diaphragms
- Float needle valve
- Pump ball valve
- Float
- Complete intermediate rod
- Intermediate pump lever
- Some cover holddown screws and washers

Gasket Kits:
- All gaskets

After cleaning and checking all components, reassembly the carburetor, using new parts and referring to the exploded view. When reassembling, make sure that all screws and jets are tight in their seats but DO NOT overtighten, for the tips will be distorted.

Tighten all screws gradually, in rotation. DO NOT tighten the needle valves into their seats; uneven jetting will result. Always use new gaskets. Be sure to adjust the float level when reassembling.

FUEL INJECTION SYSTEM

NOTE: *This book contains simple testing and service procedures for for your Van's fuel injection system. More comprehensive testing and diagnosis procedures may be found in* CHILTON'S GUIDE TO FUEL INJECTION AND FEEDBACK CARBURETORS, *book part number 7488, available at your local retailer.*

Electric Fuel Pump

The electric fuel pump is attached to the fuel sending unit, located in the fuel tank.

REMOVAL AND INSTALLATION

NOTE: *The following procedure requires the use of the GM Fuel Gauge Sending Unit Retaining Cam tool No. J-24187 or equivalent.*

1. If the fuel system has been in use, turn the ignition switch Off and allow the system time to reduce the fuel pressure.
2. Disconnect the negative battery terminal from the battery.
NOTE: *Be sure to keep a Class B (dry chemical) fire extinguisher nearby.*
CAUTION: *Due to the possibility of fire or explosion, never drain or store gasoline in an open container.*
3. Using a hand pump or a siphon hose, drain the gasoline into an approved container.

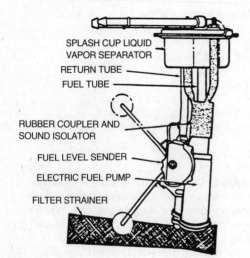

SPLASH CUP LIQUID VAPOR SEPARATOR
RETURN TUBE
FUEL TUBE
RUBBER COUPLER AND SOUND ISOLATOR
FUEL LEVEL SENDER
ELECTRIC FUEL PUMP
FILTER STRAINER

TBI fuel pump

4. Raise and support the vehicle on jackstands.
5. Support the fuel tank and remove the fuel tank-to-vehicle straps.
6. Lower the tank slightly, then remove the sender unit wires, the hoses and the ground strap.
7. Remove the fuel tank from the vehicle.
8. Using the GM Fuel Gauge Sending Unit Retaining Cam tool No. J-24187 (or equivalent) or a brass drift and a hammer, remove the cam locking ring (fuel sending unit) counterclockwise, then lift the sending unit from the fuel tank.
9. Remove the fuel pump from the fuel sending unit, by performing the following procedures:
    a. Pull the fuel pump up into the mounting tube, while pulling outward (away) from the bottom support.
    NOTE: *When removing the fuel pump from the sending unit, be careful not to damage the rubber insulator and the strainer.*
    b. When the pump assembly is clear of the bottom support, pull it out of the rubber connector.
10. Inspect the fuel pump hose and bottom sound insulator for signs of deterioration, then replace it, if necessary.
11. Push the fuel pump onto the sending tube.
12. Using a new sending unit-to-fuel tank O-ring, install the sending unit into the fuel tank.
NOTE: *When installing the sending unit, be careful not to fold or twist the fuel strainer, for it will restrict the fuel flow.*
13. Using the GM Fuel Gauge Sending Unit Retaining Cam tool No. J-24187 (or equivalent) or a brass drift and a hammer, turn the sending unit-to-fuel tank locking ring clockwise.
14. To install the fuel tank, align the insulator strips and reverse the removal procedures. Torque the inner fuel tank strap-to-vehicle bolts to 26 ft.lb. and the outer fuel tank strap-to-vehicle nuts/bolts to 26 ft.lb.

TESTING AND ADJUSTMENTS
Flow Test

1. Remove the fuel pump-to-throttle body line from the throttle body.
2. Place the fuel line in a clean container.
3. Turn the ignition switch On; approximately ½ pint of the fuel should be delivered in 15 seconds.
4. If the fuel flow is below minimum, inspect the fuel system for restrictions; if no restrictions are found, replace the fuel pump.

Pressure Test

NOTE: *The following procedure requires the use of a GM Fuel Pressure Gauge tool No. J-29658-A or equivalent.*

1. If equipped with an EFI equipped engine, refer to the Fuel Pressure Relief procedures in this section and relieve the fuel pressure.

2. Remove the air cleaner, then disconnect and plug the THERMAC vacuum port on the throttle body unit.

3. Place a rag (to catch excess fuel) under the fuel line-to-throttle body connection. Disconnect the fuel line from the throttle body.

NOTE: *When disconnecting the fuel line, use a back-up wrench to hold the fuel nut on the throttle body.*

4. Using a GM Fuel Pressure Gauge tool No. J-29658-A or equivalent, install it into the fuel line.

5. Start the engine and observe the fuel pressure, it should be 9–13 psi.

NOTE: *If the fuel pressure does not meet specifications, inspect the fuel system for restrictions or replace the fuel pump.*

6. Turn the engine Off, relieve the fuel pressure and remove the GM Fuel Pressure Gauge tool No. J-29658-A or equivalent.

7. Install a new fuel line-to-throttle body O-ring and reverse the removal procedures. Unplug from the THERMAC vacuum port. Start the engine and check for fuel leaks.

Fuel Pump Relay

The fuel pump relay is mounted on the right-side of the engine compartment. Check for loose electrical connections; no other service is possible, except replacement.

REMOVAL AND INSTALLATION

1. Disconnect the negative battery terminal from the battery.

2. Disconnect the relay/electrical connector assembly from the bracket.

3. Pull the fuel pump relay from the electrical connector.

4. If necessary, use a new fuel pump and reverse the removal procedures.

FUEL PRESSURE RELIEF

2.5L Engine

1. From the fuse block, located in the passenger compartment, remove the fuse labeled, Fuel Pump.

2. Start the engine.

NOTE: *The engine will start and run, for a short period of time, until the remaining fuel is used up.*

3. Engage the starter, a few more times, to relieve any remaining pressure.

4. Turn the ignition switch Off and install the Fuel Pump fuse into the fuse block.

4.3L EFI Engine

Allow the engine to set for 5–10 minutes; this will allow the orifice (in the fuel system) to bleed off the pressure.

Throttle Body

The Model 300 throttle body, used on the 2.5L engine (1985–87), is a single barrel, single injector type. The Model 220 throttle body, used on the 4.3L engine (1986–87), is a dual barrel, twin injector type. The operation of both types are basically the same.

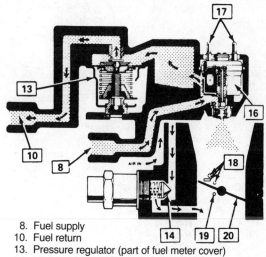

8. Fuel supply
10. Fuel return
13. Pressure regulator (part of fuel meter cover)
14. Idle air control (IAC) valve (shown open)
16. Fuel injector
17. Fuel injector terminals
18. Ported vacuum sources*
19. Manifold vacuum source*
20. Throttle valve

Operation of the TBI unit

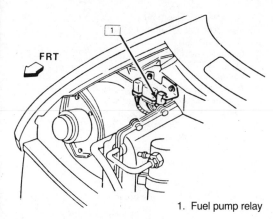

1. Fuel pump relay

Location of the fuel pump relay

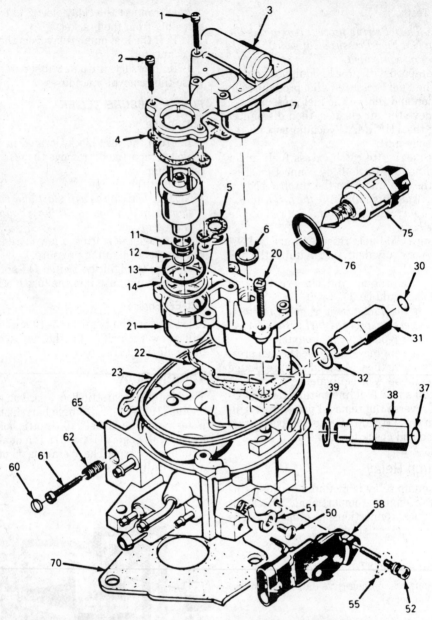

1. Screw & washer assembly—long (3)
2. Screw & washer assembly—short (2)
3. Fuel meter cover assembly
4. Gasket—fuel meter cover
5. Gasket—fuel meter outlet
6. Dust seal—pressure regulator
7. Pressure regulator
11. Filter—fuel injector nozzle
12. Lower "O" ring
13. Upper "O" ring
14. Back-up washer—fuel injector
20. Screw & washer assembly—attaching (3)
21. Fuel meter body assembly
22. Gasket—fuel meter body
23. Gasket—air filter
30. Fuel return line "O" ring
31. Nut—fuel return

32. Gasket—fuel return nut
37. Fuel inlet line "O" ring
38. Nut—fuel inlet
39. Gasket—fuel inlet nut
50. Screw—TPS lever attaching
51. Lever—TPS
52. Screw & washer assembly—attaching
55. Retainer—TPS attaching screw
58. Sensor—throttle position
60. Plug—idle stop screw
61. Screw—throttle stop
62. Spring—throttle stop screw
65. Throttle body assembly
70. Gasket—flange mounting
75. Idle air control assembly
76. Gasket—IAC to throttle body

Exploded view of the Model 300 throttle body—2.5L engine

1. Screw assembly—fuel meter cover attaching—long
2. Screw assembly—fuel meter cover attaching—short
3. Fuel meter cover assembly
4. Gasket—fuel meter cover
5. Gasket—fuel meter outlet
6. Seal—pressure regulator
7. Pressure regulator
10. Injector—fuel
11. Filter—fuel injector inlet
12. O-ring—fuel injector—lower
13. O-ring—fuel injector—upper
14. Washer—fuel injector
20. Screw assembly—fuel meter body—throttle body attaching
21. Fuel meter body assembly
22. Gasket—throttle body to fuel meter body
23. Gasket—air filter
30. O-ring—fuel return line
31. Nut—fuel outlet
37. O-ring—fuel inlet line
38. Nut—fuel inlet
40. Gasket—fuel outlet nut
41. Gasket—fuel inlet nut
50. Screw—TPS lever attaching
51. Lever—TPS
52. Screw assembly—TPS attaching
58. Sensor—throttle position (TPS)
60. Plug—idle stop screw
61. Screw assembly—idle stop
62. Spring—idle stop screw
65. Throttle body assembly
70. Gasket—flange
75. Valve assembly—idle air control (IAC)
76. Gasket—idle air control valve assembly

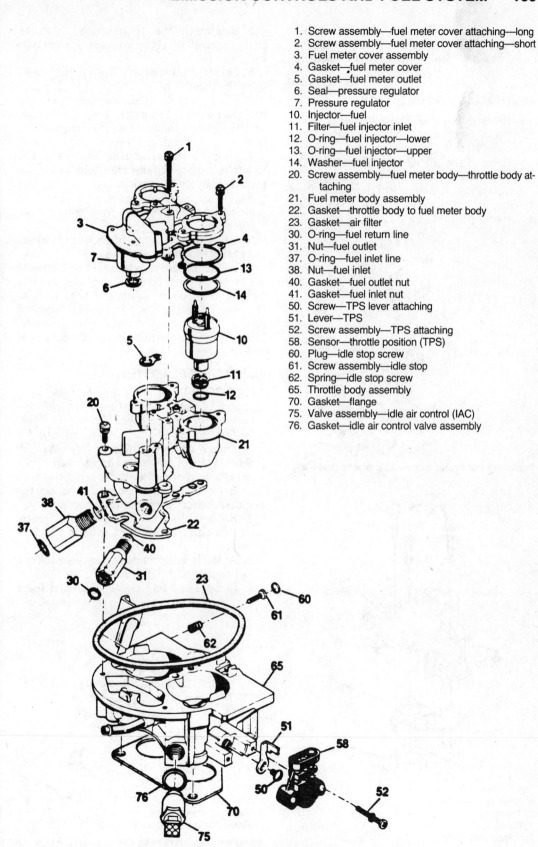

Exploded view of the Model 220 throttle body—4.3L engine

Both throttle bodies are constantly monitored by the ECM to produce a 14.7:1 air/fuel ratio, which is vital to the catalytic converter operation.

REMOVAL AND INSTALLATION

1. Refer to the Fuel Pressure Relief procedures in this section and reduce the pressure in the fuel system.
2. Remove the air cleaner. Disconnect the negative battery cable from the battery.
3. Disconnect the electrical connectors from the idle air control valve, the throttle position sensor and the fuel injector(s).

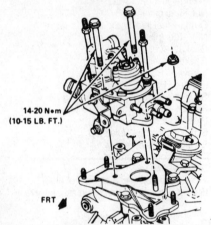

14-20 N·m (10-15 LB. FT.)

FRT

Replacing the throttle body—2.5L engine (1985–87)

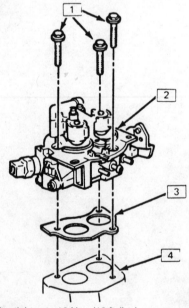

1. Bolt—tighten to 16 N·m (12 ft. lbs.)
2. TBI unit
3. Gasket
4. Engine inlet manifold

Replacing the throttle body—4.3L engine (1986–87)

4. Remove the throttle return spring(s), the cruise control (if equipped) and the throttle linkage.
5. Label and disconnect the vacuum hoses from the throttle body.
6. Place a rag (to catch the excess fuel) under the fuel line-to-throttle body connection, then disconnect the fuel line from the throttle body.
7. Remove the attaching hardware, the throttle body-to-intake manifold bolts, the throttle body and the gasket.

NOTE: *Be sure to place a cloth in the intake manifold to prevent dirt from entering the engine.*

8. Using a putty knife (if necessary), clean the gasket mounting surfaces.
9. To install, use a new gasket and reverse the removal procedures. Torque the throttle body-to-intake manifold nuts/bolts to 13 ft.lb. Depress the accelerator pedal to the floor and release it, to see if the pedal returns freely. Turn the ignition switch On and check for fuel leaks.

INJECTOR REPLACEMENT

CAUTION: *When removing the injector(s), be careful not to damage the electrical connector pins (on top of the injector), the injector fuel filter and the nozzle. The fuel injector is serviced as a complete assembly ONLY, it is an electrical component and should not be immersed in any kind of cleaner.*

1. Remove the air cleaner. Disconnect the negative battery terminal from the battery.
2. Refer to the Fuel Pressure Relief procedures in this section and relieve the fuel pressure.
3. At the injector connector, squeeze the two tabs together and pull it straight up.
4. Remove the fuel meter cover and leave the cover gasket in place.

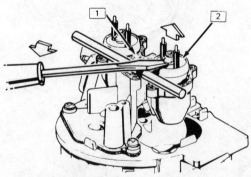

1. Fuel meter cover gasket
2. Removing fuel injector

Using a pry bar to remove the fuel injector from the throttle body—4.3L engine—2.5L is similar

55 WAYS TO IMPROVE FUEL ECONOMY

CHILTON'S
FUEL ECONOMY
& TUNE-UP TIPS

Tune-up • Spark Plug Diagnosis • Emission Controls

Fuel System • Cooling System • Tires and Wheels

General Maintenance

CHILTON'S FUEL ECONOMY & TUNE-UP TIPS

Fuel economy is important to everyone, no matter what kind of vehicle you drive. The maintenance-minded motorist can save both money and fuel using these tips and the periodic maintenance and tune-up procedures in this Repair and Tune-Up Guide.

There are more than 130,000,000 cars and trucks registered for private use in the United States. Each travels an average of 10-12,000 miles per year, and, and in total they consume close to 70 billion gallons of fuel each year. This represents nearly ⅔ of the oil imported by the United States each year. The Federal government's goal is to reduce consumption 10% by 1985. A variety of methods are either already in use or under serious consideration, and they all affect you driving and the cars you will drive. In addition to "down-sizing", the auto industry is using or investigating the use of electronic fuel delivery, electronic engine controls and alternative engines for use in smaller and lighter vehicles, among other alternatives to meet the federally mandated Corporate Average Fuel Economy (CAFE) of 27.5 mpg by 1985. The government, for its part, is considering rationing, mandatory driving curtailments and tax increases on motor vehicle fuel in an effort to reduce consumption. The government's goal of a 10% reduction could be realized — and further government regulation avoided — if every private vehicle could use just 1 less gallon of fuel per week.

How Much Can You Save?

Tests have proven that almost anyone can make at least a 10% reduction in fuel consumption through regular maintenance and tune-ups. When a major manufacturer of spark plugs sur-

TUNE-UP

1. Check the cylinder compression to be sure the engine will really benefit from a tune-up and that it is capable of producing good fuel economy. A tune-up will be wasted on an engine in poor mechanical condition.

2. Replace spark plugs regularly. New spark plugs alone can increase fuel economy 3%.

3. Be sure the spark plugs are the correct type (heat range) for your vehicle. See the Tune-Up Specifications.

Heat range refers to the spark plug's ability to conduct heat away from the firing end. It must conduct the heat away in an even pattern to avoid becoming a source of pre-ignition, yet it must also operate hot enough to burn off conductive deposits that could cause misfiring.

The heat range is usually indicated by a number on the spark plug, part of the manufacturer's designation for each individual spark plug. The numbers in bold-face indicate the heat range in each manufacturer's identification system.

Manufacturer	Typical Designation
AC	R **45** TS
Bosch (old)	WA **145** T30
Bosch (new)	HR **8** Y
Champion	RBL **15** Y
Fram/Autolite	**415**
Mopar	P-**62** PR
Motorcraft	BRF-**42**
NGK	BP **5** ES-15
Nippondenso	W **16** EP
Prestolite	14GR **5** 2A

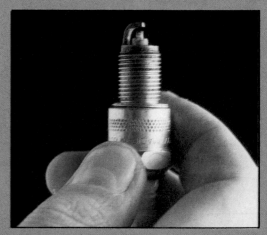

Periodically, check the spark plugs to be sure they are firing efficiently. They are excellent indicators of the internal condition of your engine.

On AC, Bosch (new), Champion, Fram/Autolite, Mopar, Motorcraft and Prestolite, a higher number indicates a hotter plug. On Bosch (old), NGK and Nippondenso, a higher number indicates a colder plug.

4. Make sure the spark plugs are properly gapped. See the Tune-Up Specifications in this book.

5. Be sure the spark plugs are firing efficiently. The illustrations on the next 2 pages show you how to "read" the firing end of the spark plug.

6. Check the ignition timing and set it to specifications. Tests show that almost all cars have incorrect ignition timing by more than 2°.

veyed over 6,000 cars nationwide, they found that a tune-up, on cars that needed one, increased fuel economy over 11%. Replacing worn plugs alone, accounted for a 3% increase. The same test also revealed that 8 out of every 10 vehicles will have some maintenance deficiency that will directly affect fuel economy, emissions or performance. Most of this mileage-robbing neglect could be prevented with regular maintenance.

Modern engines require that all of the functioning systems operate properly for maximum efficiency. A malfunction anywhere wastes fuel. You can keep your vehicle running as efficiently and economically as possible, by being aware of your vehicle's operating and performance characteristics. If your vehicle suddenly develops performance or fuel economy problems it could be due to one or more of the following:

PROBLEM	POSSIBLE CAUSE
Engine Idles Rough	Ignition timing, idle mixture, vacuum leak or something amiss in the emission control system.
Hesitates on Acceleration	Dirty carburetor or fuel filter, improper accelerator pump setting, ignition timing or fouled spark plugs.
Starts Hard or Fails to Start	Worn spark plugs, improperly set automatic choke, ice (or water) in fuel system.
Stalls Frequently	Automatic choke improperly adjusted and possible dirty air filter or fuel filter.
Performs Sluggishly	Worn spark plugs, dirty fuel or air filter, ignition timing or automatic choke out of adjustment.

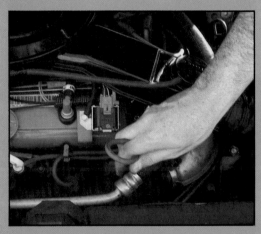

Check spark plug wires on conventional point type ignition for cracks by bending them in a loop around your finger.

Be sure that spark plug wires leading to adjacent cylinders do not run too close together. (Photo courtesy Champion Spark Plug Co.)

7. If your vehicle does not have electronic ignition, check the points, rotor and cap as specified.

8. Check the spark plug wires (used with conventional point-type ignitions) for cracks and burned or broken insulation by bending them in a loop around your finger. Cracked wires decrease fuel efficiency by failing to deliver full voltage to the spark plugs. One misfiring spark plug can cost you as much as 2 mpg.

9. Check the routing of the plug wires. Misfiring can be the result of spark plug leads to adjacent cylinders running parallel to each other and too close together. One wire tends to pick up voltage from the other causing it to fire "out of time".

10. Check all electrical and ignition circuits for voltage drop and resistance.

11. Check the distributor mechanical and/or vacuum advance mechanisms for proper functioning. The vacuum advance can be checked by twisting the distributor plate in the opposite direction of rotation. It should spring back when released.

12. Check and adjust the valve clearance on engines with mechanical lifters. The clearance should be slightly loose rather than too tight.

SPARK PLUG DIAGNOSIS

Normal

APPEARANCE: This plug is typical of one operating normally. The insulator nose varies from a light tan to grayish color with slight electrode wear. The presence of slight deposits is normal on used plugs and will have no adverse effect on engine performance. The spark plug heat range is correct for the engine and the engine is running normally.

CAUSE: Properly running engine.

RECOMMENDATION: Before reinstalling this plug, the electrodes should be cleaned and filed square. Set the gap to specifications. If the plug has been in service for more than 10-12,000 miles, the entire set should probably be replaced with a fresh set of the same heat range.

Oil Deposits

APPEARANCE: The firing end of the plug is covered with a wet, oily coating.

CAUSE: The problem is poor oil control. On high mileage engines, oil is leaking past the rings or valve guides into the combustion chamber. A common cause is also a plugged PCV valve, and a ruptured fuel pump diaphragm can also cause this condition. Oil fouled plugs such as these are often found in new or recently overhauled engines, before normal oil control is achieved, and can be cleaned and reinstalled.

RECOMMENDATION: A hotter spark plug may temporarily relieve the problem, but the engine is probably in need of work.

Incorrect Heat Range

APPEARANCE: The effects of high temperature on a spark plug are indicated by clean white, often blistered insulator. This can also be accompanied by excessive wear of the electrode, and the absence of deposits.

CAUSE: Check for the correct spark plug heat range. A plug which is too hot for the engine can result in overheating. A car operated mostly at high speeds can require a colder plug. Also check ignition timing, cooling system level, fuel mixture and leaking intake manifold.

RECOMMENDATION: If all ignition and engine adjustments are known to be correct, and no other malfunction exists, install spark plugs one heat range colder.

Photos Courtesy Fram Corporation

Carbon Deposits

APPEARANCE: Carbon fouling is easily identified by the presence of dry, soft, black, sooty deposits.

CAUSE: Changing the heat range can often lead to carbon fouling, as can prolonged slow, stop-and-start driving. If the heat range is correct, carbon fouling can be attributed to a rich fuel mixture, sticking choke, clogged air cleaner, worn breaker points, retarded timing or low compression. If only one or two plugs are carbon fouled, check for corroded or cracked wires on the affected plugs. Also look for cracks in the distributor cap between the towers of affected cylinders.

RECOMMENDATION: After the problem is corrected, these plugs can be cleaned and reinstalled if not worn severely.

MMT Fouled

APPEARANCE: Spark plugs fouled by MMT (Methycyclopentadienyl Maganese Tricarbonyl) have reddish, rusty appearance on the insulator and side electrode.

CAUSE: MMT is an anti-knock additive in gasoline used to replace lead. During the combustion process, the MMT leaves a reddish deposit on the insulator and side electrode.

RECOMMENDATION: No engine malfunction is indicated and the deposits will not affect plug performance any more than lead deposits (see Ash Deposits). MMT fouled plugs can be cleaned, regapped and reinstalled.

High Speed Glazing

APPEARANCE: Glazing appears as shiny coating on the plug, either yellow or tan in color.

CAUSE: During hard, fast acceleration, plug temperatures rise suddenly. Deposits from normal combustion have no chance to fluff-off; instead, they melt on the insulator forming an electrically conductive coating which causes misfiring.

RECOMMENDATION: Glazed plugs are not easily cleaned. They should be replaced with a fresh set of plugs of the correct heat range. If the condition recurs, using plugs with a heat range one step colder may cure the problem.

Ash (Lead) Deposits

APPEARANCE: Ash deposits are characterized by light brown or white colored deposits crusted on the side or center electrodes. In some cases it may give the plug a rusty appearance.

CAUSE: Ash deposits are normally derived from oil or fuel additives burned during normal combustion. Normally they are harmless, though excessive amounts can cause misfiring. If deposits are excessive in short mileage, the valve guides may be worn.

RECOMMENDATION: Ash-fouled plugs can be cleaned, gapped and reinstalled.

Detonation

APPEARANCE: Detonation is usually characterized by a broken plug insulator.

CAUSE: A portion of the fuel charge will begin to burn spontaneously, from the increased heat following ignition. The explosion that results applies extreme pressure to engine components, frequently damaging spark plugs and pistons.

Detonation can result by over-advanced ignition timing, inferior gasoline (low octane) lean air/fuel mixture, poor carburetion, engine lugging or an increase in compression ratio due to combustion chamber deposits or engine modification.

RECOMMENDATION: Replace the plugs after correcting the problem.

Photos Courtesy Champion Spark Plug Co.

EMISSION CONTROLS

13. Be aware of the general condition of the emission control system. It contributes to reduced pollution and should be serviced regularly to maintain efficient engine operation.

14. Check all vacuum lines for dried, cracked or brittle conditions. Something as simple as a leaking vacuum hose can cause poor performance and loss of economy.

15. Avoid tampering with the emission control system. Attempting to improve fuel econ-

FUEL SYSTEM

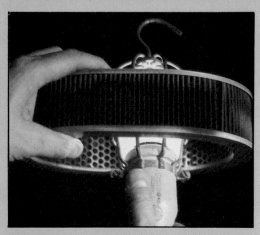

Check the air filter with a light behind it. If you can see light through the filter it can be reused.

Extremely clogged filters should be discarded and replaced with a new one.

18. Replace the air filter regularly. A dirty air filter richens the air/fuel mixture and can increase fuel consumption as much as 10%. Tests show that ⅓ of all vehicles have air filters in need of replacement.

19. Replace the fuel filter at least as often as recommended.

20. Set the idle speed and carburetor mixture to specifications.

21. Check the automatic choke. A sticking or malfunctioning choke wastes gas.

22. During the summer months, adjust the automatic choke for a leaner mixture which will produce faster engine warm-ups.

COOLING SYSTEM

29. Be sure all accessory drive belts are in good condition. Check for cracks or wear.

30. Adjust all accessory drive belts to proper tension.

31. Check all hoses for swollen areas, worn spots, or loose clamps.

32. Check coolant level in the radiator or expansion tank.

33. Be sure the thermostat is operating properly. A stuck thermostat delays engine warm-up and a cold engine uses nearly twice as much fuel as a warm engine.

34. Drain and replace the engine coolant at least as often as recommended. Rust and scale

TIRES & WHEELS

38. Check the tire pressure often with a pencil type gauge. Tests by a major tire manufacturer show that 90% of all vehicles have at least 1 tire improperly inflated. Better mileage can be achieved by over-inflating tires, but never exceed the maximum inflation pressure on the side of the tire.

39. If possible, install radial tires. Radial tires deliver as much as ½ mpg more than bias belted tires.

40. Avoid installing super-wide tires. They only create extra rolling resistance and decrease fuel mileage. Stick to the manufacturer's recommendations.

41. Have the wheels properly balanced.

omy by tampering with emission controls is more likely to worsen fuel economy than improve it. Emission control changes on modern engines are not readily reversible.

16. Clean (or replace) the EGR valve and lines as recommended.

17. Be sure that all vacuum lines and hoses are reconnected properly after working under the hood. An unconnected or misrouted vacuum line can wreak havoc with engine performance.

23. Check for fuel leaks at the carburetor, fuel pump, fuel lines and fuel tank. Be sure all lines and connections are tight.

24. Periodically check the tightness of the carburetor and intake manifold attaching nuts and bolts. These are a common place for vacuum leaks to occur.

25. Clean the carburetor periodically and lubricate the linkage.

26. The condition of the tailpipe can be an excellent indicator of proper engine combustion. After a long drive at highway speeds, the inside of the tailpipe should be a light grey in color. Black or soot on the insides indicates an overly rich mixture.

27. Check the fuel pump pressure. The fuel pump may be supplying more fuel than the engine needs.

28. Use the proper grade of gasoline for your engine. Don't try to compensate for knocking or "pinging" by advancing the ignition timing. This practice will only increase plug temperature and the chances of detonation or pre-ignition with relatively little performance gain.

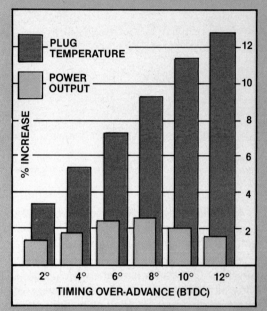

Increasing ignition timing past the specified setting results in a drastic increase in spark plug temperature with increased chance of detonation or preignition. Performance increase is considerably less. (Photo courtesy Champion Spark Plug Co.)

that form in the engine should be flushed out to allow the engine to operate at peak efficiency.

35. Clean the radiator of debris that can decrease cooling efficiency.

36. Install a flex-type or electric cooling fan, if you don't have a clutch type fan. Flex fans use curved plastic blades to push more air at low speeds when more cooling is needed; at high speeds the blades flatten out for less resistance. Electric fans only run when the engine temperature reaches a predetermined level.

37. Check the radiator cap for a worn or cracked gasket. If the cap does not seal properly, the cooling system will not function properly.

42. Be sure the front end is correctly aligned. A misaligned front end actually has wheels going in differed directions. The increased drag can reduce fuel economy by .3 mpg.

43. Correctly adjust the wheel bearings. Wheel bearings that are adjusted too tight increase rolling resistance.

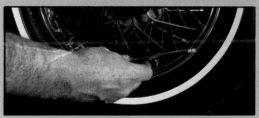

Check tire pressures regularly with a reliable pocket type gauge. Be sure to check the pressure on a cold tire.

GENERAL MAINTENANCE

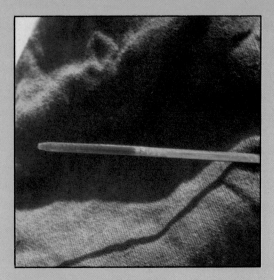

Check the fluid levels (particularly engine oil) on a regular basis. Be sure to check the oil for grit, water or other contamination.

A vacuum gauge is another excellent indicator of internal engine condition and can also be installed in the dash as a mileage indicator.

44. Periodically check the fluid levels in the engine, power steering pump, master cylinder, automatic transmission and drive axle.

45. Change the oil at the recommended interval and change the filter at every oil change. Dirty oil is thick and causes extra friction between moving parts, cutting efficiency and increasing wear. A worn engine requires more frequent tune-ups and gets progressively worse fuel economy. In general, use the lightest viscosity oil for the driving conditions you will encounter.

46. Use the recommended viscosity fluids in the transmission and axle.

47. Be sure the battery is fully charged for fast starts. A slow starting engine wastes fuel.

48. Be sure battery terminals are clean and tight.

49. Check the battery electrolyte level and add distilled water if necessary.

50. Check the exhaust system for crushed pipes, blockages and leaks.

51. Adjust the brakes. Dragging brakes or brakes that are not releasing create increased drag on the engine.

52. Install a vacuum gauge or miles-per-gallon gauge. These gauges visually indicate engine vacuum in the intake manifold. High vacuum = good mileage and low vacuum = poorer mileage. The gauge can also be an excellent indicator of internal engine conditions.

53. Be sure the clutch is properly adjusted. A slipping clutch wastes fuel.

54. Check and periodically lubricate the heat control valve in the exhaust manifold. A sticking or inoperative valve prevents engine warm-up and wastes gas.

55. Keep accurate records to check fuel economy over a period of time. A sudden drop in fuel economy may signal a need for tune-up or other maintenance.

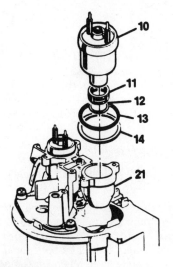

10. Injector–fuel
11. Filter–fuel injector inlet
12. "O" ring–fuel injector–lower
13. "O" ring–fuel injector–upper
14. Washer–fuel injector
21. Fuel meter body assembly

Removing the fuel injector from the throttle body—4.3L engine–2.5 L is similar

5. Using a small pry bar or tool No. J-26868, carefully lift the injector until it is free from the fuel meter body.

6. Remove the small O-ring form the nozzle end of the injector. Carefully rotate the injector's fuel filter back-and-forth to remove it from the base of the injector.

7. Discard the fuel meter cover gasket.

8. Remove the large O-ring and back-up washer from the top of the counterbore of the fuel meter body injector cavity.

9. To install, lubricate the O-rings with automatic transmission fluid and push it into the fuel injector cavity. To complete the installation, reverse the removal procedures. Start the engine and check for fuel leaks.

FUEL METER COVER REPLACEMENT

1. Remove the air cleaner. Disconnect the negative battery terminal from the battery.

2. At the injector electrical connector, squeeze the two tabs together and pull it straight up.

3. Remove the fuel meter-to-fuel meter body screws and lockwashers.

NOTE: *When removing the fuel meter cover screws, note the location of the two short screws.*

4. Remove the fuel meter cover and discard the gasket.

5. To install, use a new gasket and reverse the removal procedures.

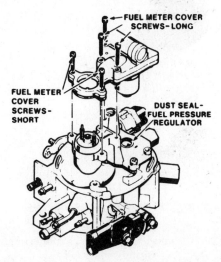

Removing the fuel meter cover from the throttle body—2.5L engine—4.3L is similar

IDLE AIR CONTROL (IAC) VALVE REPLACEMENT

NOTE: *The following procedure requires the use of the GM Removal tool No. J-33031 or equivalent.*

1. From inside the vehicle, remove the engine cover.

2. Remove the air cleaner. Disconnect the negative battery terminal from the battery.

3. Disconnect the electrical connector from the idle air control valve.

4. Using a 1¼" (32mm) wrench or the GM Removal tool No. J-33031, remove the idle air control valve.

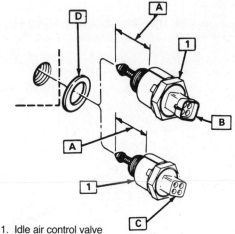

1. Idle air control valve
A. Less than 28mm (1-⅛ in.)
B. Type I (with collar)
C. Type II (without collar)
D. Gasket (part of IAC valve service kit)

Exploded view of the idle air control valve(s)

CAUTION: *Before installing a new idle air control valve, measure the distance that the valve extends (from the motor housing to the end of the cone); the distance should be no greater than 1⅛" (28mm). If it extends to far, damage will occur to the valve when it is installed.*

5. To install, use a new gasket and reverse the removal procedures. Start the engine and allow it to reach normal operating temperatures.

NOTE: *The ECM will reset the idle speed when the vehicle is driven at 30 mph.*

THROTTLE POSITION SENSOR (TPS)

1. Remove the air cleaner.
2. Disconnect the electrical connector from the throttle position sensor (TPS).
3. Remove the TPS mounting screws, the lockwashers and the retainers.
4. Remove the TPS sensor.
5. To install, make sure that the throttle

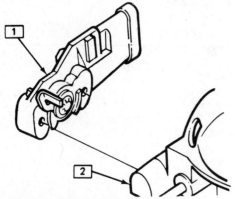

1. Throttle position sensor
2. TBI unit

Exploded view of the throttle position sensor—2.5L engine

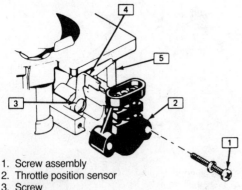

1. Screw assembly
2. Throttle position sensor
3. Screw
4. Lever
5. Throttle body assembly

Exploded view of the throttle position sensor—4.3L engine

valve is in the closed position, then install the TPS sensor.

NOTE: *Make sure the the TPS pickup lever is located ABOVE the tang on the throttle actuator lever.*

6. To complete the installation, lubricate the mounting screws with Loctite® (thread locking compound) No. 262 or equivalent, then reverse the removal procedures.

ADJUSTMENTS

Idle Speed and Mixture Adjustment

2.5L EFI ENGINE

The throttle stop screw, used in regulating the minimum idle speed, is adjusted at the factory and is not necessary to perform. This adjustment should be performed ONLY when the throttle body has been replaced.

NOTE: *The following procedures require the use a tachometer, GM tool No. J-33047, BT-8207 or equivalent, GM Torx Bit No. 20, silicone sealant, a ⁵⁄₃₂" drill bit, a prick punch and a ¹⁄₁₆" pin punch.*

NOTE: *The replacement of the complete throttle body assembly will have the minimum idle adjusted at the factory.*

1. Remove the air cleaner and the gasket. Be sure to plug the THERMAC vacuum port (air cleaner vacuum line-to-throttle body) on the throttle body.

2. Remove the throttle valve cable from the throttle control bracket to provide access to the minimum air adjustment screw.

3. Using the manufacturer's instructions, connect a tachometer to the engine.

4. Remove the electrical connector from the Idle Air Control (IAC) valve, located on the throttle body.

5. If necessary to remove the throttle stop screw cover, perform the following procedures:

   a. Using a prick punch, mark the housing at the top over the center line of the throttle stop screw.

   b. Using a ⁵⁄₃₂" drill bit, drill (on an angle) a hole through the casting to the hardened cover.

   c. Using a ¹⁄₁₆" pin punch, place it through the hole and drive out the cover to expose the throttle stop screw.

6. Place the transmission in Park (AT) or Neutral (MT), start the engine and allow the idle speed to stabilize.

7. Using the GM tool No. J-33047, BT-8207 or equivalent, install it into the idle air passage of the throttle body; be sure that the tool is fully seated in the opening and no air leaks exist.

8. Using the GM Torx Bit No. 20, turn the throttle stop screw until the engine speed is

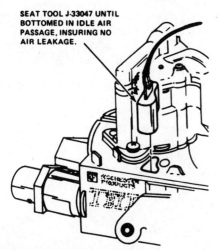

SEAT TOOL J-33047 UNTIL BOTTOMED IN IDLE AIR PASSAGE, INSURING NO AIR LEAKAGE.

Installing the tool J-33047 to adjust the idle speed— 2.5L TBI engine

475–525 rpm (AT in Park or Neutral) or 750–800 rpm (MT in Neutral).

9. With the idle speed adjusted, stop the engine, remove the tool No. J-33047, BT-8207 or equivalent, from the throttle body.

10. Reconnect the Idle Air Control (IAC) electrical connector.

11. Using silicone sealant or equivalent, cover the throttle stop screw.

12. Reinstall the gasket and the air cleaner assembly.

4.3L EFI ENGINE

NOTE: *The following procedure requires the use of a tachometer, a prick punch, a $^5/_{32}$" drill bit, a $^1/_{16}$" pin punch, a grounding wire and silicone sealant.*

1. Remove the air cleaner and the gasket.

2. If necessary to remove the throttle stop screw cover, perform the following procedures:

   a. Using a prick punch, mark the housing at the top over the center line of the throttle stop screw.

   b. Using a $^5/_{32}$" drill bit, drill (on an angle) a hole through the casting to the hardened cover.

   c. Using a $^1/_{16}$" pin punch, place it through the hole and drive out the cover to expose the throttle stop screw.

NOTE: *The following adjustment should be performed ONLY when the throttle body assembly has been replaced; the engine should be at normal operating temperatures before making this adjustment.*

3. With the Idle Air Control (IAC) connected, ground the diagnostic terminal of the Assembly Line Communications Link (ALCL) connector.

NOTE: *The Assembly Line Communications*

Link (ALCL) connector is located in the engine compartment on the left side firewall.

4. Turn the ignition switch On but DO NOT start the engine. Wait 30 seconds, this will allow the IAC valve pintle to extend and seat in the throttle body.

5. With the ignition switch turned On, disconnect the Idle Air Control (IAC) valve electrical connector.

6. Remove the ground from the Diagnostic Terminal ALCL connector and start the engine.

7. Adjust the idle stop screw to obtain 400–450 rpm (AT in Drive).

8. Turn the ignition switch Off and reconnect the IAC valve electrical connector.

9. Using silicone sealant or equivalent, cover the throttle stop screw.

10. Reinstall the gasket and the air cleaner assembly.

Throttle Position Sensor (TPS)

The throttle position sensor is non-adjustable but a test should be performed ONLY when throttle body parts have been replaced or AFTER the minimum idle speed has been adjusted.

NOTE: *The following procedure requires the use of the Digital Voltmeter tool No. J-29125-A or equivalent.*

1. Using the Digital Voltmeter tool No. J-29125-A or equivalent, set it on the 0–5.0V scale, then connect the probes to the center terminal **B** and the outside terminal **C** (2.5L engine) or **A** (4.3L engine).

NOTE: *To attach probes to the TPS electrical connector, disconnect the TPS electrical connector, install thin wires into the sockets and reconnect the connector.*

2. Turn the ignition On (engine stopped).

3. The output voltage should be 1.25V. If the voltage is more that 1.25V, replace the TPS.

4. Remove the voltmeter and the jumper wires.

FUEL TANK

The fuel tank is located under the left side, center of the vehicle and is held in place by two metal straps.

REMOVAL AND INSTALLATION

1. Disconnect the negative battery terminal from the battery.

NOTE: *Be sure to keep a Class B (dry chemical) fire extinguisher nearby.*

CAUTION: *Due to the possibility of fire or explosion, never drain or store gasoline in an open container.*

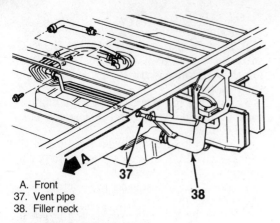

A. Front
37. Vent pipe
38. Filler neck

View of the installed fuel tank

2. Using a hand pump or a siphon hose, drain the gasoline into an approved container.
3. Raise and support the vehicle on jackstands.

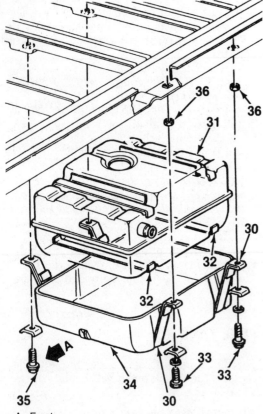

A. Front
30. Strap
31. Tank
32. Insulator
33. Bolt
34. Lower shield
35. Bolt
36. Nut

Exploded view of the fuel tank and accessories.

4. Support the fuel tank and remove the fuel tank-to-vehicle straps.
5. Lower the tank slightly, then remove the sender unit wires, the hoses and the ground strap.
6. Remove the fuel tank from the vehicle.
7. To install, align the insulator strips and reverse the removal procedures. Torque the inner fuel tank strap-to-vehicle bolts to 26 ft.lb. and the outer fuel tank strap-to-vehicle nuts/bolts to 26 ft.lb.

NOTE: *Be sure to connect the sender unit wires and the hoses before final installation of the fuel tank.*

TROUBLESHOOTING

All GM dealerships are equipped with a testing tool, known as SCAN (it connects to the ALCL diagnostic connector), which performs quick checks of the sensors and switches that provide information to the Electronic Control Module (ECM). Due to the cost factor, it is not advisable for the do-it-yourselfer to purchase one. Since these troubleshooting procedures will be limited to NON-SCAN procedures, it is advisable to schedule an appointment with a dealership to have the vehicle thoroughly checked.

Understanding the diagnostic checks and using it correctly will reduce the diagnostic time and prevent unnecessary replacement of parts.

NOTE: *This book contains simple testing procedures for your Vans's electronic ignition and fuel injection system. More comprehensive testing on your Van's systems can be found in CHILTON'S GUIDE TO ELECTRONIC ENGINE CONTROLS, book part number 7535, and CHILTON'S GUIDE TO FUEL INJECTION AND FEEDBACK CARBURETORS, book part number 7488, available at your local retailer.*

CAUTION: *If attempting to do any checking or repair of the electrical system, be very careful, for these systems are VERY delicate and major damage can occur. All work of this nature should be referred to a qualified technician.*

Non-Scan Diagnostic Checks

The following is an explanation of the NON-SCAN diagnostic circuit check:

1. With engine stopped, the ignition turned On and a steady "SERVICE ENGINE SOON" light On, at the instrument panel, indicates that there is battery and ignition voltage to the ECM.
2. Connect a jumper wire between the terminals **A** to **B** of the ALCL diagnostic connec-

tor (located beneath the instrument panel), the following instrument panel display will occur:

a. The ECM will cause the "SERVICE ENGINE SOON" lamp to flash a Code 12, which indicates that the ECM diagnostics are working.

b. The Code 12 will flash three times, followed by any other trouble codes that are stored in its memory.

c. Each additional code will flash three times, starting with the lowest code, then the cycle will start over again with the Code 12.

d. If there are no other codes, the Code 12 will flash continuously until the jumper wire is disconnected or the engine is started.

3. Record all of the stored codes, except Code 12, then consult the service shop.

4. The "Field Service Mode" may be helpful in the diagnosis, depending on the severity of the problem. With the diagnostic terminal grounded and the engine running, the ECM will respond to the O_2 sensor signal voltage and use the "SERVICE ENGINE SOON" light to display the following information:

a. CLOSED LOOP—confirms that the O_2 sensor signal is being used by the ECM to control the fuel delivery and that the system is working normally; the signal voltage will quickly change from 0.35–0.55V.

b. OPEN LOOP—indicates that the O_2 sensor voltage signal is not usable to the ECM; the signal is at a constant value between 0.35–0.55V.

NOTE: *The system will flash "Open Loop" for 1/2–2 minutes after the engine starts or until the sensor reaches normal operating temperature; if the system fails to go to "Closed Loop".*

c. SERVICE ENGINE SOON—with this light Off, the exhaust is lean; the O_2 sensor signal voltage will remain under 0.35V and steady.

d. SERVICE ENGINE SOON—with this light On and steady (not flashing), the exhaust is rich; the O_2 sensor voltage will be over 0.55V and steady.

5. Road test the vehicle, at steady speeds, using the "Field Service Mode".

Because the vehicle operations are different in the "Field Service Mode" the following conditions may be observed and should be considered normal:

• Acceleration—The light may be On too long due to acceleration enrichment.

• Deceleration—The light may be Off too long due to deceleration enleanment or fuel cut-off.

• Idle—The light may be On too long with the idle below 1,200 rpm.

6. To clear the codes, turn the ignition Off and disconnect the battery terminal or the ECM **B** fuse for ten seconds.

ECM CODE DESCRIPTIONS

2.5L EFI Engines

• Code 12—No reference code.
• Code 13—Oxygen sensor circuit open.
• Code 14—Coolant sensor circuit indicating low signal voltage.
• Code 15—Coolant sensor circuit indicating high signal voltage.
• Code 21—Throttle Position Sensor (TPS) indicating high signal voltage.
• Code 22—Throttle Position Sensor (TPS) indicating low signal voltage.
• Code 24—Vehicle Speed Sensor (VSS) defective.
• Code 33—Manifold Absolute Pressure (MAP) sensor indicating high signal voltage.
• Code 34—Manifold Absolute Pressure (MAP) sensor indicating low signal voltage.
• Code 35—Idle Air Control (IAC) valve defective.
• Code 42—Electronic Spark Timing (EST) circuit indicating an open or short in the EST or bypass circuits.
• Code 44—Lean exhaust indicating open oxygen sensor circuit.
• Code 45—Rich exhaust indicating open oxygen sensor circuit.
• Code 51—Programmable Read Only Memory (PROM) unit defective or loose terminals.
• Code 55—Electronic Control Module (ECM) unit defective.

4.3L Engines

CARBURETOR (1985)

• Code 12—No reference code.
• Code 13—Oxygen sensor circuit open.
• Code 14—Coolant sensor circuit indicating low signal voltage.
• Code 15—Coolant sensor circuit indicating high signal voltage.
• Code 21—Throttle Position Sensor (TPS) indicating high signal voltage.
• Code 22—Throttle Position Sensor (TPS) indicating low signal voltage.
• Code 23—M/C solenoid circuit open or grounded.
• Code 24—Vehicle Speed Sensor (VSS) circuit defective.
• Code 32—Barometric Pressure Sensor (BARO) circuit indicating low voltage.
• Code 34—Manifold Absolute Pressure (MAP) sensor indicating low signal voltage.
• Code 35—Idle Speed Control (ISC) switch short circuited.
• Code 41—Distributor-to-ECM circuit open.

• Code 42 – Electronic Spark Timing (EST) circuit indicating an open or short in the EST or bypass circuits.
• Code 43 – Electronic Spark Control (ESC) system defective.
• Code 44 – Lean exhaust indicating open oxygen sensor circuit.
• Code 45 – Rich exhaust indicating open oxygen sensor circuit.
• Code 51 – Programmable Read Only Memory (PROM) unit defective or loose terminals.
• Code 53 – Exhaust Gas Recirculation (EGR) system defective
• Code 54 – M/C Solenoid shorted and/or faulty ECM.
• Code 55 – Electronic Control Module (ECM) unit defective.

THROTTLE BODY (1986–87)
• Code 12 – No reference code.
• Code 13 – Oxygen sensor circuit open.
• Code 14 – Coolant sensor circuit indicating low signal voltage.
• Code 15 – Coolant sensor circuit indicating high signal voltage.
• Code 21 – Throttle Position Sensor (TPS) indicating high signal voltage.
• Code 22 – Throttle Position Sensor (TPS) indicating low signal voltage.
• Code 24 – Vehicle Speed Sensor (VSS) defective.
• Code 32 – Exhaust Gas Recirculation (EGR) system failure.
• Code 33 – Manifold Absolute Pressure (MAP) sensor indicating high signal voltage.
• Code 34 – Manifold Absolute Pressure (MAP) sensor indicating low signal voltage.
• Code 42 – Electronic Spark Timing (EST) circuit indicating an open or short in the EST or bypass circuits.
• Code 43 – Electronic Spark Control (ESC) system defective.
• Code 44 – Lean exhaust indicating open oxygen sensor circuit.
• Code 45 – Rich exhaust indicating open oxygen sensor circuit.
• Code 51 – Programmable Read Only Memory (PROM) unit defective or loose terminals.
• Code 52 – CALPAK unit defective.
• Code 55 – Electronic Control Module (ECM) unit defective.

DIAGNOSTIC INSPECTION
Initial Checks
The importance of these procedures can save valuable time by preventing any further inspections.
1. Check the hoses for splits, kinks and proper connections (see the Vehicle Emission Control Information label).
2. Inspect for air leaks at the throttle body or carburetor and the intake manifold.
3. Check the ignition wires for cracking, hardening, routing and carbon tracking.
4. Check the wiring for pinches, cuts and proper connections.

Intermittent Problems
NOTE: *These problems may or may not turn On the "SERVICE ENGINE SOON" light or store a code. DO NOT use the trouble codes in this section. If a fault is present, locate it and repair it.*
1. Most intermittent problems are caused by faulty electrical connections or wiring. Perform careful visual checks of the suspected circuits for:
• BACKED OUT CONNECTORS – Terminals not fully seated in the connector or poor mating of the connector halves.
• DAMAGED CONNECTORS – Improperly formed connectors. Reform the connectors to increase the contact tension.
• POOR TERMINAL TO WIRE CONNECTION – Remove the terminal from the connector and check the condition of the wire to the terminal.
2. Connect a voltmeter to the suspected circuit and drive it around. An abnormal voltage reading in the circuit may indicate the problem is in that circuit.
3. The trouble memory code may be lost. Disconnect the Throttle Position Sensor (TPS) and curb idle the engine until the "SERVICE ENGINE SOON" light turns On. Code 22 should be stored and kept in the memory when the ignition is turned Off (for at least 10 seconds); if not, the ECM is faulty.
4. If the problem still exists, perform the following checks:
• A sharp electrical surge occurs, usually when a faulty component is operated, such as: a relay, an Electronic Control Module (ECM) driven solenoid or a switch.
• The improper installation of optional equipment, such as: A two-way radio, lights or etc.
• Electronic Spark Timing (EST) wires may be too close to the spark plug wires, the distributor wires, the distributor housing, the coil and/or the alternator. Be sure that the distributor ground wire is grounded well.
• The secondary ignition may be shorted to ground.
• The Electronic Control Module (ECM) power wire may be grounded.

Hard Starting

The engine cranks OK but will not start for a long period of time, it eventually runs or it may start and immediately dies.

1. Check the fuel system for:
- Water in the fuel.
- Poor fuel pressure.
- A sticking or binding Throttle Position Sensor (TPS).
  - A bad fuel pump relay.
  - A poor in-tank fuel pump check valve.
2. Check the ignition system for:
- Ignition coil output.
- A worn distributor shaft.
- Bare and/or shorted wires.
- Poor pickup coil resistance and connections.
- Loose ignition coil ground.
- Moisture in the distributor cap.
- Defective spark plugs.
3. If the engine starts, then immediately stalls, open the distributor by-pass line. If it then starts and runs OK, replace the distributor pickup coil.
4. If the engine is hard to start, at normal operating temperature, check the ECM.

Surge and/or Chuggle

At normal speed, with no change in the accelerator pedal position, the engine speeds up and slows down, inspect the following:
- Vehicle Speed Sensor (VSS) using the ALCL diagnostic connector.
- Exhaust Gas Recirculation (EGR) system if the problem is intermittent at idle.
- Ignition timing (see the Vehicle Emission Control Information label).
- Inline fuel filter for restrictions.
- Fuel pressure.
- Alternator output voltage, it must between 9–16V.
- Oxygen sensor.
- Spark plugs, distributor cap and ignition wire condition.
- Transmission Convertor Clutch (TCC) operation.

Lack of Power (Sluggish)

When the accelerator is pushed part way down, there is little or no increase in speed or power.

1. Compare your vehicles performance with a similar one.
2. Check and/or replace the air cleaner.
3. Check the following equipment:
- Ignition timing (see Vehicle Emission Control Information label).
- Fuel system for a plugged fuel filter, poor fuel pressure and/or contaminated fuel.

- Poor Electronic Control Module (ECM) grounds.
- Exhaust Gas Recirculation (EGR) valve being open or partly open all of the time.
- Alternator output voltage, it must between 9–16V.
- Valve timing.
- Engine compression.
- Worn camshaft lobes.

4. To inspect the exhaust system, perform the following procedures with the engine at normal operating temperatures:

a. Using a vacuum gauge, connect it to an intake manifold port.

b. Disconnect the EGR solenoid electrical connector or connect the EGR valve directly to a vacuum source bypassing any switches or solenoids.

c. Operate the engine at 1,000 rpm and record the vacuum reading.

d. Slowly increase the engine speed to 2,500 rpm, hold the speed at 2,500 rpm and record the vacuum reading.

NOTE: *If the vacuum reading, taken at 2,500 rpm, decreases more than 3 in.Hg from the one taken at 1,000 rpm, the exhaust system should be inspected for restrictions*

e. Disconnect the exhaust pipe from the engine and repeat the Steps 4c and 4d.

NOTE: *If the reading still drops more than 3 in.Hg, check the valve timing.*

Detonation/Spark Knock

The engine makes a sharp metallic knocks, which range from mild to severe pings, usually worse under acceleration.

1. If a heating problem is noticed, check for:

a. Low engine coolant.

b. A loose water pump drive belt.

c. Restricted air or water flow through the radiator.

2. For other than heating problems, check for:

a. Poor quality fuel (low octane rating).

b. Correct Progammable Read Only Memory (PROM) unit.

c. THERMAC may be staying closed.

d. Ignition timing (see the Vehicle Emission Control Information label).

e. Low fuel pressure.

f. Exhaust Gas Recirculation (EGR) valve may be closed.

g. Transmission for proper shifting points and operation of the Transmission Convertor Clutch (TCC).

h. Incorrect engine parts, such as: camshaft, cylinder head(s), pistons and etc.

3. If the problem persists, obtain a can of en-

gine (carbon) cleaner and follow the instructions on the can.

Hesitation or Stumble

This condition is a momentary lack of response when accelerating, which can occur at all speeds but usually when trying to make the vehicle move from a stop sign; it may cause the vehicle to stall, if severe enough.

To check the systems, perform the following checks:

- Low fuel pressure.
- Water in fuel.
- Binding or sticking Throttle Position Sensor (TPS).
- Ignition timing (see Vehicle Emission Control Information label).
- Alternator output, it must be between 9–16V.
- An ungrounded in the High Energy Ignition (HEI) system.
- Non-working emissions canister purge.
- Non-working Exhaust Gas Recirculation (EGR) valve.

Misses or Cuts Out

This condition is a steady pulsation or jerking which follows the engine speed, it is usually more pronounced as the engine increases speed. At low speed or idle, the exhaust has a steady spitting sound.

1. To check for a missing cylinder, perform the following procedures:

a. Disconnect the electrical connector from the Idle Air Control (IAC) motor.

b. Start the engine.

c. Using insulated pliers, remove one spark plug wire at a time and check for an rpm drop. If no drop is noticed, check the spark plugs for cracks, wear, improper gap, burned electrodes and/or heavy deposits. NOTE: *If a drop of 50 rpm is recorded between the cylinders, replace the IAC electrical connector and proceed to the "Rough, Unstable or Incorrect Idle, Stalling" section.*

2. Using an ohmmeter, over $30,000\Omega$, check the spark plug wires and replace them, if necessary.

3. Using the Spark Tester tool No. J-26792 or equivalent, check the ignition coil's primary and secondary voltages.

4. Check the fuel system for a plugged fuel filter, water in the fuel and/or low fuel pump pressure.

5. Inspect the ignition timing (see the Vehicle Emission Control Information label).

6. Perform a compression check on the engine; if the compression is low, repair as necessary.

7. Inspect the distributor cap and rotor for dust, cracks, burns, moisture and etc. Using a fine water mist, spray the cap and plug wires to check for shorts.

8. Remove the rocker arm covers and inspect for bent pushrods, worn rocker arms, broken valve springs and/or worn camshaft lobes.

Poor Fuel Economy

By performing an actual road test, it is determined that the fuel economy is lower than some other actual road test on the same vehicle.

To determine the reason for the poor fuel economy, inspect the following items:

1. The engine thermostat for the wrong heat range or a faulty (always open) part.

2. The fuel system for low fuel pressure.

3. The ignition timing (see the Vehicle Emission Control Information label).

4. The Transmission Convertor Clutch (TCC) for proper operation.

Rough, Unstable or Incorrect Idle, Stalling

In this condition, the engine idles unevenly, it may shake (if bad enough) and/or may stall.

To determine the reason(s) for poor operation, inspect the following items:

1. The ignition timing (see the Vehicle Emission Control Informations label).

2. The Park/Neutral (P/N) switch, if equipped with an AT.

3. A leaking fuel injector.

4. A fuel injector operating too rich or lean.

If rough idle occurs ONLY when the engine is Hot, perform the additional checks:

1. To check for vacuum leaks, perform the following checks:

a. Using the GM Plug tool No. J-33047 or equivalent, block the idle air passage.

b. If the engine speed is higher than 650 rpm with the throttle closed, locate and correct the vacuum leak, such as: A disconnected thermac or cruise control hose.

2. The Park/Neutral (P/N) switch, if equipped with an AT.

3. The Throttle Position Switch (TPS) may be sticking or binding, causing the throttle to remain open.

4. Exhaust Gas Recirculation (EGR) system—if it is on while the engine is idling, roughness, stalling and hard starting will occur.

5. Battery cables and ground straps—dirty and loose battery connections will cause erratic voltage, which will cause the Idle Air Control (IAC) valve to change its position, resulting in poor idle quality. The IAC valve will not move if the system voltage is below 9V or greater than 17.8V.

6. Power Steering system—the ECM should

compensate for power steering loads; if the signal is lost, the vehicle will be difficult to park and steer with heavy loads.

7. Manifold Absolute Pressure (MAP) sensor – idle the engine and disconnect the electrical connector from the sensor, if the idle improves, substitute a known GOOD sensor and recheck.

8. The Air Conditioning (A/C) compressor and relay, also, the refrigerant pressure may be too high or have a faulty cycling switch.

9. The Positive Crankcase Ventilation (PCV) valve – place your finger over the end and release it several times, if the valve does not snap back, replace it.

10. Perform a cylinder compression check and compare the results, then repair as necessary.

11. Oxygen sensor – inspect it for sensor contamination (white, powdery coating) and high electrical conductivity; as a result, the ECM will reduce the amount of fuel to the engine.

12. Air Management system – check for intermittent air to the ports while in the "Closed Loop" operation (4.3L engines).

Abnormal Emissions (Odors)

To correct abnormal emissions, inspect or test the following items, for:

1. Excessive CO and HC emissions (odors), plus, any thing that will make the engine run rich.

2. Incorrect ignition timing (see the Vehicle Emission Control Information label).

3. Loading of the fuel emissions canister.

4. Stuck or blocked Positive Crankcase Ventilation (PCV) valve.

5. Condition of the spark plugs, ignition wires and distributor cap.

6. Lead contamination of the Catalytic Converter.

Dieseling

This condition exists when the ignition switch is turned Off and the engine continues to run roughly. If the engine runs smoothly, check and/or adjust the ignition switch.

NOTE: *The only way to prevent the engine from dieseling is to eliminate fuel leakage to the cylinders.*

To remedy this situation, turn the ignition switch On, to energize the fuel pump, then check the fuel injector(s) and the throttle body for fuel leakage. If necessary, repair or replace the leaking items.

Backfire

This condition exists when fuel ignites in the intake or exhaust manifold, making a loud popping noise.

To correct this situation, inspect and/or replace the following items:

• Exhaust Gas Recirculation (EGR) system, it must not be open all of the time.

• Output voltage of the ignition coil.

• Crossfire between the spark plugs (distributor cap, ignition wires).

• Intermittent condition in the primary ignition system.

• Ignition timing (see the Vehicle Emission Control Information label).

• Faulty spark plugs and/or ignition wires.

• Valve timing.

• Compression check – look for leaking or sticking valves.

Chassis Electrical

5

UNDERSTANDING BASIC ELECTRICITY

For any electrical system to operate, it must make a complete circuit. This simply means that the power flow from the battery must make a complete circle. When an electrical component is operating, power flows from the battery to the component, passes through the component causing it to perform its function (lighting a light bulb, for example) and then returns to the battery through the ground of the circuit. This ground is usually (but not always) the metal part of the vehicle on which the electrical component is mounted.

Perhaps the easiest way to visualize this is to think of connecting a light bulb (with two wires attached to it) to the battery. The battery has two posts (negative and positive). If one of the two wires (attached to the light bulb) is attached to the negative post of the battery and the other wire is attached to the positive post of the battery, you would have a complete circuit. Current from the battery would flow out of one post, through the wire (attached to it) and then to the light bulb, causing it to light. It would then leave the light bulb, travel through the other wire and return to the other post of the battery.

The normal automotive circuit differs from this simple example in two ways. First, instead of having a return wire from the bulb to the battery, the light bulb returns the current to the battery through the chassis of the vehicle. Since the negative battery cable is attached to the chassis and the chassis is made of electrically conductive metal, the chassis of the vehicle can serve as a ground wire to complete the circuit. Secondly, most automotive circuits contain switches to turn components On and Off as required.

There are many types of switches but the most common simply serves to prevent the passage of current when it is turned Off. Since the

switch is a part of the circle necessary for a complete circuit, it operates to leave an opening in the circuit and thus an incomplete or open circuit, when it is turned Off.

Some electrical components which require a large amount of current to operate also have a relay in their circuit. Since these circuits carry a large amount of current, the thickness of the wire (gauge size) in the circuit is also greater. If this large wire were connected from the component to the control switch on the instrument panel and then back to the component, a voltage drop would occur in the circuit. To prevent this potential drop in voltage, an electromagnetic switch (relay) is used. The large wires in the circuit are connected from the battery to one side of the relay and from the opposite side of the relay to the component. The relay is normally open, preventing current from passing through the circuit. An additional, smaller, wire is connected from the relay to the control switch for the circuit. When the control switch is turned On, it grounds the smaller wire from the relay and completes the circuit. This closes the relay and allows current to flow from the battery to the component. The horn, headlight and starter circuits are three which use relays.

You have probably noticed how the vehicle's instrument panel lights get brighter the faster you rev the engine. This happens because the alternator (which supplies current to the battery) puts out more current at speeds above idle. This is normal. However, it is possible for larger surges of current to pass through the electrical system. If this surge of current were to reach an electrical component, it could burn the component out. To prevent this from happening, fuses are connected in the current supply wires of most of the major electrical systems. The fuse serves to head off the surge at the pass. When an electrical current of excessive power passes through the component's fuse, the fuse blows out and breaks the circuit, saving it from destruction.

The fuse also protects the component from damage if the power supply wire to the component is grounded before the current reaches the component.

There is another important rule to the complete circle circuit. **Every complete circuit from a power source must include a component which is using the power from the power source.** If you were to disconnect the light bulb (from the previous example of a light bulb being connected to the battery by two wires together — take our word for it — don't try it) the result would literally be shocking. A similar thing happens (on a smaller scale) when the power supply wire to a component or the electrical component itself becomes grounded before the normal ground connection for the circuit. To prevent damage to the system, the fuse for the circuit blows to interrupt the circuit — protecting the components from damage. Because grounding a wire from a power source makes a complete circuit — less the required component to use the power — this phenomenon is called a short circuit. The most common causes of short circuits are: the rubber insulation on a wire breaking or rubbing through to expose the current carrying core of the wire to a metal part of the vehicle or a shorted switch.

Some electrical systems on the vehicle are protected by a circuit breaker which is, basically, a self-repairing fuse. When either of the above described events take place in a system which is protected by a circuit breaker, the circuit breaker opens the circuit the same way a fuse does. However, when either the short is removed from the circuit or the surge subsides, the circuit breaker may be reset and does not have to be replaced as a fuse does.

The final protective device in the chassis electrical system is a fuse link. A fuse link is a wire that acts as a fuse. It is connected between the starter relay and the main wiring harness for the vehicle. This connection is under the hood, very near a similar fuse link which protects all the chassis electrical components. It is the probable cause of trouble when none of the electrical components function, unless the battery is disconnected or dead.

HEATING AND AIR CONDITIONING

Heater Blower Motor
REMOVAL AND INSTALLATION
Front (Main) Motor

The blower motor is located in the engine compartment on the right side of the firewall.

1. Disconnect the negative battery terminal from the battery.

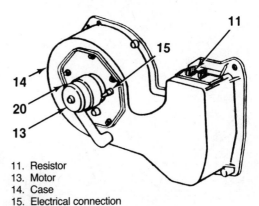

11. Resistor
13. Motor
14. Case
15. Electrical connection
20. Screws

View of the heater blower motor and case

2. Disconnect the electrical connector from the blower motor.

3. Remove the radiator coolant collecting bottle from the right side of the engine compartment.

4. Remove the windshield washer fluid bottle from the right side of the engine compartment.

5. Remove the blower motor-to-duct housing screws and the blower motor from the vehicle.

6. If necessary, replace the blower motor-to-duct housing gasket.

7. To install, reverse the removal procedures. Refill the windshield washer bottle and the radiator coolant collecting bottle.

Rear (Overhead) Motor

A rear overhead heater provides heating to the rear of the vehicle. It is located on the left side of the vehicle, in front of the wheel fender and is concealed behind a cover.

1. Disconnect the negative battery terminal from the battery.

2. Remove the cover-to-heater unit and the cover.

3. Disconnect the electrical connector from the blower motor.

4. Remove the blower motor-to-heater housing screws and the blower motor.

5. If necessary, replace the blower motor-to-heater housing gasket.

6. To install, use a new gasket (if necessary) and reverse the removal procedures.

Blower Motor Resistor

A blower motor resistor is mounted on top of each blower/heater or blower/evaporator case.

REMOVAL AND INSTALLATION

1. Disconnect the negative battery terminal from the battery.

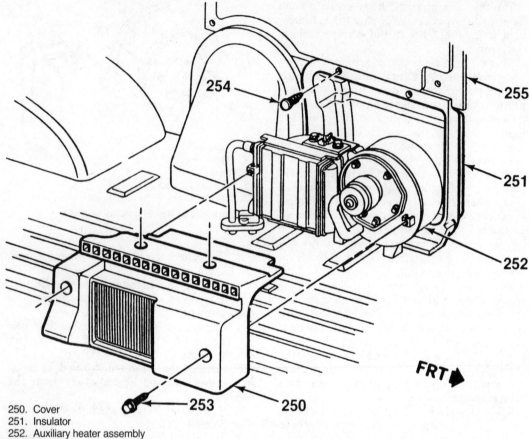

250. Cover
251. Insulator
252. Auxiliary heater assembly
253. Screw
254. Retainer
255. Arm rest assembly

View of the rear heater assembly

2. Disconnect the electrical connector from the resistor.

3. Remove the resistor-to-case screws and lift the resistor from the case.

4. To install, reverse the removal procedures.

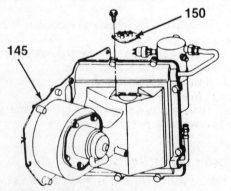

145. Blower motor and evaporator case
150. Resistor

Exploded view of a blower motor resistor—all are similar

Heater Core

REMOVAL AND INSTALLATION

Front Core

The front heater core is located on the right side of the passenger compartment, under the dash.

1. Disconnect the negative battery terminal from the battery.

2. Place a catch pan under the radiator, open the drain cock and drain the coolant to a level below the heater core.

3. Remove the radiator overflow coolant bottle and the windshield washer fluid bottle.

4. In the engine compartment, remove the inlet/outlet hose clamps from the heater core. Remove and plug the heater hoses to prevent coolant spillage.

5. From inside the vehicle, remove the engine cover to provide extra room.

6. From under the dash, remove the lower right filler panel.

7. Remove the distributor duct, for extra room.

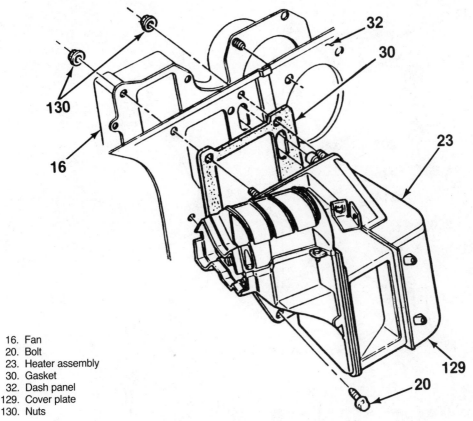

16. Fan
20. Bolt
23. Heater assembly
30. Gasket
32. Dash panel
129. Cover plate
130. Nuts

Exploded view of the front heater assembly

8. Remove the heater-to-cowl bolts and the heater assembly from the vehicle.

9. Separate the cover plate and the heater core from the heater assembly.

10. To install, reverse the removal procedures. Refill the cooling system. Start the engine, allow the engine to reach normal operating temperatures, then check for system leaks and heat output.

Rear Core

A rear heater core provides heating to the rear of the vehicle. It is located on the left side of the vehicle, in front of the wheel fender and is concealed behind a cover.

1. Disconnect the negative battery terminal from the battery.

2. Place a catch pan under the radiator, open the drain cock and drain the cooling system.

3. From under the vehicle (at the rear heating unit), remove the inlet/outlet hose clamps from the heater core. Remove and plug the heater hoses to prevent coolant excess spillage.

4. From inside the vehicle, remove the heating unit cover.

5. Remove the heater core from the blower assembly.

6. Inspect the heater hoses for deterioration, then replace (if necessary).

7. To install, reverse the removal procedures. Refill the cooling system. Start the engine, allow the engine to reach normal operating temperatures, then check the system for leaks and heat output.

Control Assembly

The control assembly is located on the instrument panel to the right side of the steering wheel.

REMOVAL AND INSTALLATION

1. Disconnect the negative battery terminal from the battery.

2. Remove the instrument panel bezel.

3. Remove the control assembly-to-instrument panel screws and pull the control assembly from the instrument panel.

4. Disconnect the electrical connectors, the control cables and the blower switch from the control assembly.

5. To install, reverse the removal proce-

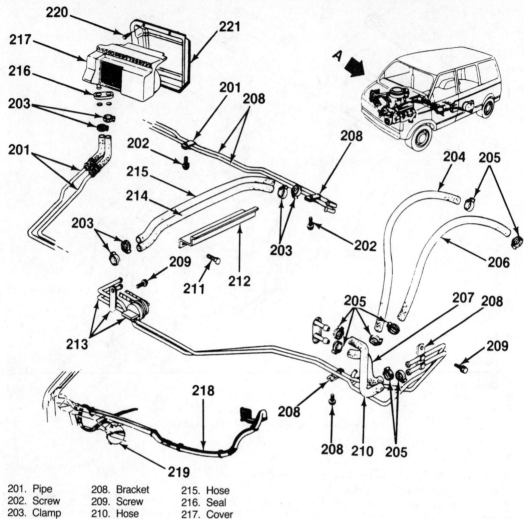

201. Pipe	208. Bracket	215. Hose
202. Screw	209. Screw	216. Seal
203. Clamp	210. Hose	217. Cover
204. Hose	211. Screw	218. Harness
205. Clamp	212. Support	219. Tank
206. Hose	213. Valve	220. Retainer
207. Hose	214. Hose	221. Insulator

Exploded view of the rear heating system

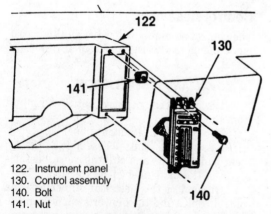

122. Instrument panel
130. Control assembly
140. Bolt
141. Nut

Removing the control assembly from the instrument panel

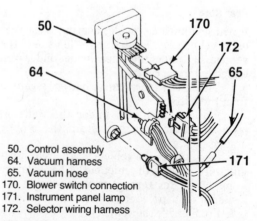

50. Control assembly
64. Vacuum harness
65. Vacuum hose
170. Blower switch connection
171. Instrument panel lamp
172. Selector wiring harness

View of the control assembly connectors

dures. Check the operation of the control cables and the switches of the control assembly.

Evaporator Blower Motor

REMOVAL AND INSTALLATION

Front System

The blower motor is located in the engine compartment on the right side of the firewall.

1. Disconnect the negative battery terminal from the battery.
2. Disconnect the electrical connector from the blower motor.
3. Remove the radiator coolant collecting bottle from the right side of the engine compartment.
4. Remove the windshield washer fluid bottle from the right side of the engine compartment.
5. Remove the relay bracket and move it aside.
6. Remove the blower motor-to-duct housing screws and the blower motor from the vehicle.
7. If necessary, replace the blower motor-to-duct housing gasket.
8. To install, reverse the removal procedures. Refill the windshield washer bottle and the radiator coolant collecting bottle.

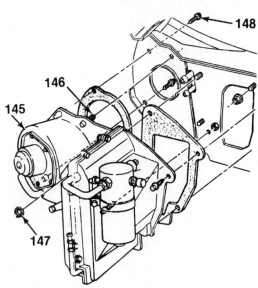

145. Blower motor and evaporator case
146. Seal
147. Nut
148. Screw

Exploded view of the heater blower/evaporator case— front A/C system

Rear Overhead System

The rear overhead blower motor is located at the rear door on the left side.

1. Disconnect the negative battery terminal from the battery.
2. Remove the rear blower motor-to-vehicle cover.
3. Disconnect the electrical connectors from the rear blower motor.
4. Remove the blower motor-to-blower case screws and the blower motor from the vehicle.
5. To install, reverse the removal procedures.

Blower Motor Relay—A/C System

The blower motor relay is located on a bracket attached to the right side of the vehicle, near the blower motor.

REMOVAL AND INSTALLATION

1. Disconnect the negative battery terminal from the battery.
2. Disconnect the electrical connector from the blower motor relay.
3. Remove the blower motor relay bracket-to-vehicle screws, lift the bracket and remove the relay from the bracket.
4. To install, reverse the removal procedures.

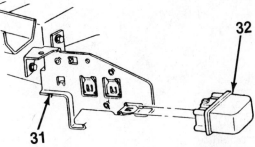

31. Bracket
32. Blower motor relay

Replacing the blower motor relay

Evaporator Core

Two evaporator cores are used, one in the front (engine compartment) and one at the rear (overhead) door. The rear overhead A/C system works in conjunction with the front system.

REMOVAL AND INSTALLATION

NOTE: *Before removing the evaporator core, the A/C system must be discharged. Refer to the A/C Discharging procedures in Chapter 1 and discharge the A/C system.*

Front System

The front evaporator core is located in the engine compartment on the right side of the

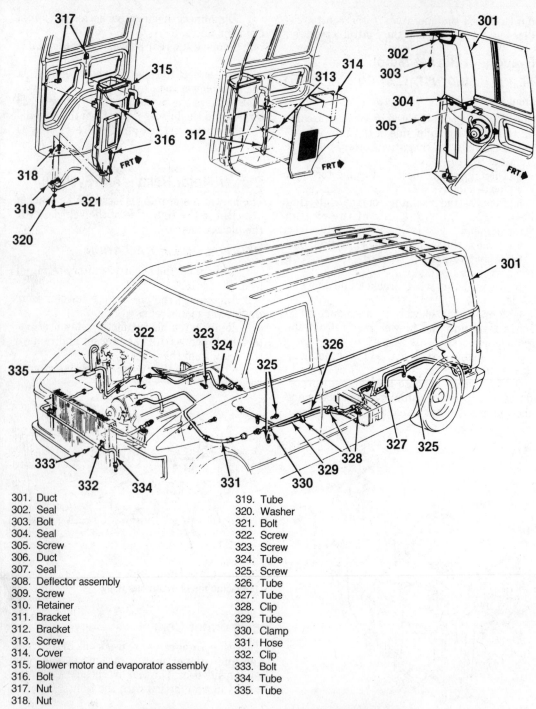

301. Duct	319. Tube
302. Seal	320. Washer
303. Bolt	321. Bolt
304. Seal	322. Screw
305. Screw	323. Screw
306. Duct	324. Tube
307. Seal	325. Screw
308. Deflector assembly	326. Tube
309. Screw	327. Tube
310. Retainer	328. Clip
311. Bracket	329. Tube
312. Bracket	330. Clamp
313. Screw	331. Hose
314. Cover	332. Clip
315. Blower motor and evaporator assembly	333. Bolt
316. Bolt	334. Tube
317. Nut	335. Tube
318. Nut	

Exploded view of the rear overhead A/C unit assembly

firewall inside the heater/evaporator/blower motor case.

1. Disconnect the negative battery terminal from the battery.

2. Remove the radiator coolant collecting bottle and the windshield washer fluid bottle.

3. Disconnect any necessary electrical connectors.

4. Disconnect the A/C refrigerant lines from the evaporator.

5. Remove the relay bracket and move it aside.

6. Remove the evaporator/blower case nuts and the case, then separate the evaporator from the case.

7. To install, reverse the removal proce-

dures. Reconnect the electrical connectors. Recharge the A/C system. Start the engine, allow it establish normal operating temperatures and check the A/C cooling operation.

Rear Overhead System

1. Disconnect the negative battery terminal from the battery.

2. Remove the rear evaporator/blower motor-to-vehicle cover.

3. Disconnect the electrical connectors from the rear blower motor and the resistor.

4. From under the left rear of the vehicle, remove the A/C line fitting-to-evaporator fitting nut.

5. Remove the evaporator/blower motor case-to-vehicle screws and the case from the vehicle.

6. Separate the A/C evaporator from the evaporator/blower motor case assembly.

7. Inspect the A/C line gaskets for damage and replace (if necessary).

8. To install, reverse the removal procedures. Torque the evaporator/blower motor case assembly-to-vehicle screws to 4 in.lb. and the A/C line fitting-to-evaporator fitting nut to 18 ft.lb. Reconnect the electrical connectors. Recharge the A/C system. Start the engine, allow it establish normal operating temperatures and check the A/C cooling operation.

RADIO

REMOVAL AND INSTALLATION

1. Disconnect the negative battery terminal from the battery.

2. Remove the instrument panel-to-engine cover assembly.

3. Remove the radio-to-instrument panel bezel.

4. Remove the radio-to-instrument panel fasteners.

5. Pull the radio (slightly) from the instrument, then disconnect the antenna and electrical connectors.

6. Remove the radio from the instrument panel.

7. To install, reverse the removal procedures. Reconnect the negative battery terminal. Turn the radio On and check the operation.

WINDSHIELD WIPERS

The windshield wiper units are of the 2-speed, non-depressed park type, a washer pump mounted under the washer bottle and turn sig-

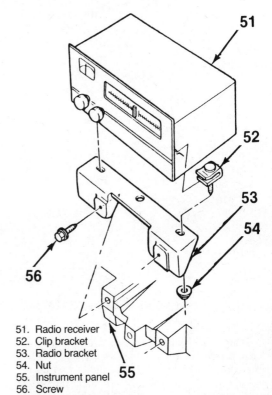

51. Radio receiver
52. Clip bracket
53. Radio bracket
54. Nut
55. Instrument panel
56. Screw

Exploded view of the radio

nal type wiper/washer switch. A single wiper motor operates both wiper blades. Rotating the switch to either **LO** or **HI** speed position completes the circuit and the wiper motor runs at that speed.

The pulse/demand wash functions are controlled by a plug-in printed circuit board enclosed in the wiper housing cover.

Blade and Arm
REMOVAL AND INSTALLATION

NOTE: *The following procedure requires the use of GM Windshield Wiper Blade/Arm Removal tool No. J-8966 or equivalent.*

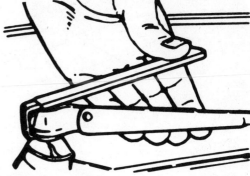

Removing the wiper arm with the special GM tool No. J-8966

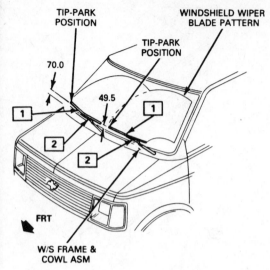

1. Blade
2. Arm

Positioning the wiper arms on the windshield

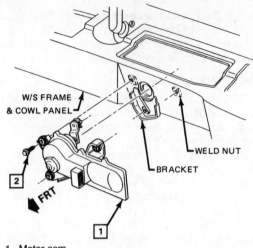

1. Motor asm
2. Bolt

Exploded view of the windshield wiper motor

If the wiper assembly has a press type release tab at the center, simply depress the tab and remove the blade. If the blade has no release tab, use a screwdriver to depress the spring at the center; this will release the assembly. To install the assembly, position the blade over the pin (at the tip of the arm) and press until the spring retainer engages the groove in the pin.

To remove the element, either depress the release button or squeeze the spring type retainer clip (at the outer end) together and slide the blade element out. To install, slide the new element in until it latches.

1. Insert the tool under the wiper arm and lever the arm off the shaft.

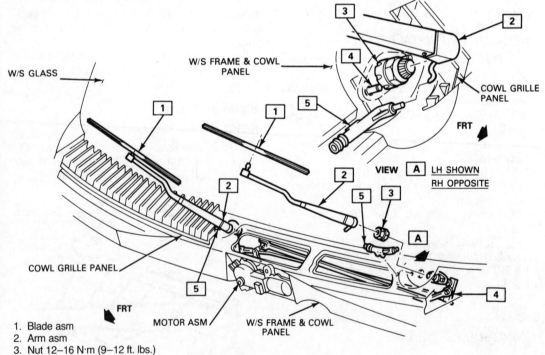

1. Blade asm
2. Arm asm
3. Nut 12–16 N·m (9–12 ft. lbs.)
4. Transmission asm
5. Connector

Exploded view of the windshield wiper blade and linkage assemblies

2. Disconnect the washer hose from the arm (if equipped), then remove the arm.

3. To install, operate the wiper motor (momentarily) to position the pivot shafts into the Park position and reverse the removal procedures. The proper Park position for the arms is with the blades apporximately 2″ (51mm) on the driver's side, or 2¾″ (70mm) on the passenger's side, above the lower windshield molding.

Windshield Wiper Motor

The windshield wiper motor is located in the engine compartment on the left side of the cowl.

REMOVAL AND INSTALLATION

1. Disconnect the electrical connector from the windshield wiper motor.

2. Remove the transmission link from the wiper motor crank arm by pulling or prying it toward the rear of the vehicle.

3. Remove the wiper motor-to-cowl bolts and the wiper motor from the vehicle.

4. To install, reverse the removal procedures.

Wiper Linkage

REMOVAL AND INSTALLATION

NOTE: *The following procedure requires the use of GM Windshield Wiper Blade/Arm Removal tool No. J-8966 or equivalent.*

1. Using the GM Windshield Wiper Blade/Arm Removal tool No. J-8966 or equivalent, remove the wiper blade/arm assemblies from the pivot shafts.

2. Remove the antenna.

3. Remove the outside air cowl ventilator grille-to-cowl screws and the grille from the cowl.

4. At the center of the cowl, remove the link rod-to-motor drive nut, then disengage the link rod from the pins.

5. Remove the arm transmission pivot shaft assembly-to-cowl nuts.

6. Remove the pivot shaft assembly (with link rod) from the plenum chamber.

7. To install, operate the wiper motor (momentarily) to position the pivot shafts into the Park position and reverse the removal procedures.

INSTRUMENTS AND SWITCHES

Instrument Cluster

REMOVAL AND INSTALLATION

1. Disconnect the negative battery terminal from the battery.

2. Remove the lower steering column cover-to-instrument panel screws and the cover.

3. Remove the instrument cluster trim plate-to-instrument cluster screws and the panel, then allow the panel to hang to the left side by the wiring.

4. Remove the A/C control-to-instrument panel screws and move the control assembly aside.

5. For access, remove the seat alarm assembly from the bracket, on the left side of the instrument panel.

6. Remove the instrument panel cluster-to-instrument panel fasteners and the cluster assembly.

7. Disconnect the speedometer cable, the speed sensor and any other necessary electrical connectors.

8. To install, reverse the removal procedures.

Instrument Panel

REMOVAL AND INSTALLATION

1. Disconnect the negative battery terminal from the battery.

2. Remove the lower steering column cover-to-instrument panel screws and the cover.

3. Remove the lower instrument panel-to-engine cover nuts/bolts and the lower instrument panel-to-dash bolts.

4. Remove the instrument cluster trim plate-to-instrument cluster screws and the panel, then allow the panel to hang to the left side by the wiring.

5. Remove the A/C control-to-instrument panel screws and move the control assembly aside.

6. For access, remove the seat alarm assembly from the bracket, on the left side of the instrument panel.

7. Remove the instrument panel cluster-to-instrument panel fasteners and the cluster assembly.

8. Disconnect the speedometer cable, the speed sensor and any other necessary electrical connectors.

9. Remove the instrument panel-to-cowl screws and the instrument panel from the vehicle.

10. To install, reverse the removal procedures.

Windshield Wiper Switch

The windshield wiper switch is located on the end of the combination switch, attached to the steering column.

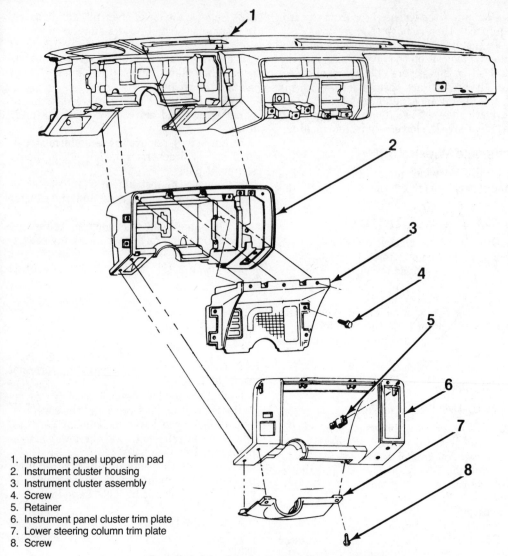

1. Instrument panel upper trim pad
2. Instrument cluster housing
3. Instrument cluster assembly
4. Screw
5. Retainer
6. Instrument panel cluster trim plate
7. Lower steering column trim plate
8. Screw

Exploded view of the instrument cluster and panel

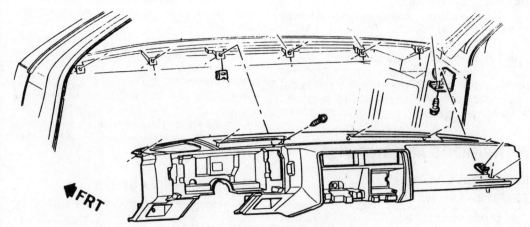

Exploded view of the instrument panel

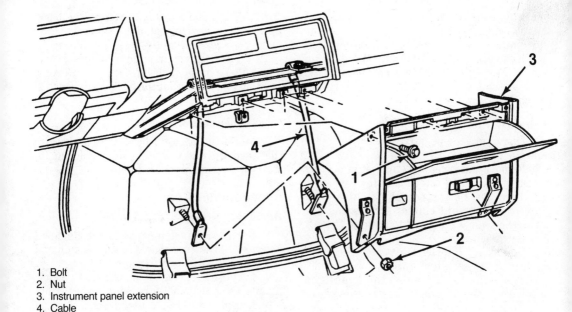

1. Bolt
2. Nut
3. Instrument panel extension
4. Cable

Removing the lower instrument panel

REMOVAL AND INSTALLATION

NOTE: *Refer to the Combination Switch, Removal and Installation procedures in Chapter 7 and replace the combination switch.*

Headlight Switch

The headlight switch, a push button switch to turn the lights On and Off, is located on the left side of the instrument panel. A rheostat dial, located just above the headlight/parking light

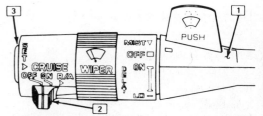

1. Directional signal lever
2. Off/on/resume/accel switch
3. Set/coast switch

View of the combination switch

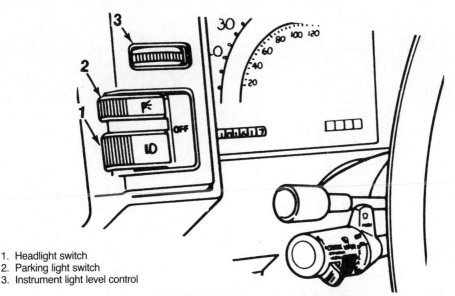

1. Headlight switch
2. Parking light switch
3. Instrument light level control

View of the headlight switch mounted on the instrument panel

switch, is used to control the illumination of the instrument panel.

A dimmer switch (part of the combination switch), to control the **Hi** and **Lo** beam operation, is located on the steering column; the lights are changed by pulling the combination switch lever toward the driver.

REMOVAL AND INSTALLATION

1. Disconnect the negative battery terminal from the battery.

2. Remove the lower steering column cover-to-instrument panel screws and the cover.

3. Remove the instrument cluster trim plate-to-instrument cluster screws and the panel, then allow the panel to hang to the left side by the wiring.

4. Disconnect the electrical connector from the rear of the headlight switch.

5. Disengage and remove the headlight switch from the instrument cluster trim plate.

6. To install, reverse the removal procedures. Check the operation of the headlight switch.

Back-Up Light Switch

REMOVAL AND INSTALLATION

Automatic Transmission

1. Disconnect the negative battery terminal from the battery.

2. From the steering column, disconnect the electrical harness connector from the back-up light switch.

3. Using a small pry bar, expand the back-up switch-to-steering column retainers and remove the switch from the steering column.

4. To install, reverse the removal procedures. Place the gear shift lever in the Reverse position and check that the back-up lights turn On.

Manual Transmission

To replace the back-up light switch, refer to the Back-Up Light Switch, Removal and Installation procedures in Chapter 6.

Speedometer Cable

REMOVAL AND INSTALLATION

1. Refer to the Instrument Cluster, Removal and Installation procedures in this section and remove the instrument cluster.

2. From the rear of the instrument cluster, remove the speedometer cable-to-head fitting.

3. If replacing ONLY the speedometer cable, perform the following procedures:

    a. Disconnect the speedometer casing from the speedometer head.

    b. Pull the speedometer cable from the speedometer casing.

    c. Using lubricant P/N 6478535 or equivalent, lubricate a new speedometer cable and install the cable into the casing.

4. If replacing the speedometer cable and the speedometer casing, perform the following procedures:

    a. Disconnect the speedometer casing from the speedometer head.

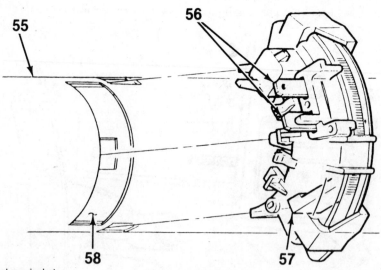

55. Steering column jacket
56. Switch terminals
57. Tangs
58. Shift tube

Removing the back-up light switch from the steering column—automatic transmission

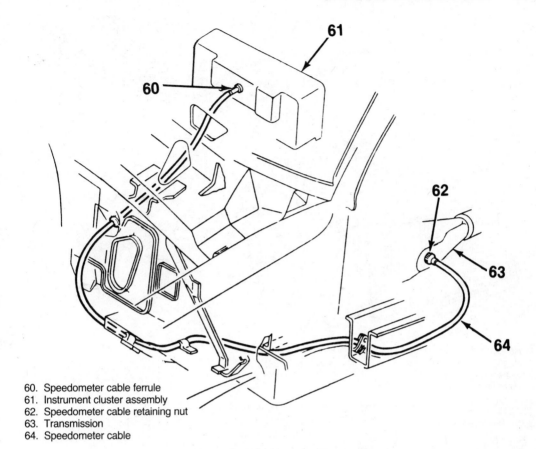

60. Speedometer cable ferrule
61. Instrument cluster assembly
62. Speedometer cable retaining nut
63. Transmission
64. Speedometer cable

View of the speedometer cable routing

b. Disconnect the speedometer casing from the transmission.

c. Remove the various speedometer cable/casing retaining clips.

d. Remove the speedometer cable/casing assembly from the vehicle.

5. To install the speedometer cable, reverse the removal procedures.

LIGHTING

Headlights

REMOVAL AND INSTALLATION

NOTE: *The following procedure may require the use of the GM Safety Aimer tool No. J-6878-01 or equivalent.*

1. Disconnect the negative battery terminal from the battery.

2. Remove the headlight bezel-to-fender screws and the bezel; allow the bezel to hang by the parking/side marker light wires.

3. Remove the headlight retaining-to-fender spring.

4. Remove the headlight retaining ring-to-fender screws and the retaining ring.

5. Disconnect the electrical connector from the headlight and remove the headlight from the vehicle.

6. To install, reverse the removal procedures. Check the headlight operation. Although, adjustment procedures may not be necessary, DO check the aim of the headlight. NOTE: *If necessary to adjust the headlight aim, use the GM Safety Aimer tool No. J-6878-01 or equivalent; the instructions are included with the instrument.*

Signal and Marker Lights

REMOVAL AND INSTALLATION

Front Turn Signal and Parking Lights

1. Disconnect the negative battery terminals from the battery.

2. Remove the headlight bezel-to-fender screws and the bezel; allow the bezel to hang by the turn signal/parking/marker light wires.

3. From the rear headlight bezel, remove the turn signal/parking/marker lamp-to-bezel screws and the turn signal/parking/marker lamp.

4. Disconnect the turn signal bulb and the

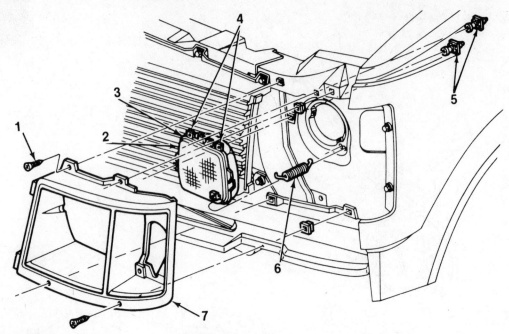

1. Headlamp bezel screws
2. Headlamp
3. Headlamp retaining ring
4. Headlamp retaining ring screws
5. Adjusting screws
6. Adjusting spring
7. Headlamp bezel

Exploded view of the headlight assembly

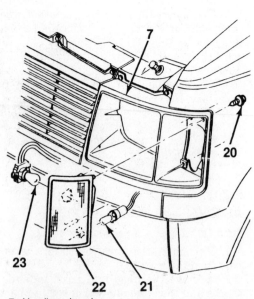

7. Headlamp bezel
20. Combination lamp housing screw
21. Marker lamp
22. Combination lamp housing
23. Park and turn signal lamp

Exploded view of the front turn signal/parking/marker lamp assembly

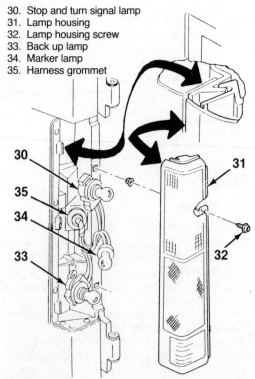

30. Stop and turn signal lamp
31. Lamp housing
32. Lamp housing screw
33. Back up lamp
34. Marker lamp
35. Harness grommet

Exploded view of the rear turn signal/brake/parking light assembly

parking/marker bulb from the lamp housing and the housing from the vehicle.

5. To install, use new bulbs (if necessary) and reverse the removal procedures. Check the turn signal and the parking/marker light operations

Rear Turn Signal, Brake and Parking Lights

1. Disconnect the negative battery terminal from the battery.

2. Remove the rear turn signal/brake/parking lamp-to-vehicle screw and the lamp housing from the vehicle.

3. Replace the defective bulb(s).

4. To install, reverse the removal procedures.

TRAILER WIRING

Wiring the van for towing is fairly easy. There are a number of good wiring kits available and these should be used, rather than trying to design your own. All trailers will need brake lights and turn signals as well as tail lights and side marker lights. Most states require extra marker lights for overly wide trailers. Also, most states have recently required back-up lights for trailers, and most trailer manufacturers have been building trailers with back-up lights for several years.

Additionally, some Class I, most Class II and just about all Class III trailers will have electric brakes.

Add to this number an accessories wire, to operate trailer internal equipment or to charge the trailer's battery, and you can have as many as seven wires in the harness.

Determine the equipment on your trailer and buy the wiring kit necessary. The kit will contain all the wires needed, plus a plug adapter set which included the female plug, mounted on the bumper or hitch, and the male plug, wired into, or plugged into the trailer harness.

When installing the kit, follow the manufacturer's instructions. The color coding of the wires is standard throughout the industry.

One point to note: some domestic vehicles, and most imported vehicles, have separate turn signals. On most domestic vehicles, the brake lights and rear turn signals operate with the same bulb. For those vehicles with separate turn signals, you can purchase an isolation unit so that the brake lights won't blink whenever the turn signals are operated, or, you can go to your local electronics supply house and buy four diodes to wire in series with the brake and turn signal bulbs. Diodes

will isolate the brake and turn signals. The choice is yours. The isolation units are simple and quick to install, but far more expensive than the diodes. The diodes, however, require more work to install properly, since they require the cutting of each bulb's wire and soldering in place of the diode.

One, final point, the best kits are those with a spring loaded cover on the vehicle mounted socket. This cover prevent dirt and moisture from corroding the terminals. Never let the vehicle socket hang loosely; always mount it securely to the bumper or hitch.

CIRCUIT PROTECTION

Fuses

The fuses are of the miniaturized (compact) size and are located on a fuse block, they provide increased circuit protection and reliability. Access to the fuse block is gained either through a swing-down unit (located on the underside of the instrument panel, near the steering column) or through the glove box opening. Each fuse receptacle is marked as to the circuit it protects and the correct amperage of the fuse.

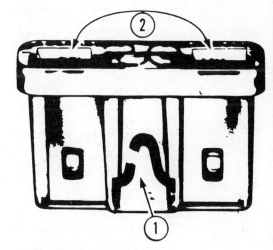

To test for blown mini-fuse:
1. Pull fuse out and check visually
2. With the circuit activated use a test light across the points shown

MINI FUSE COLOR CODES

RATING	COLOR
5 AMP	TAN
10 AMP	RED
20 AMP	YELLOW
25 AMP	WHITE

Blown Fuse

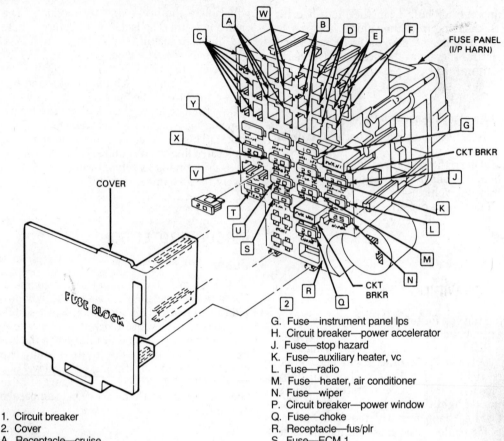

1. Circuit breaker
2. Cover
A. Receptacle—cruise
B. Receptacle—A/C switch lp, auxiliary heater lp switch
C. Receptacle—lighter, digital clock, glove box lp
D. Receptacle—dome lp, cigarette lighter lp, power mirror switch lp
E. Receptacle—power locks
F. Receptacle—auxiliary heater, rear air conditioner
G. Fuse—instrument panel lps
H. Circuit breaker—power accelerator
J. Fuse—stop hazard
K. Fuse—auxiliary heater, vc
L. Fuse—radio
M. Fuse—heater, air conditioner
N. Fuse—wiper
P. Circuit breaker—power window
Q. Fuse—choke
R. Receptacle—fus/plr
S. Fuse—ECM 1
T. Fuse—ECM B
U. Fuse—ECM B
V. Fuse—tail lamp
W. Receptacle—power window
X. Fuse—gauges
Y. Fuse—horn, lighter

View of the fuse block

REPLACEMENT

1. Pull the fuse from the fuse block.
2. Inspect the fuse element (through the clear plastic body) to the blade terminal for defects.
    NOTE: *When replacing the fuse, DO NOT use one of a higher amperage.*
3. To install, reverse the removal procedures.

Convenience Center

The Convenience Center is a swing-down unit located on the underside of the instrument panel, near the steering column. The swing-down feature provides central location and easy access to buzzers, relays and flasher units. All units are serviced by plug-in replacement.

Fusible Links

In addition to fuses, the wiring harness incorporates fusible links (in the battery feed cir-

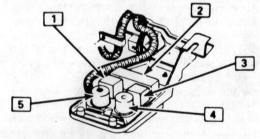

1. Horn relay
2. Seat belt—ignition key—headlight buzzer
3. Choke relay (vacant w/EFI)
4. Hazard flasher
5. Signal flasher

Convenience Center and Components

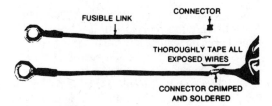

FUSIBLE LINK   CONNECTOR

THOROUGHLY TAPE ALL
EXPOSED WIRES

CONNECTOR CRIMPED
AND SOLDERED

New fusible links are spliced to the wire

cuits) to protect the wiring. Fusible links are 4″ (102mm) sections of copper wire, 4 gauges smaller than the circuit(s) they are protecting, designed to melt under electrical overload. There are four different gauge sizes used. The fusible links are color coded so that they may be installed in their original positions.

REPLACEMENT

1. Disconnect the negative battery terminal from the battery.
2. Locate the burned out link.
3. Strip away the melted insulation and cut the burned link ends from the wire.
4. Strip the wire back ½″ (12.7mm) to allow soldering of the new link.
5. Using a new fusible link 4 gauges smaller than the protected circuit (approx. 10″ [254mm] long), solder it into the circuit.
   NOTE: *Whenever splicing a new wire, always bond the splice with rosin core solder, then cover with electrical tape. Using acid core solder may cause corrosion.*
6. Tape and seal all splices with silicone to weatherproof repairs.
7. After taping the wire, tape the electrical harness leaving an exposed 5″ (127mm) loop of wire.
8. Reconnect the battery.

Circuit Breakers

A circuit breaker is an electrical switch which breaks the circuit in case of an overload. The circuit breaker is located on the lower center of the fuse block. The circuit breaker will remain open until the short or overload condition in the circuit is corrected.

RESETTING

Locate the circuit breaker on the fuse block, then push the circuit breaker in until it locks. If the circuit breaker kicks itself Off again, locate and correct the problem in the electrical circuit.

WIRING DIAGRAMS

Wiring diagrams are not included in this book. As the vehicles have become more complex and available with longer option lists, wiring diagrams have grown in size and complexity. It has become virtually impossible to provide a readable reproduction of a wiring diagram in a book this size.

TROUBLESHOOTING

Electrical problems generally fall into one of three areas:
1. The component that is not functioning is not receiving current.
2. The component itself is not functioning.
3. The component is not properly grounded.
Problems that fall into the first category are by far the most complicated. It is the current supply system to the component which contains all the switches, relays, fuses and etc.

The electrical system can be checked with a test light and a jumper wire. A test light is a device that looks like a pointed screwdriver with a wire attached to it. It has a light bulb inside its handle. A jumper wire is a piece of insulated wire with an alligator clip attached to each end.

If a light bulb is not working, you must follow a systematic plan to determine which of the three causes is the villain.
1. Turn On the switch that controls the inoperable bulb.
2. Disconnect the power supply wire from the bulb.
3. Attach the ground wire on the test light to a good metal ground.
4. Touch the probe end of the test light to the end of the power supply wire that was disconnected from the bulb. If the bulb is receiving current, the test light will turn On.
   NOTE: *If the bulb is one which works only when the ignition key is turned on (turn signal), make sure the key is turned On.*

If the test light does not turn On, then the problem is in the circuit between the battery and the bulb. As mentioned before, this includes all the switches, fuses and relays in the system. The problem is an open circuit between the battery and the bulb. If the fuse is blown and, when replaced, immediately blows again, there is a short circuit in the system which must be located and repaired. If there is a switch in the system, bypass it with a jumper wire. This is done by connecting one end of the jumper wire to the power supply wire into the switch and the other end of the jumper wire to the wire coming out of the switch. If the test light turns On with the jumper wire installed, the switch or whatever was bypassed is defective.

NOTE: *Never substitute the jumper wire for the bulb, as the bulb is the component required to use the power from the power source.*

5. If the bulb in the test light turns On, the current is getting to the bulb that is not working in the vehicle. This eliminates the first of the three possible causes. Connect the power supply wire and connect a jumper wire from the bulb to a good metal ground. Do this with the switch which controls the bulb turned On and also the ignition switch turned On (if it is required for the light to work). If the bulb works with the jumper wire installed, then it has a bad ground. This is usually caused by the metal area on which the bulb mounts to the vehicle being coated with some type of foreign matter or rust.

6. If neither test located the source of the trouble, then the light bulb itself is defective.

The above test procedures can be applied to any of the components of the chassis electrical system by substituting the component that is not working for the light bulb. Remember that for any electrical system to work, all connections must be clean and tight.

MANUAL TRANSMISSION

Identification

Manual transmissions are identified by using the following descriptions:

    a. The number of forward gears.

    b. The measured distance between the centerlines of the mainshaft and the countergear.

The 4-speed (76mm) transmission is a fully synchronized unit with blocker ring synchronizers and a sliding mesh reverse gear. The transmission case houses the various gears, bearings and shafts, a shift control cover and an extension housing. The floor-mounted gearshift lever assembly is located on top of the extension housing; the shifting mechanism is connected to the shift control cover by adjustable shifting arms. The MR2 model is used in combination with both engines.

The 5-speed (77mm) transmission is a fully synchronized unit with blocker ring synchronizers and a sliding mesh reverse gear. It has an aluminum transmission case that houses the various gears, bearings and an extension housing. The floor-mounted gearshift lever assembly is located on top of the extension housing. The ML3 model, is used with the 2.5L en-

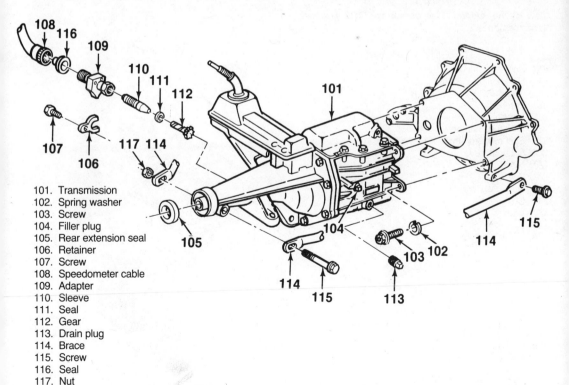

101. Transmission
102. Spring washer
103. Screw
104. Filler plug
105. Rear extension seal
106. Retainer
107. Screw
108. Speedometer cable
109. Adapter
110. Sleeve
111. Seal
112. Gear
113. Drain plug
114. Brace
115. Screw
116. Seal
117. Nut

View of the MH3/ML3, 5-speed transmission—MR2, 4-speed is similar

gine; the MH3 model is used with the 4.3L engine.

Adjustment

NOTE: *The shifter mechanism, of the 5-speed transmission, does not require adjustment and can be serviced independently.*

SHIFTER RODS

4-Speed (MR2)

NOTE: *The following procedure requires the use a 0.249-0.250" (6.32-6.35mm) Pin Gauge or equivalent.*

1. At each shifting swivel (located on the shifter sidecover), loosen the jam nuts on the shifter rods.
2. From inside the vehicle, place the floor mounted, gear shift lever in the Neutral position.

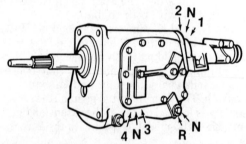

View of the shifting lever positions—MR2 4-speed transmission

3. From under the vehicle, place the shifter rods in the Neutral position.
4. Using a 0.249-0.250" (6.32-6.35mm) Pin Gauge, position it in the holes of the gear shift control levers.
5. While applying forward pressure (separately) on each shifter rod, tighten the shifter rod jam nuts, located on each side of the shifting swivel.
6. Remove the pin gauge and check the shifting operation. Lubricate the shifting levers.

CLUCH SWITCH

A clutch switch is located under the instrument panel and attached to the top of the clutch pedal.

1. Disconnect the negative battery terminal from the battery.
2. Remove the lower steering column-to-instrument panel cover.
3. Disconnect the electrical connector from the clutch switch.

NOTE: *Be sure to leave any carpets and floor mats (being used in the vehicle) in place, when making the adjustment.*

4. At the clutch switch, move the slider (adjuster) to the rear of the clutch switch shaft.
5. Push the clutch pedal to the floor.
6. While holding the clutch pedal to the floor, move the slider down the clutch switch shaft until it stops.

NOTE: *When moving the slider down the*

120. Shift lever
121. Shift control
122. Retainer
123. Washer
124. Control lever
125. Shift rod, 1st/2nd
126. Shift rod, 3rd/4th
127. Shift rod, rev.
128. Nut
129. Swivel
130. Nut
131. Shift lever
132. Washer
133. Retainer
 A. Gage pin hole

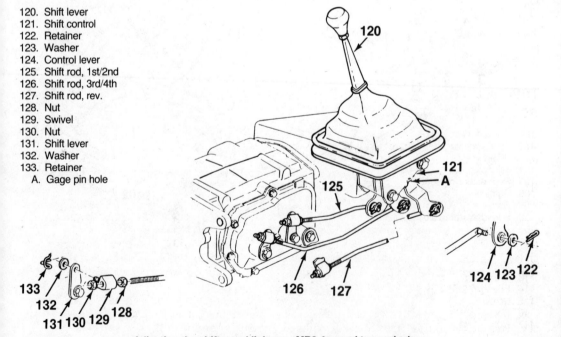

Adjusting the shifter rod linkage—MR2 4-speed transmission

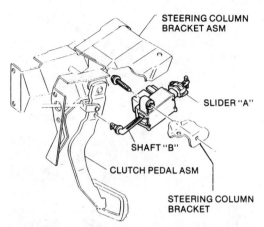

STEERING COLUMN
BRACKET ASM

SLIDER "A"

SHAFT "B"

CLUTCH PEDAL ASM

STEERING COLUMN
BRACKET

**Adjusting the clutch (neutral start) switch—manual
transmission**

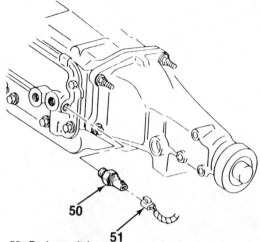

50

51

50. Backup switch
51. Backup switch connector

**Exploded view of the back-up light switch—manual
transmission**

*clutch switch shaft, a clicking noise can be
heard.*

7. Release the clutch pedal; the adjustment
is complete.

8. Reconnect the electrical connector, the
hush panel and the negative battery terminal.

Back-up Light Switch

REMOVAL AND INSTALLATION

1. Disconnect the negative battery terminal
from the battery.

2. From the left rear of the transmission,
disconnect the electrical connector from the
back-up light switch.

3. Remove the back-up light switch from the
transmission.

4. To install, reverse the removal procedures. Place the gear shift lever in the Reverse
position and check the back-up lights are
turned On.

Transmission

REMOVAL AND INSTALLATION

1. Refer to the Driveshaft, Removal and Installation procedures in this section and remove the driveshaft.

2. Using a clean catch pan, place it under
the transmission, remove the drain plug and
drain the fluid from the transmission.

3. Loosen the shifter control knob-to-shifter
control lever nut, then remove the shifter control knob. Remove the shifter control boot-to-
chassis plate and the shifter control boot.

4. If removing an MH3/ML3, 5-speed transmission, unscrew the shift lever from the control lever.

5. If removing an MR2, 4-speed transmission, remove the shifter rods, then the shifter
control assembly from the extension housing.

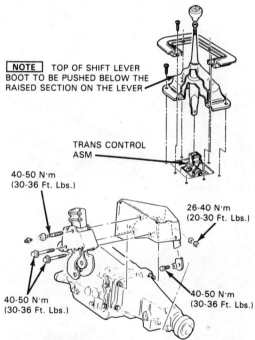

NOTE   TOP OF SHIFT LEVER
BOOT TO BE PUSHED BELOW THE
RAISED SECTION ON THE LEVER

TRANS CONTROL
ASM

40-50 N·m
(30-36 Ft. Lbs.)

26-40 N·m
(20-30 Ft. Lbs.)

40-50 N·m
(30-36 Ft. Lbs.)

40-50 N·m
(30-36 Ft. Lbs.)

**Removing the shift control assembly from the MR2,
4-speed transmission**

6. Disconnect the speedometer cable and the
seal from the transmission.

7. Disconnect the electrical connector from
the transmission.

8. If necessary, disconnect and lower the exhaust pipe(s).

9. Using a transmission jack, place it under
and connect it to the transmission, then support it with the jack.

10. Remove the transmission-to-crossmem-

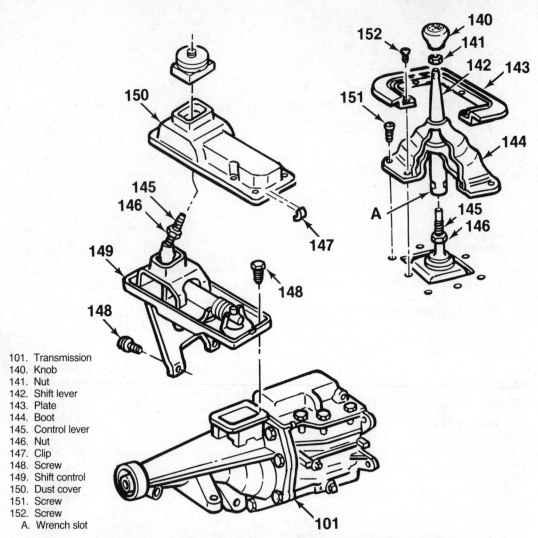

101. Transmission
140. Knob
141. Nut
142. Shift lever
143. Plate
144. Boot
145. Control lever
146. Nut
147. Clip
148. Screw
149. Shift control
150. Dust cover
151. Screw
152. Screw
 A. Wrench slot

Removing the shift control lever from the MH3/ML3, 5-speed transmission

ber nuts/bolts and the transmission-to-chassis braces nuts/bolts, then remove the braces and the crossmember.

NOTE: *If any spacers are used, make a note of them so that they may be installed in their original position.*

11. While supporting the transmission, remove the transmission-to-bellhousing bolts; DO NOT allow it to hang on the input shaft.

12. Move the transmission/jack assembly rearward and remove the transmission from the vehicle.

13. Using high temperature grease, place a thin coat on the main drive gear splines.

14. To install, align the transmission's input shaft with the bell housing/clutch assembly and slide the transmission into the clutch assembly.

NOTE: *When installing the transmission,*

shift the transmission into High gear, then turn the output shaft to align the input shaft splines with the clutch plate.

15. To complete the installation, reverse the removal procedures. Torque the transmission-to-bellhousing bolts to 50 ft.lb., the transmission-to-mount bolts to 40 ft.lb. (MR2) or 33 ft.lb. (MH3/ML3), the crossmember-to-mount bolts to 26 ft.lb. (MR2) or 18 ft.lb. (MH3/ML3), the crossmember-to-chassis bolts to 37 ft.lb., transmission-to-brace bolts 26 ft.lb., shifter control assembly-to-extension housing bolts to 23 ft.lb., the shifter rod swivel nut to 18 ft.lb. and the shifter lever nut to 35 ft.lb.

CLUTCH

The vehicles use a hydraulic clutch system which consists of a master and a slave cylinder. When pressure is applied to the clutch pedal (pedal depressed), the push rod contacts the plunger and pushes it up the bore of the master cylinder. In the first $\frac{1}{32}''$ (0.8mm) of movement, the center valve seal closes the port to the fluid reservoir tank and as the plunger continues to move up the bore of the cylinder, the fluid is forced through the outlet line to the slave cylinder mounted on the clutch housing. As fluid is pushed down the pipe from the master cylinder, this in turn forces the piston in the slave cylinder outward. A push rod is connected to the slave cylinder and rides in the pocket of the clutch fork. As the slave cylinder piston moves rearward the push rod forces the clutch fork and the release bearing to disengage the pressure plate from the clutch disc. On the return stroke (pedal released), the plunger moves back as a result of the return pressure of the clutch. Fluid returns to the master cylinder and the final movement of the plunger lifts the valve seal off the seat, allowing an unrestricted flow of fluid between the system and the reservoir.

A piston return spring in the slave cylinder preloads the clutch linkage and assures contact of the release bearing with the clutch release fingers at all times. As the driven disc wears, the diaphragm spring fingers move rearward forcing the release bearing, fork and push rod to move. This movement forces the slave cylinder piston forward in its bore, displacing hydraulic fluid up into the master cylinder reservoir, thereby providing the self-adjusting feature of the hydraulic clutch linkage system.

Before attempting to repair the clutch, transmission, hydraulic system or related linkages for any reason other than an obvious failure, the problem and probable cause should be identified. A large percentage of clutch and manual transmission problems are manifested by shifting difficulties such as high shift effort, gear clash and grinding or transmission blockout. When any of these problems occur, a careful analysis of these difficulties should be made, then the basic checks and adjustments performed before removing the clutch or transmission for repairs. Run the engine at a normal idle with the transmission in Neutral (clutch engaged). Disengage the clutch, wait about 10 seconds and shift the transmission into Reverse (no grinding noise should be heard). A grinding noise indicates incorrect clutch travel, lost motion, clutch misalignment or internal problems such as failed dampers, facings, cushion springs, diaphragm spring fingers, pressure plate drive straps, pivot rings or etc.

Adjustments

Since the hydraulic system provides automatic clutch adjustment, no adjustment of the clutch linkage or pedal height is required.

Clutch Plate and Pressure Plate
REMOVAL AND INSTALLATION

CAUTION: *The clutch plate contains asbestos, which has been determined to be a cancer causing agent. Never clean the clutch surfaces with compressed air! Avoid inhaling any dust from any clutch surface! When cleaning clutch surfaces, use a commercially available brake cleaning fluid.*

1. Refer to the Transmission, Removal and Installation procedures in this section and remove the transmission from the vehicle.

2. Remove the slave cylinder attaching bolts and the bell housing.

3. Slide the clutch fork from the ball stud and remove the fork from the dust boot.

NOTE: *The ball stud is threaded into the clutch housing and can be easily replaced.*

4. Install the Clutch Pilot tool No. J-33169 into the clutch plate to support it during removal.

5. The flywheel and clutch cover are marked with X's for correct assembly or white painted letters, if these are not visible, scribe new marks.

6. Gradually loosen the clutch-to-flywheel bolts (one turn at a time) until all of the spring pressure is released.

7. Remove the bolts and the clutch assembly.

NOTE: *The clutch pilot bearing is an oil impregnated type bearing pressed into the crankshaft. This bearing requires attention when the clutch is removed from the vehicle, at which time it should be cleaned and inspected for excessive wear or damage and should be replaced (if necessary).*

8. To install, crank the engine over by hand until the X-mark on the flywheel is on the bottom.

9. Position the clutch disc and pressure plate in the same relative location as removed and support with the clutch pilot tool.

NOTE: *The clutch disc is installed with the damper springs and slinger toward the transmission.*

10. Rotate the clutch assembly until the X-marks on the flywheel and clutch assembly align. Align the cover bolt holes with those in the flywheel.

11. Install the bolts, then tighten evenly and gradually. Install the remaining bolts.

12. Remove the clutch pilot tool.

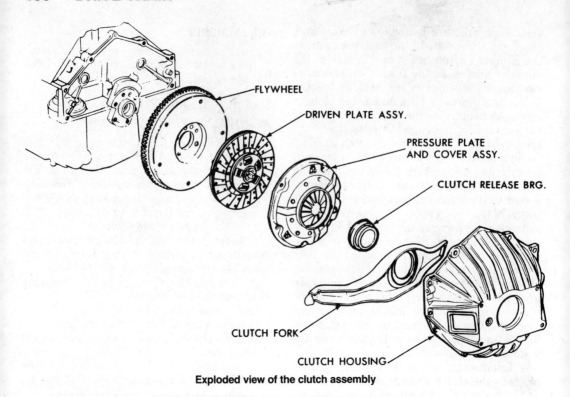

Exploded view of the clutch assembly

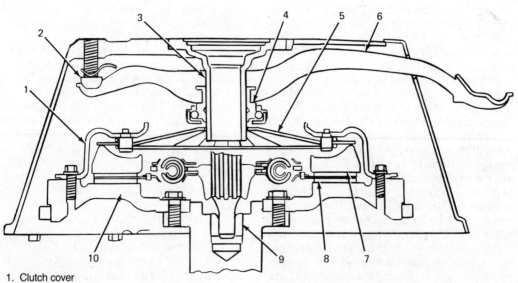

1. Clutch cover
2. Fork ball stud
3. Main drive gear bearing retainer
4. Release bearing
5. Diaphragm spring
6. Clutch fork
7. Pressure plate
8. Driven disc
9. Pilot bearing
10. Flywheel

Cross-section view of the clutch assembly

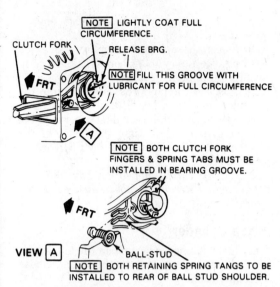

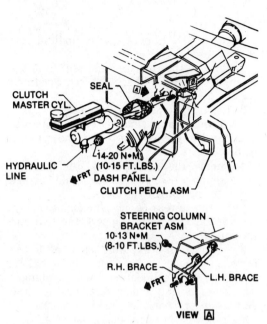

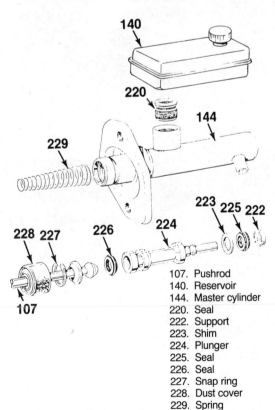

NOTE LIGHTLY COAT FULL CIRCUMFERENCE.

CLUTCH FORK

FRT

RELEASE BRG.

NOTE FILL THIS GROOVE WITH LUBRICANT FOR FULL CIRCUMFERENCE

A

NOTE BOTH CLUTCH FORK FINGERS & SPRING TABS MUST BE INSTALLED IN BEARING GROOVE.

FRT

VIEW A

BALL-STUD

NOTE BOTH RETAINING SPRING TANGS TO BE INSTALLED TO REAR OF BALL STUD SHOULDER.

Clutch release bearing lubrication points—typical

CLUTCH MASTER CYL.

SEAL

A

HYDRAULIC LINE

14-20 N•M (10-15 FT.LBS.)

FRT

DASH PANEL

CLUTCH PEDAL ASM

STEERING COLUMN BRACKET ASM 10-13 N•M (8-10 FT.LBS.)

R.H. BRACE

L.H. BRACE

FRT

VIEW A

Exploded view of the clutch master cylinder-to-cowl assembly

13. Lubricate the ball socket on the clutch fork and reinstall on the ball stud.

14. Pack the recess on the inside of the throwout bearing collar and the throwout groove with graphite grease.

15. Install the bell housing and the slave cylinder.

16. Install the throwout bearing on the fork. Lubricate the bearing groove.

17. To complete the installation, reverse the removal procedures. Torque the pressure plate-to-flywheel bolts to 15–22 ft.lb. (4-speed) or 25–35 ft.lb. (5-speed), the flywheel-to-crankshaft bolts to 60–75 ft.lb. (4-speed) or 55–75 ft.lb. (5-speed), the slave cylinder-to-bell housing bolts to 10–15 ft.lb.

NOTE: *If replacing an MR2, 4-speed transmission, lubricate and adjust the transmission shift linkages.*

Master Cylinder

The clutch master cylinder is located in the engine compartment, on the left-side of the firewall, above the steering column.

REMOVAL AND INSTALLATION

1. Disconnect negative battery cable.
2. Remove hush panel from under the dash.
3. Disconnect push rod from clutch pedal.
4. Disconnect hydraulic line from the clutch master cylinder.
5. Remove the master cylinder-to-cowl brace nuts. Remove master cylinder and overhaul (if necessary).
6. Using a putty knife, clean the master cylinder and cowl mounting surfaces.
7. To install, reverse the removal procedures. Torque the master cylinder-to-cowl

brace nuts to 10–15 ft.lb. (14–20 Nm). Fill master cylinder with new hydraulic fluid conforming to Dot 3 specifications. Bleed and check the hydraulic clutch system for leaks.

140

220

144

229

223 225 222

228 227

226

224

107

107. Pushrod
140. Reservoir
144. Master cylinder
220. Seal
222. Support
223. Shim
224. Plunger
225. Seal
226. Seal
227. Snap ring
228. Dust cover
229. Spring

Exploded view of the clutch master cylinder

OVERHAUL

1. Remove the filler cap and drain fluid from the master cylinder.

2. Remove the reservoir and seal from the master cylinder. Pull back the dust cover and remove the snapring.

3. Remove the push rod assembly. Using a block of wood, tap the master cylinder on it to eject the plunger assembly from the cylinder bore.

4. Remove the seal (carefully) from the front of the plunger assembly, ensuring no damage occurs to the plunger surfaces.

5. From the rear of the plunger assembly, remove the spring, the support, the seal and the shim.

6. Using clean brake fluid, clean all of the parts.

7. Inspect the cylinder bore and the plunger for ridges, pitting and/or scratches, the the dust cover for wear and cracking; replace the parts if any of the conditions exist.

8. To install, use new seals, lubricate all of the parts in clean brake fluid, fit the plunger

seal to the plunger and reverse the removal procedures.

9. Insert the plunger assembly, valve end leading into the cylinder bore (easing the entrance of the plunger seal).

10. Position the push rod assembly into the cylinder bore, then install a new snapring to retain the push rod. Install dust cover onto the master cylinder. Lubricate the inside of the dust cover with Girling® Rubber Grease or equivalent.

NOTE: *Be careful not to use any lubricant that will deteriorate rubber dust covers or seals.*

Slave Cylinder

The slave cylinder is located on the left side of the bellhousing and controls the clutch release fork operation.

REMOVAL AND INSTALLATION

1. Disconnect the negative battery cable.

2. Raise and support the front of the vehicle on jackstands.

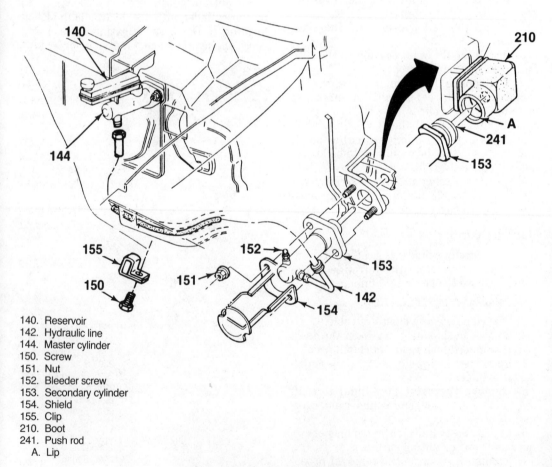

140. Reservoir
142. Hydraulic line
144. Master cylinder
150. Screw
151. Nut
152. Bleeder screw
153. Secondary cylinder
154. Shield
155. Clip
210. Boot
241. Push rod
  A. Lip

View of the hydraulic clutch assembly

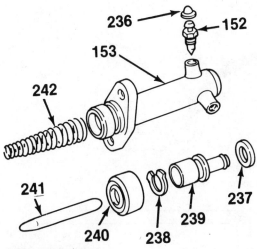

152. Bleeder screw
153. Secondary cylinder
236. Cap
237. Seal
238. Snap ring
239. Plunger
240. Dust cover
241. Pushrod
242. Spring

Exploded view of the clutch slave cylinder

3. Disconnect the hydraulic line from clutch master cylinder. Remove the hydraulic line-to-chassis screw and the clip from the chassis.

NOTE: *Be sure to plug the line opening to keep dirt and moisture out of the system.*

4. Remove the slave cylinder-to-bellhousing nuts.

5. Remove the push rod and the slave cylinder from the vehicle, then overhaul it (if necessary).

6. To install, reverse the removal procedures. Lubricate leading end of the slave cylinder with Girling® Rubber Lube or equivalent. Torque the slave cylinder-to-bellhousing nuts to 10–15 ft.lb. (14–20 Nm). Fill the master cylinder with new brake fluid conforming to Dot 3 specifications. Bleed the hydraulic system.

OVERHAUL

1. Remove the shield, the pushrod and dust cover from the slave cylinder, then inspect the cover for damage or deterioration.

2. Remove the snapring from the end of the cylinder bore.

3. Using a block of wood, tap the slave cylinder on it to eject the plunger, then remove the seal and the spring.

4. Using clean brake fluid, clean all of the parts.

5. Inspect the cylinder bore and the plunger for ridges, pitting and/or scratches, the the

dust cover for wear and cracking; replace the parts if any of the conditions exist.

6. To install, use new seals and lubricate all of the parts in clean brake fluid. Install the spring, the plunger seal and the plunger into the cylinder bore, then install a new snapring.

7. Lubricate the inside of the dust cover with Girling® Rubber Grease or equivalent, then install it into the slave cylinder.

NOTE: *Be careful not to use any lubricant that will deteriorate the rubber dust covers or seals.*

BLEEDING THE HYDRAULIC CLUTCH

Bleeding air from the hydraulic clutch system is necessary whenever any part of the system has been disconnected or the fluid level (in the reservoir) has been allowed to fall so low, that air has been drawn into the master cylinder.

1. Fill master cylinder reservoir with new brake fluid conforming to Dot 3 specifications.

CAUTION: *Never, under any circumstances, use fluid which has been bled from a system to fill the reservoir as it may be aerated, have too much moisture content and possibly be contaminated.*

2. Raise and support the front of the vehicle on jackstands.

3. Remove the slave cylinder attaching bolts.

4. Hold slave cylinder at approximately 45° with the bleeder at highest point. Fully depress clutch pedal and open the bleeder screw.

5. Close the bleeder screw and release clutch pedal.

6. Repeat the procedure until all of the air is evacuated from the system. Check and refill master cylinder reservoir as required to prevent air from being drawn through the master cylinder.

NOTE: *Never release a depressed clutch pedal with the bleeder screw open or air will be drawn into the system.*

AUTOMATIC TRANSMISSION

Identification

The THM 700-R4 is a fully automatic transmission which provides 4 forward gears and a reverse gear. The oil pressure and shifting points are controlled by the throttle opening, via a Throttle Valve (TV) cable.

Fluid Pan

REMOVAL AND INSTALLATION

NOTE: *The fluid should be drained when the transmission is warm.*

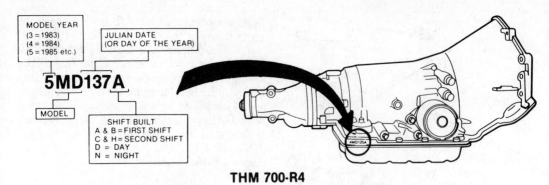

THM 700-R4

Identifcation of the THM 700-R4 transmission

1. Raise and support the front of the vehicle with jackstands.

2. Place a drain catch pan under the transmission oil pan.

3. Remove the pan bolts from the front and sides of the pan, then loosen the rear bolts 4 turns.

4. Using a small pry bar, pry the oil pan loose and allow the pan to partially drain. Remove the remaining pan bolts and carefully lower the pan away from the transmission.

NOTE: *If the transmission fluid is dark or has a burnt smell, transmission damage is indicated. Have the transmission checked professionally.*

CAUTION: *If the pan sticks, carefully tap sideways on the pan with a rubber or plastic mallet to break it loose; DO NOT dent the pan.*

5. Empty and wash the pan in solvent, then blow dry with compressed air.

6. Using a putty knife, clean the gasket mounting surfaces.

7. To install, use a new filter, a new gasket and reverse the removal procedures. Torque the pan-to-transmission bolts to 12–14 ft.lb. (in a criss-cross pattern). Recheck the bolt torque after all of the bolts have been tightened once. Add Dexron®II automatic transmission fluid through the filler tube.

CAUTION: *DO NOT OVERFILL the transmission; foaming of the fluid and subsequent transmission damage due to slippage will result.*

8. With the gear selector lever in Park, start the engine and let it idle; DO NOT race the engine.

9. Move the gear selector lever through each position, holding the brakes. Return the lever to Park and check the fluid level with the engine idling. The level should be between the two dimples on the dipstick, about ¼" (6mm) below the ADD mark. Add fluid, if necessary.

10. Check the fluid level after the vehicle has been driven enough to thoroughly warm the

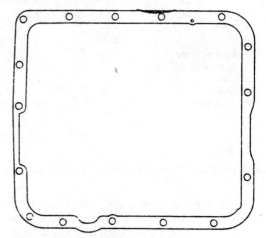

View of the THM 700-R4 oil pan gasket

transmission. Details are given under Fluid Level Checks earlier in Chapter 1. If the transmission is overfilled, the excess must be drained off. Use a suction pump, if necessary.

FILTER SERVICE

1. Refer to the Fluid Pan, Removal and Installation procedures in this section and remove the fluid pan.

2. Remove the transmission filter screws or clips and the filter from the valve body. The filter may have either a fibrous or screen filtering element and is retained by one or two fasteners.

NOTE: *If the transmission uses a filter having a fully exposed screen, it may be cleaned and reused.*

3. To install, use a new filter, a new gasket and reverse the removal procedures. Torque the pan-to-transmission bolts to 12–14 ft.lb. (in a criss-cross pattern). Recheck the bolt torque after all of the bolts have been tightened once. Add Dexron®II automatic transmission fluid through the filler tube.

Adjustments

SHIFT LINKAGE

1. Firmly apply the parking brake.
2. Raise and support the front of the vehicle on jackstands.
3. At the left side of the transmission, loosen the shift rod swivel-to-equalizer lever nut.
4. Rotate the transmission shift lever clockwise (forward) to the last detent (Park) position, then turn it counterclockwise (rearward) to the rear of the 2nd detent (Neutral) position.
5. At the steering column, place the gear selector lever into the Neutral position.

NOTE: *When positioning the gear selector lever, DO NOT use the steering column indicator to find the Neutral position.*

6. Tightly, hold the shifting rod (swivel) against the equalizer lever, then torque the adjusting nut to 11 ft.lb.
7. Using the gear selector lever (on the steering column), place it in the Park position and check the adjustment. Move the gear selector lever into the various positions; the engine must start in the Park and the Neutral positions.

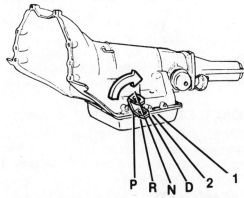

View of the shifting positions—THM 700-R4

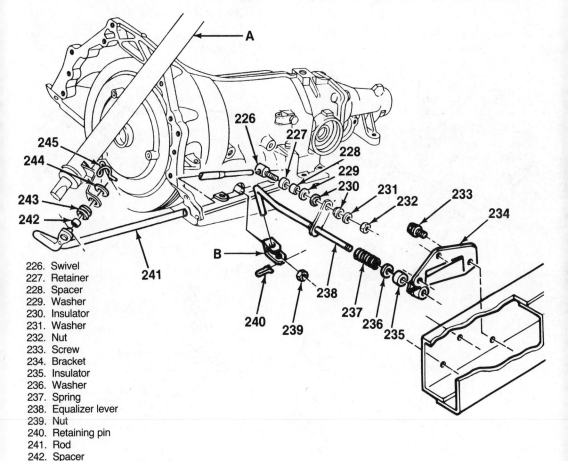

226. Swivel
227. Retainer
228. Spacer
229. Washer
230. Insulator
231. Washer
232. Nut
233. Screw
234. Bracket
235. Insulator
236. Washer
237. Spring
238. Equalizer lever
239. Nut
240. Retaining pin
241. Rod
242. Spacer
243. Insulator
244. Washer
245. Retaining pin
A. Steering column
B. Shift lever

Exploded view of the shift lever assembly—THM 700-R4

NOTE: *If the engine will not start in the Neutral and/or Park positions, refer to Back-Up Light Switch adjustment procedures in Chapter 5 and adjust the switch.*

CAUTION: *With the gear selector lever in the Park position, the parking pawl should engage the rear internal gear lugs or output ring gear lugs to prevent the vehicle from rolling and causing personal injury.*

8. Align the gear selector lever indicator, if necessary. Lower the vehicle and release the parking brake.

THROTTLE VALVE (TV) CABLE

If the TV cable is broken, sticky, misadjusted or incorrect part for the model, the vehicle may exhibit various malfunctions, such as: delayed or full throttle shifts.

Preliminary Checks

1. Inspect and/or correct the transmission fluid level.

2. Make sure that the brakes are not dragging and that the engine is operating correctly.

3. Make sure that the cable is connected at both ends.

4. Make sure that the correct cable is installed.

Adjustment

1. If necessary, remove the air cleaner.

2. If the cable has been removed and installed, check to see that the cable slider is in the zero or the fully adjusted position; if not, perform the following procedures:

a. Depress and hold the readjust tab.

b. Move the slider back through the fitting (away from the throttle lever) until it stops against the fitting.

c. Release the readjust tab.

3. Rotate the throttle lever to the Full Throttle Stop position to obtain a minimum of 1 click.

4. Release the throttle lever.

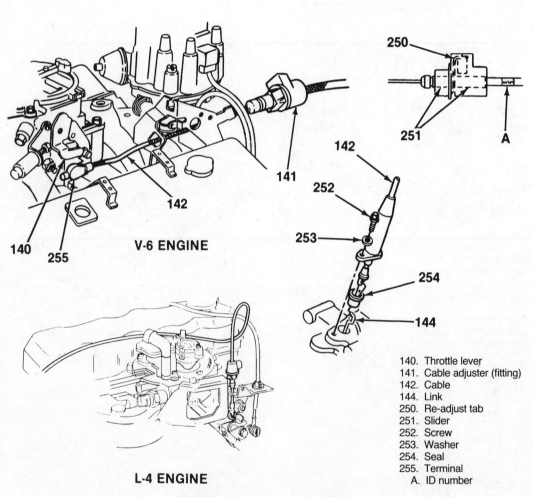

V-6 ENGINE

L-4 ENGINE

140. Throttle lever
141. Cable adjuster (fitting)
142. Cable
144. Link
250. Re-adjust tab
251. Slider
252. Screw
253. Washer
254. Seal
255. Terminal
A. ID number

Adjusting the TV cable—THM 700-R4

Neutral Safety Switch

The Neutral Safety Switch is a part of the Back-Up Light Switch. For the replacement or adjustment procedures, refer to the Back-Up Light Switch, Removal and Installation procedures in Chapter 5.

Back-up Light Switch

NOTE: *The back-up light switch is located on the steering column. To replace the back-up light switch, refer to the Back-Up Light Switch, Removal and Installation procedures in Chapter 5.*

Transmission

REMOVAL AND INSTALLATION

NOTE: *The following procedure requires the use of the Torque Converter Holding tool No. J-21366 or equivalent.*

1. Refer to the Driveshaft, Removal and Installation procedures in this section and remove the driveshaft.
2. Disconnect the negative battery terminal from the battery.
3. From inside the vehicle, remove the engine cover.
4. Disconnect the Throttle Valve (TV) cable from the throttle lever.
5. Raise and support the front of the vehicle on jackstands.
6. Disconnect the speedometer cable, the shift linkage, the electrical connectors and any electrical connector retaining clips from the transmission.
7. Remove the engine-to-transmission support braces (at the torque converter cover) bolts.
8. Disconnect the exhaust crossover pipe from the exhaust manifold(s).

9. Remove the engine-to-transmission support brackets.
10. Remove the torque converter cover, then matchmark the flywheel to the torque converter; matching of the marks will maintain the original balance.
11. Remove the torque converter-to-flywheel bolts/nuts and slide the converter back into the transmission.
12. Using a transmission jack, position it under and secure it to the transmission, then raise the transmission slightly.
13. Remove the crossmember-to-transmission mount bolts and the crossmember-to-frame bolts; if insulators are used, be sure to

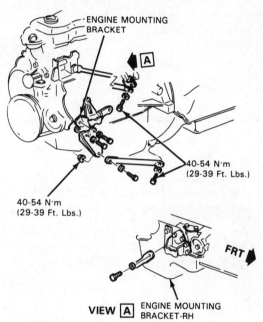

View of the automatic transmission support brackets—4-Cyl

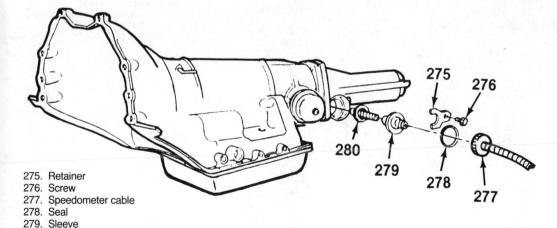

275. Retainer
276. Screw
277. Speedometer cable
278. Seal
279. Sleeve
280. Driven gear, or speed sensor

Exploded view of the speedometer cable assembly—THM 700-R4

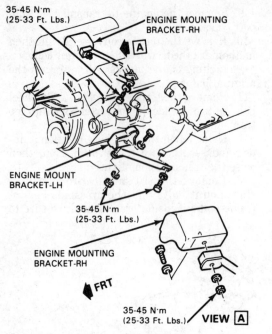

35-45 N·m
(25-33 Ft. Lbs.)

ENGINE MOUNTING
BRACKET-RH

A

ENGINE MOUNT
BRACKET-LH

35-45 N·m
(25-33 Ft. Lbs.)

ENGINE MOUNTING
BRACKET-RH

FRT

35-45 N·m
(25-33 Ft. Lbs.) VIEW A

View of the automatic transmission support brackets—V6

remove them. Remove the crossmember from the vehicle by moving it rearward.

14. Lower the transmission (slightly), then disconnect the oil cooler lines and the Throttle Valve (TV) cable from it.

NOTE: *When disconnecting the oil cooler lines and the TV cable, be sure to plug the openings to keep dirt out of the system.*

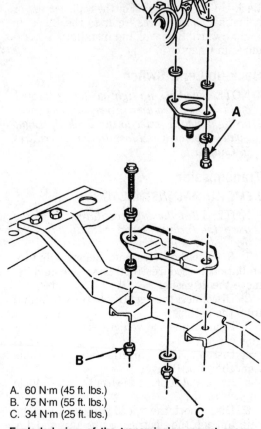

A

B

C

A. 60 N·m (45 ft. lbs.)
B. 75 N·m (55 ft. lbs.)
C. 34 N·m (25 ft. lbs.)

Exploded view of the transmission mount assembly—THM 700-R4

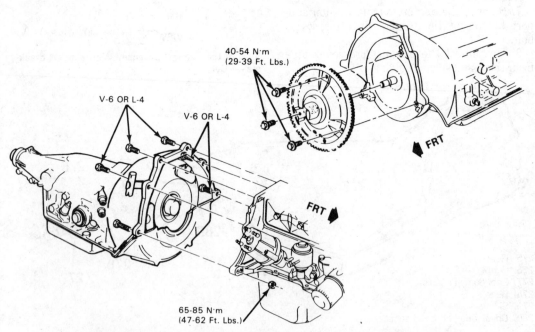

40-54 N·m
(29-39 Ft. Lbs.)

V-6 OR L-4

V-6 OR L-4

FRT

FRT

65-85 N·m
(47-62 Ft. Lbs.)

Removing the transmission and the flywheel from the engine—THM 700-R4

15. Using a block of wood and a floor jack, place them under the rear of the engine and support it.

16. Using the Torque Converter Holding tool No. J-21366 or equivalent, secure the torque converter to the transmission.

17. Remove the transmission-to-engine bolts and the transmission from the vehicle.

18. To install, reverse the removal procedures. Torque the transmission-to-engine bolts to 47–62 ft.lb. (4-Cyl.) or 29–39 ft.lb. (V6), the torque converter-to-flywheel bolts to 29–39 ft.lb., the transmission-to-support bracket bolts to 34 ft.lb., the damper-to-transmission bolt to 45 ft.lb., the crossmember-to-transmission mount support bolts to 55 ft.lb., the transmission mount-to-mount support bolts to 25 ft.lb. and the crossmember-to-frame bolts to 65 ft.lb.

NOTE: *Before installing the flywheel-to-torque converter bolts, be sure that the converter weld nuts are flush with the flywheel and the converter rotates freely by hand.*

19. Adjust the shift linkage and the TV cable. Refill the transmission with Dexron®II automatic transmission fluid.

DRIVELINE

The Astro Van's driveshaft is of the conventional, open type. Located at either end of the driveshaft is a universal joint (U-joint), which allows the driveshaft to move up and down to match the motion of the rear axle.

The front U-joint (injected nylon or internal snaprings) connects the driveshaft to a slip-jointed yoke. This yoke is internally splined and allows the driveshaft to move in and out on the transmission splines. On the production U-joints, nylon is injected through a small hole in the yoke during manufacture and flows along a circular groove between the U-joint and the yoke, creating a non-metallic snapring.

The rear U-joint is clamped to the rear axle pinion. The rear U-joint is secured in the yoke, using external snaprings (inside the yoke ears). It is attached to the rear axle pinion by use of bolted straps.

Bad U-joints, requiring replacement, will produce a clunking sound when the vehicle is put into gear and when the transmission shifts from gear-to-gear. This is due to worn needle bearings or scored trunnion end possibly caused by improper lubrication during assembly. U-joints require no periodic maintenance and therefore have no lubrication fittings.

A vibration damper is employed as part of the slip joint. This damper cannot be serviced separately from the slip joint; if either component goes bad, the two must be replaced as a unit.

Driveshaft and U-Joints
REMOVAL AND INSTALLATION

1. Raise and support the rear of the vehicle on jackstands.

10. Rear axle housing
11. Pinion flange
12. Snap ring type yoke
13. Retainer
14. Bolt
15. Propeller shaft
16. Nylon injected type yoke
17. Damper
18. Transmission

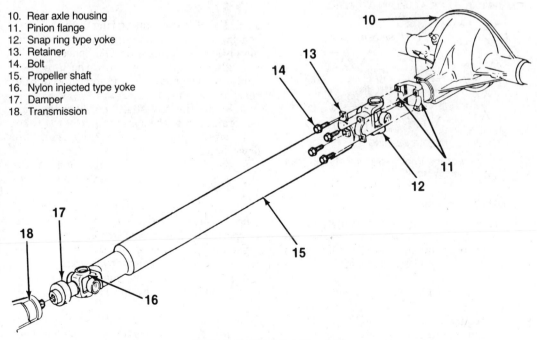

Exploded view of the driveshaft

2. Using paint, matchmark the relationship of the driveshaft-to-pinion flange.

3. Remove the universal joint-to-rear axle retainers.

NOTE: *If the bearing cups are loose, tape them together to prevent dropping or loosing the roller bearings.*

4. Remove the driveshaft by sliding it forward, to disengage it from the axle flange, and then rearward, passing it under the axle housing.

NOTE: *When removing the driveshaft, DO NOT drop it or allow the universal joints to bend at extreme angles, for this may fracture the plastic injected joints.*

5. Inspect the driveshaft splines and surfaces for burrs, damage or wear.

6. To install, position the driveshaft into the transmission, align it with the matchmarks on the axle flange and reverse the removal procedures. Torque the universal joint-to-pinion flange bolts to 12–17 ft.lb.

U-JOINT OVERHAUL

Two types of universal joints are used: The front uses an internal snapring (production is plastic injected) and the rear uses an external snapring.

NOTE: *The following procedure requires the use of an Arbor Press, the GM Cross Press tool No. J-9522-3 or equivalent, the GM Spacer tool No. J-9522-5 or equivalent, and a 1⅛" (29mm) socket.*

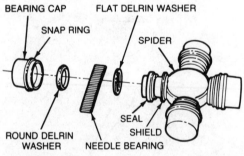

Exploded view of the front (replacement) universal joint—internal snap ring—

Internal snaring (Front)

1. While supporting the driveshaft, in the horizontal position, position it so that the lower ear of the front universal joint's shaft yoke is supported on a 1⅛" (29mm) socket.

NOTE: *DO NOT clamp the driveshaft tube in a vise, for the tube may become damaged.*

2. Using the GM Cross Press tool No. J-9522-3 or equivalent, place it on the horizontal bearing cups and press the lower bearing cup out of the yoke ear; the pressing action will

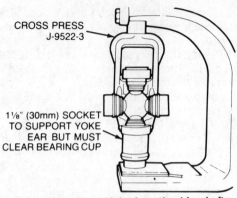

CROSS PRESS J-9522-3

1⅛" (30mm) SOCKET TO SUPPORT YOKE EAR BUT MUST CLEAR BEARING CUP

Removing the unviveral joint from the driveshaft

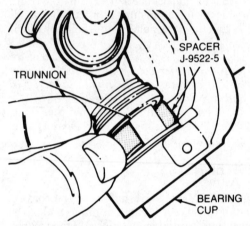

SPACER J-9522-5

TRUNNION

BEARING CUP

Using the GM Spacer tool No. J-9522-5 or equivalent, to completely remove the universal joint from the driveshaft

shear the plastic retaining ring from the lower bearing cup. If the bearing cup was not completely removed, insert the GM Spacer tool No. J-9522-5 or equivalent, onto the universal joint, then complete the pressing procedure to remove the joint.

3. Rotate the driveshaft and shear the plastic retainer from the opposite side of the yoke.

4. Disengage the slip yoke from the driveshaft.

5. To remove the universal joint from the slip yoke, perform the procedures used in Steps 1–4.

NOTE: *When the front universal joint has been disassembled, it must be discarded and replaced with a service kit joint, for the production joint is not equipped with bearing retainer grooves on the bearing cups.*

6. Clean (remove any remaining plastic particles) and inspect the slip yoke and driveshaft for damage, wear or burrs.

NOTE: *The universal joint service kit includes: A pregreased cross assembly, four bearing cups with seals, needle rollers, wash-*

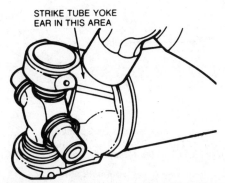

STRIKE TUBE YOKE EAR IN THIS AREA

Tapping the universal joint to seat the retaining rings—internal rings

ers, four bearing retainers and grease. Make sure that the bearing cup seals are installed to hold the needle bearings in place for handling.

7. To install, position one bearing cup assembly part way into the yoke ear (turn the ear to the bottom), insert the bearing cross (into the yoke) so that the trunnion seats freely into the bearing cup. Turn the yoke 180° and install the other bearing cup assembly.

NOTE: *When installing the bearing cup assemblies, make sure the trunnions are started straight and true into the bearing cups.*

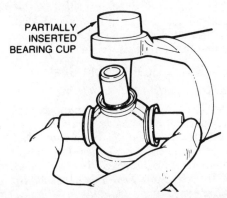

PARTIALLY INSERTED BEARING CUP

Installing the new universal joint bearing cross into the slip yoke

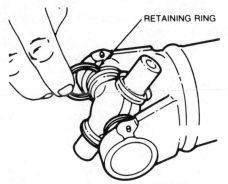

RETAINING RING

Installing the new universal joint retaining rings—internal rings

8. Using the arbor press, press the bearing cups onto the cross trunnion, until they seat.

NOTE: *While installing the bearing cups, twist the cross trunnion to work it into the bearings. If there seems to be a hangup, stop the pressing and recheck the needle roller alignment.*

9. Once the bearing cup retainer grooves have cleared the inside of the yoke, stop the pressing and install the snaprings.

10. If the other bearing cup retainer groove has not cleared the inside of the yoke, use a hammer to aid in the seating procedure.

11. To install the yoke/universal assembly to the driveshaft, perform the Steps 7–10 of this procedure.

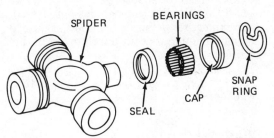

SPIDER BEARINGS SNAP RING CAP SEAL

Exploded view of the rear universal joint—external snap ring

External snapring (Rear)

1. Remove the snaprings from inside the yoke ears.

2. While supporting the driveshaft, in the horizontal position, position it so that the lower ear of the front universal joint's shaft yoke is supported on a 1⅛" (29mm) socket.

NOTE: *DO NOT clamp the driveshaft tube in a vise, for the tube may become damaged.*

3. Using the GM Cross Press tool No. J-9522-3 or equivalent, place it on the horizontal bearing cups and press the lower bearing cup out of the yoke ear. If the bearing cup was not completely removed, insert the GM Spacer tool No. J-9522-5 or equivalent, onto the universal joint, then complete the pressing procedure.

4. Rotate the driveshaft and press the bearing cup from the opposite side of the yoke.

5. Disengage the slip yoke from the driveshaft.

6. To remove the universal joint from the slip yoke, perform Steps 1–4 which were used to remove the joint from the driveshaft.

NOTE: *When the front universal joint has been disassembled, it should be discarded and replaced with a service kit joint.*

7. Clean and inspect the slip yoke and the driveshaft for damage, wear or burrs.

8. To install, position one bearing cup assembly part way into the yoke ear (turn the ear

to the bottom), insert the bearing cross (into the yoke) so that the trunnion seats freely into the bearing cup. Turn the yoke 180° and install the other bearing cup assembly.

NOTE: *When installing the bearing cup assemblies, make sure the trunnions are started straight and true into the bearing cups.*

9. Using the arbor press, press the bearing cups onto the cross trunnion, until they seat.

NOTE: *While installing the bearing cups, twist the cross trunnion to work it into the bearings. If there seems to be a hangup, stop the pressing and recheck the needle roller alignment.*

10. Once the bearing cup clears the retainer grooves (inside of the yoke ear), stop the pressing and install the snaprings.

11. If the other bearing cup has not cleared the retainer groove (inside the yoke ear), use a hammer and a brass drift punch to aid in the seating procedure.

12. To install the yoke/universal assembly to the driveshaft, perform the Steps 8–11 of this procedure.

REAR AXLE

Two types of rear axles are used: The standard and the locking. The axle is of a semi-floating type, where the vehicle weight is carried on the axle housing. It is designed for use with an open driveline and fiberglass leaf springs. All of the power transmitting parts are enclosed in a Salisbury type axle (a carrier casting with pressed tubes, welded into the carrier). A removable cover at the rear of the housing, allows the axle to be serviced without removing the entire assembly from the vehicle.

The Eaton built (locking) rear axle, equipped with a speed sensitive, multi-disc clutch pack mechanism, locks both wheels together if either wheel spins excessively during slow vehicle operation.

Identification

The rear axle identification number is located on the front, right side of the axle tube. See the Rear Axle Specification chart in Chapter 1 for information on determining the axle ratio, differential type, manufacturer and date built, from the letter codes.

Determining Axle Ratio

An axle ratio is obtained by dividing the number of teeth on the drive pinion gear into the number of teeth on the ring gear. For instance, on a 4.11:1 ratio, the driveshaft will turn 4.11 times for every turn of the rear wheels.

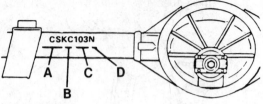

A. Axle code
B. 7½″ (190 mm) Chevrolet St. Catherines
C. Day built
D. Shift (D = Day, N = Night)

View of the rear axle identification number

The most accurate way to determine the axle ratio is to drain the differential, remove the cover and count the number of teeth on the ring and the pinion.

An easier method is raise and support the rear of the vehicle on jackstands. Make a chalk mark on the rear wheel and the driveshaft. Block the front wheels and put the transmission in Neutral. Turn the rear wheel one complete revolution and count the number of turns made by the driveshaft. The number of driveshaft rotations is the axle ratio. More accuracy can be obtained by going more than one tire revolution and dividing the result by the number of tire rotations.

The axle ratio is also identified by the axle serial number prefix on the axle; the axle ratios are listed in the dealer's parts books according to the prefix number.

Axle Shaft, Bearing and Seal
REMOVAL AND INSTALLATION

NOTE: *The following procedures requires the use of the GM Slide Hammer tool No. J-2619 or equivalent, the GM Adapter tool No. J-2619-4 or equivalent, the GM Axle Bearing Puller tool No. J-22813-01 or equivalent, the GM Axle Shaft Seal Installer tool No. J-33782 or equivalent and the Axle Shaft Bearing Installer tool No. J-34974 or equivalent.*

1. Raise and support the rear of the vehicle on jackstands.

2. Remove the rear wheel assemblies and the brake drums.

CAUTION: *Brake shoes contain asbestos, which has been determined to be a cancer causing agent. Never clean the brake surfaces with compressed air! Avoid inhaling any dust from any brake surface! When cleaning brake surfaces, use a commercially available brake cleaning fluid.*

3. Using a wire brush, clean the dirt/rust from around the rear axle cover.

4. Place a catch pan under the differential, then remove the drain plug (if equipped) or rear axle cover and drain the fluid (discard it).

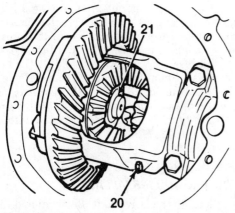

20. Lock bolt
21. "C" lock

View of the rear axle pinion shaft lock bolt and the "C" lock retainer

5. At the differential, remove the rear pinion shaft lock bolt and the pinion shaft.
6. Push the axle shaft inward and remove the C-lock from the button end of the axle shaft.
7. Remove the axle shaft from the axle housing, be careful not to damage the oil seal.
8. Using a putty knife, clean the gasket mounting surfaces.

NOTE: *It is recommended, when the axle shaft is removed, to replace the oil seal.*

9. To replace the oil seal, perform the following procedures:

a. Using a medium pry bar, pry the oil seal from the end of the rear axle housing; DO NOT damage the housing oil seal surface.

b. Clean and inspect the axle tube housing.

c. Using the GM Axle Shaft Seal Installer tool No. J-33782 or equivalent, drive the new seal into the housing until it is flush with the axle tube.

d. Using gear oil, lubricate the new seal lips.

10. If replacing the wheel bearing, perform the following procedures:

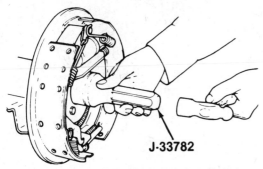

J-33782

Installing the new oil seal in the axle housing tube

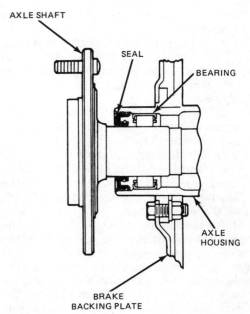

Sectional view of the rear axle, bearing and seal assembly

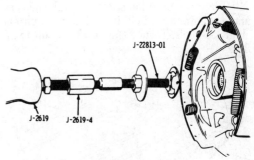

Removing the rear axle wheel bearing

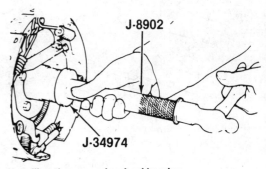

Installing the rear axle wheel bearing

a. Using the GM Slide Hammer tool No. J-2619 or equivalent, the GM Adapter tool No. J-2619-4 or equivalent and the GM Axle Bearing Puller tool No. J-22813-01 or equivalent, install the tool assembly so that the tangs engage the outer race of the bearing.

b. Using the action of the slide hammer,

pull the wheel bearing from the axle housing.

c. Using solvent, throughly clean the wheel bearing, then blow dry with compressed air. Inspect the wheel bearing for excessive wear or damage, then replace it (if necessary).

d. With a new or the reused bearing, place a blob of heavy grease in the palm of your hand, then work the bearing into the grease until it is thoroughly lubricated.

e. Using the Axle Shaft Bearing Installer tool No. J-34974 or equivalent, drive the bearing into the axle housing until it bottoms against the seat.

11. To install, slide the axle shaft into the rear axle housing and engage the splines of the axle shaft with the splines of the rear axle side gear, then install the C-lock retainer on the axle shaft button end. After the C-lock is installed, pull the axle shaft outward to seat the C-lock retainer in the counterbore of the side gears.

NOTE: *When installing the axle shaft(s), be careful not to cut the oil seal lips.*

12. Install the pinion shaft through the case and the pinions, then install a new pinion shaft lock bolt. Torque the new lock bolt to 25 ft.lb.

13. To complete the installation, use a new rear axle cover gasket and reverse the removal procedures. Torque the carrier cover-to-rear axle housing bolts to 20 ft.lb. Refill the housing with SAE-80W or SAE-80W-90 GL-5 oil to a level ⅜″ (10mm) below the filler plug hole.

NOTE: *When adding oil to the rear axle, be aware that some locking differentials require the use of a special gear lubricant additive GM No. 1052271.*

Axle Housing

REMOVAL AND INSTALLATION

1. Refer to the Driveshaft, Removal and Installation procedures in this section and disconnect the driveshaft from the rear axle housing; the driveshaft may either be removed or supported on a wire. Using a floor jack, position it under and support the rear axle housing.

NOTE: *When supporting the rear of the vehicle, be sure to place the jackstands under the frame.*

2. Remove the rear wheel assemblies.

3. Remove the shock absorber-to-axle housing nuts/bolts, then swing the shock absorbers away from the axle housing.

4. Disconnect the brake lines from the axle

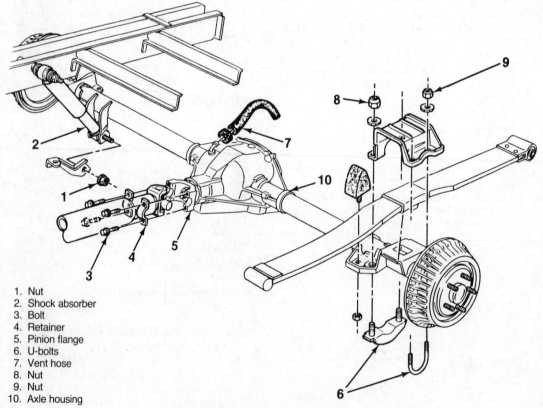

1. Nut
2. Shock absorber
3. Bolt
4. Retainer
5. Pinion flange
6. U-bolts
7. Vent hose
8. Nut
9. Nut
10. Axle housing

Exploded view of the rear axle housing

housing clips and the backing plates (wheel cylinders).

NOTE: *When disconnecting the brake lines from the wheel cylinders, be sure to plug the lines to keep dirt from entering the lines.*

5. Disconnect the axle housing-to-spring U-bolt nuts, the U-bolts and the anchor plates.

6. Remove the vent hose from the top of the axle housing.

7. Using the floor jack, lower the axle housing and remove from the vehicle.

8. To install, reverse the removal procedures. Torque the inner U-bolt-to-anchor plate nuts to 41 ft.lb., the outer U-bolt-to-anchor plate nuts to 48 ft.lb., the shock absorber-to-axle housing nuts/bolts to 74 ft.lb. and the driveshaft-to-pinion flange retainer nuts to 27 ft.lb. Check and/or refill the axle housing with SAE-80W or SAE-80W-90 GL-5 oil to a level ⅜" (10mm) below the filler plug hole. Bleed the rear brake system.

Troubleshooting the Manual Transmission

Problem	Cause	Solution
Transmission shifts hard	• Clutch adjustment incorrect • Clutch linkage or cable binding • Shift rail binding	• Adjust clutch • Lubricate or repair as necessary • Check for mispositioned selector arm roll pin, loose cover bolts, worn shift rail bores, worn shift rail, distorted oil seal, or extension housing not aligned with case. Repair as necessary.
	• Internal bind in transmission caused by shift forks, selector plates, or synchronizer assemblies • Clutch housing misalignment • Incorrect lubricant • Block rings and/or cone seats worn	• Remove, dissemble and inspect transmission. Replace worn or damaged components as necessary. • Check runout at rear face of clutch housing • Drain and refill transmission • Blocking ring to gear clutch tooth face clearance must be 0.030 inch or greater. If clearance is correct it may still be necessary to inspect blocking rings and cone seats for excessive wear. Repair as necessary.
Gear clash when shifting from one gear to another	• Clutch adjustment incorrect • Clutch linkage or cable binding • Clutch housing misalignment • Lubricant level low or incorrect lubricant • Gearshift components, or synchronizer assemblies worn or damaged	• Adjust clutch • Lubricate or repair as necessary • Check runout at rear of clutch housing • Drain and refill transmission and check for lubricant leaks if level was low. Repair as necessary. • Remove, disassemble and inspect transmission. Replace worn or damaged components as necessary.
Transmission noisy	• Lubricant level low or incorrect lubricant • Clutch housing-to-engine, or transmission-to-clutch housing bolts loose • Dirt, chips, foreign material in transmission • Gearshift mechanism, transmission gears, or bearing components worn or damaged • Clutch housing misalignment	• Drain and refill transmission. If lubricant level was low, check for leaks and repair as necessary. • Check and correct bolt torque as necessary • Drain, flush, and refill transmission • Remove, disassemble and inspect transmission. Replace worn or damaged components as necessary. • Check runout at rear face of clutch housing

Troubleshooting the Manual Transmission (cont.)

Problem	Cause	Solution
Jumps out of gear	• Clutch housing misalignment	• Check runout at rear face of clutch housing
	• Gearshift lever loose	• Check lever for worn fork. Tighten loose attaching bolts.
	• Offset lever nylon insert worn or lever attaching nut loose	• Remove gearshift lever and check for loose offset lever nut or worn insert. Repair or replace as necessary.
	• Gearshift mechanism, shift forks, selector plates, interlock plate, selector arm, shift rail, detent plugs, springs or shift cover worn or damaged	• Remove, disassemble and inspect transmission cover assembly. Replace worn or damaged components as necessary.
	• Clutch shaft or roller bearings worn or damaged	• Replace clutch shaft or roller bearings as necessary
	• Gear teeth worn or tapered, synchronizer assemblies worn or damaged, excessive end play caused by worn thrust washers or output shaft gears	• Remove, disassemble, and inspect transmission. Replace worn or damaged components as necessary.
	• Pilot bushing worn	• Replace pilot bushing
Will not shift into one gear	• Gearshift selector plates, interlock plate, or selector arm, worn, damaged, or incorrectly assembled	• Remove, disassemble, and inspect transmission cover assembly. Repair or replace components as necessary.
	• Shift rail detent plunger worn, spring broken, or plug loose	• Tighten plug or replace worn or damaged components as necessary
	• Gearshift lever worn or damaged	• Replace gearshift lever
	• Synchronizer sleeves or hubs, damaged or worn	• Remove, disassemble and inspect transmission. Replace worn or damaged components.
Locked in one gear—cannot be shifted out	• Shift rail(s) worn or broken, shifter fork bent, setscrew loose, center detent plug missing or worn	• Inspect and replace worn or damaged parts
	• Broken gear teeth on countershaft gear, clutch shaft, or reverse idler gear	• Inspect and replace damaged part
	Gearshift lever broken or worn, shift mechanism in cover incorrectly assembled or broken, worn damaged gear train components	• Disassemble transmission. Replace damaged parts or assemble correctly.
Lubricant leaking from output shaft seals or from vent	• Output shaft seals damaged or installed incorrectly	• Replace seals. Be sure seal lip faces interior of case when installed. Also be sure yoke seal surfaces are not scored or nicked. Remove scores, nicks with fine sandpaper or replace yoke(s) if necessary.
Abnormal tire wear	• Extended operation on dry hard surface (paved) roads in 4H range	• Operate in 2H on hard surface (paved) roads

Lockup Torque Converter Service Diagnosis

Problem	Cause	Solution

No lockup	• Faulty oil pump
	• Sticking governor valve
	• Valve body malfunction
	   (a) Stuck switch valve
	   (b) Stuck lockup valve
	   (c) Stuck fail-safe valve
	• Failed locking clutch
	• Leaking turbine hub seal
	• Faulty input shaft or seal ring
		• Replace oil pump
		• Repair or replace as necessary
		• Repair or replace valve body or its internal components as necessary
		
		• Replace torque converter
		• Replace torque converter
		• Repair or replace as necessary

Will not unlock	• Sticking governor valve
	• Valve body malfunction
	   (a) Stuck switch valve
	   (b) Stuck lockup valve
	   (c) Stuck fail-safe valve
		• Repair or replace as necessary
		• Repair or replace valve body or its internal components as necessary

Stays locked up at too low a speed in direct	• Sticking governor valve
	• Valve body malfunction
	   (a) Stuck switch valve
	   (b) Stuck lockup valve
	   (c) Stuck fail-safe valve
		• Repair or replace as necessary
		• Repair or replace valve body or its internal components as necessary

Locks up or drags in low or second	• Faulty oil pump
	• Valve body malfunction
	   (a) Stuck switch valve
	   (b) Stuck fail-safe valve
		• Replace oil pump
		• Repair or replace valve body or its internal components as necessary

Sluggish or stalls in reverse	• Faulty oil pump
	• Plugged cooler, cooler lines or fittings
	• Valve body malfunction
	   (a) Stuck switch valve
	   (b) Faulty input shaft or seal ring
		• Replace oil pump as necessary
		• Flush or replace cooler and flush lines and fittings
		• Repair or replace valve body or its internal components as necessary

Loud chatter during lockup engagement (cold)	• Faulty torque converter • Failed locking clutch • Leaking turbine hub seal	• Replace torque converter • Replace torque converter • Replace torque converter
Vibration or shudder during lockup engagement	• Faulty oil pump • Valve body malfunction • Faulty torque converter • Engine needs tune-up	• Repair or replace oil pump as necessary • Repair or replace valve body or its internal components as necessary • Replace torque converter • Tune engine
Vibration after lockup engagement	• Faulty torque converter • Exhaust system strikes underbody • Engine needs tune-up • Throttle linkage misadjusted	• Replace torque converter • Align exhaust system • Tune engine • Adjust throttle linkage
Vibration when revved in neutral Overheating: oil blows out of dip stick tube or pump seal	• Torque converter out of balance • Plugged cooler, cooler lines or fittings • Stuck switch valve	• Replace torque converter • Flush or replace cooler and flush lines and fittings • Repair switch valve in valve body or replace valve body
Shudder after lockup engagement	• Faulty oil pump • Plugged cooler, cooler lines or fittings • Valve body malfunction • Faulty torque converter • Fail locking clutch • Exhaust system strikes underbody • Engine needs tune-up • Throttle linkage misadjusted	• Replace oil pump • Flush or replace cooler and flush lines and fittings • Repair or replace valve body or its internal components as necessary • Replace torque converter • Replace torque converter • Align exhaust system • Tune engine • Adjust throttle linkage

Troubleshooting Basic Driveshaft and Rear Axle Problems

When abnormal vibrations or noises are detected in the driveshaft area, this chart can be used to help diagnose possible causes. Remember that other components such as wheels, tires, rear axle and suspension can also produce similar conditions.

BASIC DRIVESHAFT PROBLEMS

Problem	Cause	Solution
Shudder as car accelerates from stop or low speed	• Loose U-joint • Defective center bearing	• Replace U-joint • Replace center bearing
Loud clunk in driveshaft when shifting gears	• Worn U-joints	• Replace U-joints
Roughness or vibration at any speed	• Out-of-balance, bent or dented driveshaft • Worn U-joints • U-joint clamp bolts loose	• Balance or replace driveshaft • Replace U-joints • Tighten U-joint clamp bolts
Squeaking noise at low speeds	• Lack of U-joint lubrication	• Lubricate U-joint; if problem persists, replace U-joint
Knock or clicking noise	• U-joint or driveshaft hitting frame tunnel • Worn CV joint	• Correct overloaded condition • Replace CV joint

BASIC REAR AXLE PROBLEMS

First, determine when the noise is most noticeable.

Drive Noise: Produced under vehicle acceleration.

Coast Noise: Produced while the car coasts with a closed throttle.

Float Noise: Occurs while maintaining constant car speed (just enough to keep speed constant) on a level road.

Road Noise

Brick or rough surfaced concrete roads produce noises that seem to come from the rear axle. Road noise is usually identical in Drive or Coast and driving on a different type of road will tell whether the road is the problem.

Tire Noise

Tire noises are often mistaken for rear axle problems. Snow treads or unevenly worn tires produce vibrations seeming to originate elsewhere. **Temporarily** inflating the tires to 40 lbs will significantly alter tire noise, but will have no effect on rear axle noises (which normally cease below about 30 mph).

Engine/Transmission Noise

Determine at what speed the noise is most pronounced, then stop the car in a quiet place. With the transmission in Neutral, run the engine through speeds corresponding to road speeds where the noise was noticed. Noises produced with the car standing still are coming from the engine or transmission.

Front Wheel Bearings

While holding the car speed steady, lightly apply the footbrake; this will often decease bearing noise, as some of the load is taken from the bearing.

Rear Axle Noises

Eliminating other possible sources can narrow the cause to the rear axle, which normally produces noise from worn gears or bearings. Gear noises tend to peak in a narrow speed range, while bearing noises will usually vary in pitch with engine speeds.

Troubleshooting Basic Clutch Problems

Problem	Cause
Excessive clutch noise	Throwout bearing noises are more audible at the lower end of pedal travel. The usual causes are: • Riding the clutch • Too little pedal free-play • Lack of bearing lubrication A bad clutch shaft pilot bearing will make a high pitched squeal, when the clutch is disengaged and the transmission is in gear or within the first 2″ of pedal travel. The bearing must be replaced. Noise from the clutch linkage is a clicking or snapping that can be heard or felt as the pedal is moved completely up or down. This usually requires lubrication. Transmitted engine noises are amplified by the clutch housing and heard in the passenger compartment. They are usually the result of insufficient pedal free-play and can be changed by manipulating the clutch pedal.
Clutch slips (the car does not move as it should when the clutch is engaged)	This is usually most noticeable when pulling away from a standing start. A severe test is to start the engine, apply the brakes, shift into high gear and SLOWLY release the clutch pedal. A healthy clutch will stall the engine. If it slips it may be due to: • A worn pressure plate or clutch plate • Oil soaked clutch plate • Insufficient pedal free-play
Clutch drags or fails to release	The clutch disc and some transmission gears spin briefly after clutch disengagement. Under normal conditions in average temperatures, 3 seconds is maximum spin-time. Failure to release properly can be caused by: • Too light transmission lubricant or low lubricant level • Improperly adjusted clutch linkage
Low clutch life	Low clutch life is usually a result of poor driving habits or heavy duty use. Riding the clutch, pulling heavy loads, holding the car on a grade with the clutch instead of the brakes and rapid clutch engagement all contribute to low clutch life.

Troubleshooting Basic Automatic Transmission Problems

Problem	Cause	Solution
Fluid leakage	• Defective pan gasket	• Replace gasket or tighten pan bolts
	• Loose filler tube	• Tighten tube nut
	• Loose extension housing to transmission case	• Tighten bolts
	• Converter housing area leakage	• Have transmission checked professionally
Fluid flows out the oil filler tube	• High fluid level	• Check and correct fluid level
	• Breather vent clogged	• Open breather vent
	• Clogged oil filter or screen	• Replace filter or clean screen (change fluid also)
	• Internal fluid leakage	• Have transmission checked professionally
Transmission overheats (this is usually accompanied by a strong burned odor to the fluid)	• Low fluid level	• Check and correct fluid level
	• Fluid cooler lines clogged	• Drain and refill transmission. If this doesn't cure the problem, have cooler lines cleared or replaced.
	• Heavy pulling or hauling with insufficient cooling	• Install a transmission oil cooler
	• Faulty oil pump, internal slippage	• Have transmission checked professionally
Buzzing or whining noise	• Low fluid level	• Check and correct fluid level
	• Defective torque converter, scored gears	• Have transmission checked professionally
No forward or reverse gears or slippage in one or more gears	• Low fluid level	• Check and correct fluid level
	• Defective vacuum or linkage controls, internal clutch or band failure	• Have unit checked professionally
Delayed or erratic shift	• Low fluid level	• Check and correct fluid level
	• Broken vacuum lines	• Repair or replace lines
	• Internal malfunction	• Have transmission checked professionally

Transmission Fluid Indications

The appearance and odor of the transmission fluid can give valuable clues to the overall condition of the transmission. Always note the appearance of the fluid when you check the fluid level or change the fluid. Rub a small amount of fluid between your fingers to feel for grit and smell the fluid on the dipstick.

If the fluid appears:	It indicates:
Clear and red colored	• Normal operation
Discolored (extremely dark red or brownish) or smells burned	• Band or clutch pack failure, usually caused by an overheated transmission. Hauling very heavy loads with insufficient power or failure to change the fluid, often result in overheating. Do not confuse this appearance with newer fluids that have a darker red color and a strong odor (though not a burned odor).
Foamy or aerated (light in color and full of bubbles)	• The level is too high (gear train is churning oil) • An internal air leak (air is mixing with the fluid). Have the transmission checked professionally.
Solid residue in the fluid	• Defective bands, clutch pack or bearings. Bits of band material or metal abrasives are clinging to the dipstick. Have the transmission checked professionally.
Varnish coating on the dipstick	• The transmission fluid is overheating

Suspension and Steering

FRONT SUSPENSION

The front suspension is designed to allow each wheel to compensate for changes in the road surface without appreciably affecting the opposite wheel. Each wheel is independently connected to the frame by a steering knuckle, ball joint assemblies, and upper and lower control arms. The control arms are specifically designed and positioned to allow the steering knuckles to move in a prescribed three dimensional arc. The front wheels are held in proper relationship to each other by two tie rods which are connected to steering arms on the knuckles and to an intermediate rod.

Coil chassis springs are mounted between the spring housings on the frame and the lower control arms. Ride control is provided by double, direct acting, shock absorbers mounted inside the coil springs and attached to the lower control arms by nuts and bolts. The upper portion of each shock absorber extends through the upper control arm frame bracket and is secured with two grommets, two grommet retainers and a nut.

Side role of the front suspension is controlled by a spring steel stabilizer shaft. It is mounted in rubber bushings which are held to the frame side rails by brackets. The ends of the stabilizer are connected to the lower control arms by link bolts isolated by rubber grommets.

The upper control arm is attached to the upper control arm shaft through isolating rubber bushings. The upper control arm shaft, in turn, is bolted to frame brackets.

A ball joint assembly is riveted to the outer end of the upper control arm. It is preloaded by a rubber spring to insure proper seating of the ball in the socket. The upper ball joint is attached to the steering knuckle by a torque prevailing nut.

The inner ends of the lower control arm have pressed-in bushings. Bolts, passing through the bushings, attach the arm to the frame. The lower ball joint assembly is a press fit in the arm and attaches to the steering knuckle with a torque prevailing nut.

Rubber grease seals are provided at the ball socket assemblies to keep dirt and moisture from entering the joint and damaging the bearing surfaces.

Coil Springs

REMOVAL AND INSTALLATION

NOTE: *The following procedure requires the use of the GM Spring Remover tool No. J-23028 or equivalent.*

1. Raise and support the front of the vehicle on jackstands so that the lower control arms hang free.

2. Disconnect the shock absorber-to-lower control arm nuts, then push the shock absorber up into the coil spring.

3. Using the GM Spring Remover tool No. J-23028 or equivalent, secure it to a floor jack, then position the assembly under the lower

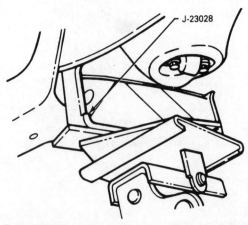

Supporting the lower control arm with the spring remover tool

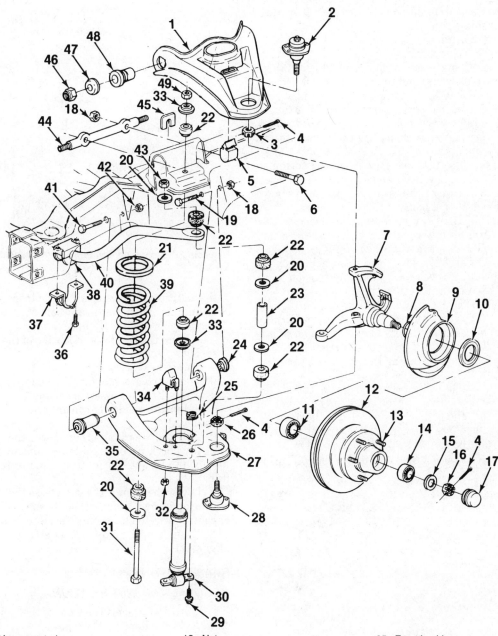

1. Upper control arm	18. Nut	35. Front bushing
2. Upper ball joint	19. Bolt	36. Bolt
3. Nut	20. Retainer	37. Bracket
4. Cotter pin	21. Insulator	38. Insulator
5. Bumper	22. Grommet	39. Spring
6. Bolt	23. Spacer	40. Stabilizer shaft
7. Steering knuckle	24. Rear bushing	41. Bolt
8. Gasket	25. Nut	42. Nut
9. Splash shield	26. Nut	43. Nut
10. Seal	27. Lower control arm	44. Upper control arm shaft
11. Inner wheel bearing	28. Lower bail joint	45. Shim
12. Rotor/hub	29. Bolt	46. Nut
13. Wheel hub bolts	30. Shock absorber	47. Retainer
14. Outer wheel bearing	31. Bolt	48. Bushing
15. Washer	32. Nut	49. Nut
16. Nut	33. Retainer	
17. Cap	34. Bumper	

Exploded view the front suspension system

control arm so that it cradles the inner bushings.

4. Disconnect the stabilizer bar from the lower control arm.

5. Using a safety chain, install it through the coil spring and the lower control arm.

CAUTION: *The coil springs are under a considerable amount of tension. Be extremely careful when removing or installing them; they can exert enough force to cause serious injury.*

6. Raise the floor jack (with the spring remover tool) to take the tension off of the lower control arm-to-chassis bolts/nuts, then remove the nuts and bolts.

NOTE: *When removing the lower control arm-to-chassis bolts/nuts, be sure to remove the rear set first, then the front set.*

7. Carefully, lower the floor jack (with the spring remover tool) until the tension is released from the coil spring.

NOTE: *When removing the coil spring, DO NOT apply force to the lower control arm or the lower ball joint. Proper maneuvering of the spring will provide easy removal.*

8. Before installing the coil spring, position it in the following order:

a. The coil spring top has a coiled, flat shape with a gripper notch at the end of the coil; the bottom has a coiled, helical shape.

b. Place the coil spring so that the tape (on the coil) is at the lowest position.

c. Position the lower end of the coil spring

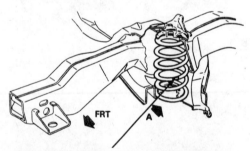

SPRING TO BE INSTALLED WITH TAPE AT LOWEST POSITION. BOTTOM OF SPRING IS COILED HELICAL, AND THE TOP IS COILED FLAT WITH A GRIPPER NOTCH NEAR END OF SPRING COIL.

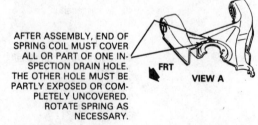

AFTER ASSEMBLY, END OF SPRING COIL MUST COVER ALL OR PART OF ONE INSPECTION DRAIN HOLE. THE OTHER HOLE MUST BE PARTLY EXPOSED OR COMPLETELY UNCOVERED. ROTATE SPRING AS NECESSARY.

Positioning the coil spring—front suspension system

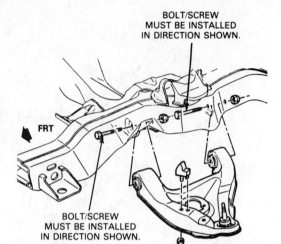

BOLT/SCREW MUST BE INSTALLED IN DIRECTION SHOWN.

FRT

BOLT/SCREW MUST BE INSTALLED IN DIRECTION SHOWN.

Replacing the lower control arm—front suspension system

so that it covers part or all of the inspection drain hole. The other drain hole MUST BE partially or completely uncovered.

d. Place the insulator at the top of the coil spring.

9. Using the GM Spring Remover tool No. J-23028 floor jack assembly, raise the lower control arm/coil spring assembly using the floor jack and install the lower control arm-to-chassis nuts/bolts.

10. Pull the shock absorber down, then install the shock absorber-to-lower control arm nuts/bolts. Torque the nuts and bolts to 18 ft.lb.

11. Lower the front of the vehicle, so that it is resting on its own weight, then torque the lower control arm-to-chassis nuts/bolts to 96 ft.lb.

12. Check and/or adjust the front end alignment.

Shock Absorbers

REMOVAL AND INSTALLATION

1. Raise and support the front of the vehicle on jackstands. Remove the wheels.

2. While holding the upper end of the shock absorber (to keep it from turning), remove the shock absorber nut, retainer and grommet.

3. Remove the shock absorber-to-lower control arm nuts and bolts, then slide the shock absorber from the bottom of the lower control arm.

4. Test the shock absorber and replace it, if necessary.

5. To install, fully extend the shock absorber, insert it through the coil spring and the upper control arm, then reverse the removal procedures. Torque the upper shock absorber nut to 15 ft.lb. and the shock absorber-to-lower control arm nuts/bolts to 18 ft.lb.

20 N·m (15 FT. LBS.)

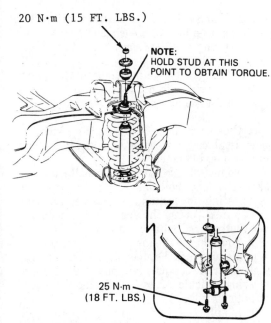

NOTE:
HOLD STUD AT THIS
POINT TO OBTAIN TORQUE.

25 N·m
(18 FT. LBS.)

Replacing the shock absorber—front suspension system

TESTING

Visually inspect the shock absorber. If there is evidence of leakage and the shock absorber is covered with oil, the shock is defective and should be replaced.

If there is no sign of excessive leakage (a small amount of weeping is normal) bounce the van at one corner by pressing down on the bumper and releasing it. When you have the van bouncing as much as you can, release the bumper. The van should stop bouncing after the first rebound. If the bouncing continues past the center point of the bounce more than once, the shock absorbers are worn and should be replaced.

Upper Ball Joint

INSPECTION

NOTE: *Before performing this inspection, make sure that the wheel bearings are adjusted correctly and that the control arm bushings are in good condition.*

1. Raise and support the front of the vehicle by placing jackstands under each lower control arm as close as possible to each lower ball joint.

NOTE: *Before performing the upper ball joint replacement, be sure that the vehicle is stable and the lower control arm bumpers are not contacting the frame.*

2. Using a dial indicator, position it so that it contacts the wheel rim.

3. To measure the horizontal deflection, perform the following procedures:

a. Grasp the tire (top and bottom), then pull outward on the top and push inward on the bottom; record the reading on the dial indicator.

b. Grasp the tire (top and bottom), then pull outward on the bottom and push inward on the top; record the reading on the dial indicator.

c. If the difference in the dial indicator reading is more than 0.125″ (3.175mm), the ball joint can be twisted in its socket (with finger pressure) or appears damaged, replace the ball joint.

REMOVAL AND INSTALLATION

NOTE: *The following procedure requires the use of the GM Ball Joint Remover tool No. J-23742 or equivalent.*

1. Raise and support the front of the vehicle by placing jackstands under the lower control arms, between the spring seat and the lower ball joint.

NOTE: *Allow the floor jack to remain under the lower control arm seat, to retain the spring and the lower control arm position.*

2. Remove the wheels assembly.

3. From the upper ball joint, remove the cotter pin, the nut and the grease fitting.

4. Using the GM Ball Joint Remover tool No. J-23742 or equivalent, separate the upper ball joint from the steering knuckle. Pull the steering knuckle free of the ball joint after removal.

NOTE: *After separating the steering knuckle from the upper ball joint, be sure to support steering knuckle/hub assembly to prevent damaging the brake hose.*

5. To remove the upper ball joint from the upper control arm, perform the following procedures:

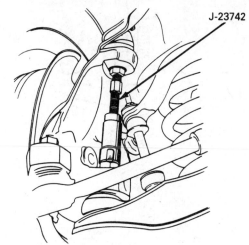

J-23742

Disconnecting the upper ball joint from the upper control arm—front suspension system

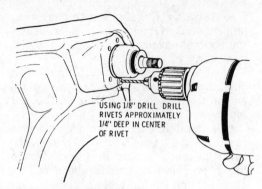

Drill the upper ball joint rivets

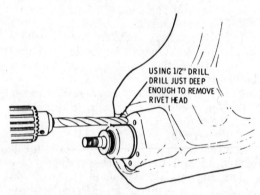

Use a ½ in. drill to drill the upper ball joint rivet heads,

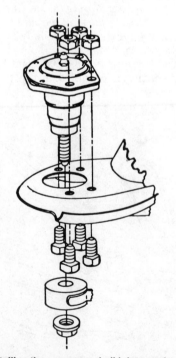

When installing the new upper ball joints, make sure that the nuts are on top

a. Using a ⅛″ (3mm) drill bit, drill a ¼″ (6mm) deep hole into each rivet.

b. Using a ½″ (13mm) drill bit, drill off the rivet heads.

c. Using a pin punch and the hammer, drive the rivets from the upper ball joint-to-upper control arm assembly and remove the upper ball joint.

6. Clean and inspect the steering knuckle hole. Replace the steering knuckle, if any out of roundness is noted.

7. To install, use a new upper ball joint, position the upper ball joint-to-upper control arm bolts facing upward and reverse the removal procedures. Torque the upper ball joint-to-upper control arm bolts to 8 ft.lb.

8. To complete the installation, seat the upper ball joint into the steering knuckle and install the nut. Torque the upper ball joint-to-steering knuckle nut to 52 ft.lb. and the wheel nuts to 90 ft.lb.

9. Install a new cotter pin to the lower ball joint stud.

NOTE: *When installing the cotter pin to the upper ball joint-to-steering knuckle nut, be sure to turn the castle nut an addition amount to expose the cotter pin hole.*

10. Using a grease gun, lubricate the upper ball joint until grease oozes from the grease seal. Inspect and/or adjust the wheel bearing and the front end alignment.

11. Remove the lower control arm support and lower the vehicle.

Lower Ball Joint

INSPECTION

NOTE: *Before performing this inspection, make sure that the wheel bearings are adjusted correctly and that the control arm bushings are in good condition.*

Visually check the wear indicator; if it is flush or inside the ball joint cover surface, replace the ball joint.

REMOVAL AND INSTALLATION

NOTE: *The following procedure requires the use of the GM Ball Joint Remover tool No. J-23742 or equivalent, the GM Ball Joint Remover tool No. J-9519-7 or equivalent, the GM Ball Joint Installer tool No. J-9519-9 or equivalent, and the GM Ball Joint Fixture tool No. J-9519-10 or equivalent.*

1. Raise and support the front of the vehicle on jackstands. Remove the wheels.

2. Using a floor jack, place it under the spring seat of the lower control arm, then raise the jack to support the arm.

NOTE: *The floor jack MUST remain under*

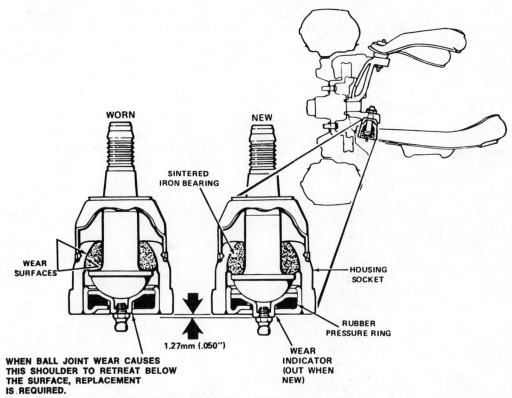

WORN

NEW

SINTERED
IRON BEARING

WEAR
SURFACES

HOUSING
SOCKET

RUBBER
PRESSURE RING

1.27mm (.050")

WHEN BALL JOINT WEAR CAUSES
THIS SHOULDER TO RETREAT BELOW
THE SURFACE, REPLACEMENT
IS REQUIRED.

WEAR
INDICATOR
(OUT WHEN
NEW)

Inspecting the lower ball joint indicator—front suspension system

the lower control arm, during the removal
and installation procedures, to retain the arm
and spring positions.

3. Remove the cotter pin (discard it) and the
ball joint nut.

4. Using the GM Ball Joint Remover tool
No. J-23742 or equivalent, disconnect the low-

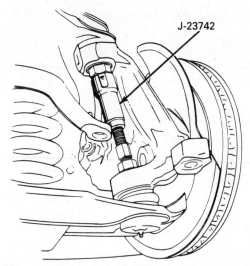

J-23742

Disconnecting the lower ball joint from the steering
knuckle/hub assembly—front suspension system

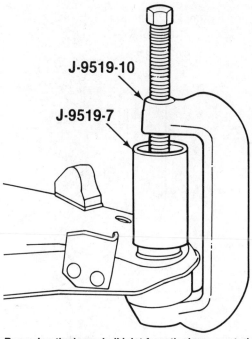

J-9519-10

J-9519-7

Removing the lower ball joint from the lower control
arm—front suspension system

er ball joint from the steering knuckle. Pull the steering knuckle away from the lower control arm, place a block of wood between the frame and the upper control arm; make sure that the brake hose is free of tension.

5. From the lower ball joint, remove the rubber grease seal and the grease fitting.

6. Using the GM Ball Joint Remover tool No. J-9519-7 or equivalent, and the GM Ball Joint Fixture tool No. J-9519-10 or equivalent, remove the lower ball joint from the lower control arm.

7. To install, position the new lower ball joint into the lower control arm. Using the GM Ball Joint Installer tool No. J-9519-9 or equivalent, and the GM Ball Joint Fixture tool No. J-9519-10 or equivalent, press the new lower ball joint into the lower control arm.

8. Install the grease fitting and the grease seal onto the lower ball joint; the grease seal MUST BE fully seated on the ball joint and the grease purge hole MUST face inboard.

9. To complete the installation, reverse the removal procedures. Torque the ball joint-to-steering knuckle nut to 81 ft.lb. and the wheel nuts to 90 ft.lb.

10. Install a new cotter pin to the lower ball joint stud.

NOTE: *When installing the cotter pin to the lower ball joint-to-steering knuckle nut, be sure to turn the castle nut an addition amount to expose the cotter pin hole.*

11. Using a grease gun, lubricate the lower

ball joint until grease oozes from the grease seal. Inspect and/or adjust the wheel bearing and the front end alignment.

12. Remove the lower control arm support and lower the vehicle.

Stabilizer Bar
REMOVAL AND INSTALLATION

1. Raise and support the front of the vehicle on jackstands. Remove the wheels.

2. Disconnect the stabilizer bar link nuts from the lower control arms.

3. Remove the stabilizer bar-to-frame clamps.

4. Remove the stabilizer bar from the vehicle.

5. To install, reverse the removal procedures. Torque the stabilizer bar link-to-lower control arm bolts to 13 ft.lb. and the stabilizer retainer-to-frame bolts to 22 ft.lb.

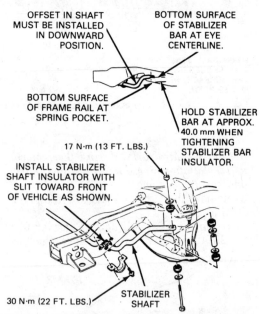

Replacing the stabilizer bar—front suspension system

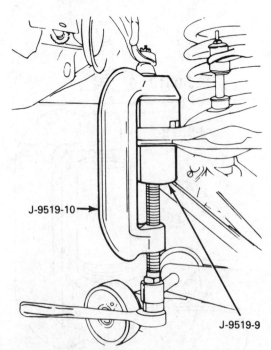

Installing the new lower ball joint into the lower control arm—front suspension system

Upper Control Arm
REMOVAL AND INSTALLATION

NOTE: *The following procedure requires the use of the GM Ball Joint Remover tool No. J-23742 or equivalent.*

1. Raise and support the front of the vehicle by placing jackstands under the lower control arms, between the spring seat and the lower ball joint.

NOTE: *Allow the floor jack to remain under the lower control arm seat, to retain the spring and the lower control arm position.*

2. Remove the wheels.

3. From the upper ball joint, remove the cotter pin and the ball joint-to-upper control arm nut.

4. Using the GM Ball Joint Remover tool No. J-23742 or equivalent, separate the upper ball joint from the steering knuckle/hub assembly. Pull the steering knuckle free of the ball joint after removal.

NOTE: *After separating the steering knuckle from the upper ball joint, be sure to support steering knuckle/hub assembly to prevent damaging the brake hose.*

5. Remove the upper control arm-to-frame nuts and bolts, then lift and remove the upper control arm from the vehicle.

NOTE: *Tape the shims together and identify them so that they can be installed in the proper positions from which they were removed.*

6. Clean and inspect the steering knuckle hole. Replace the steering knuckle, if any out of roundness is noted.

7. To install, attach the upper control arm to the frame, insert the shims in their proper po-

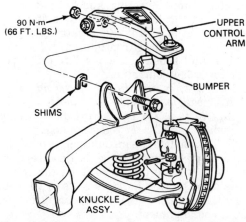

90 N·m
(66 FT. LBS.) — UPPER CONTROL ARM

BUMPER

SHIMS

KNUCKLE ASSY.

Removing the upper control arm—front suspension system

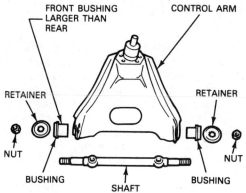

FRONT BUSHING LARGER THAN REAR

CONTROL ARM

RETAINER   RETAINER

NUT   NUT

BUSHING   BUSHING
SHAFT

Exploded view of the upper control arm—front suspension system

sitions, seat the upper ball joint into the steering knuckle and install the nut. Torque the upper control arm-to-frame bolts to 66 ft.lb., the upper ball joint-to-steering knuckle nut to 52 ft.lb. and the wheel nuts to 90 ft.lb.

8. Install a new cotter pin to the upper ball joint stud.

NOTE: *When installing the cotter pin to the upper ball joint-to-steering knuckle nut, be sure to turn the castle nut an addition amount to expose the cotter pin hole.*

9. Using a grease gun, lubricate the upper ball joint until grease oozes from the grease seal. Inspect and/or adjust the wheel bearing and the front end alignment.

10. Remove the lower control arm support and lower the vehicle.

Lower Control Arm
REMOVAL AND INSTALLATION

NOTE: *The following procedure requires the use of the GM Ball Joint Remover tool No. J-23742 or equivalent.*

1. Refer to the Coil Spring, Removal and Installation procedures in this section and remove the coil spring.

2. Remove the cotter pin (discard it) and the ball joint nut.

3. Using the GM Ball Joint Remover tool No. J-23742 or equivalent, disconnect the lower ball joint from the steering knuckle and the lower control arm from the vehicle.

NOTE: *Place a block of wood between the frame and the upper control arm; make sure that the brake hose is free of tension.*

4. To install, position the lower ball joint stud into the steering knuckle. Torque the ball joint-to-steering knuckle nut to 81 ft.lb.

5. To complete the installation, reverse the removal procedures. Lower the front of the vehicle, so that it is resting on its own weight, then torque the lower control arm-to-chassis nuts/bolts to 96 ft.lb. and the wheel nuts to 90 ft.lb.

6. Install a new cotter pin to the lower ball joint stud.

NOTE: *When installing the cotter pin to the lower ball joint-to-steering knuckle nut, be sure to turn the castle nut an addition amount to expose the cotter pin hole.*

7. Using a grease gun, lubricate the lower ball joint until grease oozes from the grease seal. Inspect and/or adjust the wheel bearing and the front end alignment.

8. Pull the shock absorber down, then install the shock absorber-to-lower control arm nuts/bolts. Torque the nuts and bolts to 18 ft.lb.

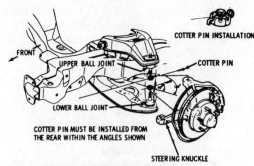

FRONT

COTTER PIN INSTALLATION

UPPER BALL JOINT

COTTER PIN

LOWER BALL JOINT

COTTER PIN MUST BE INSTALLED FROM
THE REAR WITHIN THE ANGLES SHOWN

STEERING KNUCKLE

Exploded view of the steering knuckle and the cotter
pin assembly—front suspension system

9. Remove the lower control arm support and lower the vehicle.

Knuckle and Spindle

REMOVAL AND INSTALLATION

NOTE: *The following procedure requires the use of the GM Tie Rod End Puller tool J-6627 or equivalent, and the GM Ball Joint Remover tool No. J-23742 or equivalent.*

1. Siphon some brake fluid from the brake master cylinder.

2. Raise and support the front of the vehicle on jackstands. Remove the wheels.

NOTE: *When supporting the vehicle on jackstands, DO NOT place the jackstands directly under the lower control arms for the vehicle may slip off the jackstands during the steering knuckle removal.*

3. Remove the brake caliper from the steering knuckle and support it on a wire.

4. Remove the grease cup, the cotter pin, the castle nut and the hub assembly.

5. Remove the splash shield-to-steering knuckle bolts and the shield.

6. At the tie rod end-to-steering knuckle stud, remove the cotter pin and the nut. Using

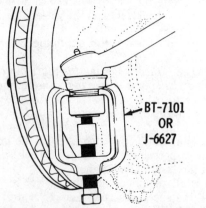

BT-7101
OR
J-6627

Disconnect the tie rod end from the steering knuckle—
front suspension system

the GM Tie Rod End Puller tool J-6627 or equivalent, separate the tie rod end from the steering knuckle.

7. From the upper and lower ball joint studs, remove the cotter pins and the nuts.

8. Using a floor jack, place it under the spring seat of the lower control arm and support the arm.

9. Using the GM Ball Joint Remover tool No. J-23742 or equivalent, separate the upper ball joint from the steering knuckle.

10. Raise the upper control arm to separate it from the steering knuckle.

11. Using the GM Ball Joint Remover tool No. J-23742 or equivalent, separate the lower ball joint from the steering knuckle, then lift the steering knuckle from the lower control arm.

12. Clean and inspect the steering knuckle and spindle for signs of wear or damage; if necessary, replace the steering knuckle.

13. To install the steering knuckle, position it onto the lower ball joint stud, then lift the upper control arm to insert the upper ball joint stud into the steering knuckle. Torque the upper ball joint-to-steering knuckle nut to 52 ft.lb. and the lower ball joint-to-steering knuckle nut to 81 ft.lb. Remove the floor jack from under the lower control arm.

14. Install a new cotter pin into the upper and lower ball joint studs.

NOTE: *When installing the cotter pin to the lower ball joint-to-steering knuckle nut, be sure to turn the castle nut an addition amount to expose the cotter pin hole.*

15. To complete the installation, reverse the removal procedures. Torque the tie rod end-to-steering knuckle nut to 30 ft.lb., the splash shield-to-steering knuckle bolts to 10 ft.lb. Check and/or adjust the wheel bearing and the front end alignment.

16. Remove the jackstands and lower the vehicle. Refill the brake master cylinder.

Front Wheel Bearings

REPLACEMENT

NOTE: *The following procedure requires the use of an Arbor Press and the GM Front Outer Race Remover tool No. J-29117 or equivalent, the GM Driver Handle tool No. J-8092 or equivalent, the GM Outer Bearing Outer Race Installer tool No. J-8457 or equivalent, the GM Inner Bearing Outer Race Installer tool No. J-8850 or equivalent, and the GM Bearing Remover tool No. J-9746-02 or equivalent.*

1. Raise and support the front of the vehicle on jackstands.

2. Remove the wheel and tire assembly.

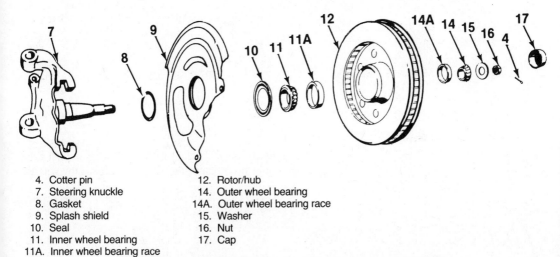

4. Cotter pin
7. Steering knuckle
8. Gasket
9. Splash shield
10. Seal
11. Inner wheel bearing
11A. Inner wheel bearing race
12. Rotor/hub
14. Outer wheel bearing
14A. Outer wheel bearing race
15. Washer
16. Nut
17. Cap

Exploded view of the disc/hub assembly—front suspension system

3. Remove the brake caliper from the steering knuckle and place a block of wood between the brake pads; using a wire, support the brake caliper (from the vehicle) without disconnecting the brake hose.

CAUTION: *Brake shoes contain asbestos, which has been determined to be a cancer causing agent. Never clean the brake surfaces with compressed air! Avoid inhaling any dust from any brake surface! When cleaning brake surfaces, use a commercially available brake cleaning fluid.*

4. Remove the dust cap, the cotter pin, the spindle nut, the thrust washer and the outer wheel bearing, then remove the disc/hub/bearing assembly.

NOTE: *When removing the disc/hub/bearing assembly, be careful not to drop the wheel bearing.*

5. Using a medium pry bar, pry the grease seal from the inner edge of the hub assembly, then remove the inner wheel bearing.

6. Using the GM Front Outer Race Remover tool No. J-29117 or equivalent, and an arbor press, remove the wheel bearing races from the hub assembly.

7. Using solvent, wash all of the parts and check for excessive wear or damage.

8. To replace the wheel bearing assemblies in the disc/hub assembly, perform the following procedures:

a. Position the disc/hub assembly (wheel studs facing downward) on the GM Bearing Remover tool No. J-9746-02 or equivalent.

b. Using the GM Driver Handle tool No. J-8092 or equivalent, and the GM Inner Bearing Outer Race Installer tool No. J-8850 or equivalent, press the inner wheel bearing

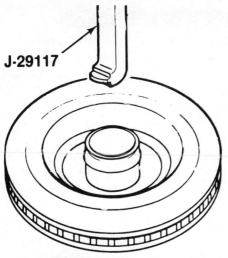

Removing the wheel bearing races from the disc/hub assembly—front suspension system

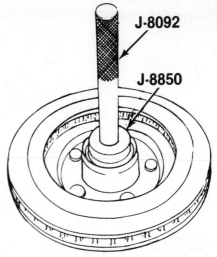

Installing the inner wheel bearing assembly into the disc/hub assembly—front suspension system

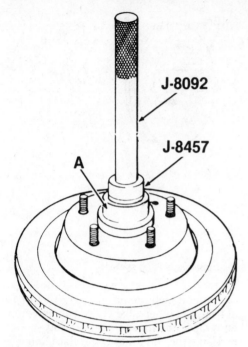

A. Outer wheel bearing race

Installing the outer wheel bearing assembly into the disc/hub assembly—front suspension system

assembly into the rear of the disc/hub assembly until the bearing seats against the shoulder.

c. Using a flat plate, drive a new grease seal into the rear of the disc/hub assembly, then lubricate the lip of the seal.

d. Turn and position the disc/hub assembly (wheel studs facing upward) on the GM Bearing Remover tool No. J-9746-02 or equivalent.

e. Using the GM Driver Handle tool No. J-8092 or equivalent, and the GM Outer Bearing Outer Race Installer tool No. J-8457 or equivalent, press the outer wheel bearing assembly into the front of the disc/hub assembly until the bearing seats against the shoulder.

9. Install the disc/hub assembly, the thrust washer and the nut onto the wheel spindle. While turning the wheel assembly in the forward direction, tighten the spindle nut to 12 ft.lb.

10. Loosen the spindle nut, then tighten it again until the slot in the nut aligns with the hole in the spindle, then install a new cotter pin.

NOTE: *When the disc/hub assembly is properly adjusted, the end play should be 0.001–0.005" (0.0254–0.127mm).*

11. After installing the cotter pin, bend the ends against the spindle nut and cut off any excess which will interfere with the dust cap.

12. To complete the installation, reverse the removal procedures. Lower the vehicle and road test.

PACKING

Clean the wheel bearings thoroughly with solvent and check their condition before installation.

NOTE: *If blow drying the wheel bearings with compressed air, DO NOT spin them, for damage may occur to the bearings.*

Apply a sizable daub of lubricant to the palm of one hand. Using your other hand, work the bearing into the lubricant so that the grease is pushed through the rollers and out the other side. Keep rotating the bearing while continuing to push the lubricant through it.

Front End Alignment
CASTER

Caster is the tilting of the front steering axis either forward or backward from the vertical.

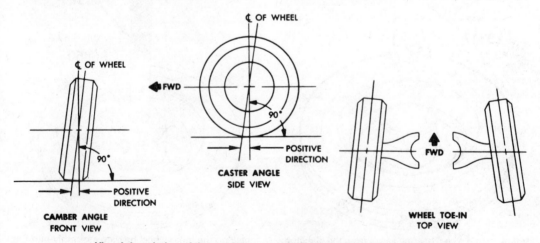

Visual description of the camber, caster and toe-in—front wheel alignment

Wheel Alignment Specifications

Years	Model	Caster (deg.)		Camber (deg.)		Toe-in (in.)	Steering Axis Inclination (deg.)
		Range	Pref.	Range	Pref.		
1985–87	Astro Van	1.7P–3.7P	2.7P	.14P–1.74P	.94P	.05P–.25P	—

A backward tilt is said to be positive (+) and a forward tilt is said to be negative (–).

CAMBER

Camber is the inward or outward tilting of the front wheels from the vertical. When the wheels tilt outward at the top, the camber is said to be positive (+). When the wheels tilt inward at the top, the camber is said to be negative (–). The amount of tilt is measured in degrees from the vertical and this measurement is called the camber angle.

TOE-IN

Toe-in is the turning in of the front wheels. The actual amount of toe-in is normally only a fraction of a degree. The purpose of toe-in is to ensure parallel rolling of the front wheels. Excessive toe-in or toe-out will cause tire wear.

REAR SUSPENSION

The rear suspension system consists of several major components: The double acting shock absorbers, variable rate single leaf fiberglass springs and various attachment parts. The single leaf fiberglass springs are connected to the frame by a hanger assembly with integral bushings in the front and a shackle assembly with integral bushings in the rear. The shackle assembly, in response to different road and

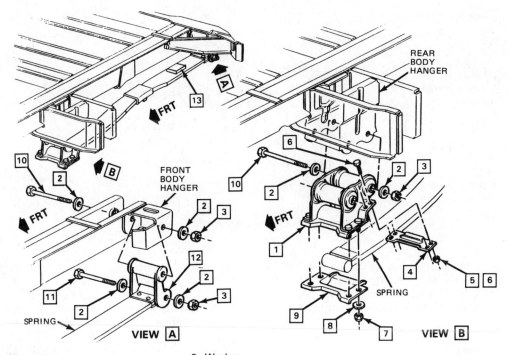

1. Hanger asm
2. Washer
3. Nut 100–120 N·m (74–88 ft. lbs.)
4. Cam asm
5. Nut 15–20 N·m (11–15 ft. lbs.)
6. Bolt 15–20 N·m (11–15 ft. lbs.)
7. Nut 20–30 N·m (15–22 ft. lbs.)
8. Washer
9. Retainer
10. Bolt
11. Bolt
12. Shackle asm
13. Mass damper

Exploded view of the fiberglass spring assembly—rear suspension system

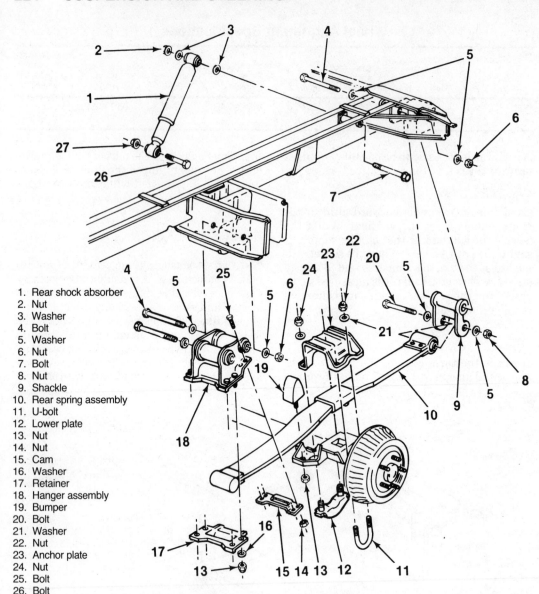

1. Rear shock absorber
2. Nut
3. Washer
4. Bolt
5. Washer
6. Nut
7. Bolt
8. Nut
9. Shackle
10. Rear spring assembly
11. U-bolt
12. Lower plate
13. Nut
14. Nut
15. Cam
16. Washer
17. Retainer
18. Hanger assembly
19. Bumper
20. Bolt
21. Washer
22. Nut
23. Anchor plate
24. Nut
25. Bolt
26. Bolt
27. Nut

Exploded view of the rear suspension system

payload conditions, allows the leaf spring to "change its length". The rear axle is connected to both the fiberglass leaf springs and the shock absorbers by various attaching parts.

Leaf Spring

REMOVAL AND INSTALLATION

NOTE: *The following procedure requires the use of two jackstands and two floor lifts.*

1. Raise and support the rear of the vehicle on jackstands.

NOTE: *When supporting the rear of the vehi-*

cle, support the axle and the body separately to relieve the load on the rear spring.

2. Remove the wheel and tire assembly.

3. At the rear of the fiberglass spring, loosen (DO NOT remove) the shackle-to-frame bolt and the shackle-to-spring.

4. Remove the shock absorber-to-axle bolt, then separate the shock absorber from the axle.

NOTE: *If removing the shock absorber from the right side, it is necessary to remove the parking brake bracket.*

5. Remove the axle U-bolt-to-anchor plate nuts, the lower plate-to-anchor plate nuts, the

U-bolts and the lower plate, then lower the axle.

NOTE: *When lowering the axle, be careful not to let the axle hang on the brake hose.*

6. At the front of the fiberglass spring, remove the retainer-to-hanger assembly nuts, the washers and the retainer(s).

7. At the rear of the fiberglass spring, remove the spring-to-shackle nut, washer and bolt. Remove the fiberglass spring from the vehicle.

8. To install, attach the spring to the shackle (DO NOT tighten the nuts/bolts), rotate the shackle forward to clear the rear bumper bracket, position the spring into the slot on the hanger and attach the retainer-to-hanger fasteners.

9. Using the axle supports, raise and position the axle housing under the fiberglass spring. Using the U-bolts and the lower plates, connect the axle housing to the spring.

NOTE: *When installing the axle housing, be sure that the full weight of the axle is resting on the supports; the fiberglass spring MUST NOT support any of the axle weight.*

10. Torque the axle U-bolt-to-spring nuts to 48 ft.lb. and the axle lower plate-to-spring nuts to 40 ft.lb.

11. To adjust the rear suspension trim height, perform the following:

　a. Raise the axle/spring assembly until the clearance between the top of the axle and the bottom of the frame is 5.3″ (135mm).

NOTE: *If the axle supports are not in complete contact with the axle housing and resting firmly on the floor, damage to the spring and axle could result.*

　b. Torque the shackle-to-spring nuts/bolts

to 81 ft.lb. and the retainer-to-hanger assembly nuts to 26 ft.lb.

12. Connect the shock absorber to the axle housing, then torque the nut/bolt to 75 ft.lb.

NOTE: *When installing the shock absorber on the right side, be sure to position the parking brake bracket on the bolt before the nut is installed.*

13. Install the wheel assemblies and lower the vehicle.

Shock Absorbers
REMOVAL AND INSTALLATION

NOTE: *The following procedure requires the use of a lifting device and two jackstands.*

1. Raise and support the rear of the vehicle on jackstands (positioned under the frame), then support the axle housing independently.

2. Remove the shock absorber-to-frame bolts.

3. Remove the shock absorber-to-axle housing bolts and shock absorber from the vehicle.

NOTE: *When removing the shock absorber-to-axle housing bolt, the parking brake bracket must be removed after the nut.*

4. Inspect and test the shock absorber, then replace them (if necessary).

5. To install, connect the shock absorber-to-frame nut/bolt (DO NOT tighten) and the shock absorber-to-axle nut/bolt.

NOTE: *If installing the shock absorber onto the right side, be sure to install the parking brake bracket.*

6. Torque the shock absorber-to-frame nut to 75 ft.lb., the shock absorber-to-frame bolt to 83 ft.lb. and the shock absorber-to-axle housing nut to 75 ft.lb. Lower the vehicle.

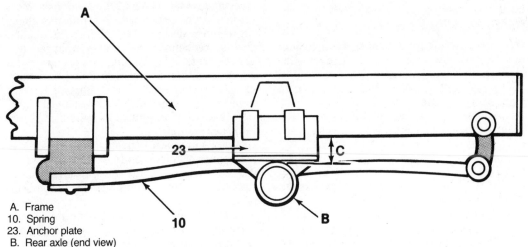

A. Frame
10. Spring
23. Anchor plate
B. Rear axle (end view)
C. Distance is approximately 135 mm (5.3-inches)

Adjusting the trim height—rear suspension system

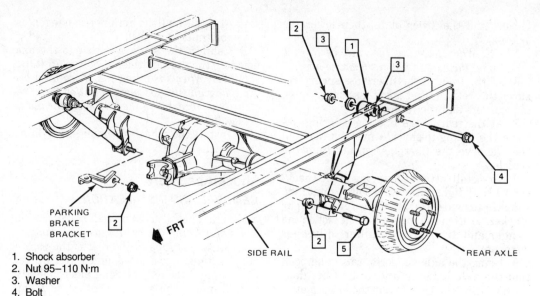

1. Shock absorber
2. Nut 95–110 N·m
3. Washer
4. Bolt
5. Bolt

Exploded view of the shock absorber assemblies—rear suspension system

TESTING

Visually inspect the shock absorber. If there is evidence of leakage and the shock absorber is covered with oil, the shock is defective and should be replaced.

If there is no sign of excessive leakage (a small amount of weeping is normal) bounce the van at one corner by pressing down on the bumper and releasing it. When you have the van bouncing as much as you can, release the bumper. The van should stop bouncing after the first rebound. If the bouncing continues past the center point of the bounce more than once, the shock absorbers are worn and should be replaced.

Rear End Alignment

If the tire wear indicates that the rear springs may be mislocated or the axle housing may be bent, check the alignment as follows:

1. Position the rear of the vehicle on an alignment machine.

2. Compensate for the wheel runout; perform the same procedure as for checking the front wheel toe-in. The toe-out should be 0–$\frac{1}{16}$" (0–1.5mm).

NOTE: *If the vehicle is backed onto an alignment machine, the toe-out will be read as the toe-in.*

3. Check the camber reading, it should be 3°N–5°P.

4. If alignment operations are necessary, they may be performed by using frame straightening equipment or relocating the spring onto the axle housing without removing the axle housing from the vehicle.

STEERING

The steering box (manual or power) consists of a recirculating balls, which transmits force from the worm gear to the sector gear. A relay type steering linkage is used with a pitman arm connected to one end of the relay rod. The relay rod is supported by two idler arms; the idler arms pivot on a support which is attached to the frame. The relay rod is connected to the steering arms by two adjustable tie rods. Most models are equipped with a collapsible steering column designed to collapse on impact, thereby reducing possible chest injuries during accidents. When making any repairs to the steering column or steering wheel, excessive pressure or force capable of collapsing the column must be avoided. The ignition lock, ignition switch and an antitheft system are built into each column.

On the automatic transmission, the ignition key cannot be removed unless the shift lever is in the Park position and the ignition switch in the Lock position. Placing the lock in the Lock position activates a rod within the column which locks the steering wheel and shift lever.

On the floor shift models, a back drive linkage between the floorshift and the column produces the same effect.

Steering Wheel

REMOVAL AND INSTALLATION

NOTE: *The following procedure requires the use of the GM Steering Wheel Puller tool No. J-1859-03 or equivalent.*

1. Disconnect the negative battery terminal from the battery.

2. Position the steering wheel so that it is in the horizontal position.

3. If equipped with a horn cap, pry the cap from the center of the steering wheel. If equipped with a steering wheel shroud, remove the screw from the rear of the steering wheel and remove the shroud.

NOTE: *If the horn cap or shroud is equipped with an electrical connector, disconnect it.*

4. Remove the steering wheel-to-steering shaft retainer (snapring) and nut.

NOTE: *Since the steering column is designed to collapse upon impact, it is recommended NEVER to hammer on it.*

5. Matchmark the relationship of the steering wheel to the steering shaft.

6. Using the GM Steering Wheel Puller tool No. J-1859-03 or equivalent, press the steering wheel from the steering column.

NOTE: *Before installing the steering wheel, be sure that the combination control switch is in the Neutral position. DO NOT misalign the steering wheel more than 1" (25.4mm) from the horizontal centerline.*

7. To install the steering wheel, align the matchmarks and push it onto the steering shaft splines, torque the steering wheel-to-steering shaft nut to 30 ft.lb. and reverse the removal procedures.

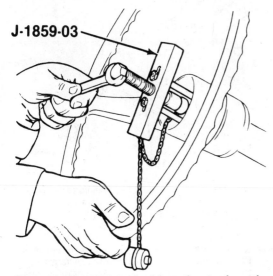

J-1859-03

Removing the steering wheel from the steering column

Combination Switch

The combination switch is a combination of the turn signal, the windshield wiper/washer, the dimmer and the cruise control switches.

REMOVAL AND INSTALLATION

NOTE: *The following procedure requires the use of the GM Lock Plate Compressor tool No. J-23653 or equivalent.*

1. Refer to the Steering Wheel, Removal and Installation procedures in this section and remove the steering wheel.

2. If necessary, remove the steering column-to-lower instrument panel cover. Disconnect the electrical harness connector from the steering column jacket (under the dash).

3. Using a screwdriver, insert into the slots between the steering shaft lock plate cover and the steering column housing, then pry upward to remove the cover from the lock plate.

4. Using the GM Lock Plate Compressor tool No. J-23653-A or equivalent, screw the center shaft onto the steering shaft (as far as it will go), then screw the center post nut clockwise until the lock plate is compressed.

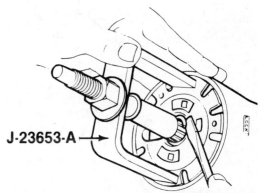

J-23653-A

Compressing the locking plate on the steering column

5. Using a small pry bar, pry the snapring from the steering shaft slot.

NOTE: *If the steering column is being disassembled on a bench, the steering shaft will slide out of the mast jacket when the snapring is removed.*

6. Remove the GM Lock Plate Compressor tool No. J-23653 or equivalent, and the lock plate.

7. Remove the multi-function lever-to-switch screw and the lever.

8. To remove the hazard warning switch, press the knob inward and unscrew it.

9. Remove the combination switch assembly-to-steering column screws.

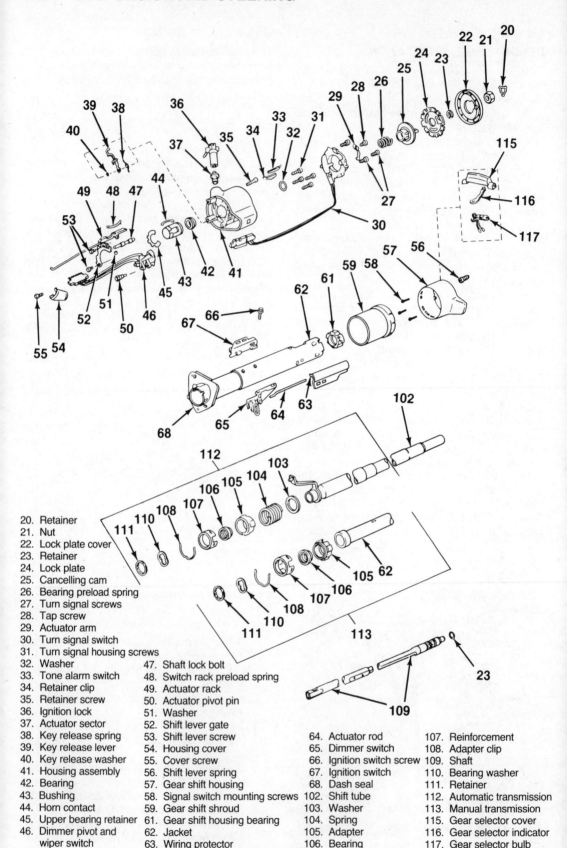

20. Retainer
21. Nut
22. Lock plate cover
23. Retainer
24. Lock plate
25. Cancelling cam
26. Bearing preload spring
27. Turn signal screws
28. Tap screw
29. Actuator arm
30. Turn signal switch
31. Turn signal housing screws
32. Washer
33. Tone alarm switch
34. Retainer clip
35. Retainer screw
36. Ignition lock
37. Actuator sector
38. Key release spring
39. Key release lever
40. Key release washer
41. Housing assembly
42. Bearing
43. Bushing
44. Horn contact
45. Upper bearing retainer
46. Dimmer pivot and
    wiper switch

47. Shaft lock bolt
48. Switch rack preload spring
49. Actuator rack
50. Actuator pivot pin
51. Washer
52. Shift lever gate
53. Shift lever screw
54. Housing cover
55. Cover screw
56. Shift lever spring
57. Gear shift housing
58. Signal switch mounting screws
59. Gear shift shroud
61. Gear shift housing bearing
62. Jacket
63. Wiring protector

64. Actuator rod
65. Dimmer switch
66. Ignition switch screw
67. Ignition switch
68. Dash seal
102. Shift tube
103. Washer
104. Spring
105. Adapter
106. Bearing

107. Reinforcement
108. Adapter clip
109. Shaft
110. Bearing washer
111. Retainer
112. Automatic transmission
113. Manual transmission
115. Gear selector cover
116. Gear selector indicator
117. Gear selector bulb

Exploded view of the standard steering column

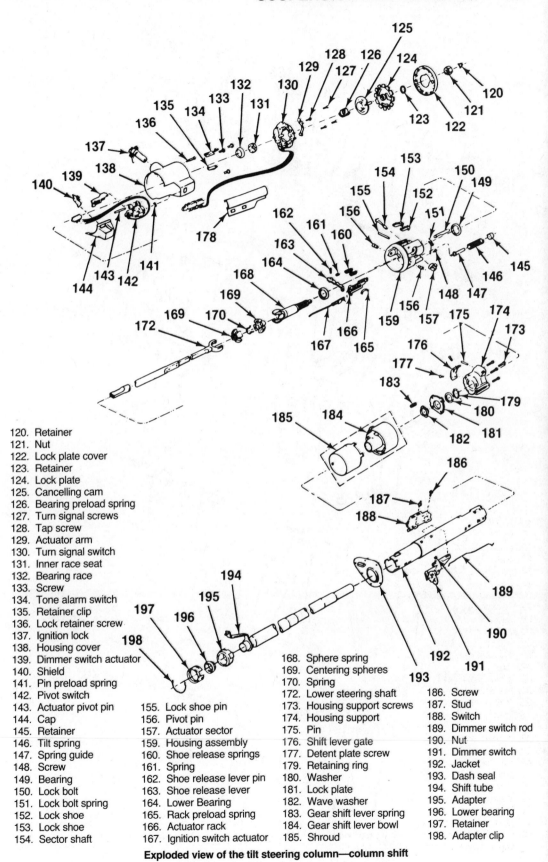

120. Retainer
121. Nut
122. Lock plate cover
123. Retainer
124. Lock plate
125. Cancelling cam
126. Bearing preload spring
127. Turn signal screws
128. Tap screw
129. Actuator arm
130. Turn signal switch
131. Inner race seat
132. Bearing race
133. Screw
134. Tone alarm switch
135. Retainer clip
136. Lock retainer screw
137. Ignition lock
138. Housing cover
139. Dimmer switch actuator
140. Shield
141. Pin preload spring
142. Pivot switch
143. Actuator pivot pin
144. Cap
145. Retainer
146. Tilt spring
147. Spring guide
148. Screw
149. Bearing
150. Lock bolt
151. Lock bolt spring
152. Lock shoe
153. Lock shoe
154. Sector shaft

155. Lock shoe pin
156. Pivot pin
157. Actuator sector
159. Housing assembly
160. Shoe release springs
161. Spring
162. Shoe release lever pin
163. Shoe release lever
164. Lower Bearing
165. Rack preload spring
166. Actuator rack
167. Ignition switch actuator

168. Sphere spring
169. Centering spheres
170. Spring
172. Lower steering shaft
173. Housing support screws
174. Housing support
175. Pin
176. Shift lever gate
177. Detent plate screw
179. Retaining ring
180. Washer
181. Lock plate
182. Wave washer
183. Gear shift lever spring
184. Gear shift lever bowl
185. Shroud

186. Screw
187. Stud
188. Switch
189. Dimmer switch rod
190. Nut
191. Dimmer switch
192. Jacket
193. Dash seal
194. Shift tube
195. Adapter
196. Lower bearing
197. Retainer
198. Adapter clip

Exploded view of the tilt steering column—column shift

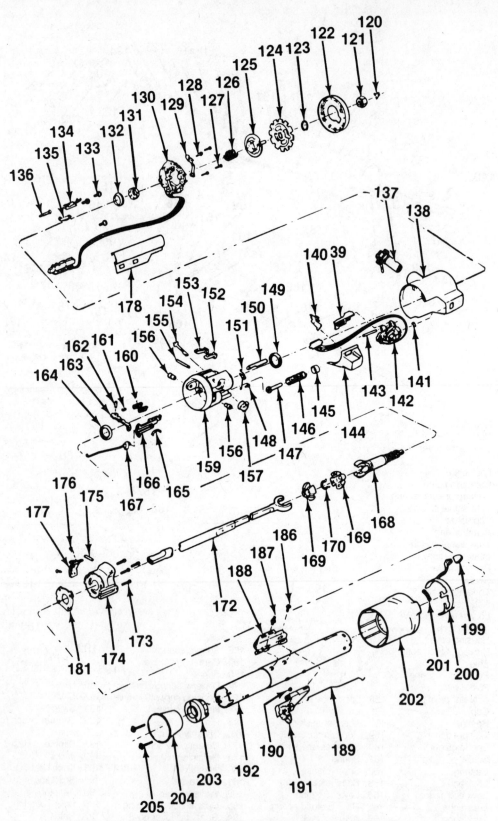

Exploded view of the tilt steering column—floor shift

120. Retainer	144. Cap	168. Sphere spring
121. Nut	145. Retainer	169. Centering spheres
122. Lock plate cover	146. Tilt spring	170. Spring
123. Retainer	147. Spring guide	172. Lower steering shaft
124. Lock plate	148. Screw	173. Housing support screws
125. Cancelling cam	149. Bearing	174. Housing support
126. Bearing preload spring	150. Lock bolt	175. Pin
127. Turn signal screws	151. Lock bolt spring	176. Shift lever gate
128. Tap screw	152. Lock shoe	177. Detent plate screw
129. Actuator arm	153. Lock shoe	181. Lock plate
130. Turn signal switch	154. Sector shaft	182. Screw
131. Inner race seat	155. Lock shoe pin	187. Stud
132. Bearing race	156. Pivot pin	188. Switch
133. Screw	157. Actuator sector	189. Dimmer switch rod
134. Tone alarm switch	159. Housing assembly	190. Nut
135. Retainer clip	160. Shoe release springs	191. Dimmer switch
136. Lock retainer screw	161. Spring	199. Pad
137. Ignition lock	162. Shoe release lever pin	200. Key release lever
138. Housing cover	163. Shoe release lever	201. Key release spring
139. Dimmer switch actuator	164. Lower bearing	202. Shroud
140. Shield	165. Rack preload spring	203. Lower bearing
141. Pin preload spring	166. Actuator rack	204. Retainer
142. Pivot switch	167. Ignition switch actuator	205. Screws
143. Actuator pivot pin		

Exploded view of the tilt steering column—floorshift

10. Lift the combination switch assembly from the steering column, then slide the electrical connector through the column housing and the protector.

NOTE: *If the steering column is the tilting type, position the steering housing into the Low position.*

11. To remove the harness cover, pull it toward the lower end of the column; be careful not to damage the wires.

12. To remove the wire protector, grab the protector's tab with a pair of pliers, then pull the protector downward, out of the steering column.

NOTE: *When assembling the steering column, use only fasteners of the correct length; overlength fasteners could prevent a portion of the assembly from compressing under impact.*

13. To install the combination switch electrical connector, perform the following procedures:

a. On the non-tilt columns, be sure that the electrical connector is on the protector,

Removing the turn signal wire protector from the steering column

then feed it and the cover down through the housing and under the mounting bracket.

b. On the tilt columns, feed the electrical connector down through the housing and under the mounting bracket, then install the cover onto the housing.

14. Install the clip the electrical connector to the clip on the jacket, the combination switch-to-steering column mounting screws, the lower instrument trim panel, the turn signal lever/screws and the hazard warning knob.

NOTE: *With the multi-function lever installed, place it into the Neutral position. With the hazard warning knob installed, pull it Outward.*

15. Onto the upper end of the steering shaft, install the washer, the upper bearing preload spring, the cancelling cam, the lock plate and a new retaining ring (snapring). Using the GM Lock Plate Compressor tool No. J-23653 or equivalent, compress the lock plate and slide the new retaining ring into the steering shaft groove.

16. To complete the installation, reverse the removal procedures. Torque the multi-function switch-to-steering column screws to 35 in.lb. and the steering wheel nut to 30 ft.lb.

Ignition Switch

The ignition switch, for anti-theft reasons, is located inside the channel section of the brake pedal support and is completely inaccessible without first lowering the steering column. The switch is actuated by a rod and rack assembly. A gear on the end of the lock cylinder engages the toothed upper end of the actuator rod.

REMOVAL AND INSTALLATION

1. Remove the lower instrument panel-to-steering column cover. Remove the steering column-to-dash bolts and lower the steering column; be sure to properly support it.

2. Place the ignition switch in the Locked position.

NOTE: *If the lock cylinder was removed, the actuating rod should be pulled up until it stops, then moved down one detent; the switch is now in the Lock position.*

3. Remove the two ignition switch-to-steering column screws and the switch assembly.

4. Before installing the ignition switch, place it in the Locked position, then make sure that the lock cylinder and actuating rod are in the Locked position (1st detent from the top).

5. Install the activating rod into the ignition switch and assemble the switch onto the steering column. Torque the ignition switch-to-steering column screws to 35 in.lb..

NOTE: *When installing the ignition switch, use only the specified screws since overlength screws could impair the collapsibility of the column.*

6. To complete the installation, install the

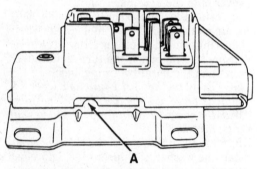

A. Switch in the lock position

Positioning the ignition switch prior to installation—1st detent from the top

steering column and the lower instrument panel cover. Torque the steering column-to-instrument bolts to 22 ft.lb.

Ignition Lock Cylinder
REMOVAL AND INSTALLATION

1. Refer to the Combination Switch, Removal and Installation procedures in this section and remove the combination switch.

2. Place the lock cylinder in the **Run** position.

3. Remove the buzzer switch, the lock cylinder screw and the lock cylinder.

CAUTION: *If the screw is dropped upon removal, it could fall into the steering column, requiring complete disassembly to retrieve the screw.*

4. To install, rotate the lock cylinder clockwise to align the cylinder key with the keyway in the housing.

5. Push the lock cylinder all the way in.

6. Install the cylinder lock-to-housing screw. Tighten the screw to 14 in.lb.

Steering Column
REMOVAL AND INSTALLATION

1. Refer to the Steering Wheel, Removal and Installation procedures in this section and remove the steering wheel.

2. Disconnect the negative battery terminal from the battery.

3. If equipped with a column shift, disconnect the transmission control linkage from the column shift tube levers.

4. From inside the engine compartment, remove the intermediate shaft-to-steering column shaft pinch bolt.

NOTE: *Before separating the intermediate shaft from the steering column shaft, mark the relationship of the two shafts.*

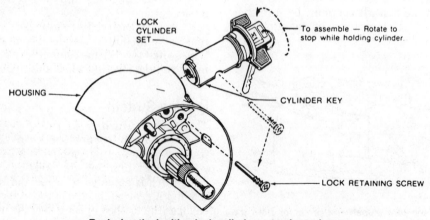

LOCK CYLINDER SET

HOUSING

To assemble — Rotate to stop while holding cylinder.

CYLINDER KEY

LOCK RETAINING SCREW

Replacing the ignition lock cylinder—steering column

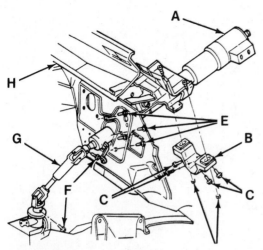

A. Steering column assembly
B. Bracket
C. 40 N·m (30 ft. lbs.)
D. Capsule nuts 34 N·m (25 ft. lbs.)
E. 9 N·m (7 ft. lbs.)
F. Pinch bolt 40 N·m (30 ft. lbs.)
G. Intermediate shaft assembly
H. Panel
Replacing the steering column

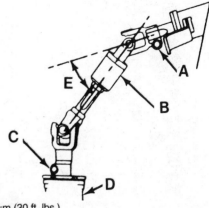

A. 40 N·m (30 ft. lbs.)
B. Intermediate shaft
C. 40 N·m (30 ft. lbs.)
D. Steering gear
E. 36–58° angle must not exceed 39 degrees maximum or 34 degrees minimum

View of the intermediate shaft with the Carden joint

5. Remove the lower instrument panel-to-steering column cover, the steering column bracket-to-dash nuts/bolts (support the steering column) and the steering column-to-firewall cover (if necessary).

6. From under the dash, disconnect the electrical harness connectors from the steering column.

NOTE: *Some models are equipped with a back-up light switch and a neutral/start switch, be sure to disconnect the electrical connectors from them.*

7. Remove the steering column from the vehicle.

NOTE: *If equipped with a column shifter, rotate the steering column so that the shift lever clears the dash opening.*

8. To install, align the matchmarks of the steering column shaft and the intermediate shaft, tighten the fasteners finger tight and reverse the removal procedures.

NOTE: *Make sure that the Carden joint (intermediate shaft) operating angle is between 34°–39°.*

9. Torque the intermediate shaft-to-steering column shaft pinch bolt to 30 ft.lb., the steering column bracket-to-dash nuts to 25 ft.lb. and the steering column-to-firewall screws to 7 ft.lb.

10. Reconnect the electrical harness-to-steering column connectors. Reinstall the steering wheel and the negative battery terminal.

NOTE: *If equipped with steering column shifter, reconnect the transmission-to-steering column linkage.*

Steering Linkage

The steering linkage consists of: a forward mounted linkage (parallelogram type), crimp nuts at the inner pivots, castellated nuts at the steering knuckle arm, a second idler arm and steering gear pitman arm-to-relay rod connecting rod to maintain proper geometry, and a steering damper (manual steering). Grease fittings are equipped with each joint, for durability.

REMOVAL AND INSTALLATION

Pitman Arm

NOTE: *The following procedure requires the use of the GM Steering Linkage Puller tool No. J-24319-01 or equivalent, the GM Pitman Arm Remover tool No. J-6632 or equivalent, and the GM Steering Linkage Installer tool No. J-29193 (12mm) or J-29194 (14mm) or equivalent.*

1. Raise and support the front of the vehicle on jackstands.

2. Disconnect the nut from the pitman arm ball joint stud.

3. Using the GM Steering Linkage Puller tool No. J-24319-01 or equivalent, separate the connecting rod from the pitman arm. Pull down on the connecting rod and separate it from the stud.

4. Remove the pitman arm-to-pitman shaft nut, mark the relationship the arm to the

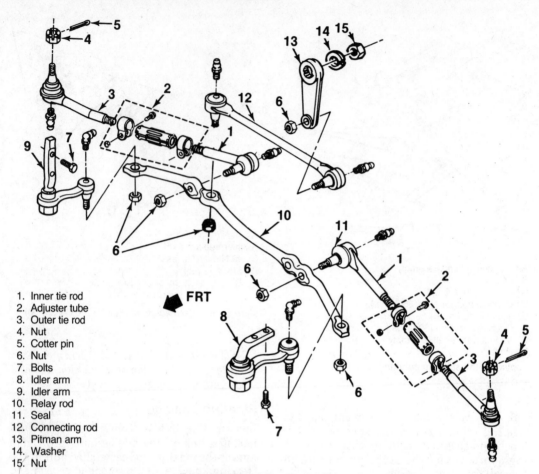

1. Inner tie rod
2. Adjuster tube
3. Outer tie rod
4. Nut
5. Cotter pin
6. Nut
7. Bolts
8. Idler arm
9. Idler arm
10. Relay rod
11. Seal
12. Connecting rod
13. Pitman arm
14. Washer
15. Nut

Exploded view of the steering linkage

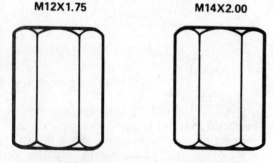

M12X1.75   **M14X2.00**

J-29193   **J-29194**

View of the special tools used to seat the pitman arm-to-pitman shaft tapers

shaft. Using the GM Pitman Arm Remover tool No. J-6632 or equivalent, separate the pitman arm from the pitman shaft.

NOTE: *When separating the pitman arm from the shaft, DO NOT use a hammer or apply heat to the arm.*

5. To install, align the pitman arm-to-pitman shaft matchmark and the pitman shaft nut; torque the pitman arm-to-pitman shaft nut to 177–185 ft.lb.

6. Connect the pitman arm to the connecting rod ball stud (make sure that the seal is on the stud. Using the GM Steering Linkage Installer tool No. J-29193 (12mm) or J-29194 (14mm) or equivalent, install the correct one onto the ball stud and torque it to 40 ft.lb. (to seat the tapers); after seating, remove the tool.

7. Install the pitman arm-to-connecting rod ball joint nut, then torque the ball joint nut to 66 ft.lb.

Idler Arm

NOTE: *The following procedure requires the use of the GM Steering Linkage Puller tool No. J-24319-01 or equivalent, the GM Pitman Arm Remover tool No. J-6632 or equivalent, the GM Steering Linkage Installer tool No. J-29193 (12mm) or J-29194 (14mm) or equivalent, and a spring scale.*

1. Raise and support the front of the vehicle on jackstands.

NOTE: *Jerking the right wheel assembly*

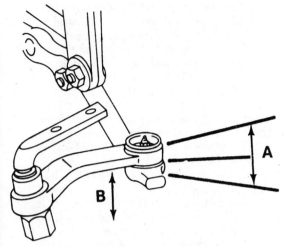

A. 6.35 mm (¼ inch)
B. Apply spring scale

Inspecting the idler arm movement

back and forth is not an acceptable testing procedure; there is not control on the amount of force being applied to the idler arm. Before suspecting idler arm shimmying complaints, check the wheels for imbalance, runout, force variation and/or road surface irregularities.

2. To inspect for a defective idler arm, perform the following procedures:

    a. Position the wheels in the straight ahead position.

    b. Using a spring scale, position it near the relay rod end of the idler arm, then exert 25 lbs. of force upward and then downward.

    c. Measure the distance between the upward and downward directions that the idler arm moves. The allowable deflection is ⅛″ (3mm) for each direction; a total difference of ¼″ (6mm); if the idler arm deflection is beyond the allowable limits, replace it.

3. Remove the idler arm-to-frame bolts and the idler arm-to-relay rod ball joint nut.

4. Using the GM Steering Linkage Puller tool No. J-24319-01 or equivalent, separate the relay rod from the ball joint stud.

5. Inspect and/or replace (if necessary) the idler arm.

6. Install the idler arm-to-frame bolts and torque them to 37 ft.lb.

7. Connect the relay rod to the idler arm ball joint stud. Using the GM Steering Linkage Installer tool No. J-29193 (12mm) or J-29194 (14mm) or equivalent, seat (torque) the relay rod-to-idler arm ball joint stud to 40 ft.lb., then remove the tool.

8. Install the idler arm-to-relay rod stud nut and torque it to 66 ft.lb.

9. Lower the vehicle. Check and/or adjust the toe-in.

Relay Rod

NOTE: *The following procedure requires the use of the GM Steering Linkage Puller tool No. J-24319-01 or equivalent, and the GM Steering Linkage Installer tool No. J-29193 (12mm) or J-29194 (14mm) or equivalent.*

1. Refer to the Tie Rod, Removal and Installation procedures in this section and disconnect the inner tie rod ends from the relay rod.

2. Remove the connecting rod stud-to-relay rod nut and the idler arm stud-to-relay rod nuts.

3. Using the GM Steering Linkage Puller tool No. J-24319-01 or equivalent, disconnect the connecting rod from the relay rod.

4. Using the GM Steering Linkage Puller tool No. J-24319-01 or equivalent, disconnect the relay rod from the idler arms, then remove the relay rod from the vehicle.

5. Clean and inspect the threads on the tie rod, the tie rod ends and the ball joints for damage, then replace them (if necessary). Inspect the ball joint seals for excessive wear, then replace them (if necessary).

6. To install, position the relay rod onto the idler arms (no mounting nuts). Using the GM Steering Linkage Installer tool No. J-29193 (12mm) or J-29194 (14mm) or equivalent, install them onto the idler arm studs and torque the idler arm-to-relay rod stud nuts to 40 ft.lb. (to seat the tapers). Remove the installer tool, then install the mounting nuts and torque the idler arm-to-relay arm stud nuts to 66 ft.lb.

7. Position the connecting rod onto the relay rod (no mounting nut). Using the GM Steering Linkage Installer tool No. J-29193 (12mm) or J-29194 (14mm) or equivalent, install one onto the connecting rod stud and torque the connecting rod-to-relay rod stud to 40 ft.lb. (to seat the taper). Remove the installer tool, then install the mounting nuts and torque the connecting rod-to-relay rod stud nuts to 66 ft.lb.

8. Position the inner tie rod ball joints onto the relay rod (no mounting nuts). Using the GM Steering Linkage Installer tool No. J-29193 (12mm) or J-29194 (14mm) or equivalent, install them onto the tie rod studs and torque the tie rod-to-relay rod stud nuts to 40 ft.lb. (to seat the tapers). Remove the installer tool, then install the mounting nuts and torque the tie rod-to-relay rod stud nuts to 66 ft.lb.

9. Lower the vehicle and check the steering linkage performance.

Connecting Rod

NOTE: *The following procedure requires the use of the GM Steering Linkage Puller tool No. J-24319-01 or equivalent, and the GM Steering Linkage Installer tool No. J-29193 (12mm) or J-29194 (14mm) or equivalent.*

1. Raise and support the front of the vehicle on jackstands.

2. Remove the connecting rod stud-to-relay rod nut and the connecting rod stud-to-pitman arm nut.

3. Using the GM Steering Linkage Puller tool No. J-24319-01 or equivalent, separate the connecting rod from the relay rod and the pitman arm, then remove the connecting rod from the vehicle.

4. Clean and inspect the ball joint threads for damage, then replace the rod (if necessary). Inspect the ball joint seals for excessive wear, then replace them (if necessary).

5. To install, position the connecting rod onto the relay rod and the pitman arm (no mounting nuts). Using the GM Steering Linkage Installer tool No. J-29193 (12mm) or J-29194 (14mm) or equivalent, install them onto the connecting rod studs and torque the connecting rod stud nuts to 40 ft.lb. (to seat the tapers). Remove the installer tools, then install the mounting nuts and torque them to 66 ft.lb.

6. Lower the vehicle and check the steering linkage performance.

Tie Rod

NOTE: *The following procedure requires the use of the Steering Linkage Installer tool No. J-29193 (12mm) or J-29194 (14mm) or equivalent, and the GM Wheel Stud and Tie Rod Remover tool No. J-6627-A or equivalent.*

1. Raise and support the front of the vehicle on jackstands.

2. Remove the cotter pin from the tie rod-to-steering knuckle stud.

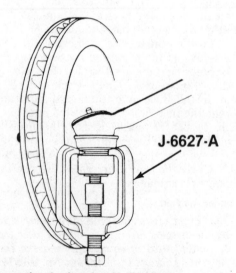

Separating the tie rod end ball joint stud

3. Remove the tie rod-to-relay rod stud nut and the tie rod-to-steering knuckle stud nut.

NOTE: *DO NOT attempt to separate the tie rod-to-steering knuckle joint using a wedge type tool for seal damage could result.*

4. Using the GM Wheel Stud Remover tool No. J-6627-A or equivalent, separate the outer tie rod stud from the steering knuckle and the inner tie rod stud from the relay rod. Remove the tie rod from the vehicle.

5. If removing ONLY the tie rod end, perform the following procedures:

a. Disconnect the defective ball joint end of the tie rod.

b. Loosen the adjuster tube clamp bolt.

c. Unscrew the tie rod end from the adjuster tube; count the number of turns necessary to remove the tie rod end.

d. Clean, inspect and lubricate the adjuster tube threads.

e. To install a new tie rod end, screw it into the adjuster tube using the same number of turns necessary to remove it.

f. Position the clamp bolts between the adjuster tube dimples (located at each end) and in the proper location (see illustration). Torque the adjuster tube clamp bolt 13 ft.lb.

6. To install, position the tie rod onto the steering knuckle and the relay rod. Using the Steering Linkage Installer tool No. J-29193 (12mm) or J-29194 (14mm) or equivalent, install them onto the studs and torque them to 40 ft.lb. (to seat the tapers). After seating the tapers, remove the tools, install the mounting nuts and torque mounting nuts to 66 ft.lb.

7. At the tie rod-to-steering knuckle stud, tighten the nut until the castle nut slot aligns with the hole in the stud, then install a new cotter pin.

8. Lower the vehicle and check the steering linkage performance.

Damper Assembly

The damper assembly is used to the remove steering wheel vibration and vehicle wonder; not all vehicles are equipped with it.

1. Raise and support the front of the vehicle on jackstands.

2. Remove the damper assembly-to-connecting rod cotter pin and nut.

3. Remove the damper assembly-to-bracket nut/bolt and remove the damper assembly from the vehicle.

4. If necessary, use a new damper assembly and reverse the removal procedures. Torque the damper assembly-to-bracket nut/bolt to 22 ft.lb. and the damper assembly-to-connecting rod nut to 41 ft.lb. Align the castle nut slot with the hole in the ball joint stud and install a new cotter pin.

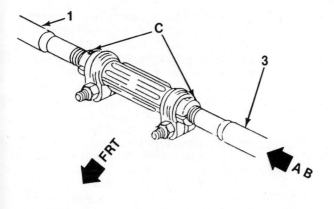

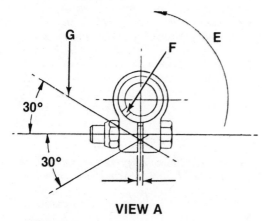

VIEW A

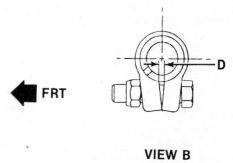

VIEW B

1. Inner tie rod
3. Outer tie rod
C. Clamp must be between and clear of dimples before
   torquing nut
D. Clamp ends must touch when nuts are torqued to
   specifications. But gap must be visible adjacent to
   adjuster tube
E. Rearward rotation
F. Adjuster tube slot
G. Center line of bolt

Proper orientation of the tie rod clamps and adjuster

Manual Steering Gear

The recirculating ball type manual steering gear is manufactured by Saginaw and is equipped with a mechanical ratio of 24:1.

ADJUSTMENTS

NOTE: *The following procedure requires the use the GM Steering Linkage Puller tool No. J-6632 or equivalent, and a 0–50 in.lb. torque wrench.*

1. Disconnect the negative battery terminal from the battery.

2. Raise and support the front of the vehicle on jackstands.

NOTE: *Before adjustments are made to the*

steering gear, be sure to check the front end alignment, the shock absorbers, the wheel balance and the tire pressure.

3. Remove the pitman arm-to-pitman shaft nut and matchmark the pitman arm to the pitman shaft. Using the GM Steering Linkage Puller tool No. J-6632 or equivalent, remove the pitman arm from the pitman shaft.

4. Loosen the steering gear adjuster plug locknut and back-off the adjuster plug ¼ turn.

5. From the steering wheel, remove the horn cap or cover.

6. Gently, turn the steering wheel (in one direction) to the stop; then, turn it back ½ turn.

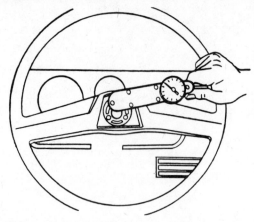

Using a dial torque wrench to measure the bearing drag

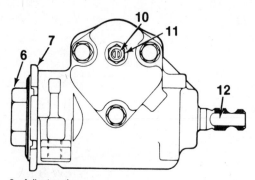

6. Adjuster plug
7. Nut
10. Adjuster screw
11. Jam nut
12. Wormshaft flat

View of the steering gear adjustment points

NOTE: *When the steering linkage is disconnected from the steering gear, DO NOT turn the steering wheel hard against the stops for damage to the ball guides may result.*

7. Using a torque wrench (0–50 in.lb.), position it onto the steering wheel nut, then measure and record the bearing drag. To measure the bearing drag, use the torque wrench to rotate the steering wheel 90°.

8. Using a torque wrench (0–50 in.lb.), tighten the adjuster plug (on the steering gear) to obtain a thrust bearing preload of 5–8 in.lb. After the thrust bearing preload is obtained, torque the adjuster plug locknut to 25 ft.lb.

NOTE: *If the steering gear feels lumpy (after adjustment), suspect damage to the bearings, probably due to the improper adjustment or severe impact.*

9. To adjust the overcenter preload, perform the following procedures:

a. Turn the steering wheel, from one stop all the way to the other stop, counting the number of turns. Turn the steering wheel back exactly ½ way, to the center position.

b. Turn the overcenter adjusting screw clockwise, until the lash is removed between the ball nut and the pitman shaft sector teeth, then tighten the locknut.

c. Using a torque wrench (0–50 in.lb.), check the highest force necessary to turn the steering wheel through the center position; the usable torque is 4–10 in.lb.

d. If necessary, loosen the locknut and readjust the overcenter adjusting screw to obtain the proper torque. Retorque the locknut to 25 ft.lb. and recheck the steering wheel torque through the center of travel.

NOTE: *If the maximum is too high, turn the overcenter adjuster screw counterclockwise, then torque the adjuster lock nut in the clockwise motion to achieve the proper torque.*

10. To install, realign the pitman arm-to-pitman shaft, torque the pitman shaft nut to 177–185 ft.lb.

REMOVAL AND INSTALLATION

NOTE: *The following procedure requires the use of the GM Pitman Arm Remover tool No. J-6632 or equivalent.*

1. Disconnect the negative battery terminal from the battery.

2. Raise and support the front of the vehicle on jackstands. Position the wheel in the straight ahead direction.

3. Remove the intermediate shaft-to-steering gear pinch bolt.

4. Remove the pitman arm-to-pitman shaft nut, mark the relationship the arm to the shaft. Using the GM Pitman Arm Remover tool No. J-6632 or equivalent, separate the pitman arm from the pitman shaft.

NOTE: *When separating the pitman arm from the shaft, DO NOT use a hammer or apply heat to the arm.*

5. Remove the steering gear-to-frame bolts and the gear from the vehicle.

NOTE: *When installing the steering gear, be sure that the intermediate shaft bottoms on the worm shaft, so that the pinch bolt passes through the undercut on the worm shaft. Check and/or adjust the alignment of the pitman arm-to-pitman shaft.*

6. To install, align the matchmarks and reverse the removal procedures. Torque the steering gear-to-frame bolts to 70 ft.lb., the pitman arm-to-pitman shaft nut to 177–185 ft.lb. and the intermediate steering shaft-to-steering gear bolt to 30 ft.lb.

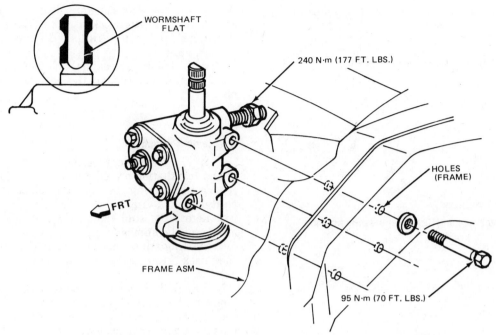

Replacing the manual steering gear

Power Steering Gear

The recirculating ball type power steering gear is basically the same as the manual steering gear, except that it uses a mechanical advantage.

The power steering gear control valve directs the power steering fluid to either side of the rack piston. The steering rack converts the hydraulic pressure into mechanical force. Should the vehicle loose the hydraulic pressure, it can still be controlled mechanically.

ADJUSTMENTS

NOTE: *To perform adjustments to the power steering gear, it is recommended to remove the power steering gear from the vehicle and place it in a vise. Before adjustments are performed to the system, be sure to check problems relating to hydraulic pressures and performance.*

Worm Bearing Preload

NOTE: *The following procedure requires the use of the GM Adjustable Spanner Wrench tool No. J-7624 or equivalent.*

1. Refer to the Power Steering Gear, Removal and Installation procedures in this section, remove the steering gear from the vehicle and position it in a vise.
2. Using a hammer and a brass punch, drive the adjuster plug counterclockwise and remove it from the end of the steering gear.

Removing the adjuster jam nut—power steering gear

3. Using the GM Adjustable Spanner Wrench tool No. J-7624 or equivalent, turn the adjuster plug inward, until it firmly bottoms in the housing with a torque of 20 ft.lb.
4. Using a scribing tool, place a matchmark (on the housing) next to the one of the spanner wrench holes in the adjuster plug.
5. Using a ruler, measure ½" (12.7mm) counterclockwise from the scribed mark (on the housing) and place another mark.
6. Using the GM Adjustable Spanner

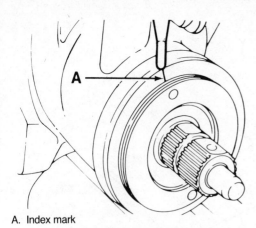

A. Index mark

Match-marking the power steering housing

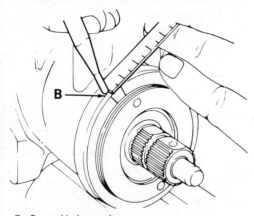

B. Second index mark

Remarking the power steering housing

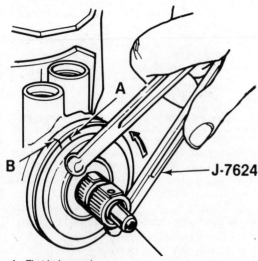

A. First index mark
B. Second index mark

Using the spanner wrench to align the adjuster with the 2nd mark—power steering gear

Wrench tool No. J-7624 or equivalent, turn the adjuster plug (counterclockwise) until the hole in the adjuster plug aligns with the 2nd scribed mark.

7. While holding the adjuster plug in alignment, install and tighten the adjuster plug nut.

8. Perform the overcenter preload adjustment.

Overcenter Preload

1. Refer to the Power Steering Gear, Removal and Installation procedures in this section, remove the steering gear from the vehicle and position it in a vise.

2. Rotate the stud shaft from stop-to-stop and count the number of turns necessary.

3. Starting from one stop, turn the stub shaft back ½ the number of turns (center of the gear).

NOTE: *With the stub gear centered, the flat on top of the shaft should face upward and be parallel with the side cover; the master spline on the pitman shaft should be in line with the adjuster screw.*

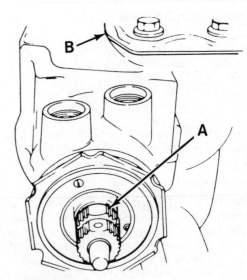

A. Stub shaft flat
B. Side cover

Aligning the stub shaft—power steering gear

4. Loosen the pitman shaft adjuster screw locknut and turn the adjuster screw counterclockwise until it is fully extended, then turn it clockwise one full turn.

5. Using a torque wrench (0–50 in.lb.), position it onto the stub shaft, rotate it 45° (to each side) and record the highest drag measured near or on the center.

6. Turn the adjuster screw inward until the

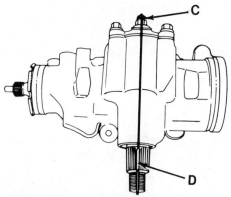

C. Adjuster screw
D. Master spline on the pitman shaft

Aligning the master spline on the pitman arm shaft—power steering gear

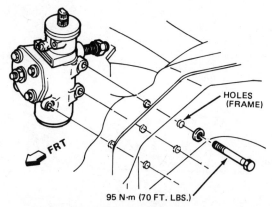

HOLES (FRAME)

FRT

95 N·m (70 FT. LBS.)

Replacing the power steering gear

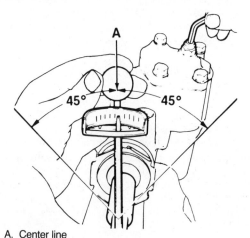

45°   45°

A. Center line

Checking the over-center rotational torque—power steering gear

torque on the stub shaft is 6–10 in.lb. greater than the initial reading.

7. Install the adjuster screw jam nut and torque it to 20 ft.lb. Reinstall the power steering gear into the vehicle.

REMOVAL AND INSTALLATION

1. Refer to the Pitman Arm, Removal and Installation procedures in this section and disconnect the pitman arm from the power steering gear.

2. Position a fluid catch pan under the power steering gear.

3. At the power steering gear, disconnect and plug the pressure hoses; any excess fluid will be caught by the catch pan.

NOTE: *Be sure to plug the pressure hoses and the openings of the power steering pump to keep dirt out of the system.*

4. Remove the intermediate shaft-to-steering gear bolt. Matchmark the intermediate

shaft-to-power steering gear and separate the shaft from the gear.

5. Remove the power steering gear-to-frame bolts, washers and the steering gear from the vehicle.

6. To install, reverse the removal procedures. Torque the power steering gear-to-frame bolts to 55 ft.lb., the intermediate shaft-to-power steering gear bolt to 30 ft.lb. and the pitman arm-to-pitman shaft nut to 177–185 ft.lb.

7. Connect the pressure hoses to the power steering gear, refill the power steering reservoir and bleed the power steering system.

8. Road test the vehicle.

Power Steering Pump
REMOVAL AND INSTALLATION

NOTE: *The following procedure requires the use of the GM Puller tool No. J-29785-A or equivalent, and the GM Pulley Installer tool No. J-25033-B or equivalent.*

1. Position a fluid catch pan under the power steering pump.

2. Remove the pressure hoses from the power steering pump and drain the excess fluid into the catch pan.

NOTE: *On models equipped with a remote fluid reservoir, disconnect and plug the hose(s).*

3. Loosen the power steering pump adjusting bolt, the washer and the pivot bolt, then remove the drive belt.

4. Using the GM Puller tool No. J-29785-A or equivalent, install it onto the power steering pump pulley. While holding the tool body, turn the pilot bolt counterclockwise to press the drive pulley from the pump.

NOTE: *When installing the puller tool onto the power steering pump pulley, be sure that the pilot bolt bottoms in the pump shaft by turning the head of the pilot bolt.*

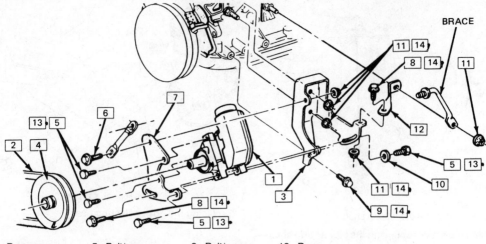

1. Pump asm
2. Belt
3. Bracket asm
4. Pulley asm
5. Bolt/screw
6. Bolt/screw
7. Bracket
8. Bolt/screw
9. Bolt/screw
10. Washer
11. Nut
12. Brace
13. 25 N·m (18 ft. lbs.)
14. 50 N·m (37 ft. lbs.)

Exploded view of the power steering pump assembly—4 Cyl engine

5. Remove the power steering pump-to-bracket bolts and the pump from the vehicle.

6. To install, reverse the removal procedures. Torque the power steering pump-to-bracket bolts to 18 ft.lb.

7. Using the GM Pulley Installer tool No. J-25033-B or equivalent, press the drive pulley onto the power steering pump. While holding the tool body, turn the pilot bolt clockwise to press the drive pulley onto the pump.

NOTE: *When installing the installer tool onto the power steering pump pulley, be sure that the pilot bolt bottoms in the pump shaft by turning the head of the pilot bolt.*

8. Hand tighten the pivot bolt, the adjusting bolt and the washer.

9. Install the drive belt and adjust the drive belt tension. Torque the mounting bolts and nut to 30 ft.lb. Install the pressure hoses (to the pump), refill the power steering reservoir and bleed the system.

NOTE: *Be sure to secure any hoses which*

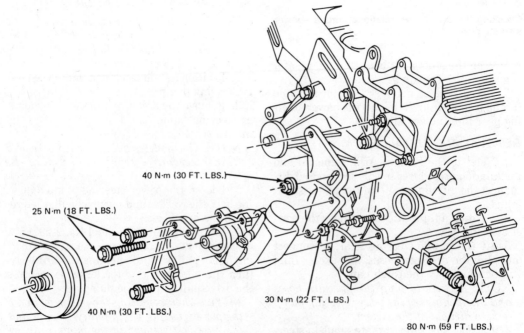

Exploded view of the power steering pump assembly—V6 engine

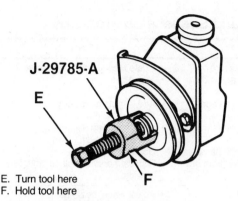

E. Turn tool here
F. Hold tool here

Removing the power steering pump pulley

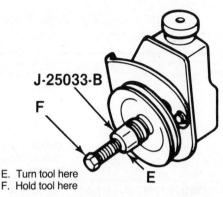

E. Turn tool here
F. Hold tool here

Installing the power steering pump pulley

may get in the way or rub other components.
10. Test drive the vehicle.

SYSTEM BLEEDING

1. Run the engine until the power steering fluid reaches normal operating temperature, approximately 170°F (76°C), then shut the engine Off. Remove the reservoir filler cap and check the oil level.

2. If the oil level is low, add power steering fluid to proper level and replace the filler cap. When adding or making a complete fluid change, always use GM No. 1050017 or equivalent, power steering fluid. DO NOT use transmission fluid.

3. Start the engine and turn the wheels in both directions (to the stops) several times. Stop the engine and add power steering fluid to the level indicated on the reservoir.

NOTE: *Maintain the fluid level just above the internal pump casting. Fluid with air in it will have a light tan or milky appearance. This air must be eliminated from the fluid before normal steering action can be obtained.*

4. Return the wheels to the center position and continue to run it for 2–3 minutes, then shut the engine Off.

5. Road test the vehicle to make sure the steering functions normally and is free from noise.

6. Allow the vehicle to stand for 2–3 hours, then recheck the power steering fluid.

NOISE DIAGNOSIS

The Noise Is	Most Probably Produced By
• Identical under Drive or Coast	• Road surface, tires or front wheel bearings
• Different depending on road surface	• Road surface or tires
• Lower as the car speed is lowered	• Tires
• Similar with car standing or moving	• Engine or transmission
• A vibration	• Unbalanced tires, rear wheel bearing, unbalanced driveshaft or worn U-joint
• A knock or click about every 2 tire revolutions	• Rear wheel bearing
• Most pronounced on turns	• Damaged differential gears
• A steady low-pitched whirring or scraping, starting at low speeds	• Damaged or worn pinion bearing
• A chattering vibration on turns	• Wrong differential lubricant or worn clutch plates (limited slip rear axle)
• Noticed only in Drive, Coast or Float conditions	• Worn ring gear and/or pinion gear

Troubleshooting Basic Steering and Suspension Problems

Problem	Cause	Solution
Hard steering (steering wheel is hard to turn)	• Low or uneven tire pressure • Loose power steering pump drive belt • Low or incorrect power steering fluid • Incorrect front end alignment • Defective power steering pump • Bent or poorly lubricated front end parts	• Inflate tires to correct pressure • Adjust belt • Add fluid as necessary • Have front end alignment checked/adjusted • Check pump • Lubricate and/or replace defective parts
Loose steering (too much play in the steering wheel)	• Loose wheel bearings • Loose or worn steering linkage • Faulty shocks • Worn ball joints	• Adjust wheel bearings • Replace worn parts • Replace shocks • Replace ball joints
Car veers or wanders (car pulls to one side with hands off the steering wheel)	• Incorrect tire pressure • Improper front end alignment • Loose wheel bearings • Loose or bent front end components • Faulty shocks	• Inflate tires to correct pressure • Have front end alignment checked/adjusted • Adjust wheel bearings • Replace worn components • Replace shocks
Wheel oscillation or vibration transmitted through steering wheel	• Improper tire pressures • Tires out of balance • Loose wheel bearings • Improper front end alignment • Worn or bent front end components	• Inflate tires to correct pressure • Have tires balanced • Adjust wheel bearings • Have front end alignment checked/adjusted • Replace worn parts
Uneven tire wear	• Incorrect tire pressure • Front end out of alignment • Tires out of balance	• Inflate tires to correct pressure • Have front end alignment checked/adjusted • Have tires balanced

Troubleshooting the Steering Column

Problem	Cause	Solution
Will not lock	• Lockbolt spring broken or defective	• Replace lock bolt spring
High effort (required to turn ignition key and lock cylinder)	• Lock cylinder defective • Ignition switch defective • Rack preload spring broken or deformed • Burr on lock sector, lock rack, housing, support or remote rod coupling • Bent sector shaft • Defective lock rack • Remote rod bent, deformed • Ignition switch mounting bracket bent • Distorted coupling slot in lock rack (tilt column)	• Replace lock cylinder • Replace ignition switch • Replace preload spring • Remove burr • Replace shaft • Replace lock rack • Replace rod • Straighten or replace • Replace lock rack
Will stick in "start"	• Remote rod deformed • Ignition switch mounting bracket bent	• Straighten or replace • Straighten or replace
Key cannot be removed in "off-lock"	• Ignition switch is not adjusted correctly • Defective lock cylinder	• Adjust switch • Replace lock cylinder
Lock cylinder can be removed without depressing retainer	• Lock cylinder with defective retainer • Burr over retainer slot in housing cover or on cylinder retainer	• Replace lock cylinder • Remove burr
High effort on lock cylinder between "off" and "off-lock"	• Distorted lock rack • Burr on tang of shift gate (automatic column) • Gearshift linkage not adjusted	• Replace lock rack • Remove burr • Adjust linkage
Noise in column	• One click when in "off-lock" position and the steering wheel is moved (all except automatic column) • Coupling bolts not tightened • Lack of grease on bearings or bearing surfaces • Upper shaft bearing worn or broken • Lower shaft bearing worn or broken • Column not correctly aligned • Coupling pulled apart • Broken coupling lower joint • Steering shaft snap ring not seated • Shroud loose on shift bowl. Housing loose on jacket—will be noticed with ignition in "off-lock" and when torque is applied to steering wheel.	• Normal—lock bolt is seating • Tighten pinch bolts • Lubricate with chassis grease • Replace bearing assembly • Replace bearing. Check shaft and replace if scored. • Align column • Replace coupling • Repair or replace joint and align column • Replace ring. Check for proper seating in groove. • Position shroud over lugs on shift bowl. Tighten mounting screws.
High steering shaft effort	• Column misaligned • Defective upper or lower bearing • Tight steering shaft universal joint • Flash on I.D. of shift tube at plastic joint (tilt column only) • Upper or lower bearing seized	• Align column • Replace as required • Repair or replace • Replace shift tube • Replace bearings
Lash in mounted column assembly	• Column mounting bracket bolts loose • Broken weld nuts on column jacket • Column capsule bracket sheared	• Tighten bolts • Replace column jacket • Replace bracket assembly

Troubleshooting the Steering Column (cont.)

Problem	Cause	Solution
Lash in mounted column assembly (cont.)	• Column bracket to column jacket mounting bolts loose	• Tighten to specified torque
	• Loose lock shoes in housing (tilt column only)	• Replace shoes
	• Loose pivot pins (tilt column only)	• Replace pivot pins and support
	• Loose lock shoe pin (tilt column only)	• Replace pin and housing
	• Loose support screws (tilt column only)	• Tighten screws
Housing loose (tilt column only)	• Excessive clearance between holes in support or housing and pivot pin diameters	• Replace pivot pins and support
	• Housing support-screws loose	• Tighten screws
Steering wheel loose—every other tilt position (tilt column only)	• Loose fit between lock shoe and lock shoe pivot pin	• Replace lock shoes and pivot pin
Steering column not locking in any tilt position (tilt column only)	• Lock shoe seized on pivot pin	• Replace lock shoes and pin
	• Lock shoe grooves have burrs or are filled with foreign material	• Clean or replace lock shoes
	• Lock shoe springs weak or broken	• Replace springs
Noise when tilting column (tilt column only)	• Upper tilt bumpers worn	• Replace tilt bumper
	• Tilt spring rubbing in housing	• Lubricate with chassis grease
One click when in "off-lock" position and the steering wheel is moved	• Seating of lock bolt	• None. Click is normal characteristic sound produced by lock bolt as it seats.
High shift effort (automatic and tilt column only)	• Column not correctly aligned	• Align column
	• Lower bearing not aligned correctly	• Assemble correctly
	• Lack of grease on seal or lower bearing areas	• Lubricate with chassis grease
Improper transmission shifting—automatic and tilt column only	• Sheared shift tube joint	• Replace shift tube
	• Improper transmission gearshift linkage adjustment	• Adjust linkage
	• Loose lower shift lever	• Replace shift tube

Troubleshooting the Ignition Switch

Problem	Cause	Solution
Ignition switch electrically inoperative	• Loose or defective switch connector	• Tighten or replace connector
	• Feed wire open (fusible link)	• Repair or replace
	• Defective ignition switch	• Replace ignition switch
Engine will not crank	• Ignition switch not adjusted properly	• Adjust switch
Ignition switch wil not actuate mechanically	• Defective ignition switch	• Replace switch
	• Defective lock sector	• Replace lock sector
	• Defective remote rod	• Replace remote rod
Ignition switch cannot be adjusted correctly	• Remote rod deformed	• Repair, straighten or replace

Troubleshooting the Turn Signal Switch

Problem	Cause	Solution
Turn signal will not cancel	• Loose switch mounting screws • Switch or anchor bosses broken • Broken, missing or out of position detent, or cancelling spring	• Tighten screws • Replace switch • Reposition springs or replace switch as required
Turn signal difficult to operate	• Turn signal lever loose • Switch yoke broken or distorted • Loose or misplaced springs • Foreign parts and/or materials in switch • Switch mounted loosely	• Tighten mounting screws • Replace switch • Reposition springs or replace switch • Remove foreign parts and/or material • Tighten mounting screws
Turn signal will not indicate lane change	• Broken lane change pressure pad or spring hanger • Broken, missing or misplaced lane change spring • Jammed wires	• Replace switch • Replace or reposition as required • Loosen mounting screws, reposition wires and retighten screws
Turn signal will not stay in turn position	• Foreign material or loose parts impeding movement of switch yoke • Defective switch	• Remove material and/or parts • Replace switch
Hazard switch cannot be pulled out	• Foreign material between hazard support cancelling leg and yoke	• Remove foreign material. No foreign material impeding function of hazard switch—replace turn signal switch.
No turn signal lights	• Inoperative turn signal flasher • Defective or blown fuse • Loose chassis to column harness connector • Disconnect column to chassis connector. Connect new switch to chassis and operate switch by hand. If vehicle lights now operate normally, signal switch is inoperative • If vehicle lights do not operate, check chassis wiring for opens, grounds, etc.	• Replace turn signal flasher • Replace fuse • Connect securely • Replace signal switch • Repair chassis wiring as required
Instrument panel turn indicator lights on but not flashing	• Burned out or damaged front or rear turn signal bulb • If vehicle lights do not operate, check light sockets for high resistance connections, the chassis wiring for opens, grounds, etc. • Inoperative flasher • Loose chassis to column harness connection • Inoperative turn signal switch • To determine if turn signal switch is defective, substitute new switch into circuit and operate switch by hand. If the vehicle's lights operate normally, signal switch is inoperative.	• Replace bulb • Repair chassis wiring as required • Replace flasher • Connect securely • Replace turn signal switch • Replace turn signal switch
Stop light not on when turn indicated	• Loose column to chassis connection • Disconnect column to chassis connector. Connect new switch into system without removing old.	• Connect securely • Replace signal switch

Troubleshooting the Turn Signal Switch (cont.)

Problem	Cause	Solution
Stop light not on when turn indicated (cont.)	Operate switch by hand. If brake lights work with switch in the turn position, signal switch is defective.	
	• If brake lights do not work, check connector to stop light sockets for grounds, opens, etc.	• Repair connector to stop light circuits using service manual as guide
Turn indicator panel lights not flashing	• Burned out bulbs • High resistance to ground at bulb socket	• Replace bulbs • Replace socket
	• Opens, ground in wiring harness from front turn signal bulb socket to indicator lights	• Locate and repair as required
Turn signal lights flash very slowly	• High resistance ground at light sockets	• Repair high resistance grounds at light sockets
	• Incorrect capacity turn signal flasher or bulb	• Replace turn signal flasher or bulb
	• If flashing rate is still extremely slow, check chassis wiring harness from the connector to light sockets for high resistance	• Locate and repair as required
	• Loose chassis to column harness connection	• Connect securely
	• Disconnect column to chassis connector. Connect new switch into system without removing old. Operate switch by hand. If flashing occurs at normal rate, the signal switch is defective.	• Replace turn signal switch
Hazard signal lights will not flash— turn signal functions normally	• Blow fuse • Inoperative hazard warning flasher	• Replace fuse • Replace hazard warning flasher in fuse panel
	• Loose chassis-to-column harness connection	• Conect securely
	• Disconnect column to chassis connector. Connect new switch into system without removing old. Depress the hazard warning lights. If they now work normally, turn signal switch is defective.	• Replace turn signal switch
	• If lights do not flash, check wiring harness "K" lead for open between hazard flasher and connector. If open, fuse block is defective	• Repair or replace brown wire or connector as required

Troubleshooting the Manual Steering Gear

Problem	Cause	Solution
Hard or erratic steering	• Incorrect tire pressure	• Inflate tires to recommended pressures
	• Insufficient or incorrect lubrication	• Lubricate as required (refer to Maintenance Section)
	• Suspension, or steering linkage parts damaged or misaligned	• Repair or replace parts as necessary
	• Improper front wheel alignment	• Adjust incorrect wheel alignment angles
	• Incorrect steering gear adjustment	• Adjust steering gear
	• Sagging springs	• Replace springs
Play or looseness in steering	• Steering wheel loose	• Inspect shaft spines and repair as necessary. Tighten attaching nut and stake in place.
	• Steering linkage or attaching parts loose or worn	• Tighten, adjust, or replace faulty components
	• Pitman arm loose	• Inspect shaft splines and repair as necessary. Tighten attaching nut and stake in place
	• Steering gear attaching bolts loose	• Tighten bolts
	• Loose or worn wheel bearings	• Adjust or replace bearings
	• Steering gear adjustment incorrect or parts badly worn	• Adjust gear or replace defective parts
Wheel shimmy or tramp	• Improper tire pressure	• Inflate tires to recommended pressures
	• Wheels, tires, or brake rotors out-of-balance or out-of-round	• Inspect and replace or balance parts
	• Inoperative, worn, or loose shock absorbers or mounting parts	• Repair or replace shocks or mountings
	• Loose or worn steering or suspension parts	• Tighten or replace as necessary
	• Loose or worn wheel bearings	• Adjust or replace bearings
	• Incorrect steering gear adjustments	• Adjust steering gear
	• Incorrect front wheel alignment	• Correct front wheel alignment
Tire wear	• Improper tire pressure	• Inflate tires to recommended pressures
	• Failure to rotate tires	• Rotate tires
	• Brakes grabbing	• Adjust or repair brakes
	• Incorrect front wheel alignment	• Align incorrect angles
	• Broken or damaged steering and suspension parts	• Repair or replace defective parts
	• Wheel runout	• Replace faulty wheel
	• Excessive speed on turns	• Make driver aware of conditions
Vehicle leads to one side	• Improper tire pressures	• Inflate tires to recommended pressures
	• Front tires with uneven tread depth, wear pattern, or different cord design (i.e., one bias ply and one belted or radial tire on front wheels)	• Install tires of same cord construction and reasonably even tread depth, design, and wear pattern
	• Incorrect front wheel alignment	• Align incorrect angles
	• Brakes dragging	• Adjust or repair brakes
	• Pulling due to uneven tire construction	• Replace faulty tire

Troubleshooting the Power Steering Gear

Problem	Cause	Solution
Hissing noise in steering gear	• There is some noise in all power steering systems. One of the most common is a hissing sound most evident at standstill parking. There is no relationship between this noise and performance of the steering. Hiss may be expected when steering wheel is at end of travel or when slowly turning at standstill.	• Slight hiss is normal and in no way affects steering. Do not replace valve unless hiss is extremely objectionable. A replacement valve will also exhibit slight noise and is not always a cure. Investigate clearance around flexible coupling rivets. Be sure steering shaft and gear are aligned so flexible coupling rotates in a flat plane and is not distorted as shaft rotates. Any metal-to-metal contacts through flexible coupling will transmit valve hiss into passenger compartment through the steering column.
Rattle or chuckle noise in steering gear	• Gear loose on frame	• Check gear-to-frame mounting screws. Tighten screws to 88 N·m (65 foot pounds) torque.
	• Steering linkage looseness	• Check linkage pivot points for wear. Replace if necessary.
	• Pressure hose touching other parts of car	• Adjust hose position. Do not bend tubing by hand.
	• Loose pitman shaft over center adjustment **NOTE:** A slight rattle may occur on turns because of increased clearance off the "high point." This is normal and clearance must not be reduced below specified limits to eliminate this slight rattle.	• Adjust to specifications
	• Loose pitman arm	• Tighten pitman arm nut to specifications
Squawk noise in steering gear when turning or recovering from a turn	• Damper O-ring on valve spool cut	• Replace damper O-ring
Poor return of steering wheel to center	• Tires not properly inflated • Lack of lubrication in linkage and ball joints	• Inflate to specified pressure • Lube linkage and ball joints
	• Lower coupling flange rubbing against steering gear adjuster plug	• Loosen pinch bolt and assemble properly
	• Steering gear to column misalignment	• Align steering column
	• Improper front wheel alignment • Steering linkage binding • Ball joints binding • Steering wheel rubbing against housing	• Check and adjust as necessary • Replace pivots • Replace ball joints • Align housing
	• Tight or frozen steering shaft bearings	• Replace bearings
	• Sticking or plugged valve spool	• Remove and clean or replace valve
	• Steering gear adjustments over specifications	• Check adjustment with gear out of car. Adjust as required.
	• Kink in return hose	• Replace hose
Car leads to one side or the other (keep in mind road condition and wind. Test car in both directions on flat road)	• Front end misaligned • Unbalanced steering gear valve **NOTE:** If this is cause, steering effort will be very light in direction of lead and normal or heavier in opposite direction	• Adjust to specifications • Replace valve

Troubleshooting the Power Steering Gear (cont.)

Problem	Cause	Solution
Momentary increase in effort when turning wheel fast to right or left	• Low oil level • Pump belt slipping • High internal leakage	• Add power steering fluid as required • Tighten or replace belt • Check pump pressure. (See pressure test)
Steering wheel surges or jerks when turning with engine running especially during parking	• Low oil level • Loose pump belt • Steering linkage hitting engine oil pan at full turn • Insufficient pump pressure • Pump flow control valve sticking	• Fill as required • Adjust tension to specification • Correct clearance • Check pump pressure. (See pressure test). Replace relief valve if defective. • Inspect for varnish or damage, replace if necessary
Excessive wheel kickback or loose steering	• Air in system • Steering gear loose on frame • Steering linkage joints worn enough to be loose • Worn poppet valve • Loose thrust bearing preload adjustment • Excessive overcenter lash	• Add oil to pump reservoir and bleed by operating steering. Check hose connectors for proper torque and adjust as required. • Tighten attaching screws to specified torque • Replace loose pivots • Replace poppet valve • Adjust to specification with gear out of vehicle • Adjust to specification with gear out of car
Hard steering or lack of assist	• Loose pump belt • Low oil level **NOTE:** Low oil level will also result in excessive pump noise • Steering gear to column misalignment • Lower coupling flange rubbing against steering gear adjuster plug • Tires not properly inflated	• Adjust belt tension to specification • Fill to proper level. If excessively low, check all lines and joints for evidence of external leakage. Tighten loose connectors. • Align steering column • Loosen pinch bolt and assemble properly • Inflate to recommended pressure
Foamy milky power steering fluid, low fluid level and possible low pressure	• Air in the fluid, and loss of fluid due to internal pump leakage causing overflow	• Check for leak and correct. Bleed system. Extremely cold temperatures will cause system aeriation should the oil level be low. If oil level is correct and pump still foams, remove pump from vehicle and separate reservoir from housing. Check welsh plug and housing for cracks. If plug is loose or housing is cracked, replace housing.
Low pressure due to steering pump	• Flow control valve stuck or inoperative • Pressure plate not flat against cam ring	• Remove burrs or dirt or replace. Flush system. • Correct
Low pressure due to steering gear	• Pressure loss in cylinder due to worn piston ring or badly worn housing bore • Leakage at valve rings, valve body-to-worm seal	• Remove gear from car for disassembly and inspection of ring and housing bore • Remove gear from car for disassembly and replace seals

Troubleshooting the Power Steering Pump

Problem	Cause	Solution
Chirp noise in steering pump	• Loose belt	• Adjust belt tension to specification
Belt squeal (particularly noticeable at full wheel travel and stand still parking)	• Loose belt	• Adjust belt tension to specification
Growl noise in steering pump	• Excessive back pressure in hoses or steering gear caused by restriction	• Locate restriction and correct. Replace part if necessary.
Growl noise in steering pump (particularly noticeable at stand still parking)	• Scored pressure plates, thrust plate or rotor • Extreme wear of cam ring	• Replace parts and flush system • Replace parts
Groan noise in steering pump	• Low oil level • Air in the oil. Poor pressure hose connection.	• Fill reservoir to proper level • Tighten connector to specified torque. Bleed system by operating steering from right to left—full turn.
Rattle noise in steering pump	• Vanes not installed properly • Vanes sticking in rotor slots	• Install properly • Free up by removing burrs, varnish, or dirt
Swish noise in steering pump	• Defective flow control valve	• Replace part
Whine noise in steering pump	• Pump shaft bearing scored	• Replace housing and shaft. Flush system.
Hard steering or lack of assist	• Loose pump belt • Low oil level in reservoir **NOTE:** Low oil level will also result in excessive pump noise • Steering gear to column misalignment • Lower coupling flange rubbing against steering gear adjuster plug • Tires not properly inflated	• Adjust belt tension to specification • Fill to proper level. If excessively low, check all lines and joints for evidence of external leakage. Tighten loose connectors. • Align steering column • Loosen pinch bolt and assemble properly • Inflate to recommended pressure
Foaming milky power steering fluid, low fluid level and possible low pressure	• Air in the fluid, and loss of fluid due to internal pump leakage causing overflow	• Check for leaks and correct. Bleed system. Extremely cold temperatures will cause system aeriation should the oil level be low. If oil level is correct and pump still foams, remove pump from vehicle and separate reservoir from body. Check welsh plug and body for cracks. If plug is loose or body is cracked, replace body.
Low pump pressure	• Flow control valve stuck or inoperative • Pressure plate not flat against cam ring	• Remove burrs or dirt or replace. Flush system. • Correct
Momentary increase in effort when turning wheel fast to right or left	• Low oil level in pump • Pump belt slipping • High internal leakage	• Add power steering fluid as required • Tighten or replace belt • Check pump pressure. (See pressure test)
Steering wheel surges or jerks when turning with engine running especially during parking	• Low oil level • Loose pump belt • Steering linkage hitting engine oil pan at full turn • Insufficient pump pressure	• Fill as required • Adjust tension to specification • Correct clearance • Check pump pressure. (See pressure test). Replace flow control valve if defective.

Troubleshooting the Power Steering Pump (cont.)

Problem	Cause	Solution
Steering wheel surges or jerks when turning with engine running especially during parking (cont.)	• Sticking flow control valve	• Inspect for varnish or damage, replace if necessary
Excessive wheel kickback or loose steering	• Air in system	• Add oil to pump reservoir and bleed by operating steering. Check hose connectors for proper torque and adjust as required.
Low pump pressure	• Extreme wear of cam ring • Scored pressure plate, thrust plate, or rotor • Vanes not installed properly • Vanes sticking in rotor slots • Cracked or broken thrust or pressure plate	• Replace parts. Flush system. • Replace parts. Flush system. • Install properly • Freeup by removing burrs, varnish, or dirt • Replace part

Brakes

BRAKE SYSTEM

The Astro Vans are equipped with independent front and rear brake systems. The systems consist of a power booster, a master cylinder, a combination valve, front disc and rear drum assemblies.

The master cylinder, mounted on the left firewall or power booster, consists of two fluid reservoirs, a primary (rear) cylinder, a secondary (front) cylinder and springs. The reservoirs, being independent of one another, are contained within the same housing; fluid cannot pass from one to the other. The rear reservoir supplies fluid to the front brakes while the front reservoir supplies fluid to the rear brakes.

During operation, fluid drains from the reservoirs to the master cylinder. When the brake pedal is applied, fluid from the master cylinder is sent to the combination valve (mounted on the left front fender or frame side rail beneath the master cylinder), here it is monitored and proportionally distributed to the front or rear brake systems. Should a loss of pressure occur in one system, the other system will provide enough braking pressure to stop the vehicle. Also, should a loss of pressure in one system occur, the differential warning switch (located on the combination valve) will turn ON the brake warning light (located on the dash board).

As the fluid enters each brake caliper or wheel cylinder, the pistons are forced outward. The outward movement of the pistons force the brake pads against a round flat disc or the brake shoes against a round metal drum. The brake lining attached to the pads or shoes comes in contact with the revolving disc or drum, causing friction, which brings the wheel to a stop.

In time, the brake linings wear down. If not replaced, their metal support plates (bonded type) or rivet heads (riveted type) will come in contact with the disc or drum; damage to the disc or drum will occur. Never use brake pads or shoes with a lining thickness less than $\frac{1}{32}''$ (0.8mm).

Most manufacturers provide a wear sensor, a piece of spring steel, attached to the rear edge of the inner brake pad. When the pad wears to the replacement thickness, the sensor will produce a high pitched squeal.

Adjustments

REAR DRUM BRAKES

Normal adjustments of the rear drum brakes are automatic and are made during the reverse applications of the brakes. ONLY, if the lining has been renewed, should the following procedure be performed.

NOTE: *The following procedure requires the use of the GM Brake Adjustment tool No. J-4735 or equivalent.*

1. Raise and support the rear of the vehicle on jackstands.

2. Using a punch and a hammer, at the rear of the backing plate, knock out the lanced metal area near the starwheel assembly.

NOTE: *When knocking out the lanced metal area from the backing plate, the wheels must be removed and all of the metal pieces discarded.*

3. Using the GM Brake Adjustment tool No. J-4735 or equivalent, insert it into the slot and engage the lowest possible tooth on the starwheel. Move the end of the brake tool downward to move the starwheel upward and expand the adjusting screw. Repeat this operation until the brakes lock the wheel.

4. Insert a small screwdriver or piece of firm wire (coathanger wire) into the adjusting slot and push the automatic adjuster lever out and free of the starwheel on the adjusting screw.

5. While holding the adjusting lever out of the way, engage the topmost tooth possible on

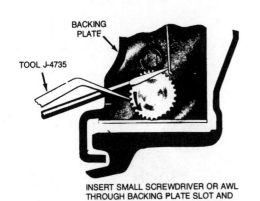

INSERT SMALL SCREWDRIVER OR AWL
THROUGH BACKING PLATE SLOT AND
HOLD ADJUSTER LEVER AWAY FROM
SPROCKET BEFORE BACKING OFF
BRAKE SHOE ADJUSTMENT

Adjusting the rear brake shoes

the starwheel (with the brake tool). Move the end of the adjusting tool upward to move the adjusting screw starwheel downward and contact the adjusting screw. Back off the adjusting screw starwheel until the wheel spins freely with a minimum of drag. Keep track of the number of turns the starwheel is backed off.

6. Repeat this operation for the other side. When backing off the brakes on the other side, the adjusting lever must be backed off the same number of turns to prevent side-to-side brake pull.

NOTE: *Backing off the starwheel 12 notches (clicks) is usually enough to eliminate brake drag.*

7. Repeat this operation on the other side of the rear brake system.

8. After the brakes are adjusted, install a rubber hole cover into the backing plate slot. To complete the brake adjustment operation, make several stops while backing the vehicle to equalize the wheels.

9. Road test the vehicle.

BRAKE PEDAL TRAVEL

The brake pedal travel is the distance the pedal moves toward the floor from the fully released position. Inspection should be made with 90 lbs. pressure on the brake pedal, when the brake system is Cold. The brake pedal travel should be 4½" (114mm) for manual, or 3½" (89mm).

NOTE: *If equipped with power brakes, be sure to pump the brake pedal at least 3 times with the engine Off, before making the brake pedal check.*

1. From under the dash, remove the pushrod-to-pedal clevis pin and separate the pushrod from the brake pedal.

2. Loosen the pushrod adjuster lock nut, then adjust the pushrod.

3. After the correct travel is established, reverse the removal procedure.

Brake Light Switch
REMOVAL AND INSTALLATION

1. Disconnect the negative battery terminal from the battery.

2. Disconnect the electrical connector from the brake light switch.

3. Turn the brake light switch retainer (to align the key with the bracket slot), then remove the switch with the retainer.

4. To install, reverse the removal procedures. Adjust the brake light switch.

ADJUSTMENT

1. Depress the brake pedal and press the brake light switch inward until it seats firmly against the clip.

NOTE: *As the switch is being pushed into the clip, audible clicks can be heard.*

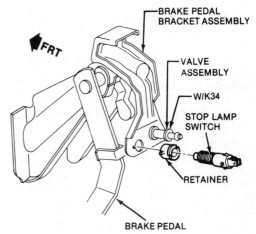

Exploded view of the brake light switch assembly

2. Release the brake pedal, then pull it back against the pedal stop until the audible click can no longer be heard.

3. The brake light switch will operate when the pedal is depressed 0.53" (13mm) from the fully released position.

Master Cylinder
REMOVAL AND INSTALLATION

1. Apply the parking brakes or block the wheels.

2. Using a siphon, remove and discard some of the brake fluid from the master cylinder reservoirs.

3. Disconnect and plug the hydraulic lines from the master cylinder.

4. If equipped with a manual brake system, disconnect the pushrod from the brake pedal.

5. Remove the master cylinder-to-bracket (manual) or vacuum booster (power) nuts, then separate the combination valve/bracket from the master cylinder.

6. Remove the master cylinder, the gasket and the rubber boot from the vehicle.

7. To install, bench bleed the master cylinder and reverse the removal procedures. Torque the master cylinder mounting nuts to 28 ft.lb. Refill the master cylinder with clean brake fluid, bleed the brake system and check the brake pedal travel.

NOTE: *If equipped with manual brakes, be sure to reconnect the pushrod to the brake pedal.*

OVERHAUL

1. Refer to the Master Cylinder, Removal and Installation procedures in this section and remove the master cylinder from the vehicle.

2. At the rear of the master cylinder, depress the primary piston and remove the lock ring.

3. Block the rear outlet hole on the master cylinder. Using compressed air, gently direct it into the front outlet hole to remove the primary and secondary pistons from the master cylinder. If compressed air is not available, use a hooked wire to pull out the secondary piston.

CAUTION: *If using compressed air to remove the pistons from the master cylinder, DO NOT stand in front of the pistons, for too much air will cause the pistons to be fired from the master cylinder, causing bodily harm.*

4. From the secondary piston, remove the spring retainer and the seals.

5. Using the mounting flange (ear) on the master cylinder, clamp it into a vise.

6. Using a medium pry bar, pry the reservoirs from the master cylinder. Remove the reservoir grommets.

NOTE: *DO NOT attempt to remove the quick*

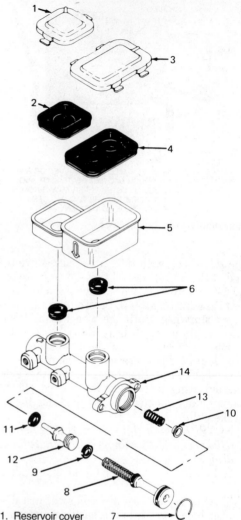

1. Reservoir cover
2. Reservoir diaphragm
3. Reservoir cover
4. Reservoir diaphragm
5. Reservoir
6. Reservoir grommet
7. Lock ring
8. Primary piston assembly
9. Secondary seal
10. Spring retainer
11. Primary seal
12. Secondary piston
13. Spring
14. Cylinder body

Exploded view of the master cylinder assembly

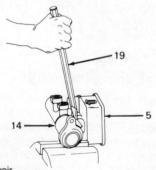

5. Reservoir
14. Cylinder body
19. Pry bar

Removing the reservoirs from the master cylinder

take-up valve from the master cylinder body; the valve is not serviceable separately.

7. Using denatured alcohol, clean and blow dry all of the master cylinder parts.

8. Inspect the master cylinder bore for corrosion or scratches; if damaged, replace the master cylinder with a new one.

9. To install, use new reservoir grommets (lubricated with silicone brake lube) and press

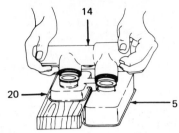

5. Reservoir
14. Cylinder body
20. Block

Installing the reservoirs onto the master cylinder

them into the master cylinder body. Install new seals onto the primary and secondary pistons.

10. Position the reservoirs on flat, hard surfaces (block of wood), then press the master cylinder onto the reservoirs, using a rocking motion.

11. Using heavy duty brake fluid, meeting Dot 3 specifications, lubricate the primary and secondary pistons, then install them into the master cylinder. While depressing the primary piston, install the lock ring.

12. Install new diaphragms onto the reservoir covers.

13. To complete the installation, reverse the removal procedures.

Power Brake Booster

The power brake booster is a tandem vacuum suspended unit, equipped with a single or dual function vacuum switch that activates a brake warning light should low booster vacuum be present. Under normal operation, vacuum is present on both sides of the diaphragms. When the brakes are applied, atmospheric air is admitted to one side of the diaphragms to provide power assistance.

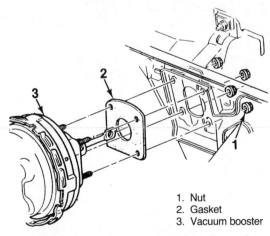

1. Nut
2. Gasket
3. Vacuum booster

Removing the power brake booster from the cowl

REMOVAL AND INSTALLATION

1. Apply the parking brake or block the wheels.

2. Remove the master cylinder-to-power brake booster nuts and move the master cylinder out of the way; if necessary, support the master cylinder on a wire.

NOTE: *When removing the master cylinder from the power brake booster, it is not necessary to disconnect the hydraulic lines.*

3. Disconnect the vacuum hose from the power brake booster.

4. From under the dash, disconnect the pushrod from the brake pedal.

5. From under the dash, remove the power brake booster-to-cowl nuts.

6. From the engine compartment, remove the power brake booster and the gasket from the vehicle.

7. To install, use a new gaskets and reverse the removal procedures. Torque the power brake booster-to-cowl nuts and the master cylinder-to-power brake booster nuts to 28 ft.lb. Start the engine and check the brake system operation.

Combination Valve

The combination valve is located in the engine compartment, directly under the master cylinder. It consists of three sections: the metering valve, the warning switch and the proportioning valve.

The metering section limits the pressure to the front disc brakes until a predetermined front input pressure is reached, enough to overcome the rear shoe retractor springs. Under 3 psi, there is no restriction of the inlet pressures; the pressures are allowed to equalize during the no brake period.

The proportioning section controls the outlet pressure to the rear brakes after a predetermined rear input pressure has been reached; this feature is provided for vehicles with light loads, to prevent rear wheel lock-up. The Bypass feature of this valve assures full system pressure to the rear brakes in the event of a front brake system malfunction. Also, full front pressure is retained if the rear system malfunctions.

The pressure differential warning switch is designed to constantly compare the front and the rear brake pressures; if one should malfunction, the warning light (on the dash) will turn On. The valve and switch are designed to lock On the warning position once the malfunction has occurred. The only way the light can be turned Off is to repair the malfunction and apply a brake line force of 450 psi.

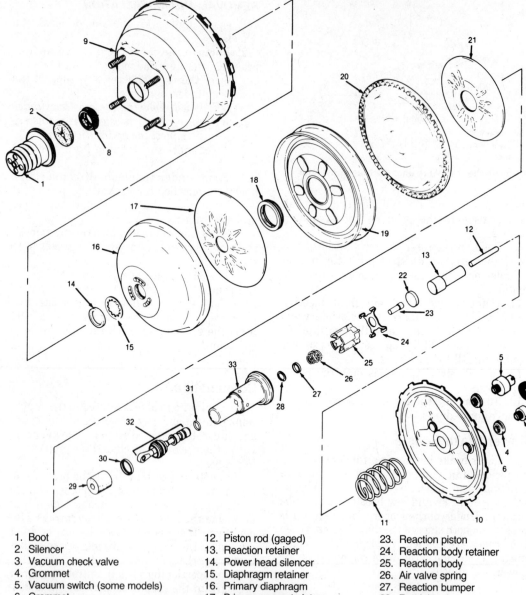

1. Boot
2. Silencer
3. Vacuum check valve
4. Grommet
5. Vacuum switch (some models)
6. Grommet
7. Front housing seal
8. Primary piston bearing
9. Rear housing
10. Front housing
11. Return spring
12. Piston rod (gaged)
13. Reaction retainer
14. Power head silencer
15. Diaphragm retainer
16. Primary diaphragm
17. Primary support plate
18. Secondary piston bearing
19. Housing divider
20. Secondary diaphragm
21. Secondary support plate
22. Reaction disc
23. Reaction piston
24. Reaction body retainer
25. Reaction body
26. Air valve spring
27. Reaction bumper
28. Retaining ring
29. Filter
30. Retainer
31. O-ring
32. Air valve push rod assembly
33. Power piston

Exploded view of the tandem power brake booster

REMOVAL AND INSTALLATION

1. Disconnect and plug the hydraulic lines from the combination valve to prevent the loss of brake fluid or dirt from entering the system.

2. Disconnect the electrical connector from the combination valve.

3. Remove the combination valve-to-bracket nuts and the combination valve from the vehicle.

NOTE: *The combination valve is not repairable and must be replaced as a complete assembly.*

4. To install, use a new combination valve (if defective) and reverse the removal procedures. Torque the combination valve-to-bracket nuts to 37 ft.lb. Reconnect the electrical connector to the combination valve. Bleed the brake system.

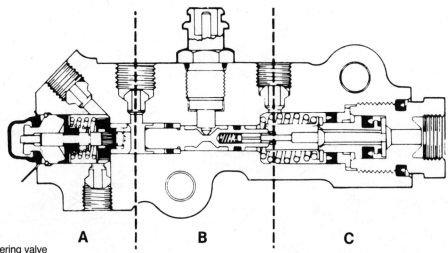

A. Metering valve
B. Warning switch
C. Proportioner

Cross-sectional view of the combination valve

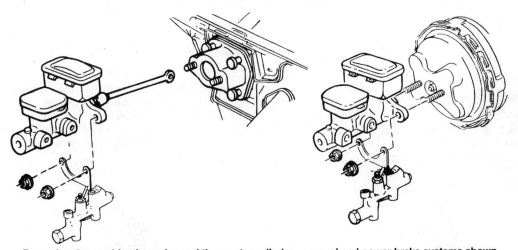

Removing the combination valve and the master cylinder—manual and power brake systems shown

Brake Pipes and Hoses

REMOVAL AND INSTALLATION

Flexible Hoses

Flexible hoses are installed between the frame-to-front calipers and the frame-to-rear differential.

1. Using a wire brush, clean the dirt and/or grease from both ends of the hose fittings.

2. Disconnect the steel pipes from the flexible hose.

3. To remove the brake hose from the front brake caliper or the rear differential, perform the following procedures:

   a. Remove the brake hose-to-frame bracket retaining clip.

   b. Remove the brake hose-to-brake caliper or differential junction block bolt.

   c. Remove the brake hose and the gaskets from the vehicle.

NOTE: *After disconnecting the brake hose(s) from the fittings, be sure to plug the fittings to keep the fluid from discharging or dirt from entering the system.*

5. Clean and inspect the brake hose(s) for cracking, chafing or road damage; replace the hose(s) if any signs are observed.

6. Using new flexible hose-to-caliper gaskets, install the flexible hose(s) and reverse the removal procedures. Torque the flexible hose(s)-to-front caliper bolt(s) to 32 ft.lb. and all other brake pipe fittings to 13 ft.lb. Bleed the brake system.

NOTE: *Be sure that the hoses do not make contact with any of the suspension components.*

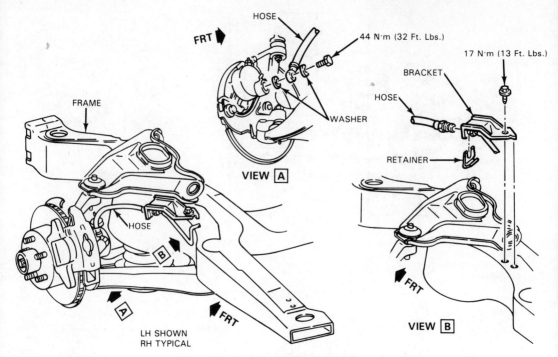

View of the front brake hose assemblies

Steel Pipes

When replacing the steel brake pipes, always use steel piping which is designed to withstand high pressure, resist corrosion and is of the same size.

CAUTION: *Never use copper tubing, for it is* *subject to fatigue, cracking, and/or corrosion,* *which will result in brake line failure.*

NOTE: *The following procedure requires the use of the GM Tube Cutter tool No. J-23533 or equivalent, and the GM Flaring tool No. J-23530 or equivalent.*

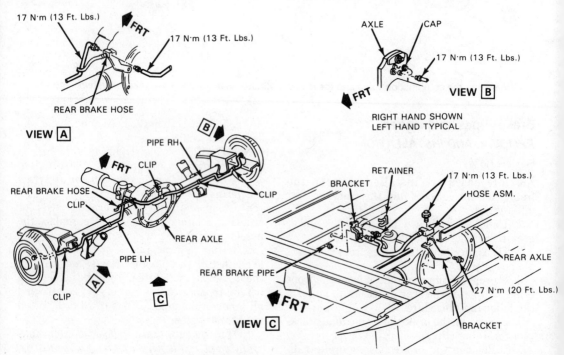

View of the rear brake hose and steel tube assemblies

1. Disconnect the steel brake pipe(s) from the flexible hose connections or the rear wheel cylinders; be sure to remove any retaining clips.

2. Remove the steel brake pipe from the vehicle.

3. Using new steel pipe (same size) and the GM Tube Cutter tool No. J-23533 or equivalent, cut the pipe to length; be sure to add ⅛″ (3mm) for each flare.

NOTE: *Be sure to install the correct pipe fittings onto the tube before forming any flares.*

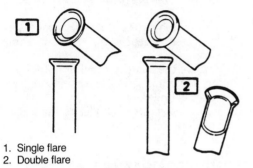

1. Single flare
2. Double flare

View of the single and the double flare fittings

4. Using the Flaring tool No. J-23530 or equivalent, follow the instructions equipped with the tool to form double flares on the ends of the pipes.

5. Using the small pipe bending tool, bend the pipe to match the contour of the pipe which was removed.

6. To install, reverse the removal procedures. Bleed the hydraulic system.

Bleeding

The hydraulic brake system must be bled any time one of the lines is disconnected or any time air enters the system. If the brake pedal feels spongy upon application, and goes almost to the floor but regains height when pumped, air has entered the system. It must be bled out. Check for leaks that would have allowed the entry of air and repair them before bleeding the system. The correct bleeding sequence is; right rear, left rear, right front and left front.

MANUAL

This method of bleeding requires two people, one to depress the brake pedal and the other to open the bleeder screws.

NOTE: *The following procedure requires the use of a clear vinyl hose, a glass jar and clean brake fluid.*

1. Clean the top of the master cylinder, remove the cover and fill the reservoirs with clean fluid. To prevent squirting fluid, replace the cover.

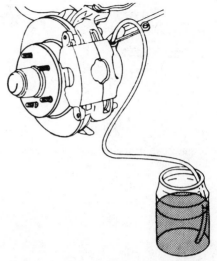

Installing a clear vinyl bleeder hose to the wheel caliper

NOTE: *On vehicles equipped with front disc brakes, it will be necessary to hold in the metering valve pin during the bleeding procedure. The metering valve is located beneath the master cylinder and the pin is situated under the rubber boot on the end of the valve housing. This may be tapped in or held by an assistant.*

2. Fill the master cylinder with brake fluid.

3. Install a box end wrench onto the bleeder screw on the right rear wheel.

4. Attach a length of small diameter, clear vinyl tubing to the bleeder screw. Submerge the other end of the tubing in a glass jar partially filled with clean brake fluid. Make sure the tube fits on the bleeder screw snugly or you may be squirted with brake fluid when the bleeder screw is opened.

5. Have your assistant slowly depress the brake pedal. As this is done, open the bleeder screw ½ turn and allow the fluid to run through the tube. Close the bleeder screw, then return the brake pedal to its fully released position.

6. Repeat this procedure until no bubbles appear in the jar. Refill the master cylinder.

7. Repeat this procedure on the left rear, right front and the left front wheels, in that order. Periodically, refill the master cylinder so that it does not run dry.

8. If the brake warning light is On, depress the brake pedal firmly. If there is no air in the system, the light will go Off.

PRESSURE

NOTE: *The following procedure requires the use of the GM Brake Bleeder Adapter tool No. J-29567 or equivalent, and the GM Combina-*

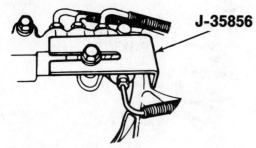

J-35856

View of the valve depressor tool connected to the combination valve

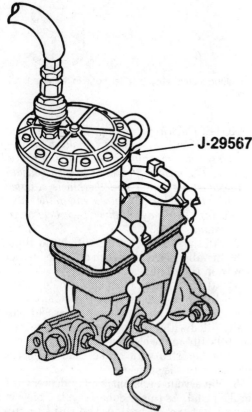

J-29567

View of the bleeder adapter tool connected to the master cylinder reservoir

tion Valve Depressor tool No. J-35856 or equivalent.

1. Using the GM Brake Bleeder Adapter tool No. J-29567 or equivalent, fill the pressure tank to at least ⅓ full of brake fluid. Using compressed air, charge the pressure tank to 20–25 psi., then install it onto the master cylinder.

2. Using the GM Combination Valve Depressor tool No. J-35856 or equivalent, install it onto the combination valve to hold the valve open during the bleeding operation.

3. Bleed each wheel cylinder or caliper in the following sequence: right rear, left rear, right front and left front.

4. Connect a hose from the bleeder tank to the adapter at the master cylinder, then open the tank valve.

5. Attach a clear vinyl hose to the brake bleeder screw, then immerse the opposite end into a container partially filled with clean brake fluid.

6. Open the bleeder screw ¾ turn and allow the fluid to flow until no air bubbles are seen in the fluid, then close the bleeder screw.

7. Repeat the bleeding process to each wheel.

8. Inspect the brake pedal for sponginess and if necessary, repeat the entire bleeding procedure.

9. Remove the depressor tool from the combination valve and the bleeder adapter from the master cylinder.

10. Refill the master cylinder to the proper level with brake fluid.

FRONT DISC BRAKES

CAUTION: *Brake shoes contain asbestos, which has been determined to be a cancer causing agent. Never clean the brake surfaces with compressed air! Avoid inhaling any dust from any brake surface! When cleaning brake surfaces, use a commercially available brake cleaning fluid.*

Brake Pads
INSPECTION

Brake pads should be inspected once a year or at 7,500 miles, which ever occurs first. Check both ends of the outboard shoe, looking in at each end of the caliper; then check the lining thickness on the inboard shoe, looking down through the inspection hole. The lining should be more than 0.032″ (0.8mm) thick above the rivet (so that the lining is thicker than the metal backing). Keep in mind that any applicable state inspection standards that are more stringent, take precedence. All four pads must be replaced if one shows excessive wear.

NOTE: *All models have a wear indicator that makes a noise when the linings wear to a degree where replacement is necessary. The spring clip is an integral part of the inboard shoe and lining. When the brake pad reaches a certain degree of wear, the clip will contact the rotor and produce a warning noise.*

REMOVAL AND INSTALLATION

NOTE *The following procedure requires the use of a C-clamp and channel lock pliers.*

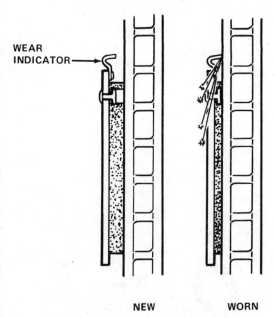

WEAR INDICATOR

NEW   WORN

Front disc brake pad wear indicator

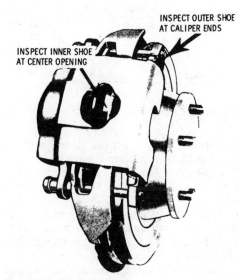

INSPECT OUTER SHOE AT CALIPER ENDS

INSPECT INNER SHOE AT CENTER OPENING

Disc brake pad inspection

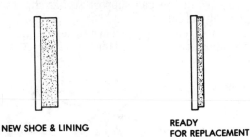

NEW SHOE & LINING

READY FOR REPLACEMENT

New and worn brake pads

1. Siphon off about ⅔ of the brake fluid from the master cylinder reservoirs.

CAUTION: *The insertion of thicker replacement pads will push the piston back into its*

bore *and will cause a full master cylinder reservoir to overflow, possibly causing paint damage. In addition to siphoning off fluid, it would be wise to keep the reservoir cover on during pad replacement.*

2. Raise and support the front of the vehicle on jackstands. Remove the wheels.

NOTE: *When replacing the pads on just one wheel, uneven braking will result; always replace the pads on both wheels.*

3. Install a C-clamp on the caliper so that the frame side of the clamp rests against the back of the caliper and so the screw end rests against the metal part (shoe) of the outboard pad.

4. Tighten the clamp until the caliper moves

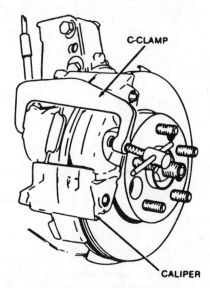

C-CLAMP

CALIPER

Install a C-clamp to retract the brake pads

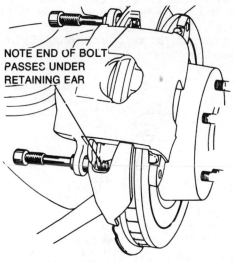

NOTE END OF BOLT PASSES UNDER RETAINING EAR

Caliper bolts must go under the pad retaining ears

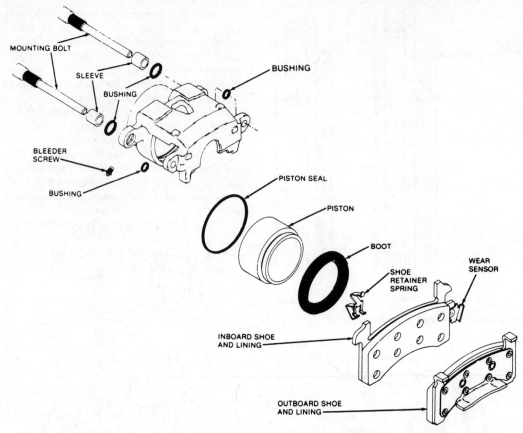

MOUNTING BOLT

SLEEVE

BUSHING

BLEEDER
SCREW

BUSHING

BUSHING

PISTON SEAL

PISTON

BOOT

WEAR
SENSOR

SHOE
RETAINER
SPRING

INBOARD SHOE
AND LINING

OUTBOARD SHOE
AND LINING

Exploded View of the Front Disc Brake Caliper

enough to bottom the piston in its bore. Remove the clamp.

5. Remove the two Allen head caliper mounting bolts enough to allow the caliper to be pulled off the disc.

6. Remove the inboard pad and loosen the outboard pad. Place the caliper where it will not strain the brake hose; it would be best to wire it out of the way.

7. Remove the pad support spring clip from the piston.

8. Remove the two bolt ear sleeves and the four rubber bushings from the ears.

9. Brake pads should be replaced when they are worn to within $\frac{1}{32}''$ (0.8mm) of the rivet heads.

10. Check the inside of the caliper for leakage and the condition of the piston dust boot.

11. Lubricate the two new sleeves and four bushings with a silicone spray.

12. Install the bushings in each caliper ear. Install the two sleeves in the two inboard ears.

13. Install the pad support spring clip and the old pad into the center of the piston. You will then push this pad down to get the piston flat against the caliper. This part of the job is a

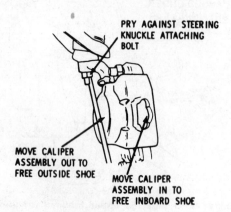

PRY AGAINST STEERING
KNUCKLE ATTACHING
BOLT

MOVE CALIPER
ASSEMBLY OUT TO
FREE OUTSIDE SHOE

MOVE CALIPER
ASSEMBLY IN TO
FREE INBOARD SHOE

Compressing caliper with pry bar

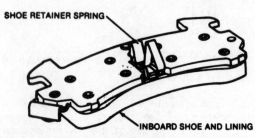

SHOE RETAINER SPRING

INBOARD SHOE AND LINING

Proper retaining spring installation

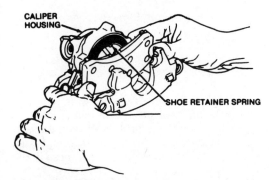

Install inboard brake shoe and linings

hassle and requires an assistant. While the assistant holds the caliper and loosens the bleeder valve to relieve the pressure, obtain a medium pry bar and try to force the old pad inward, making the piston flush with the caliper surface. When it is flush, close the bleeder valve so that no air gets into the system.

NOTE: *Make sure that the wear sensor is facing toward the rear of the caliper.*

14. Place the outboard pad in the caliper with its top ears over the caliper ears and the bottom tab engaged in the caliper cutout.

15. After both pads are installed, lift the caliper and place the bottom edge of the outboard pad on the outer edge of the disc to make sure that there is no clearance between the tab on the bottom of the shoes and the caliper abutment.

16. Place the caliper over the disc, lining up the hole in the caliper ears with the hole in the mounting bracket. Make sure that the brake hose is not kinked.

17. Start the caliper-to-mounting bracket

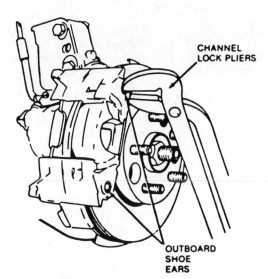

Bend the outboard pad ears into place with a large pair of slipjoint pliers

bolts through the sleeves in the inboard caliper ears and through the mounting bracket, making sure that the ends of the bolts pass under the retaining ears of the inboard shoe.

18. Push the mounting bolts through to engage the holes in the outboard shoes and the outboard caliper ears and then threading them into the mounting bracket.

19. Torque the mounting bolts to 37 ft.lb. Pump the brake pedal to seat the linings against the rotors.

20. Using a pair of channel lock pliers, place them on the notch on the caliper housing, bend the caliper upper ears until no clearance exists between the shoe and the caliper housing.

21. Install the wheels, lower the vehicle and refill the master cylinder reservoirs with brake fluid. Pump the brake pedal to make sure that it is firm. If it is not, bleed the brakes.

Brake Caliper
REMOVAL AND INSTALLATION

1. Refer to the Brake Pads, Removal and Installation procedures in this section and remove the brake caliper from the steering knuckle.

2. Disconnect the flexible brake hose-to-caliper bolt, discard the pressure fitting washers, then remove the brake caliper from the vehicle and place it on a work bench.

3. To inspect the caliper assembly, perform the following procedures:

   a. Check the inside of the caliper assembly for signs of leakage; if necessary, replace or rebuild the caliper.

   b. Check the mounting bolts and sleeves for signs of corrosion; if necessary, replace the bolts.

NOTE: *If the mounting bolts have signs of corrosion, DO NOT attempt to polish away the corrosion.*

4. To install, use new caliper bushing and sleeves, use Delco® Silicone Lube or equivalent to lubricate the mounting bolts and new brake pads (if necessary).

5. After both pads are installed, lift the caliper and place the bottom edge of the outboard pad on the outer edge of the disc to make sure that there is no clearance between the tab on the bottom of the shoes and the caliper abutment.

6. Place the caliper over the disc, lining up the hole in the caliper ears with the hole in the mounting bracket.

7. Start the caliper-to-mounting bracket bolts through the sleeves in the inboard caliper ears and through the mounting bracket, making sure that the ends of the bolts pass under the retaining ears of the inboard shoe.

8. Push the mounting bolts through to engage the holes in the outboard shoes and the outboard caliper ears, then thread them into the mounting bracket.

9. To complete the installation, use new flexible brake hose-to-caliper washers and reverse the removal procedures. Torque the caliper-to-steering knuckle bolts to 30–45 ft.lb. and the flexible brake hose-to-caliper bolt to 18–30 ft.lb. Refill the master cylinder reservoirs and bleed the brake system. Pump the brake pedal to seat the linings against the rotors.

10. Using a pair of channel lock pliers, place them on the caliper housing notch, bend the caliper upper ears until no clearance exists between the shoe and the caliper housing.

11. Install the wheels, lower the vehicle. Pump the brake pedal to make sure that it is firm. Road test the vehicle.

OVERHAUL

1. Refer to the Brake Caliper, Removal and Installation procedures in this section and remove the brake caliper from the vehicle.

2. Remove the inlet fitting from the brake caliper.

3. Position the caliper on a work bench and place clean shop cloths in the caliper opening.

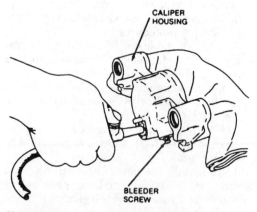

Use air pressure to remove the piston from the bore

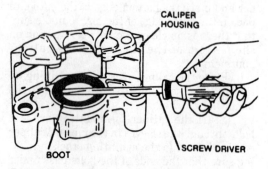

Remove the piston boot with an awl

Using compressed air, force the piston from it's bore.

CAUTION: *DO NOT apply too much air pressure to the bore, for the piston may jump out, causing damage to the piston and/or the operator.*

4. Remove and discard the piston boot and seal (with a plastic or wooden tool).

5. Clean all of the parts with non-mineral based solvent and blow dry with compressed air. Replace the rubber parts with those in the brake service kit.

6. Inspect the piston and the caliper bore for damage or corrosion. Replace the caliper and/or the piston (if necessary).

7. Remove the bleeder screw and it's rubber cap.

8. Inspect the guide pins for corrosion, replace them (if necessary). When installing the guide pins, coat them with silicone grease.

9. To install, perform the following procedures:

   a. Maintain the proper tolerances by referring to the following chart.

   b. Lubricate the piston, caliper and seal with clean brake fluid.

NOTE: *When positioning the piston seal on the piston, it goes in the groove nearest the piston's flat end with the lap facing the largest end. If placement is correct, the seal lips will be in the groove and not extend over the groove's step.*

   c. Replace the mounting bolts and torque to 22–25 ft.lb.

10. To complete the installation, reverse the removal procedures. Bleed the brake system after installation.

Brake Disc (Rotor)

The brake disc rotor and the wheel bearing hub assembly are designed from one piece of material; therefore, to remove the brake disc, remove the wheel bearing assembly.

REMOVAL AND INSTALLATION

NOTE: *Refer to the Wheel Bearing, Removal, Packing and Installation procedures in Chapter One and replace the brake disc rotor.*

INSPECTION

1. Raise and support the front of the vehicle on jackstands. Remove the wheels.

2. To check the disc runout, perform the following procedures:

   a. Using a dial indicator, secure and position it so that the button contacts the disc about 1" (25.4mm) from the outer edge.

   b. Rotate the disc. The lateral reading

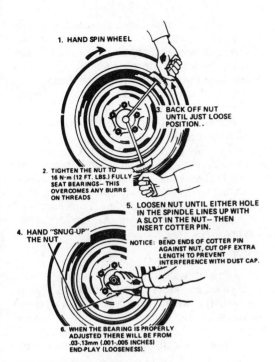

1. HAND SPIN WHEEL

3. BACK OFF NUT UNTIL JUST LOOSE POSITION.

2. TIGHTEN THE NUT TO 16 N·m (12 FT. LBS.) FULLY SEAT BEARINGS— THIS OVERCOMES ANY BURRS ON THREADS

4. HAND "SNUG-UP" THE NUT

5. LOOSEN NUT UNTIL EITHER HOLE IN THE SPINDLE LINES UP WITH A SLOT IN THE NUT— THEN INSERT COTTER PIN.

NOTICE: BEND ENDS OF COTTER PIN AGAINST NUT, CUT OFF EXTRA LENGTH TO PREVENT INTERFERENCE WITH DUST CAP.

6. WHEN THE BEARING IS PROPERLY ADJUSTED THERE WILL BE FROM .03-.13mm (.001-.005 INCHES) END-PLAY (LOOSENESS).

Wheel bearing adjustment

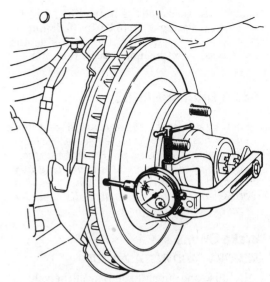

Use a dial indicator to determine brake disc run-out

should not exceed 0.004″ (0.1mm). If the reading is excessive, recondition or replace the disc.

3. To check the disc parallelism, perform the following procedures:

a. Using a micrometer, check the disc thickness at 4 locations around the disc, at the same distance from the edge.

b. The thickness should not vary more than 0.0005″ (0.0127mm). If the readings are excessive, recondition or replace the disc.

4. The surface finish must be relatively smooth to avoid pulling and erratic perfor-

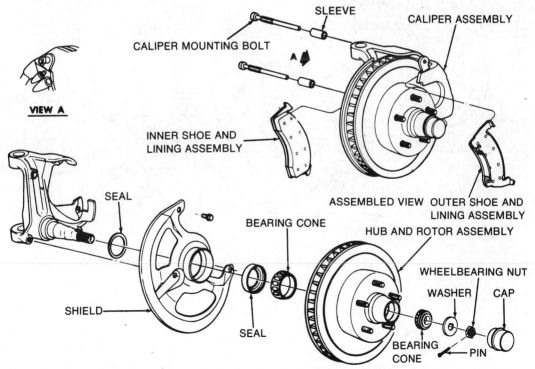

VIEW A

SLEEVE

CALIPER ASSEMBLY

CALIPER MOUNTING BOLT

INNER SHOE AND LINING ASSEMBLY

SEAL

BEARING CONE

ASSEMBLED VIEW OUTER SHOE AND LINING ASSEMBLY

HUB AND ROTOR ASSEMBLY

WHEELBEARING NUT

WASHER   CAP

SHIELD

SEAL

BEARING CONE

PIN

Exploded view of the disc brake assembly

mance, also, to extend the lining life. Light rotor surface scoring of up to 0.015" (0.38mm) in depth, can be tolerated. If the scoring depths are excessive, refinish or replace the rotor.

REAR DRUM BRAKES

CAUTION: *Brake shoes contain asbestos, which has been determined to be a cancer causing agent. Never clean the brake surfaces with compressed air! Avoid inhaling any dust from any brake surface! When cleaning brake surfaces, use a commercially available brake cleaning fluid.*

Brake Drums
REMOVAL AND INSTALLATION

1. Raise and support the rear of the vehicle on jackstands.
2. Remove the wheel and tire assemblies.
3. Pull the brake drum off. It may by necessary to gently tap the rear edges of the drum to start it off the studs.

4. If extreme resistance to removal is encountered, it will be necessary to retract the adjusting screw. Remove the access hole cover from the backing plate and turn the adjuster to retract the linings away from the drum.
5. Install a replacement hole cover before reinstalling the drum.
6. Install the drums in the same position on the hub as removed.

NOTE: *The rear wheel bearings are not adjustable, they are serviced by replacement ONLY. If necessary to replace the rear wheel bearings, refer to the Axle Shaft, Bearing and Seal, Removal and Installation procedures in Chapter 6 and follow the replacement procedures.*

INSPECTION

1. Check the drums for any cracks, scores, grooves or an out-of-round condition; if it is cracked, replace it. Slight scores can be removed with fine emery cloth while extensive scoring requires turning the drum on a lathe.
2. Never have a drum turned more than 0.060" (1.5mm).

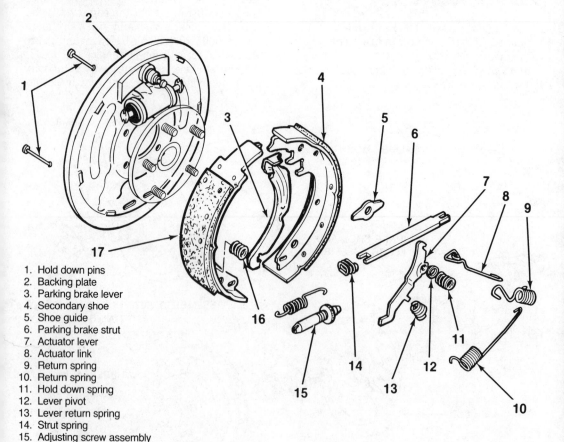

1. Hold down pins
2. Backing plate
3. Parking brake lever
4. Secondary shoe
5. Shoe guide
6. Parking brake strut
7. Actuator lever
8. Actuator link
9. Return spring
10. Return spring
11. Hold down spring
12. Lever pivot
13. Lever return spring
14. Strut spring
15. Adjusting screw assembly
16. Adjusting screw spring
17. Primary shoe

Exploded view of the rear brake assembly

Brake Shoes
INSPECTION

Remove the drum and inspect the lining thickness of both brake shoes. The rear brake shoes should be replaced if the lining is less than $\frac{1}{16}''$ (1.5mm) at the lowest point (bonded linings) or above the rivet heads (riveted linings) on the brake shoe. However, these lining thickness measurements may disagree with your state inspections laws.

NOTE: *Brake shoes should always be replaced in sets.*

REMOVAL AND INSTALLATION

NOTE: *The following procedure requires the use of the GM Brake Spring Pliers tool No. J-8057 or equivalent.*

1. Raise and support the rear of the vehicle on jackstands.
2. Slacken the parking brake cable.
3. Remove the rear wheels and the brake drum.
4. Using the GM Brake Spring Pliers tool No. J-8057 or equivalent, disconnect the brake shoe return springs, the actuator pullback spring, the holddown pins/springs and the actuator assembly.

NOTE: *Special brake spring tools are available from the auto supply stores, which will ease the replacement of the spring and anchor pin, but the job may still be performed with common hand tools.*

5. Disconnect the adjusting mechanism and spring, then remove the primary shoe. The primary shoe has a shorter lining than the secondary and is mounted at the front of the wheel.
6. Disconnect the parking brake lever from the secondary shoe and remove the shoe.
7. Clean and inspect all of the brake parts.
8. Check the wheel cylinders for seal condition and leaking.
9. If necessary, repack the wheel bearings and replace the oil seals.
10. Inspect the replacement shoes for nicks or burrs, lubricate the backing plate contact points, the brake cable, the levers and adjusting screws, then reassemble them.
11. Make sure that the right and left hand adjusting screws are not mixed. You can prevent this by working on one side at a time. This will also provide you with a reference for reassembly. The star wheel should be nearest to the secondary shoe when correctly installed.
12. Using lithium grease or equivalent, lubricate the shoe pads (on the backing plate) and the adjusting screw threads.
13. To complete the installation, reverse the removal procedures. When completed, make an initial adjustment as previously described.

Wheel Cylinders
REMOVAL AND INSTALLATION

1. Refer to the Brake Shoe, Removal and Installation procedures in this section and remove the brake shoe assembly from the backing plate.
2. Clean away all of the dirt, crud and foreign material from around the wheel cylinder.

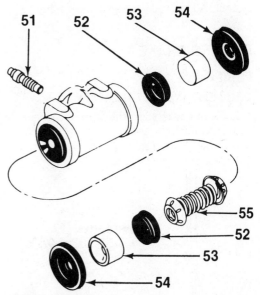

51. Bleeder valve
52. Seal
53. Piston
54. Boot
55. Spring assembly

Exploded view of the rear wheel cylinder

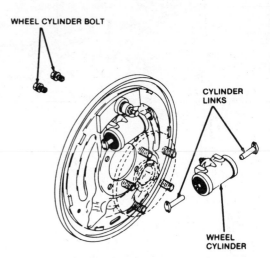

Replacing the wheel cylinder at the backing plate

It is important that dirt be kept away from the brake line when the cylinder is disconnected.

3. Disconnect and plug the inlet tube at the wheel cylinder.

4. Remove the wheel cylinder-to-backing plate bolts and the wheel cylinder from the backing plate.

NOTE: *If the wheel cylinder is sticking, use a hammer and a punch to drive the wheel cylinder from the backing plate.*

5. To install, reverse the removal procedures. Torque the wheel cylinder-to-backing plate bolts to 160 in.lb. Bleed the rear brake system. Adjust the rear brake assembly.

PARKING BRAKE

Front Cable

REMOVAL AND INSTALLATION

1. Raise and support the front of the vehicle on jackstands.

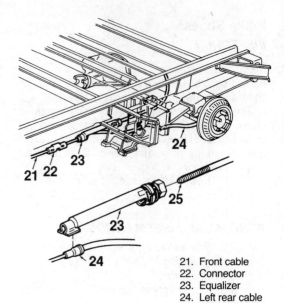

21. Front cable
22. Connector
23. Equalizer
24. Left rear cable
25. Right rear cable

Exploded view of the parking brake cable assembly

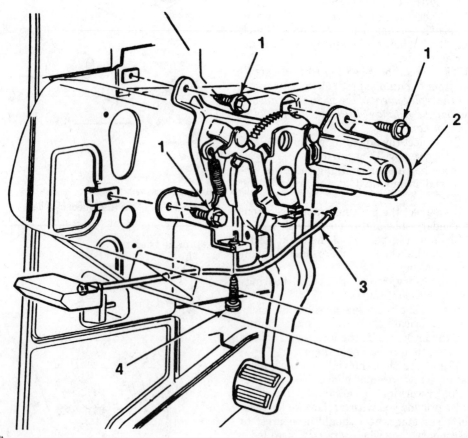

1. Bolt
2. Pedal assembly
3. Release rod
4. Bolt

Exploded view of the parking brake pedal assembly

Brake Specifications

All Specifications in inches

Years	Model	Master Cyl. Bore	Brake Disc			Brake Drum			Wheel Cyl. or Caliper Bore	
			Original Thickness	Minimum Thickness	Maximum Run-out	Orig. Inside Dia.	Max. Wear Limit	Maximum Machine O/S	Front	Rear
1985–86	Astro Van	—	1.04	0.980	0.004	9.5	9.59	9.56	—	—

2. Under the left center of the vehicle, loosen the cable equalizer assembly.

3. Separate the front cable connector from the equalizer cable.

4. Remove the front cable retaining bolts and clips, then bend the retaining fingers.

5. Disconnect the front cable from the parking pedal assembly and the cable from the vehicle.

6. To install the front cable, attach a piece of wire to the cable, fish it through the cowl and reverse the removal procedures. Adjust the parking brake.

7. Lower the vehicle and check the parking brake operation.

Rear Cable

REMOVAL AND INSTALLATION

1. Raise and support the rear of the vehicle on jackstands.

2. Under the left center of the vehicle, loosen the cable equalizer assembly.

3. Separate the front cable connector from the equalizer cable.

4. Refer to the Brake Shoe, Removal and Installation procedures in this section and remove the brake shoes.

5. At the backing plate, bend the cable retaining fingers.

6. Disconnect the rear cable(s) from the secondary brake shoe(s) and the cable(s) from the vehicle.

7. To install the rear cable(s), reverse the removal procedures. Adjust the parking brake.

NOTE: *When installing the rear parking brake cables, make sure that the retaining fingers are completely through the backing plate.*

8. Lower the vehicle and check the parking brake operation.

ADJUSTMENT

NOTE: *Before adjusting the parking brakes, check the condition of the service brakes; replace any necessary parts.*

1. Block the front wheels.

2. Raise and support the rear of the vehicle on jackstands.

3. Under the left center of the vehicle, loosen the equalizer.

4. Position the parking brake pedal on the second click (two ratchet clicks).

5. Turn the cable equalizer until the rear wheel drags (when turned by hand).

6. Tighten the equalizer lock nut.

7. Release the parking brake pedal, then test it; the correct adjustment should be 9–16 clicks.

Troubleshooting the Brake System

Problem	Cause	Solution
Low brake pedal (excessive pedal travel required for braking action.)	• Excessive clearance between rear linings and drums caused by inoperative automatic adjusters	• Make 10 to 15 alternate forward and reverse brake stops to adjust brakes. If brake pedal does not come up, repair or replace adjuster parts as necessary.
	• Worn rear brakelining	• Inspect and replace lining if worn beyond minimum thickness specification
	• Bent, distorted brakeshoes, front or rear	• Replace brakeshoes in axle sets
	• Air in hydraulic system	• Remove air from system. Refer to Brake Bleeding.
Low brake pedal (pedal may go to floor with steady pressure applied.)	• Fluid leak in hydraulic system	• Fill master cylinder to fill line; have helper apply brakes and check calipers, wheel cylinders, differential valve tubes, hoses and fittings for leaks. Repair or replace as necessary.
	• Air in hydraulic system	• Remove air from system. Refer to Brake Bleeding.
	• Incorrect or non-recommended brake fluid (fluid evaporates at below normal temp).	• Flush hydraulic system with clean brake fluid. Refill with correct-type fluid.
	• Master cylinder piston seals worn, or master cylinder bore is scored, worn or corroded	• Repair or replace master cylinder
Low brake pedal (pedal goes to floor on first application—o.k. on subsequent applications.)	• Disc brake pads sticking on abutment surfaces of anchor plate. Caused by a build-up of dirt, rust, or corrosion on abutment surfaces	• Clean abutment surfaces
Fading brake pedal (pedal height decreases with steady pressure applied.)	• Fluid leak in hydraulic system	• Fill master cylinder reservoirs to fill mark, have helper apply brakes, check calipers, wheel cylinders, differential valve, tubes, hoses, and fittings for fluid leaks. Repair or replace parts as necessary.
	• Master cylinder piston seals worn, or master cylinder bore is scored, worn or corroded	• Repair or replace master cylinder
Decreasing brake pedal travel (pedal travel required for braking action decreases and may be accompanied by a hard pedal.)	• Caliper or wheel cylinder pistons sticking or seized	• Repair or replace the calipers, or wheel cylinders
	• Master cylinder compensator ports blocked (preventing fluid return to reservoirs) or pistons sticking or seized in master cylinder bore	• Repair or replace the master cylinder
	• Power brake unit binding internally	• Test unit according to the following procedure: (a) Shift transmission into neutral and start engine (b) Increase engine speed to 1500 rpm, close throttle and fully depress brake pedal (c) Slow release brake pedal and stop engine (d) Have helper remove vacuum check valve and hose from power unit. Observe for backward movement of brake pedal. (e) If the pedal moves backward, the power unit has an internal bind—replace power unit

Troubleshooting the Brake System (cont.)

Problem	Cause	Solution
Spongy brake pedal (pedal has abnormally soft, springy, spongy feel when depressed.)	• Air in hydraulic system • Brakeshoes bent or distorted • Brakelining not yet seated with drums and rotors • Rear drum brakes not properly adjusted	• Remove air from system. Refer to Brake Bleeding. • Replace brakeshoes • Burnish brakes • Adjust brakes

Hard brake pedal (excessive pedal pressure required to stop vehicle. May be accompanied by brake fade.)	• Loose or leaking power brake unit vacuum hose
	• Incorrect or poor quality brakelining
	• Bent, broken, distorted brakeshoes
	• Calipers binding or dragging on mounting pins. Rear brakeshoes dragging on support plate.
	
	• Caliper, wheel cylinder, or master cylinder pistons sticking or seized
	• Power brake unit vacuum check valve malfunction
	
	• Power brake unit has internal bind
	
	• Master cylinder compensator ports (at bottom of reservoirs) blocked by dirt, scale, rust, or have small burrs (blocked ports prevent fluid return to reservoirs).
	• Brake hoses, tubes, fittings clogged or restricted
	
	• Brake fluid contaminated with improper fluids (motor oil, transmission fluid, causing rubber components to swell and stick in bores
	• Low engine vacuum
		• Tighten connections or replace leaking hose
		• Replace with lining in axle sets
		
		• Replace brakeshoes
		• Replace mounting pins and bushings. Clean rust or burrs from rear brake support plate ledges and lubricate ledges with molydisulfide grease.
		NOTE: If ledges are deeply grooved or scored, do not attempt to sand or grind them smooth—replace support plate.
		• Repair or replace parts as necessary
		
		• Test valve according to the following procedure:
		  (a) Start engine, increase engine speed to 1500 rpm, close throttle and immediately stop engine
		  (b) Wait at least 90 seconds then depress brake pedal
		  (c) If brakes are not vacuum assisted for 2 or more applications, check valve is faulty
		• Test unit according to the following procedure:
		  (a) With engine stopped, apply brakes several times to exhaust all vacuum in system
		  (b) Shift transmission into neutral, depress brake pedal and start engine
		  (c) If pedal height decreases with foot pressure and less pressure is required to hold pedal in applied position, power unit vacuum system is operating normally. Test power unit. If power unit exhibits a bind condition, replace the power unit.
		• Repair or replace master cylinder
		CAUTION: Do not attempt to clean blocked ports with wire, pencils, or similar implements. Use compressed air only.
		• Use compressed air to check or unclog parts. Replace any damaged parts.
		• Replace all rubber components, combination valve and hoses. Flush entire brake system with DOT 3 brake fluid or equivalent.
		
		• Adjust or repair engine

Troubleshooting the Brake System (cont.)

Problem	Cause	Solution
Grabbing brakes (severe reaction to brake pedal pressure.)	• Brakelining(s) contaminated by grease or brake fluid	• Determine and correct cause of contamination and replace brakeshoes in axle sets
	• Parking brake cables incorrectly adjusted or seized	• Adjust cables. Replace seized cables.
	• Incorrect brakelining or lining loose on brakeshoes	• Replace brakeshoes in axle sets
	• Caliper anchor plate bolts loose	• Tighten bolts
	• Rear brakeshoes binding on support plate ledges	• Clean and lubricate ledges. Replace support plate(s) if ledges are deeply grooved. Do not attempt to smooth ledges by grinding.
	• Incorrect or missing power brake reaction disc	• Install correct disc
	• Rear brake support plates loose	• Tighten mounting bolts
Dragging brakes (slow or incomplete release of brakes)	• Brake pedal binding at pivot	• Loosen and lubricate
	• Power brake unit has internal bind	• Inspect for internal bind. Replace unit if internal bind exists.
	• Parking brake cables incorrrectly adjusted or seized	• Adjust cables. Replace seized cables.
	• Rear brakeshoe return springs weak or broken	• Replace return springs. Replace brakeshoe if necessary in axle sets.
	• Automatic adjusters malfunctioning	• Repair or replace adjuster parts as required
	• Caliper, wheel cylinder or master cylinder pistons sticking or seized	• Repair or replace parts as necessary
	• Master cylinder compensating ports blocked (fluid does not return to reservoirs).	• Use compressed air to clear ports. Do not use wire, pencils, or similar objects to open blocked ports.
Vehicle moves to one side when brakes are applied	• Incorrect front tire pressure	• Inflate to recommended cold (reduced load) inflation pressure
	• Worn or damaged wheel bearings	• Replace worn or damaged bearings
	• Brakelining on one side contaminated	• Determine and correct cause of contamination and replace brakelining in axle sets
	• Brakeshoes on one side bent, distorted, or lining loose on shoe	• Replace brakeshoes in axle sets
	• Support plate bent or loose on one side	• Tighten or replace support plate
	• Brakelining not yet seated with drums or rotors	• Burnish brakelining
	• Caliper anchor plate loose on one side	• Tighten anchor plate bolts
	• Caliper piston sticking or seized	• Repair or replace caliper
	• Brakelinings water soaked	• Drive vehicle with brakes lightly applied to dry linings
	• Loose suspension component attaching or mounting bolts	• Tighten suspension bolts. Replace worn suspension components.
	• Brake combination valve failure	• Replace combination valve
Chatter or shudder when brakes are applied (pedal pulsation and roughness may also occur.)	• Brakeshoes distorted, bent, contaminated, or worn	• Replace brakeshoes in axle sets
	• Caliper anchor plate or support plate loose	• Tighten mounting bolts
	• Excessive thickness variation of rotor(s)	• Refinish or replace rotors in axle sets
Noisy brakes (squealing, clicking, scraping sound when brakes are applied.)	• Bent, broken, distorted brakeshoes	• Replace brakeshoes in axle sets
	• Excessive rust on outer edge of rotor braking surface	• Remove rust

Troubleshooting the Brake System (cont.)

Problem	Cause	Solution
Noisy brakes (squealing, clicking, scraping sound when brakes are applied.) (cont.)	• Brakelining worn out—shoes contacting drum of rotor	• Replace brakeshoes and lining in axle sets. Refinish or replace drums or rotors.
	• Broken or loose holdown or return springs	• Replace parts as necessary
	• Rough or dry drum brake support plate ledges	• Lubricate support plate ledges
	• Cracked, grooved, or scored rotor(s) or drum(s)	• Replace rotor(s) or drum(s). Replace brakeshoes and lining in axle sets if necessary.
	• Incorrect brakelining and/or shoes (front or rear).	• Install specified shoe and lining assemblies
Pulsating brake pedal	• Out of round drums or excessive lateral runout in disc brake rotor(s)	• Refinish or replace drums, re-index rotors or replace

Body and Trim

EXTERIOR

Front Doors

REMOVAL AND INSTALLATION

NOTE: *The following procedure requires the use of the GM Door Hinge Spring Compressor tool No. J-28625-A or equivalent.*

1. If equipped with power door components, perform the following procedures:

   a. Disconnect the negative battery cable from the battery.

   b. Refer to the "Door Panel, Removal and Installation" procedures in this section and remove the door panel.

   c. Disconnect the electrical harness connector from the power door lock motor and/or the power window regulator.

   d. Remove the electrical harness from the door.

CAUTION: *Before removing the hinge spring from the door, be sure to cover it (to keep it from flying); it could cause personal injury.*

2. Using the GM Door Hinge Spring Compressor tool No. J-28625-A or equivalent, compress the door hinge spring and remove it.

3. To remove the door hinge pin clips, spread the clips and move them above the recess on the pin; when the pin is removed, the clip will ride on the pin and fall free of it.

4. Using a soft-head hammer and a pair of locking pliers, remove the lower pin from the door hinge; then, install a bolt (in the lower pin hole) to hold the door in place until the upper hinge pin is removed.

5. Remove the upper door hinge pin and support the door, then remove the bolt from the lower hinge pin hole and the door from the vehicle.

6. To install the door, position the door onto the hinges and insert a bolt through the lower hinge pin hole.

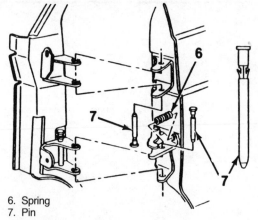

6. Spring
7. Pin

Replacing the door spring and the hinge pin

7. Using a new hinge pin clip, install the upper hinge pin.

8. Remove the bolt from the lower hinge pin hole. Using a new hinge pin, install it into the lower hinge pin holes.

9. Using the GM Door Hinge Spring Compressor tool No. J-28625-A or equivalent, compress the door hinge spring and install it into the door hinge.

10. If equipped with power door components, reconnect the electrical harness connector(s), install the door panel and the reconnect the negative battery terminal.

ADJUSTMENTS

Factory installed hinges are welded in place, so no adjustment of the system is necessary or recommended.

Front Door Hinges

NOTE: *The following procedure requires the use of an ⅛" (3mm) drill bit, ½" (13mm) drill bit, a center punch, a cold chisel, a portable body grinder, a putty knife, a scribing tool.*

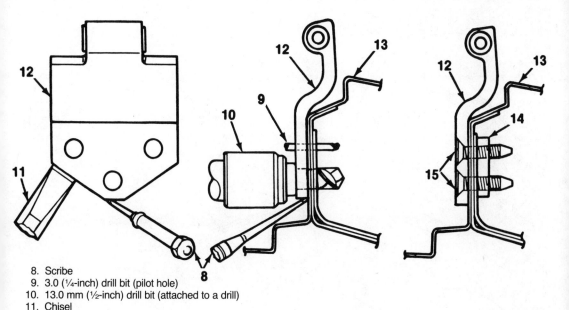

8. Scribe
9. 3.0 (¼-inch) drill bit (pilot hole)
10. 13.0 mm (½-inch) drill bit (attached to a drill)
11. Chisel
12. Hinge
13. Door frame
14. Tapped anchor plate
15. Screws

Installing replacement door hinges onto the vehicle

REMOVAL AND INSTALLATION

1. Refer to the "Door, Removal and Installation" procedures in this section and remove the door(s), then place the door on a padded workbench.

2. Using a putty knife, remove the sealant from the around the edge of the hinge.

3. Using a scribing tool, outline the position of the hinge(s) on the door and the body pillar.

4. Using a center punch, mark the center position of the hinge-to-door and the hinge-to-body pillar welds.

5. Using a ⅛" (3mm) drill bit, drill a pilot hole completely through each weld.

NOTE: *When drilling the holes through the hinge welds, DO NOT drill through the door or the body pillar.*

6. Using a ½" (13mm) drill bit, drill a hole through the hinge base, following the ⅛" (3mm) pilot hole.

7. Using a cold chisel and a hammer, separate the hinge from the door and/or the body pillar. Using a portable grinder, clean off any welds remaining on the door or the body pillar.

8. To fasten the replacement hinge(s) to the door and/or body pillar, perform the following procedures:

a. Align the replacement hinge, with the scribe lines, previously made.

b. Using a center punch and the new hinge as a template, mark the location of each bolt hole.

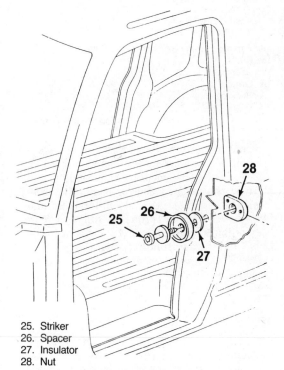

25. Striker
26. Spacer
27. Insulator
28. Nut

Exploded view of the front door stricker

c. Using a ½" (13mm) drill bit, drill holes (using the center marks) through the door and body pillar.

d. If the upper body side hinge is to be re-

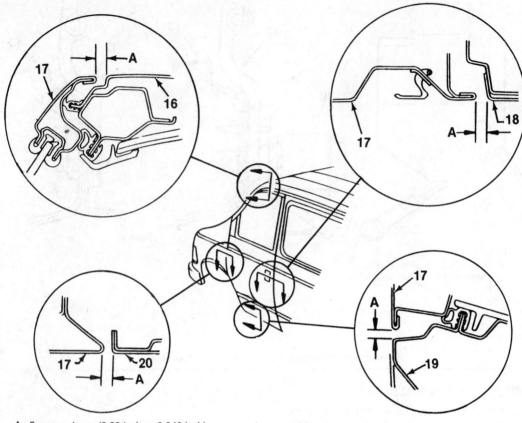

A. 5 mm ± 1 mm (0.20-inch ± 0.040-inch)
16. Roof
17. Door
18. Side panel
19. Rocker panel

Exploded view of the front door alignment points

placed, remove the instrument panel fasteners, pull the panel outwards and support it.

9. To install, use medium body sealant (apply it to the hinge-to-door or body pillar surface), the hinge-to-door/body pillar bolts and tapped anchor plate. Torque the hinge-to-door/body pillar bolts to 20 ft.lb. Apply paint to the hinge and the surrounding area.

NOTE: *If the instrument panel was removed, replace it.*

ADJUSTMENT

NOTE: *The ½" (13mm) drill hinge holes provide for some adjustment.*

1. Loosen, adjust, then tighten the hinge-to-door/body pillar bolts; close the door, then check the door gap, it should be 0.157–0.235" (4–6mm) between the door and the door frame.

2. With the door closed, it should be flush (± 0.039" [± 1.0mm]) with the body; if not, enlarge the striker hole.

Sliding Door

REMOVAL AND INSTALLATION

1. Remove the track cover.

2. Using a marking tool, mark the alignment of the lower roller bracket-to-door position.

3. Remove the upper roller bracket-to-door screws, then the lower roller bracket-to-sliding door bolts.

4. Using an assistant, to support the sliding door, open the door and roll the center roller bracket off the end of the track.

5. To install, use an assistant to roll the center roller bracket onto the end of the track. Align the lower roller bracket-to-door marks and install the mounting bolts. Torque all of the door roller bracket bolts to 20 ft.lb.

ADJUSTMENT

Although the sliding door is designed without any adjustment provisions, it is possible to rework certain portions of the system.

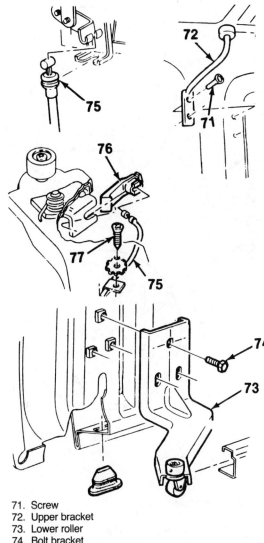

71. Screw
72. Upper bracket
73. Lower roller
74. Bolt bracket
75. Cable
76. Grommet
77. Screw

Exploded view of the upper/lower roller brackets and cable latch—sliding door

• Using the rear striker, at the center rear of the door, adjust the height and flushness.
• Using the lower roller bracket, adjust the parallel gap at the base of the door.
• To obtain flushness and vertical support, at the front of the door, adjust the door locator pins and sockets.
• To obtain proper gap and a level swing-in, at the rear of the door, adjust the center roller track fore and aft.
• Using Lubriplate® or equivalent, lubricate the roller track contact surfaces.
1. To obtain the height (up/down) and the flushness (in/out) movements, between the

door and the rear quarter panel, enlarge the rear striker hole.

NOTE: *When making the rear striker adjustments, DO NOT bend the striker to obtain the adjustment.*

2. To obtain a parallel gap between the base of the door and the rocker panel, loosen the lower roller bracket bolts. Check and/or adjust the gap between the quarter panel and the door; the gap should be parallel from the window area down to the rocker panel. Tighten the lower bracket mounting bolts to 20 ft.lb.

NOTE: *To obtain the parallel adjustment, the upper bracket hole may have to be enlarged; enlarging the hole may mean that the feature alignment of the door may have to be compromised.*

3. To obtain flushness between the door and the rocker panel, adjust the lower locating pin so that its surface is in contact with the outer edges of the locator guide. If you are having trouble obtaining the flushness, perform the following procedures:

a. Using a rubber hammer, strike the locator pin (while in position) to bend the sheet metal slightly.

b. Using a portable grinder, remove some of the material from the top or bottom of the locator guide; DO NOT remove too much material that a hole is ground through the guide.

c. Readjust the door height at the lower roller bracket.

4. Adjust the upper locator pin until it is flush with the locator guide; the locator should rub the outer edge of the locator guide. If you are having trouble obtaining the adjustment, perform the following procedures:

a. Using a rubber hammer, strike the locator pin (while in position) to bend the sheet metal slightly.

b. Using a portable grinder, remove some of the material from the top or bottom of the locator guide; DO NOT remove too much material that a hole is ground through the guide.

5. To obtain equal gaps between the door, the quarter panel and the door pillar, perform the following procedures:

a. For access to the center roller track, remove the right rear tail light bezel, the interior trim from around the track and the track cover.

b. Inspect the track rollers; the bottom rollers should ride on the track base and the side roller should ride on the outer flange of the track.

c. Loosen the track fasteners and slide the track rearward until it comes in contact the center rollers, then center the door in the

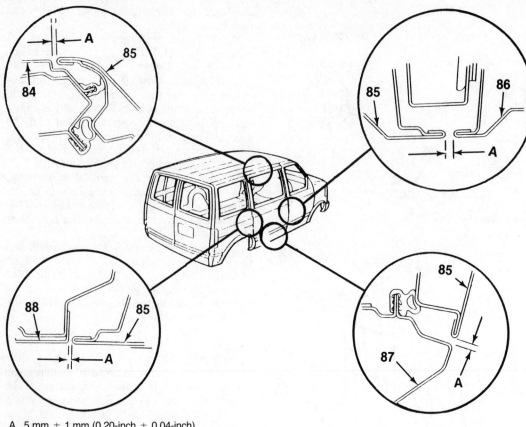

A. 5 mm ± 1 mm (0.20-inch ± 0.04-inch)
84. Roof
85. Door
86. Door pillar
87. Rocker panel
88. Rear quarter panel

View of the sliding door gap adjustments

opening. Tighten the track fasteners by starting with the one closest to the rear door striker.

d. Loosen the forward track fastener, then push the track up or down until the rear

latch rolls onto the striker in a level position; if necessary, elongate the hole.

e. Install the track cover, the interior trim and the rear tail light bezel.

6. Adjust the upper roller bracket so that

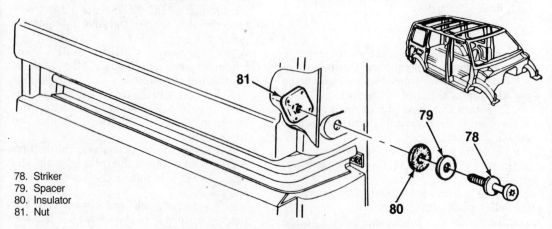

78. Striker
79. Spacer
80. Insulator
81. Nut

Exploded view of the door striker—sliding door

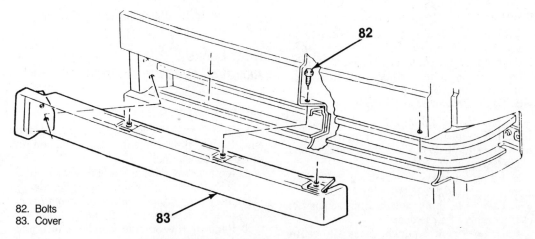

82. Bolts
83. Cover

Exploded view of the center roller track cover—sliding door

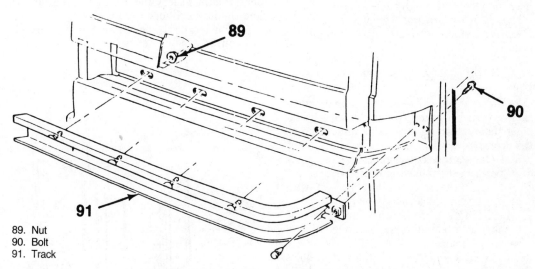

89. Nut
90. Bolt
91. Track

Exploded view of the center roller track—sliding door

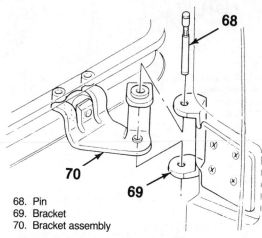

68. Pin
69. Bracket
70. Bracket assembly

Exploded view of the center roller bracket—sliding door

the roller runs in the middle of the track; it must not touch the upper or lower edge of the track. If necessary physically adjust it, remove it from the bracket and bend it at its base.

Roller Brackets
REMOVAL AND INSTALLATION
Upper

1. Remove the upper roller bracket trim.
2. Remove the front cap.
3. Remove the upper bracket-to-door screws and the bracket from the vehicle.
4. To install, reverse the removal procedures. Torque the upper roller bracket-to-door screws to 20 ft.lb. Adjust the door gap, if necessary.

Center

NOTE: *The following procedure requires the use of an ⅛" (3mm) drill bit, ½" (13mm) drill bit, a center punch, a cold chisel, a portable body grinder, a putty knife, a scribing tool.*

REMOVAL AND INSTALLATION

1. Refer to the "Sliding Door, Removal and Installation" procedures in this section and remove the sliding door, then place the door on a padded workbench.
2. Using a putty knife, remove the sealant from the around the edge of the bracket.
3. Using a scribing tool, outline the position of the bracket on the door.
4. Using a center punch, mark the center position of the bracket base welds.
5. Using a ⅛" (3mm) drill bit, drill a pilot hole completely through each weld.
NOTE: *When drilling the holes through the bracket welds, DO NOT drill through the door.*
6. Using a ½" (13mm) drill bit, drill a hole through the bracket base, following the ⅛" (3mm) pilot hole.
7. Using a cold chisel and a hammer, separate the bracket from the door. Using a portable grinder, clean off any welds remaining on the door.
8. To fasten the replacement bracket to the door, perform the following procedures:
   a. Align the replacement bracket, with the scribe lines, previously made.
   b. Using a center punch and the new bracket as a template, mark the location of each bolt hole.
   c. Using a ½" (13mm) drill bit, drill holes (using the center marks) through the door.
9. To install, use medium body sealant (apply it to the bracket-to-door surface), the brakcet-to-door bolts and tapped anchor plate. Torque the bracket-to-door bolts to 20 ft.lb. Apply paint to the bracket and the surrounding area. Adjust the sliding door-to-body gap, if necessary.

Lower

1. Remove the lower striker from the door.
2. Using a scribing tool, mark the lower roller bracket-to-door position.
3. Remove the lower roller bracket-to-door bolts and the catch cable from the bracket.
4. Slide the door to the fully back position.
5. Remove the lower roller bracket-to-body fasteners, pull the bracket from the body and slide the roller bracket out through the rear of the track.
6. To install, reverse the removal procedures. Torque the lower roller bracket-to-door

bolts to 20 ft.lb. Adjust the door-to-body gap, if necessary.

Door Locks

REMOVAL AND INSTALLATION

Front Door Manual Locks

OUTSIDE HANDLE AND LOCK CYLINDER

1. Refer to the "Door Panel, Removal and Installation" procedures in this section and remove the door panel.
2. Remove the outside handle-to-door nuts.
NOTE: *Removing the soft plug at the edge of the door may provide additional room to access the bottom door handle nut.*
3. Remove the outside handle-to-lock rod and the handle from the door.
4. Remove the lock rod from the lock cylinder, then the lock cylinder retainer, the gasket and the lock cylinder from the door.
5. To install, reverse the removal procedures.

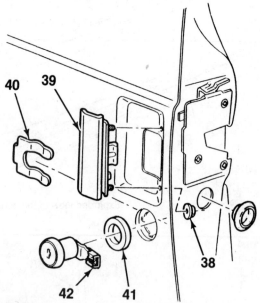

38. Nut
39. Outside handle
40. Retainer
41. Gasket
42. Lock cylinder

Exploded view of the outside handle and lock cylinder assembly—front door

LOCK ASSEMBLY

1. Refer to the "Door Panel, Removal and Installation" procedures in this section and remove the door panel.
2. Remove the outside handle-to-lock assembly rod.

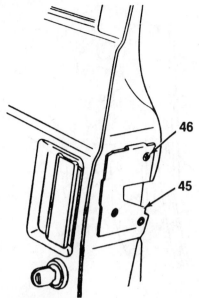

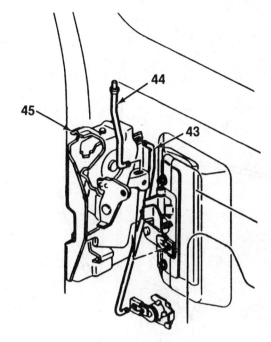

43. Lock cylinder rod
44. Outside handle rod
45. Lock assembly
46. Screw

View of the lock assembly—front door

3. Remove the lock cylinder-to-lock assembly rod.

4. Remove the inside handle-to-lock assembly rod.

5. Remove the inside lock-to-lock assembly rod.

6. Remove the lock assembly-to-door screws and the lock assembly from door.

INSIDE HANDLE

NOTE: *The following procedure requires the use of a ³⁄₁₆" (5mm) drill bit, ¼" by ½" (6mm by 13mm) pop rivets and the pop rivet gun.*

1. Refer to the "Door Panel, Removal and Installation" procedures in this section and remove the door panel.

2. Remove the inside handle-to-lock rod.

3. Using a ³⁄₁₆" (5mm) drill bit, drill the out

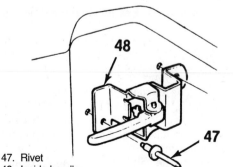

47. Rivet
48. Inside handle

Exploded view of the inside door handle—front door

the inside handle-to-door rivets, the remove the inside handle from the door.

4. To install, use ¼" by ½" (6mm by 13mm) pop rivets and a pop rivet gun, then install the inside handle to the door. To complete the installation, reverse the removal procedures.

Front Door w/Power Locks

REMOTE LOCK LEVER

NOTE: *The following procedure requires the use of a ³⁄₁₆" (5mm) drill bit, ¼" by ½" (6mm by 13mm) pop rivets and the pop rivet gun.*

1. Refer to the "Door Panel, Removal and Installation" procedures in this section and remove the door panel.

2. Remove the power door lock motor to remove the lever rod.

3. Remove the remote lever-to-lock assembly rod.

4. Remove the remote lever-to-inside lock lever rod.

5. Using a ³⁄₁₆" (5mm) drill bit, drill the out the inside handle-to-door rivets, the remove the inside handle from the door.

6. To install, use ¼" by ½" (6mm by 13mm) pop rivets and a pop rivet gun, then install the inside handle to the door. To complete the installation, reverse the removal procedures.

POWER DOOR LOCK MOTOR

1. Refer to the "Door Panel, Removal and Installation" procedures in this section and re-move the door panel.

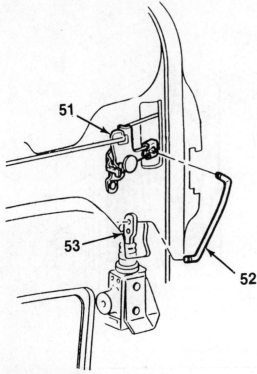

51. Lever assembly
52. Control rod
53. Door lock motor

**Exploded view of the power door lock compo-
nents—sliding door**

2. Remove the power door lock motor to remove the lever rod.
3. Disconnect the electrical connector from
the power door lock motor.
4. Remove the motor-to-door bolts and the
motor from the door.
5. To install, reverse the removal
procedures.

Sliding Door

LOCK ASSEMBLY

1. Refer to the "Sliding Door Panel, Removal and Installation" procedures in this section
and remove the door panel.
2. To remove the upper control-to-lock rods,
perform the following procedures:
   a. Using a small pry bar, pry the anchor
   clip out of the hole and push the clip away
   from the lever.
   b. Pull the rod and clip away from the
   lever.
3. To remove the remote control-to-locks
rods from the remote control, perform the following procedures:
   a. Using a small pry bar, pry the anchor
   clip out of the hole and push the clip away
   from the lever.

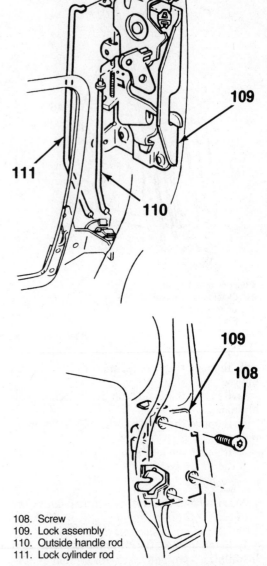

108. Screw
109. Lock assembly
110. Outside handle rod
111. Lock cylinder rod

View of the lock assembly—sliding door

   b. Pull the rod and clip away from the
   lever.
4. Remove the lock screws and the lock from
the door.
5. To install, reverse the removal
procedures.

POWER DOOR LOCK MOTOR

NOTE: *The following procedure requires the
use of a $^{3}/_{16}$" (5mm) drill bit, ¼" by ½" (6mm
by 13mm) pop rivets and the pop rivet gun.*

1. Disconnect the negative battery cable
from the battery.
2. Refer to the "Sliding Door Panel, Removal and Installation" procedures in this section
and remove the door panel.

CHILTON'S
AUTO BODY
REPAIR TIPS

**Tools and Materials • Step-by-Step Illustrated Procedures
How To Repair Dents, Scratches and Rust Holes
Spray Painting and Refinishing Tips**

With a little practice, basic body repair procedures can be mastered by any do-it-yourself mechanic. The step-by-step repairs shown here can be applied to almost any type of auto body repair.

TOOLS & MATERIALS

You may already have basic tools, such as hammers and electric drills. Other tools unique to body repair — body hammers, grinding attachments, sanding blocks, dent puller, half-round plastic file and plastic spreaders — are relatively inexpensive and can be obtained wherever auto parts or auto body repair parts are sold. Portable air compressors and paint spray guns can be purchased or rented.

Auto Body Repair Kits

The best and most often used products are available to the do-it-yourselfer in kit form, from major manufacturers of auto body repair products. The same manufacturers also merchandise the individual products for use by pros.

Kits are available to make a wide variety of repairs, including holes, dents and scratches and fiberglass, and offer the advantage of buying the materials you'll need for the job. There is little waste or chance of materials going bad from not being used. Many kits may also contain basic body-working tools such as body files, sanding blocks and spreaders. Check the contents of the kit before buying your tools.

BODY REPAIR TIPS

Safety

Many of the products associated with auto body repair and refinishing contain toxic chemicals. Read all labels before opening containers and store them in a safe place and manner.
• Wear eye protection (safety goggles) when using power tools or when performing any operation that involves

the removal of any type of material.
• Wear lung protection (disposable mask or respirator) when grinding, sanding or painting.

Sanding

1 Sand off paint before using a dent puller. When using a non-adhesive sanding disc, cover the back of the disc with an overlapping layer or two of masking tape and trim the edges. The disc will last considerably longer.

2 Use the circular motion of the sanding disc to grind *into* the edge of the repair. Grinding or sanding away from the jagged edge will only tear the sandpaper.

3 Use the palm of your hand flat on the panel to detect high and low spots. Do not use your fingertips. Slide your hand slowly back and forth.

WORKING WITH BODY FILLER

Mixing The Filler

Cleanliness and proper mixing and application are extremely important. Use a clean piece of plastic or glass or a disposable artist's palette to mix body filler.

1 Allow plenty of time and follow directions. No useful purpose will be served by adding more hardener to make it cure (set-up) faster. Less hardener means more curing time, but the mixture dries harder; more hardener means less curing time but a softer mixture.

2 Both the hardener and the filler should be thoroughly kneaded or stirred before mixing. Hardener should be a solid paste and dispense like thin toothpaste. Body filler should be smooth, and free of lumps or thick spots.

Getting the proper amount of hardener in the filler is the trickiest part of preparing the filler. Use the same amount of hardener in cold or warm weather. For contour filler (thick coats), a bead of hardener twice the diameter of the filler is about right. There's about a 15% margin on either side, but, if in doubt use less hardener.

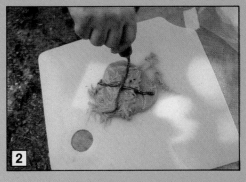

3 Mix the body filler and hardener by wiping across the mixing surface, picking the mixture up and wiping it again. Colder weather requires longer mixing times. Do not mix in a circular motion; this will trap air bubbles which will become holes in the cured filler.

Applying The Filler

1 For best results, filler should not be applied over ¼" thick.

Apply the filler in several coats. Build it up to above the level of the repair surface so that it can be sanded or grated down.

The first coat of filler must be pressed on with a firm wiping motion.

Apply the filler in one direction only. Working the filler back and forth will either pull it off the metal or trap air bubbles.

REPAIRING DENTS

Before you start, take a few minutes to study the damaged area. Try to visualize the shape of the panel before it was damaged. If the damage is on the left fender, look at the right fender and use it as a guide. If there is access to the panel from behind, you can reshape it with a body hammer. If not, you'll have to use a dent puller. Go slowly and work the metal a little at a time. Get the panel as straight as possible before applying filler.

1 This dent is typical of one that can be pulled out or hammered out from behind. Remove the headlight cover, headlight assembly and turn signal housing.

2 Drill a series of holes ½ the size of the end of the dent puller along the stress line. Make some trial pulls and assess the results. If necessary, drill more holes and try again. Do not hurry.

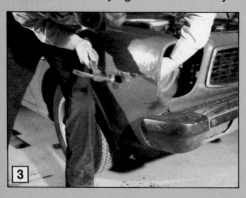

3 If possible, use a body hammer and block to shape the metal back to its original contours. Get the metal back as close to its original shape as possible. Don't depend on body filler to fill dents.

4 Using an 80-grit grinding disc on an electric drill, grind the paint from the surrounding area down to bare metal. Use a new grinding pad to prevent heat buildup that will warp metal.

5 The area should look like this when you're finished grinding. Knock the drill holes in and tape over small openings to keep plastic filler out.

6 Mix the body filler (see Body Repair Tips). Spread the body filler evenly over the entire area (see Body Repair Tips). Be sure to cover the area completely.

7 Let the body filler dry until the surface can just be scratched with your fingernail. Knock the high spots from the body filler with a body file ("Cheesegrater"). Check frequently with the palm of your hand for high and low spots.

8 Check to be sure that trim pieces that will be installed later will fit exactly. Sand the area with 40-grit paper.

9 If you wind up with low spots, you may have to apply another layer of filler.

10 Knock the high spots off with 40-grit paper. When you are satisfied with the contours of the repair, apply a thin coat of filler to cover pin holes and scratches.

11 Block sand the area with 40-grit paper to a smooth finish. Pay particular attention to body lines and ridges that must be well-defined.

12 Sand the area with 400 paper and then finish with a scuff pad. The finished repair is ready for priming and painting (see Painting Tips).

Materials and photos courtesy of Ritt Jones Auto Body, Prospect Park, PA.

REPAIRING RUST HOLES

There are many ways to repair rust holes. The fiberglass cloth kit shown here is one of the most cost efficient for the owner because it provides a strong repair that resists cracking and moisture and is relatively easy to use. It can be used on large and small holes (with or without backing) and can be applied over contoured areas. Remember, however, that short of replacing an entire panel, no repair is a guarantee that the rust will not return.

1 Remove any trim that will be in the way. Clean away all loose debris. Cut away all the rusted metal. But be sure to leave enough metal to retain the contour or body shape.

2 Grind away all traces of rust with a 24-grit grinding disc. Be sure to grind back 3-4 inches from the edge of the hole down to bare metal and be sure all traces of paint, primer and rust are removed.

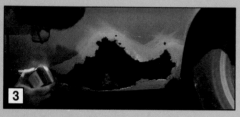

3 Block sand the area with 80 or 100 grit sandpaper to get a clear, shiny surface and feathered paint edge. Tap the edges of the hole inward with a ball peen hammer.

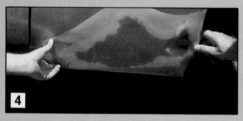

4 If you are going to use release film, cut a piece about 2-3″ larger than the area you have sanded. Place the film over the repair and mark the sanded area on the film. Avoid any unnecessary wrinkling of the film.

5 Cut 2 pieces of fiberglass matte to match the shape of the repair. One piece should be about 1″ smaller than the sanded area and the second piece should be 1″ smaller than the first. Mix enough filler and hardener to saturate the fiberglass material (see Body Repair Tips).

6 Lay the release sheet on a flat surface and spread an even layer of filler, large enough to cover the repair. Lay the smaller piece of fiberglass cloth in the center of the sheet and spread another layer of filler over the fiberglass cloth. Repeat the operation for the larger piece of cloth.

7 Place the repair material over the repair area, with the release film facing outward. Use a spreader and work from the center outward to smooth the material, following the body contours. Be sure to remove all air bubbles.

8 Wait until the repair has dried tack-free and peel off the release sheet. The ideal working temperature is 60°-90° F. Cooler or warmer temperatures or high humidity may require additional curing time. Wait longer, if in doubt.

9 Sand and feather-edge the entire area. The initial sanding can be done with a sanding disc on an electric drill if care is used. Finish the sanding with a block sander. Low spots can be filled with body filler; this may require several applications.

10 When the filler can just be scratched with a fingernail, knock the high spots down with a body file and smooth the entire area with 80-grit. Feather the filled areas into the surrounding areas.

11 When the area is sanded smooth, mix some topcoat and hardener and apply it directly with a spreader. This will give a smooth finish and prevent the glass matte from showing through the paint.

12 Block sand the topcoat smooth with finishing sandpaper (200 grit), and 400 grit. The repair is ready for masking, priming and painting (see Painting Tips).

Materials and photos courtesy Marson Corporation, Chelsea, Massachusetts

PAINTING TIPS

Preparation

1 SANDING — Use a 400 or 600 grit wet or dry sandpaper. Wet-sand the area with a ¼ sheet of sandpaper soaked in clean water. Keep the paper wet while sanding. Sand the area until the repaired area tapers into the original finish.

2 CLEANING — Wash the area to be painted thoroughly with water and a clean rag. Rinse it thoroughly and wipe the surface dry until you're sure it's completely free of dirt, dust, fingerprints, wax, detergent or other foreign matter.

3 MASKING — Protect any areas you don't want to overspray by covering them with masking tape and newspaper. Be careful not get fingerprints on the area to be painted.

4 PRIMING — All exposed metal should be primed before painting. Primer protects the metal and provides an excellent surface for paint adhesion. When the primer is dry, wet-sand the area again with 600 grit wet-sandpaper. Clean the area again after sanding.

Painting Techniques

P aint applied from either a spray gun or a spray can (for small areas) will provide good results. Experiment on an old piece of metal to get the right combination before you begin painting.

SPRAYING VISCOSITY (SPRAY GUN ONLY) — Paint should be thinned to spraying viscosity according to the directions on the can. Use only the recommended thinner or reducer and the same amount of reduction regardless of temperature.

AIR PRESSURE (SPRAY GUN ONLY) — This is extremely important. Be sure you are using the proper recommended pressure.

TEMPERATURE — The surface to be painted should be approximately the same temperature as the surrounding air. Applying warm paint to a cold surface, or vice versa, will completely upset the paint characteristics.

THICKNESS — Spray with smooth strokes. In general, the thicker the coat of paint, the longer the drying time. Apply several thin coats about 30 seconds apart. The paint should remain wet long enough to flow out and no longer; heavier coats will only produce sags or wrinkles. Spray a light (fog) coat, followed by heavier color coats.

DISTANCE — The ideal spraying distance is 8"-12" from the gun or can to the surface. Shorter distances will produce ripples, while greater distances will result in orange peel, dry film and poor color match and loss of material due to overspray.

OVERLAPPING — The gun or can should be kept at right angles to the surface at all times. Work to a wet edge at an even speed, using a 50% overlap and direct the center of the spray at the lower or nearest edge of the previous stroke.

RUBBING OUT (BLENDING) FRESH PAINT — Let the paint dry thoroughly. Runs or imperfections can be sanded out, primed and repainted.

Don't be in too big a hurry to remove the masking. This only produces paint ridges. When the finish has dried for at least a week, apply a small amount of fine grade rubbing compound with a clean, wet cloth. Use lots of water and blend the new paint with the surrounding area.

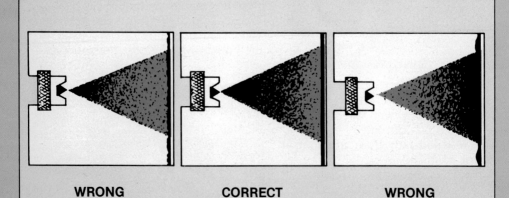

WRONG	CORRECT	WRONG
Thin coat. Stroke too fast, not enough overlap, gun too far away.	*Medium coat. Proper distance, good stroke, proper overlap.*	*Heavy coat. Stroke too slow, too much overlap, gun too close.*

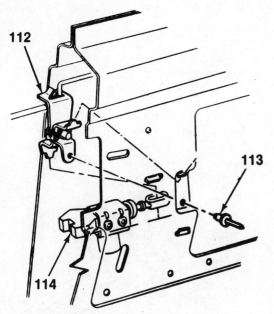

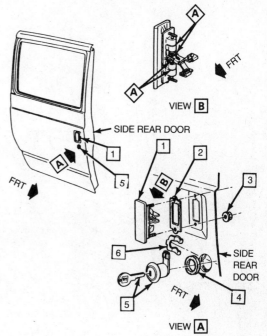

112. Lever assembly
113. Rivet
114. Power lock motor

Exploded view of the power door lock motor assembly—sliding door

1. Handle
2. Gasket
3. Nut
4. Gasket
5. Lock cylinder
5. Retainer

Rear door lock cylinder removal

3. Disconnect the electrical wiring harness from the power door lock motor.

4. Using a $\frac{3}{16}$″ (5mm) drill bit, drill the out the power door lock motor-to-door rivets, then remove the motor from the door.

5. To install, use ¼″ by ½″ (6mm by 13mm) pop rivets and a pop rivet gun, then install the inside handle to the door. To complete the installation, reverse the removal procedures.

Rear Door w/Manual Locks

OUTSIDE HANDLE AND LOCK CYLINDER

1. Refer to the "Door Panel, Removal and Installation" procedures in this section and remove the door panel.

2. Remove the control rod from the outside handle by prying the clip anchor out of the hole and pushing the clip away from the lever. Then pull the rod and the clip away from the lever.

3. Remove the outside handle-to-lock nuts and remove the rod and the handle from the door.

4. Remove the license plate housing bolts, and the license plate housing.

5. Remove the door lock shield.

6. Remove the lock control rod from the lock cylinder by prying the clip anchor out of the hole and pushing the clip away from the lever. Then pull the rod and the clip away from the lever.

7. Remove the lock cylinder retainer, and the lock cylinder from the door.

8. To install, reverse the removal procedures.

LOCK ASSEMBLY

1. Refer to the "Door Panel, Removal and Installation" procedures in this section and remove the door panel.

2. Remove the outside handle-to-lock assembly rod.

3. Remove the lock cylinder-to-lock assembly rod.

4. Remove the inside handle-to-lock assembly rod.

5. Remove the inside lock-to-lock assembly rod.

6. Remove the lock assembly-to-door screws and the lock assembly from door.

UPPER AND LOWER LATCH REPLACEMENT

1. Refer to the "Door Panel, Removal and Installation" procedures in this section and remove the door panel.

2. Remove the control rods from the remote control by prying the clip anchor out of the hole and pushing the clip away from the lever. Then pull the rod and the clip away from the lever.

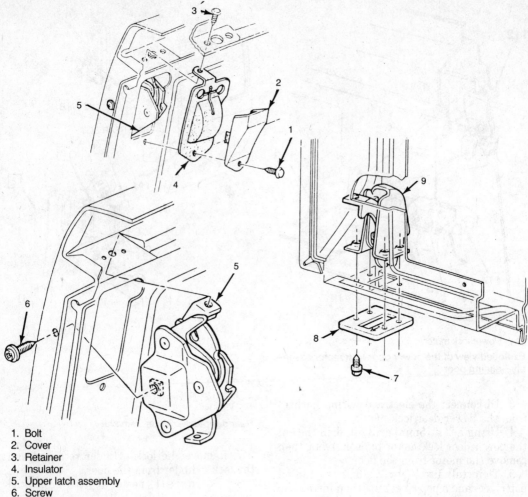

1. Bolt
2. Cover
3. Retainer
4. Insulator
5. Upper latch assembly
6. Screw
7. Bolt
8. Reinforcement
9. Lower latch assembly

Upper and lower door latches

3. Remove the upper latch screws.

4. Remove the upper latch insulator cover.

5. Pry the plastic nails holding the weatherstrip away from the door and remove the weatherstrip from around the latch area.

6. Remove the door latch insulator.

7. Remove the upper latch and rod from the door.

8. Remove the lower latch screws.

9. Remove the lower latch reinforcement plate.

10. Remove the lower latch and rod from the door.

Rear Door w/Power

REMOTE LOCK LEVER

1. Refer to the "Door Panel, Removal and Installation" procedures in this section and remove the door panel.

2. Disconnect the negative battery cable and remove the actuator to lever rod.

3. Using a $^3/_{16}$" (5mm) drill bit, drill out the the head of the actuator-to-door rivets.

4. Remove the actuator from the door.

5. To install, use ¼" diameter bolt (½" long) with a spring washer and nut to attach the actuator to the door. To complete the installation, reverse the removal procedures.

POWER LOCK ACTUATOR

1. Refer to the "Door Panel, Removal and Installation" procedures in this section and remove the door panel.

2. Remove the power door lock actuator to remove the lever rod.

3. Disconnect the electrical connector from the power door lock actuator.

4. Remove the actuator-to-door bolts and the actuator from the door.

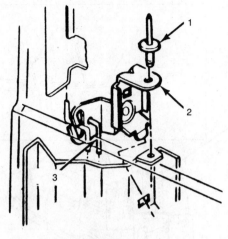

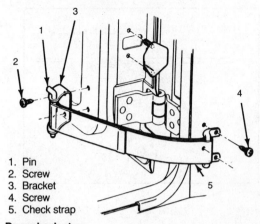

1. Pin
2. Screw
3. Bracket
4. Screw
5. Check strap

Door check strap

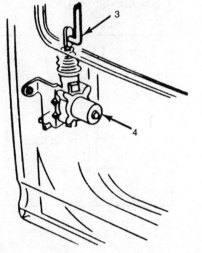

1. Rivet
2. Lever
3. Lock rod
4. Power lock actuator

Lock actuator components

5. To install, reverse the removal procedures.

Hood

REMOVAL AND INSTALLATION

1. Mark the area around the hinges to make installation easier.
2. Support the hood and remove the hinge to hood frame bolts.
3. Remove the hood from the truck.
4. Installation is the reverse of the removal procedure.

Rear Doors

REMOVAL AND INSTALLATION

1. Disconnect the negative battery cable. Open the door, remove the door trim panel and

disconnect the electrical wiring harness (if equipped).

2. Remove the check strap. Drive the hinge pins from the hinges while an assistant holds the door in place.
3. Remove the door from the vehicle.
4. Installation is the reverse of the removal procedure.

ADJUSTMENT

Van door hinges are welded in place, and adjustment of this system is not recommended. However with service bolt on hinges service is possible.

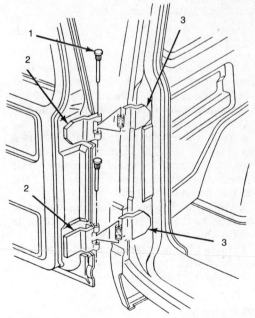

1. Hinge pin
2. Door side hinge half
3. Body side hinge half

Door hinge system

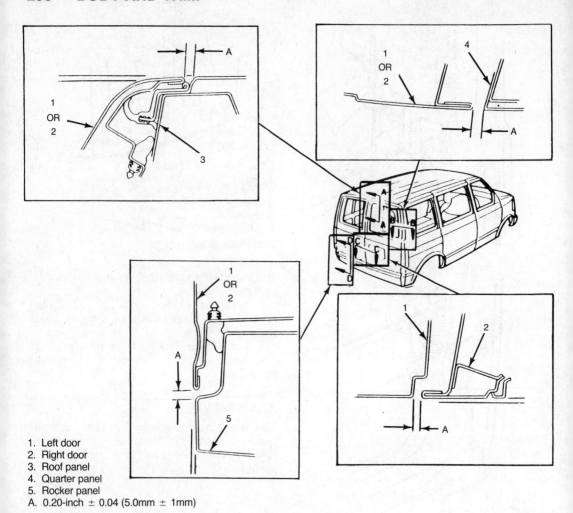

1. Left door
2. Right door
3. Roof panel
4. Quarter panel
5. Rocker panel
A. 0.20-inch ± 0.04 (5.0mm ± 1mm)

Door adjustment gaps

1. Loosen the door striker, the left door first then the right. Adjust the left door height so that there is a gap of 0.196″ ± 0.039″ (5.0mm ± 1.0mm) between the door frame at the top, bottom and side of the door.

2. Adjust the right door so that there is a gap of 0.196″ ± 0.039″ (5.0mm ± 1.0mm) between the doors. This same gap should exist between the right door and the frame at the top, bottom and side of the door.

3. Adjust both doors so that the surface of the doors to the door frame and each other is flush within 0.039″ (± 1.0mm).

4. Adjust the door striker to hold the right door flush with the left door within 0.039″ (± 1.0mm).

Windshield

NOTE: *Bonded windshields require special tools and special removal procedures to be removed without being broken. For this reason* *we recommend that you refer all removal and installation to a qualified technician.*

CAUTION: *Always wear heavy gloves when handling glass to reduce the risk of injury.*

When replacing a cracked windshield, it is important that the cause of the crack be determined and the condition corrected, before a new glass is installed.

The cause of the crack may be an obstruction or a high spot somewhere around the flange of the opening; cracking may not occur until pressure from the high spot or obstruction becomes particularly high due to winds, extremes of temperature, or rough terrain.

Suggestions of what to look for are described later in this section under inspection.

REMOVAL

When a windshield is broken, the glass may have already have fallen or been removed from the weatherstrip. Often, however, it is necessary to remove a cracked or otherwise imperfect windshield that is still intact. In this case, it is a good practise to crisscross the glass with strips of masking tape before removing the it; this will help hold the glass together and minimize the risk of injury.

If a crack extends to the edge of the glass, mark the point where the crack meets the weather strip. (Use a piece of chalk and mark the point on the cab, next to the weatherstrip.) Later, when examining the flange of the opening for a cause of the crack start at the point marked.

The higher the temperature of the work area, the more pliable the weather strip will be. The more pliable the weather strip, the more easily the windshield can be removed.

Before removing the glass, cover the instrument panel, and the surrounding sheet metal with protective covering and remove the wiper arms.

There are two methods of windshield removal, depending on the method of windshield replacement chosen. When using the short method of installation, it is important to cut the glass from the urethane adhesive as close to the glass as possible. This is due to the fact that the urethane adhesive will be used to provide a base for the replacement windshield.

When using the extended method of windshield replacement, all the urethane adhesive must be removed from the pinchweld flange so, the process of cutting the window from the adhesive is less critical.

Special tool J-24402-A, Glass Sealant Re-

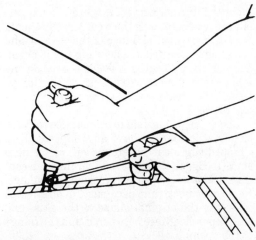

Cutting the window from the frame

mover Knife, or its equivalent is required to perform this procedure. To remove the windshield:

1. Place the protective covering around the area where the glass will be removed.

2. Remove the windshield wiper arms, and the interior garnish moldings.

3. Remove the exterior reveal moldings and the support support molding from the urethane adhesive by prying one end of the molding from the adhesive. Pull the free end of the molding away from the windshield or the pinchweld flange until the molding is completely free of the windshield.

4. Using J-24402-A cut the windshield from the urethane adhesive. If the short method of glass replacement is to be used, keep the knife as close to the glass as possible in order to leave a base for the replacement glass.

5. With the help of an assistant, remove the glass.

6. If the original glass is to be reinstalled, place it on a protected bench or a holding or holding fixture. Remove any remaining adhesive with a razor blade or a sharp scraper. Any remaining traces of adhesive material can be removed with denatured alcohol or lacqure thinner.

NOTE: *When cleaning windshield glass, avoid contacting the edge of the plastic laminate material (on the edge of the glass) with volatile cleaner. Contact may cause discoloration and deterioration of the plastic laminate. Do not use a petroleum based solvent such as gasoline or kerosene. The presence of oil will prevent the adhesion of new material.*

INSPECTION

An inspection of the windshield opening, the weather strip, and the glass may reveal the cause of a broken windshield. This can help

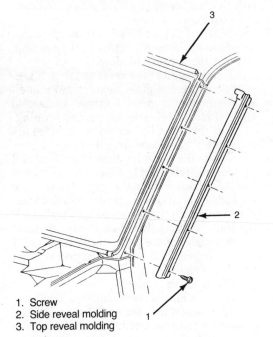

1. Screw
2. Side reveal molding
3. Top reveal molding

Windshield reveal molding

prevent future breakage. If there is no apparent cause of breakage, the weatherstrip should be removed from the flange of the opening and the flange inspected. Look for high weld or solder spots, hardened spot welds sealer, or any other obstruction or irregularity in the flange. Check the weatherstrip for irregularities or obstructions in it.

Check the windshield to be installed to make sure that it does not have any chipped edges. Chipped edges can be ground off, restoring a smooth edge to the glass, and minimizing concentrations of pressure that cause breakage. Remove no more than necessary, in an effort to maintain the original shape of the glass and the proper clearance between it and the flange of the opening.

INSTALLATION METHODS

There are two methods used for windshield replacement. The short method described previously in the removal procedure is used when the urethane adhesive can be used as a base for the new glass. This method would be used in the case of a cracked glass, if, no other service needs to be done to the windshield frame such as sheet metal or repainting work.

The extended method should be used when work must be done to the windshield frame such as straightening or repairing sheet metal or repainting the windshield frame. In this method all of the urethane adhesive must be removed from the pinchweld flange.

INSTALLATION

To replace a urethane adhered windshield, GM adhesive service kit No. 9636067 contains some of the materials needed, and must be used to insure the original integrity of the windshield design. Materials in this kit include:

1. One tube of adhesive material.
2. One dispensing nozzle.
3. Steel music wire.
4. Rubber cleaner.
5. Rubber Primer.
6. Pinchweld primer.
7. Blackout primer.
8. Filler strip (for use on windshield installations for vehicles equipped with embedded windshield antenna).
9. Primer applicators.
Other materials are required for windshield installation which are not included in the service kit. These include:
1. GM rubber lubricant No. 1051717.
2. Alcohol for cleaning the edge of the glass.
3. Adhesive dispensing gun J-24811 or its equivalent.

4. A commercial type razor knife.
5. Two rubber support spacers.

Extended Method

1. Clean all metal surrounding the windshield opening with a clean alcohol dampened cloth. Allow the alcohol to air dry.
2. Apply the pinchweld primer found in the service kit to the pinchweld area. Do not let any of the primer touch any of the exposed paint because damage to the finish may occur. Allow thirty minutes for the primer to dry.
3. Follow the steps listed under Short Method for the remainder of the procedure.

Short Method

1. Install the support molding onto the pinchweld flange from inside the vehicle. The joint of the molding should be located at the bottom center of the moulding.
2. Thoroughly clean the edge of the glass to which the adhesive material will be applied with a clean alcohol dampened cloth. Allow the alcohol to dry.
3. Apply the clear glass primer in the kit to the inner edge of the windshield from the edge of the glass inward 0.04" (1.0mm). Apply the primer around the entire perimeter of the glass. Allow the primer to cure for thirty minutes.
4. Apply the blackout primer to the glass in the same area as the clear primer. Allow the blackout primer to dry to the touch.
5. Place two rubber blocks onto the base of the pinchweld flange. Place the blocks in line with the last screw on either side of the cowl grille cover.
6. With the aid of a helper, lift the glass into the opening. Center the glass in the opening, on top of the support molding.
7. Check the fit of the revel molding. If necessary remove the glass and cut away additional urethane to give the proper windshield height. Place the glass in the window opening.
8. Cut the tip of the adhesive cartridge approximately $^3/_{16}$" (5mm) from the end of the tip.
9. Apply the adhesive first in and around the spacer blocks. Apply a smooth continuous bead of adhesive into the gap between the glass edge and the sheet metal. Use a flat bladed tool to paddle the material into position if necessary. Be sure that the adhesive contacts the entire edge of the glass, and extends to fill the gap between the glass and the primer sheet metal (extended method) or solidified urethane base (short method).
10. Spray a mist of water onto the urethane. Water will assist in the curing process. Dry the area where the reveal molding will contact the body and glass.

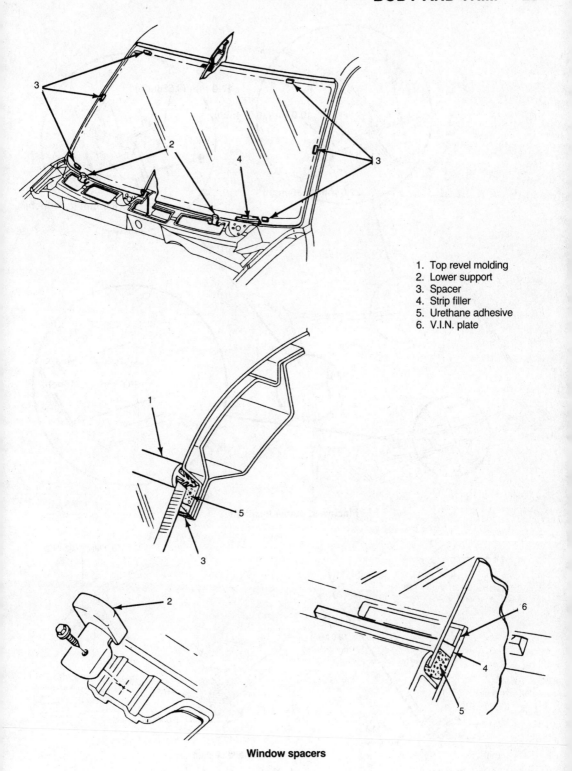

1. Top revel molding
2. Lower support
3. Spacer
4. Strip filler
5. Urethane adhesive
6. V.I.N. plate

Window spacers

11. Install new reveal moldings. Remove the protective tape covering the butyl adhesive on the underside of the molding. Push the molding caps onto each end of one of the reveal moldings. Press the lip of the molding into the urethane adhesive while holding it against the edge of the windshield. Take care to seat the molding in the corners. The lip must fully con-

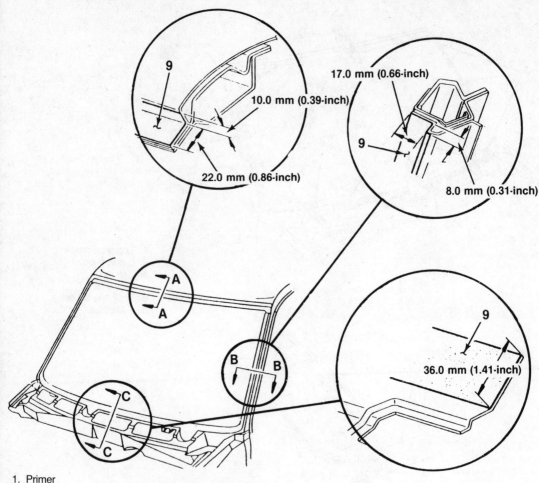

1. Primer

Pinchweld primer locations

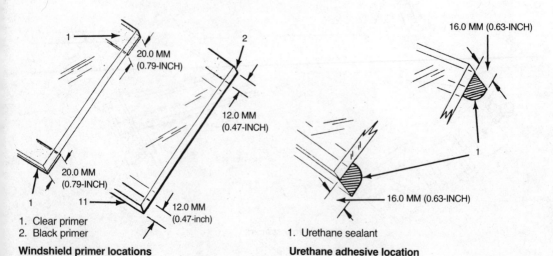

1. Clear primer
2. Black primer

Windshield primer locations

1. Urethane sealant

Urethane adhesive location

tact the adhesive and the gap must be entirely covered by the crown of the molding. Slide the molding caps onto the adjacent moldings. Use tape to hold the molding in position until the adhesive cures.

12. Install the wiper arms and the interior garnish moldings.
NOTE: *The vehicle should not be driven and should remain at room temperature for six hours to allow the adhesive to cure.*

1. Screw
2. Retainer
3. Bushing
4. Nut
5. Window assembly

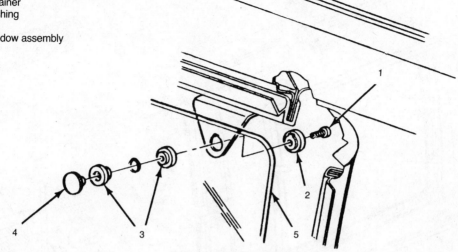

Swing out window hinge

Rear Window Glass

REMOVAL AND INSTALLATION

Swing Out Window

Special Tool J-34946 Window Roll Pin Remover is required to perform this procedure.

1. Remove the latch to window screws.
2. While an assistant holds the glass in place, remove the hinge to glass screws, retainers, bushings and nuts.
3. Remove the glass from the door.
4. Remove the window roll pin usig tool J-34964.

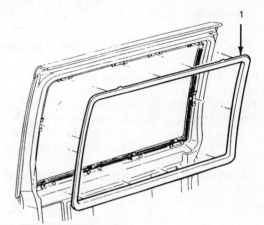

1. Window garnish modling

Window garnish molding

5. Remove the window latch.
6. Remove the latch retainer screws.
7. Remove the bearing, bushings, and nut.
8. Installation is the reverse of the removal procedure.

Stationary Window

Special tool J-28628 Adnhesive Push/Pull Knife is required to perform this procedure.

1. Remove the door garnish molding.
2. Remove the window molding.
3. Remove the window retainers.
4. Remove the window assembly from the vehicle using tool J-28628. Cut through the urethane adhesive from the inside of the vehicle.
5. Remove all the urethane from the pinchweld.
6. Clean the pinchweld flange and the new

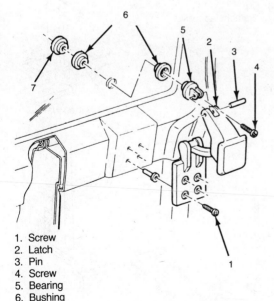

1. Screw
2. Latch
3. Pin
4. Screw
5. Bearing
6. Bushing
7. Nut

Swing out window latch

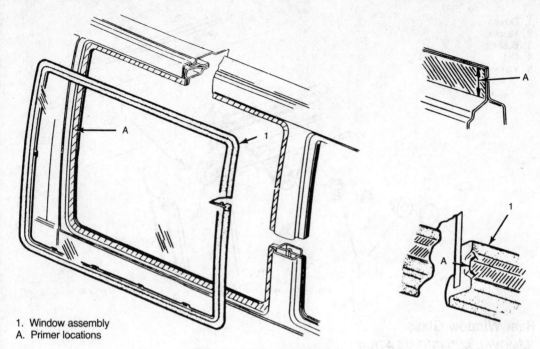

1. Window assembly
A. Primer locations

Primer locations, fixed windows

window assembly with solvent and allow it to air dry.

7. Apply urethane adhesive primer to the pinchweld flange and the window assembly molding in the area shown in the figure. Allow the primer to dry at least 30 minutes before applying the adhesive.

8. Apply a triangle bead of urethane adhesive $\frac{3}{8}''$ (10mm) high into the trough of the window assembly molding.

9. Install the window assembly in the pinchweld flange.

10. Install the window assembly retainers.

11. Apply a light mist of water to the window to check for leaks and to enhance the cure of the urethane.

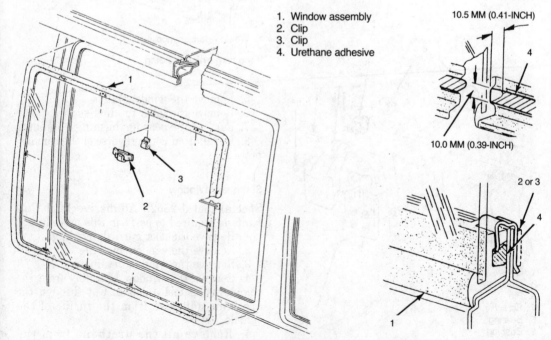

1. Window assembly
2. Clip
3. Clip
4. Urethane adhesive

10.5 MM (0.41-INCH)

10.0 MM (0.39-INCH)

2 or 3

Fixed window components

12. Install the window molding.
13. Install the door garnish molding.
14. Allow the urethane adhesive six hours to cure before moving the vehicle.

INTERIOR

Door Panels

Special tool J-9886-01, Door Handle Clip Remover, is required to perform the following procedure.

REMOVAL AND INSTALLATION

1. Remove the window regulator handle using tool J-9886-01.
2. Remove the window regulator handle bezel.
3. Remove the door lock assembly handle using J-9886-01.
4. Remove the control assembly handle bezel.
5. Remove the assist handle.
6. Remove the arm rest.
7. Remove the door trim outer panel screws and pull the panel away from the retainer.
8. Remove the door trim inner panel screws and remove the trim inner panel.
9. Installation is the reverse of the removal.

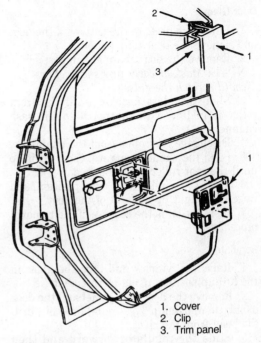

1. Cover
2. Clip
3. Trim panel

Assist handle cover

Door Glass and Regulator
REMOVAL AND INSTALLATION

CAUTION: *Always wear heavy gloves when handling glass to minimize the risk of injury.*

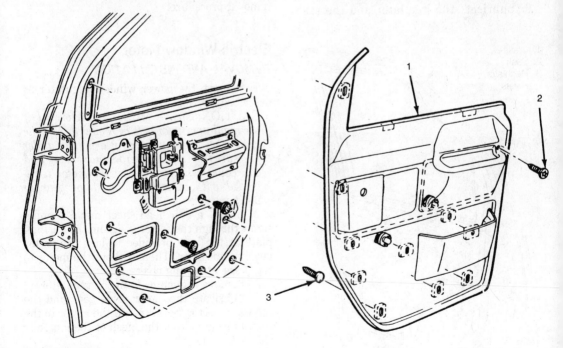

1. Trim panel
2. Screw
3. Retainer

Front door trim panel

Door Glass

1. Lower the glass to the bottom of the door and remove the door trim panel.
2. Remove the door channel run assembly. NOTE: *Mask or cover any sharp edges that could scratch the glass.*
3. Slide the glass forward until the front roller is in line with the notch in the sash channel.
4. Disengage the roller from the channel.
5. Push the window forward, then tilt it up until the rear roller is disengaged.
6. Place the window in a level position, and raise it straight up and out of the door.
7. Installation is the reverse of the removal procedure.

Regulator

1. Raise the window and tape the glass in the full up position using cloth body tape.
2. Remove the door trim panel and the door panel, then, using a $\frac{3}{16}$" (5mm) drill bit, drill the head from the rivet.
3. Slide the regulator forward and then rearward to disengage the rear roller from the sash channel. Then disengage the lower roller from the regulator rail.
4. Disengage the forward roller from the sash channel at the notch in the sash channel.
5. Collapse the regulator and remove it through the access hole in the door.
6. Lubricate the regulator and the sash channel and regulator rails with Lubriplate® or its equivalent.
7. Install the regulator in the reverse of the removal procedure.

Power Window Regulator

1. Remove the negative battery cable.
2. Remove the door trim panel.
3. Remove the armrest bracket and water deflector.
4. Raise the window and tape the glass in the full up position using cloth body tape.
5. Remove the wiring harness from the regulator motor.
6. Remove the regulator to door rivets, using a $\frac{3}{16}$" (5mm) drill bit to drill the heads from the rivets.
7. Slide the regulator forward and then rearward to disengage the rear roller from the sash channel. Then disengage the lower roller from the regulator rail.
8. Disengage the forward roller from the sash channel at the notch in the sash channel.
9. Collapse the regulator and remove it through the access hole in the door.
10. Lubricate the regulator and the sash channel and regulator rails with Lubriplate® or its equivalent.
11. Install the regulator in the reverse of the removal procedure.

Electric Window Motor
REMOVAL AND INSTALLATION

1. Remove the power window regulator as described above.
CAUTION: *Step 2 MUST be performed if the regulator motor is to be removed from the regulator. The regulator lift arms are under pressure from the counterbalance spring and can cause serious injury if the motor is removed without locking the sector gear in position.*
2. Install a pan head sheet metal tapping screw through the sector gear and the backing plate at the hole provided to lock the sector gear into position. Then drill out the motor to regulator attaching rivets.
3. Remove the motor from the regulator.
4. Lubricate the motor drive gear and the regulator sector teeth. Install the motor to the regulator and check the mesh of the motor to the regulator.
5. Install rivets to the motor and the regulator.
6. Remove the sheet metal tapping screw.
7. Install the power window regulator.

1. Glass
2. Sash
3. Regulator
4. Rivets

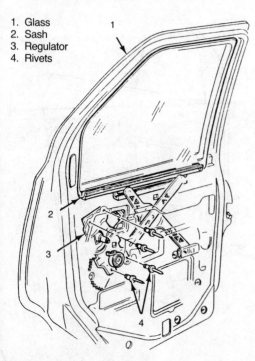

Window regulator components

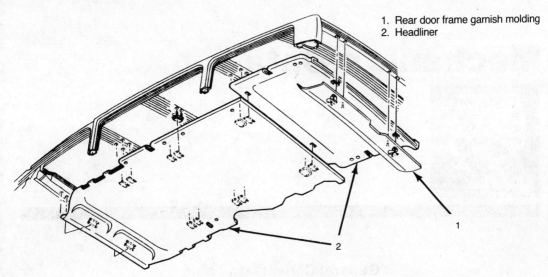

1. Rear door frame garnish molding
2. Headliner

Headliner attachment

Headliner

REMOVAL AND INSTALLATION

1. Remove the upper window trim that supports the headliner.

2. Remove the sunvisors and the door opening garnish moldings. Pull the headliner bow from the retainer (if equipped).

3. Remove the retainer bolts and the retainers.

4. Shift the headliner from side to side to disengage the headliner from the clips.

5. Remove the headliner from the vehicle.

6. Install in the reverse order of the removal procedure.

Mechanic's Data

General Conversion Table

Multiply By	To Convert	To	
		LENGTH	
2.54	Inches	Centimeters	.3937
25.4	Inches	Millimeters	.03937
30.48	Feet	Centimeters	.0328
.304	Feet	Meters	3.28
.914	Yards	Meters	1.094
1.609	Miles	Kilometers	.621
		VOLUME	
.473	Pints	Liters	2.11
.946	Quarts	Liters	1.06
3.785	Gallons	Liters	.264
.016	Cubic inches	Liters	61.02
16.39	Cubic inches	Cubic cms.	.061
28.3	Cubic feet	Liters	.0353
		MASS (Weight)	
28.35	Ounces	Grams	.035
.4536	Pounds	Kilograms	2.20
—	To obtain	From	Multiply by

Multiply By	To Convert	To	
		AREA	
.645	Square inches	Square cms.	.155
.836	Square yds.	Square meters	1.196
		FORCE	
4.448	Pounds	Newtons	.225
.138	Ft./lbs.	Kilogram/meters	7.23
1.36	Ft./lbs.	Newton-meters	.737
.112	In./lbs.	Newton-meters	8.844
		PRESSURE	
.068	Psi	Atmospheres	14.7
6:89	Psi	Kilopascals	.145
		OTHER	
1.104	Horsepower (DIN)	Horsepower (SAE)	.9861
.746	Horsepower (SAE)	Kilowatts (KW)	1.34
1.60	Mph	Km/h	.625
.425	Mpg	Km/1	2.35
—	To obtain	From	Multiply by

Tap Drill Sizes

National Coarse or U.S.S.

Screw & Tap Size	Threads Per Inch	Use Drill Number
No. 5	40	39
No. 6	32	36
No. 8	32	29
No. 10	24	25
No. 12	24	17
1/4	20	8
5/16	18	F
3/8	16	5/16
7/16	14	U
1/2	13	27/64
9/16	12	31/64
5/8	11	17/32
3/4	10	21/32
7/8	9	49/64

National Coarse or U.S.S.

Screw & Tap Size	Threads Per Inch	Use Drill Number
1	8	7/8
1 1/8	7	63/64
1 1/4	7	1 7/64
1 1/2	6	1 11/32

National Fine or S.A.E.

Screw & Tap Size	Threads Per Inch	Use Drill Number
No. 5	44	37
No. 6	40	33
No. 8	36	29
No. 10	32	21

National Fine or S.A.E.

Screw & Tap Size	Threads Per Inch	Use Drill Number
No. 12	28	15
1/4	28	3
6/16	24	1
3/8	24	Q
7/16	20	W
1/2	20	29/64
9/16	18	33/64
5/8	18	37/64
3/4	16	11/16
7/8	14	13/16
1 1/8	12	1 3/64
1 1/4	12	1 11/64
1 1/2	12	1 27/64

Drill Sizes In Decimal Equivalents

Inch	Decimal	Wire	mm	Inch	Decimal	Wire	mm	Inch	Decimal	Wire & Letter	mm	Inch	Decimal	Letter	mm	Inch	Decimal	mm
1/64	.0156		.39		.0730	49			.1614		4.1		.2717		6.9		.4331	11.0
	.0157		.4		.0748		1.9		.1654		4.2		.2720	I		7/16	.4375	11.11
	.0160	78			.0760	48			.1660	19			.2756		7.0		.4528	11.5
	.0165		.42		.0768		1.95		.1673		4.25		.2770	J		29/64	.4531	11.51
	.0173		.44	5/64	.0781		1.98		.1693		4.3		.2795		7.1	15/32	.4688	11.90
	.0177		.45		.0785	47			.1695	18			.2810	K			.4724	12.0
	.0180	77			.0787		2.0	11/64	.1719		4.36	9/32	.2812		7.14	31/64	.4844	12.30
	.0181		.46		.0807		2.05		.1730	17			.2835		7.2		.4921	12.5
	.0189		.48		.0810	46			.1732		4.4		.2854		7.25	1/2	.5000	12.70
	.0197		.5		.0820	45			.1770	16			.2874		7.3		.5118	13.0
	.0200	76			.0827		2.1		.1772		4.5		.2900	L		33/64	.5156	13.09
	.0210	75			.0846		2.15		.1800	15			.2913		7.4	17/32	.5312	13.49
	.0217		.55		.0860	44			.1811		4.6		.2950	M			.5315	13.5
	.0225	74			.0866		2.2		.1820	14			.2953		7.5	35/64	.5469	13.89
	.0236		.6		.0886		2.25		.1850	13		19/64	.2969		7.54		.5512	14.0
	.0240	73			.0890	43			.1850		4.7		.2992		7.6	9/16	.5625	14.28
	.0250	72			.0906		2.3		.1870		4.75		.3020	N			.5709	14.5
	.0256		.65		.0925		2.35	3/16	.1875		4.76		.3031		7.7	37/64	.5781	14.68
	.0260	71			.0935	42			.1890		4.8		.3051		7.75		.5906	15.0
	.0276		.7	3/32	.0938		2.38		.1890	12			.3071		7.8	19/32	.5938	15.08
	.0280	70			.0945		2.4		.1910	11			.3110		7.9	39/64	.6094	15.47
	.0292	69			.0960	41			.1929		4.9	5/16	.3125		7.93		.6102	15.5
	.0295		.75		.0965		2.45		.1935	10			.3150		8.0	5/8	.6250	15.87
	.0310	68			.0980	40			.1960	9			.3160	O			.6299	16.0
1/32	.0312		.79		.0981		2.5		.1969		5.0		.3189		8.1	41/64	.6406	16.27
	.0315		.8		.0995	39			.1990	8			.3228		8.2		.6496	16.5
	.0320	67			.1015	38			.2008		5.1		.3230	P		21/32	.6562	16.66
	.0330	66			.1024		2.6		.2010	7			.3248		8.25		.6693	17.0
	.0335		.85		.1040	37		13/64	.2031		5.16		.3268		8.3	43/64	.6719	17.06
	.0350	65			.1063		2.7		.2040	6		21/64	.3281		8.33	11/16	.6875	17.46
	.0354		.9		.1065	36			.2047		5.2		.3307		8.4		.6890	17.5
	.0360	64			.1083		2.75		.2055	5			.3320	Q		45/64	.7031	17.85
	.0370	63		7/64	.1094		2.77		.2067		5.25		.3346		8.5		.7087	18.0
	.0374		.95		.1100	35			.2087		5.3		.3386		8.6	23/32	.7188	18.25
	.0380	62			.1102		2.8		.2090	4			.3390	R			.7283	18.5
	.0390	61			.1110	34			.2126		5.4		.3425		8.7	47/64	.7344	18.65
	.0394		1.0		.1130	33			.2130	3		11/32	.3438		8.73		.7480	19.0
	.0400	60			.1142		2.9		.2165		5.5		.3445		8.75	3/4	.7500	19.05
	.0410	59			.1160	32		7/32	.2188		5.55		.3465		8.8	49/64	.7656	19.44
	.0413		1.05		.1181		3.0		.2205		5.6		.3480	S			.7677	19.5
	.0420	58			.1200	31			.2210	2			.3504		8.9	25/32	.7812	19.84
	.0430	57			.1220		3.1		.2244		5.7		.3543		9.0		.7874	20.0
	.0433		1.1	1/8	.1250		3.17		.2264		5.75		.3580	T		51/64	.7969	20.24
	.0453		1.15		.1260		3.2		.2280	1			.3583		9.1		.8071	20.5
	.0465	56			.1280		3.25		.2283		5.8	23/64	.3594		9.12	13/16	.8125	20.63
3/64	.0469		1.19		.1285	30			.2323		5.9		.3622		9.2		.8268	21.0
	.0472		1.2		.1299		3.3		.2340	A			.3642		9.25	53/64	.8281	21.03
	.0492		1.25		.1339		3.4	15/64	.2344		5.95		.3661		9.3	27/32	.8438	21.43
	.0512		1.3		.1360	29			.2362		6.0		.3680	U			.8465	21.5
	.0520	55			.1378		3.5		.2380	B			.3701		9.4	55/64	.8594	21.82
	.0531		1.35		.1405	28			.2402		6.1		.3740		9.5		.8661	22.0
	.0550	54		9/64	.1406		3.57		.2420	C		3/8	.3750		9.52	7/8	.8750	22.22
	.0551		1.4		.1417		3.6		.2441		6.2		.3770	V			.8858	22.5
	.0571		1.45		.1440	27			.2460	D			.3780		9.6	57/64	.8906	22.62
	.0591		1.5		.1457		3.7		.2461		6.25		.3819		9.7		.9055	23.0
	.0595	53			.1470	26			.2480		6.3		.3839		9.75	29/32	.9062	23.01
	.0610		1.55		.1476		3.75	1/4	.2500	E	6.35		.3858		9.8	59/64	.9219	23.41
1/16	.0625		1.59		.1495	25			.2520		6.		.3860	W			.9252	23.5
	.0630		1.6		.1496		3.8		.2559		6.5		.3898		9.9	15/16	.9375	23.81
	.0635	52			.1520	24			.2570	F		25/64	.3906		9.92		.9449	24.0
	.0650		1.65		.1535		3.9		.2598		6.6		.3937		10.0	61/64	.9531	24.2
	.0669		1.7		.1540	23			.2610	G			.3970	X			.9646	24.5
	.0670	51		5/32	.1562		3.96		.2638		6.7		.4040	Y		31/32	.9688	24.6
	.0689		1.75		.1570	22		17/64	.2656		6.74	13/32	.4062		10.31		.9843	25.0
	.0700	50			.1575		4.0		.2657		6.75		.4130	Z		63/64	.9844	25.0
	.0709		1.8		.1590	21			.2660	H			.4134		10.5	1	1.0000	25.4
	.0728		1.85		.1610	20			.2677		6.8	27/64	.4219		10.71			

GLOSSARY OF TERMS

AIR/FUEL RATIO: The ratio of air to gasoline by weight in the fuel mixture drawn into the engine.

AIR INJECTION: One method of reducing harmful exhaust emissions by injecting air into each of the exhaust ports of an engine. The fresh air entering the hot exhaust manifold causes any remaining fuel to be burned before it can exit the tailpipe.

ALTERNATOR: A device used for converting mechanical energy into electrical energy.

AMMETER: An instrument, calibrated in amperes, used to measure the flow of an electrical current in a circuit. Ammeters are always connected in series with the circuit being tested.

AMPERE: The rate of flow of electrical current present when one volt of electrical pressure is applied against one ohm of electrical resistance.

ANALOG COMPUTER: Any microprocessor that uses similar (analogous) electrical signals to make its calculations.

ARMATURE: A laminated, soft iron core wrapped by a wire that converts electrical energy to mechanical energy as in a motor or relay. When rotated in a magnetic field, it changes mechanical energy into electrical energy as in a generator.

ATMOSPHERIC PRESSURE: The pressure on the Earth's surface caused by the weight of the air in the atmosphere. At sea level, this pressure is 14.7 psi at 32°F (101 kPa at 0°C).

ATOMIZATION: The breaking down of a liquid into a fine mist that can be suspended in air.

AXIAL PLAY: Movement parallel to a shaft or bearing bore.

BACKFIRE: The sudden combustion of gases in the intake or exhaust system that results in a loud explosion.

BACKLASH: The clearance or play between two parts, such as meshed gears.

BACKPRESSURE: Restrictions in the exhaust system that slow the exit of exhaust gases from the combustion chamber.

BAKELITE: A heat resistant, plastic insulator material commonly used in printed circuit boards and transistorized components.

BALL BEARING: A bearing made up of hardened inner and outer races between which hardened steel ball roll.

BALLAST RESISTOR: A resistor in the primary ignition circuit that lowers voltage after the engine is started to reduce wear on ignition components.

BEARING: A friction reducing, supportive device usually located between a stationary part and a moving part.

BIMETAL TEMPERATURE SENSOR: Any sensor or switch made of two dissimilar types of metal that bend when heated or cooled due to the different expansion rates of the alloys. These types of sensors usually function as an on/off switch.

BLOWBY: Combustion gases, composed of water vapor and unburned fuel, that leak past the piston rings into the crankcase during normal engine operation. These gases are removed by the PCV system to prevent the build-up of harmful acids in the crankcase.

BRAKE PAD: A brake shoe and lining assembly used with disc brakes.

BRAKE SHOE: The backing for the brake lining. The term is, however, usually applied to the assembly of the brake backing and lining.

BUSHING: A liner, usually removable, for a bearing; an anti-friction liner used in place of a bearing.

BYPASS: System used to bypass ballast resistor during engine cranking to increase voltage supplied to the coil.

CALIPER: A hydraulically activated device in a disc brake system, which is mounted straddling the brake rotor (disc). The caliper contains at least one piston and two brake pads. Hydraulic pressure on the piston(s) forces the pads against the rotor.

CAMSHAFT: A shaft in the engine on which are the lobes (cams) which operate the valves. The camshaft is driven by the crankshaft, via a belt, chain or gears, at one half the crankshaft speed.

CAPACITOR: A device which stores an electrical charge.

CARBON MONOXIDE (CO): a colorless, odorless gas given off as a normal byproduct of combustion. It is poisonous and extremely dangerous in confined areas, building up slowly to toxic levels without warning if adequate ventilation is not available.

CARBURETOR: A device, usually mounted on the intake manifold of an engine, which mixes the air and fuel in the proper proportion to allow even combustion.

CATALYTIC CONVERTER: A device installed in the exhaust system, like a muffler, that converts harmful byproducts of combustion into carbon dioxide and water vapor by means of a heat-producing chemical reaction.

CENTRIFUGAL ADVANCE: A mechanical method of advancing the spark timing by using flyweights in the distributor that react to centrifugal force generated by the distributor shaft rotation.

CHECK VALVE: Any one-way valve installed to permit the flow of air, fuel or vacuum in one direction only.

CHOKE: A device, usually a moveable valve, placed in the intake path of a carburetor to restrict the flow of air.

CIRCUIT: Any unbroken path through which an electrical current can flow. Also used to describe fuel flow in some instances.

CIRCUIT BREAKER: A switch which protects an electrical circuit from overload by opening the circuit when the current flow exceeds a predetermined level. Some circuit breakers must be reset manually, while other reset automatically

COIL (IGNITION): A transformer in the ignition circuit which steps of the voltage provided to the spark plugs.

COMBINATION MANIFOLD: An assembly which includes both the intake and exhaust manifolds in one casting.

COMBINATION VALVE: A device used in some fuel systems that routes fuel vapors to a charcoal storage canister instead of venting them into the atmosphere. The valve relieves fuel tank pressure and allows fresh air into the tank as fuel level drops to prevent a vapor lock situation.

COMPRESSION RATIO: The comparison of the total volume of the cylinder and combustion chamber with the piston at BDC and the piston at TDC.

CONDENSER: 1. An electrical device which acts to store an electrical charge, preventing voltage surges.
2. A radiator-like device in the air conditioning system in which refrigerant gas condenses into a liquid, giving off heat.

CONDUCTOR: Any material through which an electrical current can be transmitted easily.

CONTINUITY: Continuous or complete circuit. Can be checked with an ohmmeter.

COUNTERSHAFT: An intermediate shaft which is rotated by a mainshaft and transmits, in turn, that rotation to a working part.

CRANKCASE: The lower part of an engine in which the crankshaft and related parts operate.

CRANKSHAFT: The main driving shaft of an engine which receives reciprocating motion from the pistons and converts it to rotary motion.

CYLINDER: In an engine, the round hole in the engine block in which the piston(s) ride.

CYLINDER BLOCK: The main structural member of an engine in which is found the cylinders, crankshaft and other principal parts.

CYLINDER HEAD: The detachable portion of the engine, fastened, usually, to the top of the cylinder block, containing all or most of the combustion chambers. On overhead valve engines, it contains the valves and their operating parts. On overhead cam engines, it contains the camshaft as well.

DEAD CENTER: The extreme top or bottom of the piston stroke.

DETONATION: An unwanted explosion of the air fuel mixture in the combustion chamber caused by excess heat and compression, advanced timing, or an overly lean mixture. Also referred to as "ping".

DIAPHRAGM: A thin, flexible wall separating two cavities, such as in a vacuum advance unit.

DIESELING: A condition in which hot spots in the combustion chamber cause the engine to run on after the key is turned off.

DIFFERENTIAL: A geared assembly which allows the transmission of motion between drive axles, giving one axle the ability to turn faster than the other.

DIODE: An electrical device that will allow current to flow in one direction only.

DISC BRAKE: A hydraulic braking assembly consisting of a brake disc, or rotor, mounted on an axle, and a caliper assembly containing, usually two brake pads which are activated by hydraulic pressure. The pads are forced against the sides of the disc, creating friction which slows the vehicle.

DISTRIBUTOR: A mechanically driven device on an engine which is responsible for electrically firing the spark plug at a predetermined point of the piston stroke.

DOWEL PIN: A pin, inserted in mating holes in two different parts allowing those parts to maintain a fixed relationship.

DRUM BRAKE: A braking system which consists of two brake shoes and one or two wheel cylinders, mounted on a fixed backing plate, and a brake drum, mounted on an axle, which revolves around the assembly. Hydraulic action applied to the wheel cylinders forces the shoes outward against the drum, creating friction and slowing the vehicle.

DWELL: The rate, measured in degrees of shaft rotation, at which an electrical circuit cycles on and off.

ELECTRONIC CONTROL UNIT (ECU): Ignition module, module, amplifier or igniter. See Module for definition.

ELECTRONIC IGNITION: A system in which the timing and firing of the spark plugs is controlled by an electronic control unit, usually called a module. These systems have not points or condenser.

ENDPLAY: The measured amount of axial movement in a shaft.

ENGINE: A device that converts heat into mechanical energy.

EXHAUST MANIFOLD: A set of cast passages or pipes which conduct exhaust gases from the engine.

FEELER GAUGE: A blade, usually metal, of precisely predetermined thickness, used to measure the clearance between two parts. These blades usually are available in sets of assorted thicknesses.

F-Head: An engine configuration in which the intake valves are in the cylinder head, while the camshaft and exhaust valves are located in the cylinder block. The camshaft operates the intake valves via lifters and pushrods, while it operates the exhaust valves directly.

FIRING ORDER: The order in which combustion occurs in the cylinders of an engine. Also the order in which spark is distributed to the plugs by the distributor.

FLATHEAD: An engine configuration in which the camshaft and all the valves are located in the cylinder block.

FLOODING: The presence of too much fuel in the intake manifold and combustion chamber which prevents the air/fuel mixture from firing, thereby causing a no-start situation.

FLYWHEEL: A disc shaped part bolted to the rear end of the crankshaft. Around the outer perimeter is affixed the ring gear. The starter drive engages the ring gear, turning the flywheel, which rotates the crankshaft, imparting the initial starting motion to the engine.

FOOT POUND (ft.lb. or sometimes, ft. lbs.): The amount of energy or work needed to raise an item weighing one pound, a distance of one foot.

FUSE: A protective device in a circuit which prevents circuit overload by breaking the circuit when a specific amperage is present. The device is constructed around a strip or wire of a lower amperage rating than the circuit it is designed to protect. When an amperage higher than that stamped on the fuse is present in the circuit, the strip or wire melts, opening the circuit.

GEAR RATIO: The ratio between the number of teeth on meshing gears.

GENERATOR: A device which converts mechanical energy into electrical energy.

HEAT RANGE: The measure of a spark plug's ability to dissipate heat from its firing end. The higher the heat range, the hotter the plug fires.

HUB: The center part of a wheel or gear.

HYDROCARBON (HC): Any chemical compound made up of hydrogen and carbon. A major pollutant formed by the engine as a byproduct of combustion.

HYDROMETER: An instrument used to measure the specific gravity of a solution.

INCH POUND (in.lb. or sometimes, in. lbs.): One twelfth of a foot pound.

INDUCTION: A means of transferring electrical energy in the form of a magnetic field. Principle used in the ignition coil to increase voltage.

INJECTION PUMP: A device, usually mechanically operated, which meters and delivers fuel under pressure to the fuel injector.

INJECTOR: A device which receives metered fuel under relatively low pressure and is activated to inject the fuel into the engine under relatively high pressure at a predetermined time.

INPUT SHAFT: The shaft to which torque is applied, usually carrying the driving gear or gears.

INTAKE MANIFOLD: A casting of passages or pipes used to conduct air or a fuel/air mixture to the cylinders.

JOURNAL: The bearing surface within which a shaft operates.

KEY: A small block usually fitted in a notch between a shaft and a hub to prevent slippage of the two parts.

MANIFOLD: A casting of passages or set of pipes which connect the cylinders to an inlet or outlet source.

MANIFOLD VACUUM: Low pressure in an engine intake manifold formed just below the throttle plates. Manifold vacuum is highest at idle and drops under acceleration.

MASTER CYLINDER: The primary fluid pressurizing device in a hydraulic system. In automotive use, it is found in brake and hydraulic clutch systems and is pedal activated, either directly or, in a power brake system, through the power booster.

MODULE: Electronic control unit, amplifier or igniter of solid state or integrated design which controls the current flow in the ignition primary circuit based on input from the pickup coil. When the module opens the primary circuit, the high secondary voltage is induced in the coil.

NEEDLE BEARING: A bearing which consists of a number (usually a large number) of long, thin rollers.

OHM: (Ω) The unit used to measure the resistance of conductor to electrical flow. One ohm is the amount of resistance that limits current flow to one ampere in a circuit with one volt of pressure.

OHMMETER: An instrument used for measuring the resistance, in ohms, in an electrical circuit.

OUTPUT SHAFT: The shaft which transmits torque from a device, such as a transmission.

OVERDRIVE: A gear assembly which produces more shaft revolutions than that transmitted to it.

OVERHEAD CAMSHAFT (OHC): An engine configuration in which the camshaft is mounted on top of the cylinder head and operates the valve either directly or by means of rocker arms.

OVERHEAD VALVE (OHV): An engine configuration in which all of the valves are located in the cylinder head and the camshaft is located in the cylinder block. The camshaft operates the valves via lifters and pushrods.

OXIDES OF NITROGEN (NOx): Chemical compounds of nitrogen produced as a byproduct of combustion. They combine with hydrocarbons to produce smog.

OXYGEN SENSOR: Used with the feedback system to sense the presence of oxygen in the exhaust gas and signal the computer which can reference the voltage signal to an air/fuel ratio.

PINION: The smaller of two meshing gears.

PISTON RING: An open ended ring which fits into a groove on the outer diameter of the piston. Its chief function is to form a seal between the piston and cylinder wall. Most automotive pistons have three rings: two for compression sealing; one for oil sealing.

PRELOAD: A predetermined load placed on a bearing during assembly or by adjustment.

PRIMARY CIRCUIT: Is the low voltage side of the ignition system which consists of the ignition switch, ballast resistor or resistance wire, bypass, coil, electronic control unit and pick-up coil as well as the connecting wires and harnesses.

PRESS FIT: The mating of two parts under pressure, due to the inner diameter of one being smaller than the outer diameter of the other, or vice versa; an interference fit.

RACE: The surface on the inner or outer ring of a bearing on which the balls, needles or rollers move.

REGULATOR: A device which maintains the amperage and/or voltage levels of a circuit at predetermined values.

RELAY: A switch which automatically opens and/or closes a circuit.

RESISTANCE: The opposition to the flow of current through a circuit or electrical device, and is measured in ohms. Resistance is equal to the voltage divided by the amperage.

RESISTOR: A device, usually made of wire, which offers a preset amount of resistance in an electrical circuit.

RING GEAR: The name given to a ring-shaped gear attached to a differential case, or affixed to a flywheel or as part a planetary gear set.

ROLLER BEARING: A bearing made up of hardened inner and outer races between which hardened steel rollers move.

ROTOR: 1. The disc-shaped part of a disc brake assembly, upon which the brake pads bear; also called, brake disc.
2. The device mounted atop the distributor shaft, which passes current to the distributor cap tower contacts.

SECONDARY CIRCUIT: The high voltage side of the ignition system, usually above 20,000 volts. The secondary includes the ignition coil, coil wire, distributor cap and rotor, spark plug wires and spark plugs.

SENDING UNIT: A mechanical, electrical, hydraulic or electromagnetic device which transmits information to a gauge.

SENSOR: Any device designed to measure engine operating conditions or ambient pressures and temperatures. Usually electronic in nature and designed to send a voltage signal to an on-board computer, some sensors may operate as a simple on/off switch or they may provide a variable voltage signal (like a potentiometer) as conditions or measured parameters change.

SHIM: Spacers of precise, predetermined thickness used between parts to establish a proper working relationship.

SLAVE CYLINDER: In automotive use, a device in the hydraulic clutch system which is activated by hydraulic force, disengaging the clutch.

SOLENOID: A coil used to produce a magnetic field, the effect of which is produce work.

SPARK PLUG: A device screwed into the combustion chamber of a spark ignition engine. The basic construction is a conductive core inside of a ceramic insulator, mounted in an outer conductive base. An electrical charge from the spark plug wire travels along the conductive core and jumps a preset air gap to a grounding point or points at the end of the conductive base. The resultant spark ignites the fuel/air mixture in the combustion chamber.

SPLINES: Ridges machined or cast onto the outer diameter of a shaft or inner diameter of a bore to enable parts to mate without rotation.

TACHOMETER: A device used to measure the rotary speed of an engine, shaft, gear, etc., usually in rotations per minute.

THERMOSTAT: A valve, located in the cooling system of an engine, which is closed when cold and opens gradually in response to engine heating, controlling the temperature of the coolant and rate of coolant flow.

TOP DEAD CENTER (TDC): The point at which the piston reaches the top of its travel on the compression stroke.

TORQUE: The twisting force applied to an object.

TORQUE CONVERTER: A turbine used to transmit power from a driving member to a driven member via hydraulic action, providing changes in drive ratio and torque. In automotive use, it links the driveplate at the rear of the engine to the automatic transmission.

TRANSDUCER: A device used to change a force into an electrical signal.

TRANSISTOR: A semi-conductor component which can be actuated by a small voltage to perform an electrical switching function.

TUNE-UP: A regular maintenance function, usually associated with the replacement and adjustment of parts and components in the electrical and fuel systems of a vehicle for the purpose of attaining optimum performance.

TURBOCHARGER: An exhaust driven pump which compresses intake air and forces it into the combustion chambers at higher than atmospheric pressures. The increased air pressure allows more fuel to be burned and results in increased horsepower being produced.

VACUUM ADVANCE: A device which advances the ignition timing in response to increased engine vacuum.

VACUUM GAUGE: An instrument used to measure the presence of vacuum in a chamber.

VALVE: A device which control the pressure, direction of flow or rate of flow of a liquid or gas.

VALVE CLEARANCE: The measured gap between the end of the valve stem and the rocker arm, cam lobe or follower that activates the valve.

VISCOSITY: The rating of a liquid's internal resistance to flow.

VOLTMETER: An instrument used for measuring electrical force in units called volts. Voltmeters are always connected parallel with the circuit being tested.

WHEEL CYLINDER: Found in the automotive drum brake assembly, it is a device, actuated by hydraulic pressure, which, through internal pistons, pushes the brake shoes outward against the drums.

ABBREVIATIONS AND SYMBOLS

A: Ampere

AC: Alternating current

A/C: Air conditioning

A-h: Ampere hour

AT: Automatic transmission

ATDC: After top dead center

μA: Microampere

bbl: Barrel

BDC: Bottom dead center

bhp: Brake horsepower

BTDC: Before top dead center

BTU: British thermal unit

C: Celsius (Centigrade)

CCA: Cold cranking amps

cd: Candela

cm^2: Square centimeter

cm^3, cc: Cubic centimeter

CO: Carbon monoxide

CO_2: Carbon dioxide

cu.in., in^3: Cubic inch

CV: Constant velocity

Cyl.: Cylinder

DC: Direct current

ECM: Electronic control module

EFE: Early fuel evaporation

EFI: Electronic fuel injection

EGR: Exhaust gas recirculation

Exh.: Exhaust

F: Fahrenheit

F: Farad

pF: Picofarad

μF: Microfarad

FI: Fuel injection

ft.lb., ft. lb., ft. lbs.: foot pound(s)

gal: Gallon

g: Gram

HC: Hydrocarbon

HEI: High energy ignition

HO: High output

hp: Horsepower

Hyd.: Hydraulic

Hz: Hertz

ID: Inside diameter

in.lb.; in. lb.; in. lbs: inch pound(s)

Int.: Intake

K: Kelvin

kg: Kilogram

kHz: Kilohertz

km: Kilometer

km/h: Kilometers per hour

kΩ: Kilohm

kPa: Kilopascal

kV: Kilovolt

kW: Kilowatt

l: Liter

l/s: Liters per second

m: Meter

mA: Milliampere

mg: Milligram

mHz: Megahertz

mm: Millimeter

mm^2: Square millimeter

m^3: Cubic meter

$M\Omega$: Megohm

m/s: Meters per second

MT: Manual transmission

mV: Millivolt

μm: Micrometer

N: Newton

N-m: Newton meter

NOx: Nitrous oxide

OD: Outside diameter

OHC: Over head camshaft

OHV: Over head valve

Ω: Ohm

PCV: Positive crankcase ventilation

psi: Pounds per square inch

pts: Pints

qts: Quarts

rpm: Rotations per minute

rps: Rotations per second

R-12: A refrigerant gas (Freon)

SAE: Society of Automotive Engineers

SO_2: Sulfur dioxide

T: Ton

t: Megagram

TBI: Throttle Body Injection

TPS: Throttle Position Sensor

V: 1. Volt; 2. Venturi

μV: Microvolt

W: Watt

$\propto$: Infinity

$<$: Less than

$>$: Greater than

Index